CLASSICA AMERICANA

MEYER REINHOLD

CLASSICA AMERICANA

The Greek and Roman Heritage in the United States

WAYNE STATE UNIVERSITY PRESS
Detroit 1984

Library of Congress Cataloging in Publication Data

Reinhold, Meyer, 1909–
  Classica Americana.

  Bibliography: p.
  Includes index.
  1. Greece—Study and teaching—United States—
History.   2. Rome—Study and teaching—United States
—History.   3. Classical philology—Study and teaching
—United States.   4. United States—Civilization—
Greek influences.   5. United States—Civilization—
Roman influences.   I. Title.
DE15.5.U6R44   1984   001.3′0973   83-19779
ISBN 0–8143–1744–8

To the memory of

David Stanley Wiesen
brilliant collaborator in the
American classical tradition

Contents

7

VII.

"A New Morning": Edward Everett's Contributions to
Classical Learning   *204*

VIII.

Philhellenism in America in the Early National Period   *214*

IX.

Vergil in the American Experience from Colonial Times
to 1882   *221*

X.

Plutarch's Influence in America from Colonial Times
to 1890   *250*

XI.

American Visitors to Pompeii, Herculaneum, and Paestum in
the Nineteenth Century   *265*

XII.

Survey of the Scholarship on Classical Traditions in
Early America   *280*

Foreword

$\mathbf{M}$eyer Reinhold is one of those rare and fortunate scholars—I recall M. P. Nilsson and Sir John Beazley— who has created a new discipline. *Vixere fortes ante Agamemnona multi.* Men before Reinhold devoted attention to the reception of the classical authors and of ancient history in colonial and early national America. One need only recall the beloved figure of Dr. Richard M. Gummere, Harvard College's longtime dean of admissions, an amiable, cultivated eighteenth-century gentleman, who believed Seneca's *Moral Epistles* and shared an intimate, anecdotal familiarity with the great authors. Here is the crux of the matter. Arnaldo Momigliano has justly complained that *Wissenschaftsgeschichte* has remained "work for Sunday afternoons," what one does when the serious stuff of editing Pseudo-Scylax is over. Wilamowitz warned James Loeb in 1910: "One can't do it any more without scholarship."

Meyer Reinhold began, aged twenty-three, with a famous Columbia dissertation, *Marcus Agrippa: A Biography* (Geneva, N.Y., 1933). The child is father of the man. Already one found mastery of ancient sources—literary, epigraphical, archaeological, numismatic —command of a vast secondary literature, lucid exposition, enthusiasm tempered by considered judgment. I may remark for readers not classicists that the author of these studies has distinguished publications in the fields of Latin literature, Roman history, and Judaica. He has not been idle. I do not know what turned him to the study of classics in early America. It was not Bicentennial fever

9

and all that. Perhaps he wished to remind forgetful Americans how much they owed their classical past in a banausic age ignorant of that great legacy. Perhaps too, like many thoughtful classicists, he saw that traditional philology had been played out and sought a subject not trivial and where much original work awaited a scholar of his generation and capacity.

In 1968, the author's sixtieth year, "Opponents of Classical Learning in America during the Revolutionary Period" appeared in the *Proceedings of the American Philosophical Society* and began a new epoch in the study of the subject, and a new career for its author. Reinhold brought a great classicist's breadth and erudition to a field whose experts no longer could read Latin and had little idea who Polybius was or what he had achieved. They lacked in short the control of Greek and Latin that the subjects of their study possessed. At age sixty, Reinhold did what a young man does at age twenty. He learned a whole new subject well enough to add to it. This tremendous achievement must never be ignored. The firm methodology of his later studies is already in evidence. There are resort to original sources, attention to detail, the instinct for precise and comprehensive documentation, the tendency to allow sources to speak for themselves, an enviable historicism that surrenders preconceptions to present the past's own view of itself. This is Lachmann's "Nur wer sich willig ergibt, befreit sein Urteil." With one stroke Reinhold replaced genteel dilettantism with the cruel requirement of professional expertise. Nineteen sixty-eight is the beginning of the scientific study of classics in early America. That is what I mean when I say that Meyer Reinhold created a new discipline. He applied to American documents of the eighteenth century the same standards that he had earlier applied to Roman documents of the first century.

Reinhold's initiative coincided with an intense renewal of interest on the continent in the history of scholarship and interpretation and the discovery by Jauss and others of *Rezeptionsgeschichte*. Later generations do not distort an ancient original. The *Aeneid* does not only mean what Vergil intended it to mean. *Nachleben* is not a perversion of *Leben*. Each generation interprets the classics in their own terms and our task is *sine ira et studio* to determine how and why each did. The studies in this volume on Plutarch, Vergil, and visitors to Pompeii, Herculaneum, and Paestum are *Rezeptionsgeschichte*. They provide models for imitation by younger scholars.

Classical scholarship did not exist in this country during Reinhold's period (1620–1880). There were no research libraries. Harvard, Yale, and Princeton were as provincial as contemporary Oxford and Cambridge, finishing schools for young gentlemen, not Prussian research institutions dedicated to the accumulation of new truth. Teaching meant elementary drilling, exhausting, repetitive, and uninspiring. Recall Gildersleeve's disappointment at Princeton ("My American teachers did not understand their business") and his sobering years at Charlottesville ("The situation is grim and there is little help from without"). Between the end of the Revolutionary period (1789) with its impassioned pursuit of classical, especially Roman, precedent, "the lamp of experience," and the founding of Johns Hopkins expressly after the Prussian model in 1876, something extraordinarily important for American classicists, if they wish to understand their plight historically, happened. American intellectuals ceased to *believe* the classics. In June 1789 Benjamin Rush declares: "We shall never equal the sublime and original authors of antiquity unless we cease to study them." It is the philistine antithesis of Winckelmann's "Der einzige Weg für uns, gross, ja, wenn möglich ist, unnachahmlich zu werden, ist der Nachahmung der Alten" (1755). The only way for us to become inimitable is by imitation of the ancients. Winckelmann and Rush unite remarkably in the figure of Werner Jaeger, German and American, whose Third Humanism was the last and surely misguided attempt to make the values of Greece central to European, especially German, education of his day. He wrote in despair after twenty-five years in the United States that teaching in America he learned what classical scholarship meant in a land where classical humanism did not exist. Reinhold, the historian of ideas, documents this crucial change and in a typically indirect fashion explains historically what Oldfather stated empirically, that classicists are not important in this country. The villain is the Fata Morgana of useful knowledge. One must know this and live with it. It is the plight not only of American classics but of American humanities. It is why defenses of classics by classicists are bland and ineffective. They defend their cause within the enemy's terms, the useful. They lack courage to say that one learns Greek to read Greek books, not to increase our English vocabulary.

Professor Reinhold draws attention to the lack of an American Hellenism during his period, of the sort one finds in Germany as a post-Napoleonic reaction against French cultural hegemony. He shows that the Founding Fathers distrusted Periclean democracy in a way Socrates might have and exalted Roman oligarchy. American Hellenism began with Greek Revival architecture. It was encouraged at the end of the nineteenth century and early twentieth by brilliant German-trained academic Hellenists, B. L. Gildersleeve, Paul Shorey, and William A. Oldfather, or by humanists like Paul Elmer More. The expatriate modernists, Pound and Eliot, made Greek chic. After World War II the movement culminated with the introduction of mass undergraduate courses on Greek literature in American translation and through the influence on American thought of German thinkers like Marx, Nietzsche, and Freud, themselves deeply influenced by Greek ideas. The history of American Hellenism has yet to be written by a scholar who will start from Reinhold's achievement.

I do not know when I have learned so much from one book. There are so many new facts here, facts that stimulate rather than banish further thought. Throughout the learned author suggests modestly and indirectly how much more there is to be done. We are debtors, as classicists and Americans, to the industry and scholarship of Professor Reinhold. He guides us with his own "lamp of experience." I think the only way we can repay him is by absorbing his wisdom, by sharing it with our students, and perhaps even—with his help—by adding a bit to it.

William M. Calder III

Acknowledgments

The author is keenly aware of debts to numerous scholars, both classicists and American intellectual historians, whose published work has been helpful to him, even indispensable in some cases. A pleasing opportunity is afforded here to record and acknowledge special obligations accumulated in the course of preparing and publishing the essays collected in this volume. Three of the chapters have not previously been published: the studies on Plutarch, Vergil, and American travelers to classical sites near Naples. Permission to reprint the others is gratefully acknowledged to the American Philological Association, the American Philosophical Society, Cambridge University Press, *Classical Outlook*, and the University of Michigan. In these essays some alterations have been made throughout for the sake of consistency and accuracy in details, but no substantive changes have been introduced. It was not deemed advisable or necessary to eliminate the repetitions of detail and documentation in these studies which appeared over a period of fifteen years and in varied publications.

The reprinted articles and chapters of books originally appeared as follows: "Opponents of Classical Learning in America during the Revolutionary Period," *Proceedings of the American Philosophical Society* 112 (1968), pp. 221–234; "The Quest for Useful Knowledge in Eighteenth-Century America," *Proceedings of the American Philosophical Society* 119 (1975), pp. 108–132; "The Cult of Antiquity in America," in *The Classick Pages: Classical Reading of Eighteenth-Century Americans* (University Park, Pa.: American

Philological Association, 1975), pp. 1–27; "The Classics and the Quest for Virtue in Eighteenth-Century America," in *The Usefulness of Classical Learning in the Eighteenth Century*, ed. Susan Ford Wiltshire (University Park, Pa.: American Philological Association, 1976), pp. 6–26; "Survey of the Scholarship on the Classical Traditions in Early America," in *The Classical Traditions in Early America*, ed. John W. Eadie (Ann Arbor: Center for the Coördination of Ancient and Modern Studies, 1976), pp. 1–48; "The Silver Age of Classical Studies in America, 1790–1830," in *Ancient and Modern: Essays in Honor of Gerald F. Else*, ed. John H. D'Arms and John W. Eadie (Ann Arbor: Center for Coördination of Ancient and Modern Studies, 1977), pp. 181–213; "The Classics and Eighteenth-Century American Political Thought," in *Classical Influences on Western Thought A.D. 1650–1870*, ed. R. R. Bolgar (Cambridge: Cambridge University Press, 1979), pp. 223–243; "Philhellenism in America in the Early National Period," *Classical Outlook* 55 (1978), pp. 86–88; " 'A New Morning': Edward Everett's Contributions to Classical Learning," *Classical Outlook* 59 (1981–82), pp. 37–41.

The work on these studies was done without the aid of grants, and with only one subvention (from the American Council of Learned Societies for travel in 1977 to Cambridge, England, for participation in the conference on "Classical Influences on Western Thought A.D. 1650–1870"). The library of the University of Missouri, at Columbia, and Widener Library at Harvard have been invaluable to me, both for their collections and the assistance of their staffs. I owe particular thanks to Professors Michael Kammen of Cornell University and Charles F. Mullett of the University of Missouri, at Columbia, each of them for reading and commenting on one of the papers, to Carol Altman Bromberg of Wayne State University Press for her editorial deftness and her good humor, and a continuing debt of gratitude to Professor George A. Kennedy of the University of North Carolina for his meticulous and generous piloting of *The Classick Pages* through the press and for his understanding and unfailing encouragement of my work on the classical heritage in America.

*In Company with Sallust, Cicero, Tacitus, and Livy, you will
learn Wisdom and Virtue. You will see them represented with
all the Charms which Language and Imagination can exhibit,
and Vice and Folly painted in all their Deformity and Horror. You will ever remember that all the End of Study is to
make you a good Man and a useful Citizen.*

—John Adams to John Quincy Adams

*Is it not the glory of Americans that, whilst they have paid
a decent regard to the opinions of former times and other
nations, they have not suffered a blind veneration to antiquity to overrule the suggestions of their good sense . . .
and the lessons of their own experience?*

—James Madison

*Nothing restores and humanizes antiquity—and makes it
blithe—as the discovery of some natural sympathy between
it and the present.*

—Henry David Thoreau

*A precious—mouldering pleasure—'tis—
To meet an Antique Book—
In just the Dress his Century wore—.*

—Emily Dickinson

Introduction

Until recently scant attention was directed to the role of the Greek and Roman tradition in the American experience before classical studies became a professional discipline in the last quarter of the nineteenth century. In our neglect to study and evaluate the nature and evolution of earlier experience with the classical heritage we have been left far behind by almost all other countries which absorbed classical learning in their cultures. In the last two decades, however, notable progress has been made in researching, describing, and explicating its role in America.

The task was a formidable one. Those who sought to contribute to an understanding of this subject were conscious of plunging into and opening up a new field in American intellectual and cultural history. There were no American intellectual historians with sufficient training in Greek and Roman antiquity, and no classicists with sophisticated knowledge of American cultural history. Moreover, the range was spacious: about 250 years of American life and thought. This extended from the importation of the cultural baggage and standards of Elizabethan England and the naturalization of the traditional classical curriculum on American soil in the early seventeenth century, through the colonial age, the Revolutionary period, and the first century of nationhood, ending with the waning of the classical presence.

Fortunately, research in this previously neglected field was not launched in the heat of Bicentennial fever, though the recent commemoration of the Declaration of Independence produced a surge

17

of interest and scholarly contributions by both classicists and Americanists. And the imminent new bicentennials, especially of the promulgation of the Constitution, are already stimulating scholarly conferences and contributions on the part of both. Indeed, research in this field, which is both interdisciplinary and multidisciplinary, has been fortified by dialogue between classical scholars and American intellectual historians, beginning with a pioneering working conference on "Classical Traditions in Early America" held at the University of Michigan in October, 1970, under the sponsorship of the Center for Coördination of Ancient and Modern Studies. This organization was also host to an interdisciplinary conference on the same subject in October, 1975, at which various contributions on specific subjects were presented and discussed.

It was clear that the first problem that needed to be addressed was the polarization of the perspectives of both groups of scholars. Classicists, with enthusiasm and rose-colored glasses, tend to claim too much for influences of the classics, and are prone to investigate the data of antiquity in America largely as aspects of the *Nachleben* of the classics. Contrariwise, many Americanists are inclined to undervalue the classical tradition in America as mere window dressing and status badge of the elite. But progress has been made in bridging this gap. Classicists have been learning to evaluate evidences of the classics in their specific American contexts. In particular, classicists now are wary of overestimating the influence of classical theory and practice on American political history and constitutional theory. Not just in the political sphere, but in every aspect of early American life—intellectual, educational, literary, religious, artistic—we are more and more conscious that the classical tradition in America was multifarious and multivalent, responding to sectarian, sectional, political, social pluralism, as well as varying in the lives of individual Americans. We have also come to discern three major periods: the earliest, from 1635 to 1735, in which the classical languages served to train servants of church and state, with emphasis on formal elements and moral instruction; the second, from about 1735 to 1800, when political adaptation was dominant, reaching its peak in the Revolutionary Age; the third, from 1800 to about 1875, when its role was that of the basic liberal arts discipline and the training school of elite orators and lawyers. In clarifying the flux of changes one of the important advances has been our understanding of the American disenchantment with ancient history and the abandonment of the search for parallels and analogies from antiquity so prized by the Founding Fathers, and by the Federalists and Whigs in the early national period.

The pursuit of fruitful scholarly investigations in the field has been fostered by the introduction of sound methodological principles. Americans did not need to be told by Samuel Johnson that "Classical quotation is the parole of literary men all over the world," and it is clearly an exercise in futility merely to hunt for and amass lists of classical tags, quotations and allusions used by Americans. Many people today can quote Shakespeare and de Tocqueville's *Democracy in America*, for example, without having read much of either. More important, we need to eschew using the conception "influence" in evaluating and dealing with the uses of "classical" phenomena. This is far more than a problem in terminology, for "influence" is a color word that is misleading and exceedingly difficult to prove. The existence of a catalogue of books in a library does not certify that the books were ever read; even if a specific book is known to have been read, it is difficult, or impossible, to prove that the contents moved the reader to action or even meditation. Indeed, it cannot be demonstrated that the galaxy of political leaders in the Revolutionary Age and the early national period was the product of a classical education.

It is now acknowledged that the *function* that knowledge of classical antiquity served should be our prime concern: how the classics functioned in early America, how Americans used, even misused and abused antiquity. This concentration on patterns of function directs us to look at many complexities in the American uses of the classics: how the classics and antiquity in general reached Americans through the Renaissance and British filters; how they were refracted also by the texts used, the translations of the classics, and by books on ancient history and antiquities; what principles and biases operated in the American "pick and choose" preferences, that is, the principles in the selective use of the classics from period to period, group to group, individual to individual; what form the resonances of the classics took in the latent Greek and Roman values mediated through secondary sources and the literature of British and continental thought from the Renaissance to the eighteenth and early nineteenth centuries; how Americans transmuted and transvalued their selective borrowings in the contemporary contexts and evolving climates of early America. In short, this historical approach enables us to understand both the direct and indirect uses, the diversity of ways in which Americans perceived and absorbed the ancient world, the biases that influenced the precise ways they constructed their models of antiquity, and, finally, the uniqueness in America of some of the ways they used the classics in colonial, Revolutionary, post-Revolutionary, and early national culture.

We understand much more today how Americans, in their selective borrowings from the pluralistic ancient world, ordered their classical models and how these functioned as symbols and role models. Needless to say, their knowledge of the ancient world was not only limited by their biases but was very slender as compared with ours, and their own world and cultural climate differed not only from the ancient world but from ours. Moreover, there were in each period, and even in many individual Americans, tensions, felt and unconscious, contradictions and paradoxes in their perception and uses of the classics. For example, in the Revolutionary Age, at a time when appeal to classical models of society was at its peak, there was a deeply perceived tension between the resort to classical models of government and the need to cut the classical umbilical cord to achieve progress into the future of a dynamic society. It is necessary also to clarify the mix of admiration for and hostility to the classics. Though classical learning was venerated by many as one of the most valuable forms of "useful knowledge," there was a persistent stream of antagonism to the classics in America throughout these centuries. It is illuminating to explore the nature and motives of this hostility by opponents of classical learning in America, and why and how the classics survived. It is also intriguing to understand why there was no neo-Hellenic period in America as there was in Germany and Britain in the late eighteenth and the nineteenth centuries, and why neoclassicism in American sculpture and painting did not survive in America, though Hellenic Revival architecture swept the country.

Great strides have been made in a relatively short time in elucidating the role of classical knowledge in early America. Many more areas and topics need to be researched, analyzed, and synthesized from accumulated data. The essays gathered in this volume will, it is hoped, serve not only to clarify many aspects of our classical heritage but also give guidance for coping with the interdisciplinary complexities of the subject, and underscore the importance of continued exploration and analytical study of the primary sources. It is also hoped that these essays will stimulate other contributions toward the history of the mission of the classical heritage in the intellectual landscape of America from 1620 to 1880.

Abbreviations Used in Notes and Bibliography

Class. World	*Classical World*
Mem. Amer. Acad. Arts & Sci.	*Memoirs of the American Academy of Arts and Sciences*
New Engl. Quart.	*New England Quarterly*
Pa. Mag. Hist. & Biog.	*Pennsylvania Magazine of History and Biography*
Proc. Amer. Antiq. Soc.	*Proceedings of the American Antiquarian Society*
Proc. Amer. Philos. Soc.	*Proceedings of the American Philosophical Society*
Proc. Mass. Hist. Soc.	*Proceedings of the Massachusetts Historical Society*
Publ. Colon. Soc. Mass.	*Publications of the Colonial Society of Massachusetts*
Trans. Amer. Philolog. Assn.	*Transactions of the American Philological Association*
Trans. Amer. Philos. Soc.	*Transactions of the American Philosophical Society*
Wm. & Mary Quart.	*William and Mary Quarterly*
Va. Mag. Hist. & Biog.	*Virginia Magazine of History and Biography*

I. The Cult of Antiquity in America

Early Americans lived in the afterglow of the Renaissance. Despite the distance from the great centers of humanistic learning, the absence of visible relics of the Greek and Roman presence[1] to memorialize the continuity with classical antiquity and excite feelings of pride in the cultural heritage,[2] and sporadic opposition on religious and utilitarian grounds, classical learning was swiftly naturalized on American soil, and in consequence a fair number of colonial and Revolutionary Americans were nurtured and molded by the humanistic tradition. Though, as on the other side of the Atlantic, the immediate beneficiaries of this learning constituted a small intellectual elite, the markedly higher level of literacy in America provided a wider audience for the classics.

Nevertheless, the overriding needs imposed on Americans by the winning and developing of a new country on the edge of the wilderness and the priorities obtruding in the practical and political domains affected Americans differently than was the experience of their classically educated counterparts in Europe. Americans did not, for instance, produce a single great classical scholar in two hundred years;[3] they did not make a single significant contribution to classical scholarship. But while adding nothing to the fund of classical learning, they plundered the classics liberally for the advantage of their own lives and the national good. For many Americans,

23

there is no doubt, classical learning was a superficial veneer, the indispensable hallmark of gentlemen's culture, yet many of them drew inspiration throughout their lives from the study and reading of the classics. They knew far less about the ancient world than we do today, but the learning they acquired, circumscribed though it was, affected their thought and action far more. Their reading in and meditation upon the classics was eminently practical and purposeful; and it contributed substantially to the development and motivation of an unparalleled concentration of political giants in world history.

Evidence abounds for an American cult of antiquity during the eighteenth century,[4] particularly during the second half: the ubiquitous classical quotations and tags; the common use of classical pseudonyms; the revival of classical place names; the constant adducing of classical parallels; even the frequent use of classical names for slaves in the southern states. Overshadowing all these was the tireless and purposeful reading by early Americans of the classics as a repository of timeless models for guidance in republicanism and private and civic virtue.

Jefferson exulted in the diffusion of classical learning in America. In 1787, when he heard that an English newspaper had put forth a claim that an English workman had invented a new wheel, reviving a Greek idea (from a passage in Homer), Jefferson, with a mixture of national pride, advocacy of agrarianism over artisan culture, and tongue in cheek, claimed the invention for a Jersey farmer. "But it is more likely," he wrote, "that the Jersey farmer got the idea from thence, because ours are the only farmers who can read Homer."[5] Even if Jefferson embroidered the tale, it is nevertheless probable that never since antiquity were the classics, in one form or other, read by a greater proportion of a population.[6]

The influence of the classics in America reached its acme in such political and intellectual giants as Thomas Jefferson and John Adams,[7] and in the debates attending the promulgation and ratification of the Constitution. But a host of lesser luminaries acknowledged the American debt to the classics. For example, in 1766 Jonathan Mayhew, in a thanksgiving sermon on the repeal of the Stamp Act, testified to his personal indebtedness: "Having been initiated, in youth, in the doctrines of civil liberty, as they were taught by such men as Plato, Demosthenes, and Cicero, and other renowned persons among the ancients, and such as Sidney and Milton, Locke and Hoadley among the moderns; I liked them; they seemed rational."[8] A more conservative minister, the arch-Tory

Jonathan Boucher, deplored the influence of classical reading on "an abundance of men, of liberal, generous and cultivated minds, lost and undone by the habit, first acquired at school, of reading only classics."[9]

It is well known that most of the Founding Fathers were beneficiaries of a classical education, and that some were steeped in classical learning.[10] Their reading in the classics was highly purposeful, adaptive, and selective; but their imitation was never slavish. Jefferson in 1814 expressed the prevailing viewpoint of many of his generation: "For classical learning I have ever been a zealous advocate. . . . I have not, however, . . . [been interested in] a hypercritical knowledge of the Latin and Greek languages. I have believed it sufficient to possess a substantial understanding of their authors."[11]

It is characteristic of eighteenth-century Americans that in their eclectic reading in the classics they were interested principally in the prose authors—the moralists and the historians[12]—for their practical value in promoting moral and political wisdom. There was little taste for belles lettres as such, especially poetry, except insofar as such reading afforded moral instruction, as in Homer, Vergil, and Horace, among others. Characteristic is the observation of the patriot William Bradford in 1774 that "this does not seem the proper time for poetry, unless it be such as Tyrtaeus wrote,"[13] and John Adams's exhortation to himself in 1759: "Labour to get distinct Ideas of Law, Right, Wrong, Justice, Equity. Search for them in your own mind, in Roman, grecian, French, English Treatises."[14]

But it is Jefferson who towers above all the others as the advocate par excellence of the classics. Whether we look in his commonplace books, with their varied and comprehensive interests, or in his letters and other writings, especially those dealing with education, he bestrode the American scene like a giant—the last great humanist.[15] In 1800 he wrote Joseph Priestley how much he enjoyed Homer in Greek (though he felt self-conscious enough to assure that it was "an innocent enjoyment"): "I thank on my knees," he said, "him who directed my early education, for having put into my possession this rich source of delight: and I would not exchange it for anything."[16]

Curriculum of Schools and Colleges

"The child of two continents, America" (in Vernon Parrington's phrase) was created out of a many-faceted pluralism of traditions and values. But the decisive sectors of the population succeeded in establishing here the model of the British educational system, which had at its core the study of the Latin and Greek languages, literatures, and antiquities. By 1650 over 130 graduates of Cambridge and Oxford had emigrated to New England; similarly, of 640 clergymen known in Virginia from 1607–85, 125 had been educated in the two British universities.[17] In Massachusetts the concern of the leaders of the Bay Colony for an educated ministry and corps of public servants swiftly led to the establishment of the first grammar (i.e., secondary) school in the New World, the Boston Latin School (founded 1635), and the first college, Harvard (1636).[18] By 1776 there were nine colleges from New Hampshire to Virginia (Harvard, William and Mary, Yale, New Jersey [later Princeton], Philadelphia [University of Pennsylvania], King's [Columbia], Rhode Island [Brown], Queen's [Rutgers], Dartmouth), as well as numerous grammar schools which prepared college-bound American youths in the colonies.

The list of classical authors first encountered by American school boys, in the grammar schools, was determined both by tradition and by the admission requirements of the colleges, especially Harvard. It was, for example, prescribed by the trustees of William and Mary for its grammar school that "as for Rudiments and Grammars, and Classick Authors of each Tongue, let them teach the same Books which by Law or Custom are used in the Schools of England."[19] In the stay of seven years in the grammar schools (until Boston Latin School in 1789 reduced its program to four years), students were prepared for college principally through the medium of the classics. The curriculum varied little throughout the eighteenth century; the principal authors read were: "Cato"'s *Distichs*; Aesop's *Fables;* Ovid's *Metamorphoses* and *Tristia;* Cicero's orations, letters, and *De Officiis;* Florus (or Eutropius or Justin); Vergil's *Aeneid;* Horace; Terence; Homer; Isocrates; Xenophon's *Memorabilia.*[20] These, and some others reserved for the college level, were the books James Madison called "the common list of School classics."[21]

Educational tradition prescribed a highly formal training for the acquisition of the languages, with emphasis on memorization (of forms, rules of grammar, phrases, sentences, long passages), construing and parsing, and writing Latin prose. But the ideal was the molding of liberally educated youths through access to the contents of the classics. The original theological and religious focus in the study of the classics in the seventeenth century yielded by the 1730s to new plural goals of a more secular nature: besides the inculcation of piety and moral truths, and the acquisition of classical learning as an adornment for an educated elite, social and civic ends increasingly loomed large. As William Livingston's *Independent Reflector* put it in 1753: "Boys in the Study of the Languages [i.e., Latin and Greek], are employed in a Manner Best suited for their Capacities. Plain Rules of Morality and History are generally the Subjects of the Books put into their Hands."[22]

What the students read in grammar schools was virtually mandated by the admission requirements of the colleges; and these remained solidly classical from the beginning throughout the eighteenth century, virtually unchanged for close to two centuries.[23] Harvard's entrance requirements set the pattern. Cotton Mather tells us in 1702: "When scholars had so far profited at the *grammar schools*, that they could read any *classical author* into English, and readily make and speak true *Latin* and write it in *verse*, as well as *prose*; and perfectly decline the *paradigms* of *nouns* and *verbs* in the Greek tongue, they were judged capable of admission to Harvard-Collidge."[24]

But Cotton Mather's statement is somewhat imprecise. The Harvard College Laws of 1655, for example, read as follows: "When any Scholler is able to read and understand Tully, Virgil or any such ordinary Classicall Authors, and can readily make and speake or write true Latin prose and hath skill in making verse, and is Competently grounded in the Greeke Language; so as to be able to Construe and Grammatically to resolve ordinary Greeke, as in the Greeke Testament, Isocrates, and the minor poets, or such like, having withall meet Testimony of his towardlinesse, hee shall be capable of admission into the Colledge."[25] Similarly, the Yale Laws of 1745 provided: "That none may Expect to be admitted into this College unless upon Examination of the Praesident and Tutors, They shall be found able Extempore to Read, Construe and Parse Tully, Virgil, and the Greek Testament: and to write True Latin Prose and to understand the Rules of Prosodia and Common Arithmetic, and shall bring Sufficient Testimony of his Blameless and inoffensive Life." In 1755 the Laws and Orders of King's College stipulated that "none shall be admitted . . . but such as can read the first three of Tully's Select Orations and the three first books of Virgil's Aeneid into English, and the ten first chapters of St. John's Gospel in Greek, into Latin and such as are well versed in all the rules of Clarke's Introduction so as to make true grammatical Latin and are expert in arithmetic as far as the rule of reduction."[26] There was thus a basic uniformity among the colleges, though variations occurred; by the end of the eighteenth century, for admission to college, students were expected to be able to read Cicero's orations, Vergil's *Aeneid*, Sallust or Caesar, ordinary Greek such as Isocrates, and the Greek Testament.[27]

In the colleges themselves the course of study continued aspects of classical training and provided for an extensive program of reading in the classical authors, as well as in ancient history, and Greek and Roman antiquities.[28] Authors commonly read in the last decade of the eighteenth century were: Sallust, Livy, Horace, Cicero, Terence, Vergil (*Georgics*), Xenophon, Homer, Lucian, Demosthenes, and Isocrates.[29]

Books and Libraries

The books owned by and accessible to early Americans enable us not only to evaluate the intellectual patterns of the age but also in particular to appreciate the scope of classical reading. The "bestsellers" of the times in classical authors, ancient history, and antiquities are known to us from wills and probate court records of estates, diaries, autobiographies, letters, and commonplace books. Another invaluable clue comes from the activities of book dealers in many cities along the seaboard, notably Boston and Philadephia: catalogues, invoices of purchases, inventories of stock, advertisements in newspapers and in broadsides, records of sales, and estates of bookmen themselves. We are fortunate, too, in possessing inventories of libraries of considerable size, both public and private, and catalogues of college libraries.

The famous and extensive libraries of early America all contained books on the classics: college libraries, especially those of Harvard (which owned ca. 3,000 volumes in 1732–35) and Yale; public libraries, notably the Library Company of Philadelphia (established 1732; it had 375 titles in 1741) and the Redwood Library Company at Newport, Rhode Island (opened 1750 with 866 titles);[30] private libraries, for example, those of John Harvard, Cotton Mather, Benjamin Franklin, the Virginians John Carter II, Robert "King" Carter, Ralph Wormeley II, Richard Lee II, and William Byrd of Westover (3,600 volumes), James Logan of Philadelphia (the best classical library in colonial times), James Bowdoin of Massachusetts (ca. 1,200 volumes), and Thomas Jefferson's great libraries. Those collections still in existence today are the Loganian Library in Philadelphia, called by Edwin Wolf "the greatest single intellectual monument of colonial America which has survived,"[31]

Thomas Jefferson's second library (in the Library of Congress), his third library (at Monticello), and John Adams's books, now in Boston.

Early Americans were on the whole avid readers; this has been demonstrated beyond question.[32] But most of the books they read were not natively produced. Until the end of the century almost all books on the classics owned by Americans were imported from England and the continent. For example, in the first century of printing in Pennsylvania only twelve titles dealing with classics were printed in Pennsylvania.[33] Before 1776 the only acceptable American-written and American-printed school text used in teaching the classics was a Latin grammar, Ezekiel Cheever's famous *Accidence*. Beginning about 1780 a few school texts began to be printed on this side of the Atlantic (texts of Aesop, beginners' books in Latin and Greek, and Latin readers), mostly reprints of books of foreign origin. But by 1804 American authors for all sorts of textbooks used in this country outnumbered the British three to one.[34] It is interesting in this connection to note that in 1760 the American patriot James Otis wrote a work on Greek prosody, but it could not be printed because, as Otis told John Adams, "there were no Greek types in the country, or, if there were, there was no printer who knew how to use them."[35]

American libraries, both public and private, reveal an evolving focus of interest—at first theological and devotional; then, beginning about 1730, secular. The reading interests turned to utilitarian subjects in many fields; and in the humanities the concentration was on moral writings and history.[36] Besides Greek and Latin texts and dictionaries, more often than not there were to be found in the libraries translations of classical authors,[37] works on ancient history, and books on classical antiquities. With regard to books on classical subjects, both college libraries, other large libraries, and those of more educated Americans contained a fair representation, but in a minority: the average holdings in classics were about 10–12 percent.

It is interesting to note that Jefferson, for all his devotion to the classics, when he recommended titles for the library of Robert Skipwith in 1771, suggested 140 titles of which only 16 were on classical subjects, mostly ancient history.[38] Noteworthy also is that of 417 books given to Yale in 1719 by Elihu Yale, only 19 were on classical topics—Greek and Latin texts.[39] Viewed overall, the major interests in college libraries throughout the century were: theological works—50 percent; history—12–15 percent; belles lettres—11–15 percent; science—7–12 percent; philosophy—3–8 percent.[40] As an additional corrective to the tendency of many to believe that the classics were the dominant interest of early Americans, we should take note of the inventory of stock of the Boston bookseller Richard Perry, who died in 1700. Of 6,000 volumes, only 300 were on classical subjects. Farther south, more than a half century later, we read of a dispute about books on classics in connection with the budget of the Charleston Library, founded in 1745. Christopher Gadsden resigned from the Library Society because his proposal to spend 70 percent of the annual appropriation on Greek and Roman classics was rejected. The librarian had reported to the members that no one had requested the classical works already in the library.[41]

Translations of the Classics

Pushkin once called translators "the post-horses of enlightenment." About the same time Goethe wrote to Carlyle, "Say what one will of the inadequacy of translation, it remains one of the most important and worthiest concerns in the totality of world affairs." For most Americans of the eighteenth century it was through translations of the classics that they gained access to the classical heritage. Despite their long training in Latin and Greek in grammar schools and colleges, few educated Americans read the classical languages with ease;[42] and, of course, most Americans simply did not have the benefit of a classical education. It is true that Jefferson preferred, and recommended, going to the originals rather than to translations,[43] but, like most American readers of the classics, he himself possessed a wide array of the best available translations of Greek and Latin authors, as his libraries reveal. Characteristic was the practice of Alexander Hamilton, who, though he possessed a good classical education, preferred to use a translation of Plutarch's *Lives*.[44] In 1752–53 William Livingston's *Independent Reflector* garnished each issue with Latin mottoes and quotations, but a letter to the editor reported that this caused grumbling among the readers. "It is . . . the Language in which they are delivered," said the writer, "and not the Sense of the Mottos, which has given Umbrage; and that for no less substantial a reason, than because many of your Betters are unprovided with Dictionaries."[45]

There is, indeed, nothing inconsistent in the fact that though many Americans possessed some facility in Latin (less in Greek),[46] there prevailed the widespread practice of reading translations of the classics in adult life.[47] William Duke might proclaim in 1795 that Latin and Greek "are still properly esteemed the originals of literature and the sources of learning," that translations are always inadequate, and that "the Latin is the common language of the learned in Europe, and I would fain add, in America."[48] The evidence, however, gathered from library holdings, letters, diaries, polemical literature, is overwhelming that most Americans read their classics in translation, and used other short cuts to antiquity.[49] As early as 1749 Franklin proposed the teaching of ancient history through translations of Greek and Roman historians.[50]

It is true that one might instance the Virginian William Byrd of Westover, who had one of the largest colonial libraries (3,600 volumes). He read some Hebrew, Greek, and Latin almost every morning, from a wide variety of authors (with preference for Homer, Lucian, and Plutarch), "just to keep in practice," as it were.[51] Or one might single out such learned classicists as Cotton Mather, James Logan, Thomas Jefferson, Samuel Adams, John Adams, and James Wilson, or some of the famous teachers of Latin and Greek, but the actuality is that most Americans had recourse to imported translations of the classics. Indeed, in 1803 Samuel Miller called eighteenth-century America "THE AGE OF TRANSLATIONS," and commented on their widespread use, "particularly within the last sixty or seventy years."[52]

The use of translations of the classics should not by any means be regarded as peculiarly American. The reading of translations was in line with tradition since the sixteenth century, when, particularly in England, there began to appear a veritable flood of translations of the classics. These effectively brought the Renaissance and the benefits of the classics to the whole country, to the broad English reading public which knew no Latin or Greek, and this was done "as an act of patriotism."[53] When Matthew Prior in 1685 assailed contemporary translators of the classics,

> In long oblivion may they happy lie,
> And with their Writings, may their Folly die,[54]

he was not criticizing translation itself but the lack of fidelity and the styles of the translators, including Dryden, "the head of this Gang." It was indeed Dryden who promulgated the neoclassic theory of translation. Rejecting what he called metaphrase (i.e., literal translation), he favored next in order paraphrase, but mostly free imitation, to enrich the vernacular through creative works and to fulfill contemporary moral aims. And, in keeping with the ideal of decorum and propriety, expurgations and other appropriate changes were justified.[55] In translating classical poetry the use of the rhymed heroic couplet was almost universal, a practice that Walt Whitman was later to ridicule as writing "like a see-saw." The translations read by early Americans, mostly imported from England, were created in this intellectual and literary tradition across the Atlantic.

The Classics as Useful Knowledge

As has been said, the classical reading of eighteenth-century Americans was selective, the range being circumscribed by a broad American pragmatic humanism, the immediate goals of freedom and the establishment of a new republic, and the contemporary nationwide quest for useful knowledge.[56] A popular maxim of the time was Horace's dictum, *Omne tulit punctum qui miscuit utile dulci* ("He is the most successful who combines the useful with the pleasurable").[57] The content both of formal instruction and of adult reading in the classics was consciously practical and purposeful. This reading served effectively as an agent of individual and social progress, directed as it was toward the inculcation of virtue and moral duties, the development of taste, and toward social utility, particularly in the political sphere, for the promotion of freedom and the prosperity of the country. This exaltation of utility in learning had many roots: the tradition of the ideals of civic humanism fostered by the Renaissance; Puritan and Quaker insistence on the utilitarian value of knowledge; and the emphasis on science and the social function of knowledge promoted by Bacon, Locke, and the Royal Society. For early Americans "the study of Greek and Latin literature [was] eminently practical [as] preparation for intelligent living. The classics provided not merely ornaments and delight, but useful guidance in the affairs of daily life."[58]

On May 1, 1783, the Reverend David M'Clure, at the inauguration of Phillips Exeter Academy, noted that "a growing taste for useful knowledge is an important characteristic of the people of this new world."[59] Actually, the pursuit and propagation of useful knowledge took shape in the seventeenth century and reached a crescendo of intensity in the second half of the eighteenth. During the extended preliminaries preceding the founding of the Royal Society (in the 1660s), the famous chemist Robert Boyle wrote of "human studies . . . that value no knowledge but as it has a tendency to use."[60] In 1760 Benjamin Franklin rephrased this as follows: "What signifies Philosophy but does not apply to some Use?"[61] And Landon Carter in 1774, when elected to the newly formed Virginian Society for the Promotion of useful Knowledge, wrote: "With me the very idea of useful knowledge must animate every endeavour; so very evident does the real emolument of it appear to every community."[62]

William Smith, later provost of the College of Philadelphia, put it this way in 1753: "A great Stock of Learning without knowing how to make it useful in the Conduct of Life, is of little Significancy"; and "the Knowledge of what tends neither directly nor indirectly to make better Men and better Citizens is but a Knowledge of Trifles; it is not Learning but a specious and Ingenious sort of Idleness."[63] In 1755 an anonymous American declared: "Use is the Soul of Study," writing in support of practical as against abstract knowledge. "Rome was never wiser," he wrote, "or more virtuous than when moderately learned and meddled with none but the useful sciences. Athens was never more foolish than when it swarmed with philosophers."[64]

On January 2, 1769, the American Philosophical Society Held at Philadelphia for Promoting Useful Knowledge was established, through the union of two older societies, the American Philosophical Society and the American Society held at Philadelphia for promoting useful Knowledge. In the preface to the first volume of its *Transactions* (1771) the new Society proclaimed its commitment as follows:

> Knowledge is of little use, when confined to mere speculation: But when speculative truths are reduced to practice, when theories grounded upon experiments, are applied to the common purposes of life; and when by these agriculture is improved, trade enlarged, the arts of living made more easy and comfortable, and, of course, the increase of happiness of mankind promoted; knowledge then becomes really useful. That this Society, therefore, may, in some degree, answer the aims of its institution, the members propose to confine their disquisitions, principally to such subjects as tend to the improvement of their country, and advancement of its interest and prosperity.

A decade later the Society formulated the national purpose in its Charter, promulgated in 1780, thus: "The cultivation of useful knowledge, and the advancement of the liberal arts and sciences in any country, have the most direct tendency towards the improvement of agriculture, the enlargement of trade, the ease and comfort of life, the ornament of society, and the increase and happiness of mankind."[65]

About this time, John Adams, in a justly celebrated passage, proclaimed with all deliberateness: "It is not indeed the fine Arts, which our Country requires. The Usefull, the mechanic Arts, are those which We have occasion for in a young Country. . . . I must study Politicks and War that my sons may have liberty to study Mathematicks and Philosophy. My sons ought to study Mathematicks, and Philosophy, Geography, natural History, Naval Architecture, navigation, Commerce and Agriculture, in order to give their Children a right to study Painting, Poetry, Musick, Architecture, Statuary, Tapestry and Porcelaine."[66] It is not surprising, therefore, to find in the constitutions of Pennsylvania and North Carolina, both promulgated in 1776, the following identical provision: "all useful learning shall be duly encouraged and promoted in one or more universities."[67]

Accordingly, when a perceptive Englishman, Leman Thomas Rede, traveled here to survey the American book trade, he wrote as follows about the reading public in America in 1789:

> North America may want some of the fopperies of literature. She boasts not those dignified literati, who in Europe obtain adulation from the learned parasite, and applause from the uninformed multitude, for pursuits which terminate in no addition to the real elegancies or conveniences of living. She may, however, claim the possession of all useful learning. . . . Whatever is useful, sells; but publications on subjects merely speculative, or rather curious than important, and generally such on arts and sciences, as are voluminous and expensive, lie upon the bookseller's hands. They have no ready money to spare for anything but what they *want*; and in literary purchases, look for the present, or future *use*.[68]

While men like Boyle and Franklin, partial to scientific experimentation and investigation, as well as numerous other American proponents of useful learning, were thinking principally of the advancement of science, the concept "useful knowledge" was applied equally to the classics. As early as 1658 the people of New York petitioned Peter Stuyvesant as follows: "the burghers and inhabitants are . . . inclined to have their children instructed in the most useful languages, the chief of which is the Latin tongue."[69] An announcement for a boarding school in Boston in 1727 stated: "It is also intended, That in Three Languages [i.e., Latin, French, English] they shall read Books, in which they may learn Sciences and Useful things, besides the Language."[70]

In response probably to Franklin's proposal to establish an English School at the Academy of Philadelphia, Richard Peters in 1750 reaffirmed the importance of the teaching of Greek and Latin at the Academy, maintaining that "there is an Abundance of useful Knowledge which can be acquired in no other Language; it is absolutely incumbent on those who study to capacitate themselves for Professions or who aim at a general Education and Acquaintance with Books, to gain a thorough Knowledge of *Latin* and *Greek*."[71] John Adams at a busy time abroad in 1780, when his sons were being educated in Europe, insisted that they "bend all the rest of their Time and attention, to Latin, Greek and French, which will be more useful and necessary for them in their own Country, where they are to spend their Lives."[72] An anonymous Rhode Islander, writing on the study of Latin and Greek in 1786, defended them as useful in the highest degree to the extent of being even "useful amusement for old Age."[73]

Though Benjamin Rush was intensely hostile to the classics from 1789 to the end of his life, he conceded in 1795 that, though ancient poets and orators "are calculated to impart pleasure only . . . , [the historians and philosophers] contain much useful knowledge, capable of being applied to many useful purposes in life."[74] A few years before, in 1791, in an exchange of letters with James Muir, principal of the Academy of Alexandria in Virginia, Rush was delighted to learn that only a few boys at the Academy (nineteen out of ninety) were studying Latin, and that they preferred more useful studies. Muir chose to elevate this statistic into evidence for a national trend, holding it as "proof of the taste of Americans in the present day, who prefer the *useful* to the *ornamental*."[75]

Thomas Jefferson, whose love of the classics continued unabated through life, side by side with his passion for science, in the choice of classical books for teaching the languages at the grammar school and college of the University of Virginia, insisted that they "be such as will at the same time impress the mind with useful facts and good principles."[76] And in 1819, in a justly celebrated letter to John Brazier on the usefulness of Greek and Latin studies, he said: "But to whom are these things useful? Certainly not to all men. There are conditions of life to which they must be forever estranged. . . . [Jefferson then expands in detail on many specific uses of classical languages and literatures.] To sum the whole, . . . it may truly be said that the classical languages are a solid basis for most, and an ornament to all the sciences."[77]

Yet not all Americans agreed that the classics were being properly taught, or that the long discipline required to learn the languages was worth while, or that what was read in the classical authors and in ancient history was useful knowledge. Sporadically throughout the century, and with greater intensity from about 1787 to 1805, a vociferous minority, the most vigorous of whom was Benjamin Rush, assailed the classics as useless for the new society.[78] As early as 1768 William Livingston of New York, fervent critic of established institutions, principal editor of the short-lived *Independent Reflector*, later first governor of New Jersey, argued that the imperatives of building a new country required more practical knowledge than the classics: "We want hands . . . more than heads. The most intimate acquaintance with the classics, will not remove our oaks; nor a taste for the *Georgics* cultivate our lands. Many of our young people are knocking their heads against the Iliad, who should employ their hands in clearing our swamps and draining our marshes. Others are musing, in cogitation profound, on the arrangement of a syllogism, while they ought to be guiding the tail of a plow."[79] Much earlier, in 1753, Livingston had warned that purely formal study of Greek and Latin was not acceptable. The purpose of education and reading, he argued, is to improve morals, inculcate public spirit, zeal for liberty, and love of and service to the community. "Whatever literary Acquirement cannot be reduced to Practice, or exerted to the Benefit of Mankind, may perhaps procure its Possessor the Name of a Scholar, but is in Reality no more than a specious Kind of Ignorance. This, therefore, I will venture to lay down for a capital Maxim, that unless the Education we propose be calculated to render our Youth better Members of Society, and useful to the Public in Proportion to the Expence, we had better be without it."[80]

Such doubt and dissent led an anonymous defender of the classics to argue in 1791—almost a century ahead of his time—that, in learning, utility should *not* be the guiding principle: he assailed "the short-sighted and superficial reason of the present day, [which] will not allow any merit or importance in pursuits of which the utility is not present immediately before their eyes."[81] Indeed, there was in fact at the end of the century the beginnings of a retreat from the concept of the classics as useful knowledge to the study of the languages as ornamental and ends in themselves. This provoked Samuel Miller to observe in 1803: "The more judicious had cause to lament that such a disproportionate share of regard was bestowed on language, to the neglect of studies more immediately practical," with the consequence that in the end many considered knowledge of the classics as "among the most useless objects of pursuit."[82] James Russell Lowell was later to castigate the pursuit of useful knowledge in America in his definition of a university as "a place where nothing useful is taught."[83]

As early as 1749 Benjamin Franklin had expressed the view in a famous passage in his *Proposals Relating to the Education of the Youth in Pennsylvania* that "as to their Studies, it would be well if they could be taught *every Thing* that is useful, and *every Thing* that is ornamental. But Art is long, and their Time is short. It is therefore proposed that they learn those things that are likely to be *most useful* and *most ornamental*, Regard being had to the several professions for which they are intended."[84] At the end of the century Jefferson's favorite architect, Benjamin Latrobe, a man of decided utilitarian bent, attacked "pretended knowledge" in Greek and Latin dress, the growing emphasis on philological study, and the choice of the authors read in the schools. "It is impossible," he said, "not to combine the acquisition of the language with that of the useful knowledge conveyed in it. But when Terence, Phaedrus, Ovid, and other poets, from whom no one ever learned a single useful fact, should be rejected," then some progress could be made. Homer especially should be rejected because he glorifies war and military heroes, and "conveys no information that can ever be practically useful."[85]

For all the incipient dissent, can anyone doubt that *"America was the land that took the ancients seriously"*?[86] Some even venerated the masterpieces of the Greeks and Romans as "the Sacred Classicks."[87]

The Uses of Ancient History

History, especially ancient history,[88] was a central interest of eighteenth-century Americans. "They lived history,"[89] and they studied it intensively, confident of its utility for their own lives. Early in the century an Englishman wrote: "No study is so useful to mankind as History, where, as in a glass, men may see the virtues and vices of great persons in former ages, and be taught to pursue the one, and avoid the other."[90] Two decades later, William Smith expressed the prevailing American view that history is "a Lesson of *Ethics* and *Politics*—an useful Rule of Conduct and Manners thro' Life. . . . The Youth are thus sent into the World well acquainted with the History of those Nations they are likely to be most concerned with in Life; and also the History of *Greece* and *Rome*, which may be justly called the History of *Heroism, Virtue,* and *Patriotism*. . . . It is History that, by presenting those bright Patterns to the eyes of Youth, awakes Emulation and calls them forth steady Patriots to fill the Offices of State."[91]

There is no better summary of the nature of the study of ancient history in Revolutionary America than that of Carl Becker, in his charming essay "The Spirit of '76," for which he invented the fictitious American patriot Jeremiah Wynkoop:

> Of all books, histories of the ancient and modern times were his favorite study. It was an interest which he acquired in college, and never afterward lost. In college of course we all read the standard Greek and Roman writers, and acquired the usual knowledge of classical history. . . . The Parallel Lives of Plutarch he knew almost by heart, and was never weary of discanting on the austere morality and virtuous republicanism of those heroic times. For Jeremiah a kind of golden age was pictured there, a lost world which forever disappeared when Caesar crossed the Rubicon. The later Roman times never interested him much—"five hundred years," he used to say, "in which the civilized world groaned under the heavy load of tyrants, relieved only by the reigns of five good emperors."[92]

No American of the time would have thought of asking, "What is the use of history?"

Though the Founding Fathers were saturated with ancient history, there was no formal course in the subject in the standard curriculum. Students read directly in the ancient historians, with supplementary perusal of histories of Rome and Greece. It was deemed a useful and entertaining study, too, but "cannot be considered a severe application of the mind," John Clarke concluded.[93] Jefferson once wrote a young man about how to study history: "It would be a waste of time to attend a professor of [history]. . . . It is to be acquired from books, and if you pursue it by yourself, you can accommodate it to your other reading so as to fill up those chasms of time not otherwise appropriated. . . . Particularly after dinner [the mind] should be applied to lighter occupations. History is of this kind. . . . The histories of Greece and Rome are worthy a good degree of attention. They should be read in the original authors."[94]

The study of ancient history by the Founding Fathers was thus not a mere antiquarian interest. It was indeed "the lamp of experience" to them, and their search for guidance and parallels from antiquity served two purposes: they increased their sense of legitimacy and dignity by linking their private and political lives with a cultural ancestry reaching back into antiquity;[95] and they thereby tested their own innovative views on the building of a new society and a new man by the criteria of the ancient republics and ancient heroes as ideal models. Knowledge of the great republics of the ancient world had utility for the present issues: they were the fountains of liberty, of republican forms, and civic virtues, as epitomized in the great classical heroes. Americans did not invent this interest in antiquity, which reflects the values of English neoclassical thought in the eighteenth century and was embodied in the historical works and commentaries written by Englishmen which Americans read. Their utilitarian selectivity was further influenced by the fact that most American patriots tended to view the lessons of ancient history as refracted through radical Whig eyes.[96]

Jefferson several times outlined a proper course of reading in the ancient historians. In 1785, for example, writing from Paris to young Peter Carr,[97] he advised on Greek history his "reading everything in the original and not in translations" and covering Goldsmith's history of Greece, Herodotus, Thucydides, Xenophon's *Hellenica* and *Anabasis*, Quintus Curtius, and Justin. Much later, in 1825, writing on the study of ancient history at the University of Virginia, he advised that "in all cases I prefer original authors to compilers" and listed the following: Herodotus, Thucydides, Xenophon, Diodorus, Livy, Caesar, Suetonius, Tacitus, and Dio Cassius, to be read "in their originals if understood, and in translations if not," also Arrian, Quintus Curtius, Polybius, Sallust, Plutarch, and Dionysius of Halicarnassus, as well as Gibbon and a universal history.[98]

This was an ideal program of reading in ancient history, accomplished by relatively few. The ancient historical works most frequently read by the adult population were Plutarch's *Lives*, Tacitus, Sallust, Polybius, Thucydides, Livy, Dionysius of Halicarnassus, and Diodorus Siculus. We also know today what were the best-sellers of the eighteenth century in ancient history, from the works most frequently recurring in American college libraries, and public and private book collections.[99]

Golden Age of the Classical Tradition in America

Few in the American colonies may have known—and not all would have agreed with—the well-known pronouncement of Lord

Chesterfield, "Classical knowledge is absolutely necessary because everybody has agreed to think and call it so," and that of Samuel Johnson, "Classical quotation is the parole of literary men all over the world." It is true that most of the leaders of the Revolutionary generation had a classical education, and many possessed facility with classical tags.[100] But in fact how deeply did classical knowledge penetrate and affect their lives? Was it mere window dressing, mere "pedantry in politics,"[101] or was it so thoroughly internalized as to be a substantive motivating force in thought and action?

Some have scanted the classical influence as a superficial veneer —a gentlemen's culture for an elite minority is Howard Mumford Jones's evaluation.[102] Similarly, Clinton Rossiter held that the ancient authors taught the Founding Fathers nothing new. "The Americans would have believed just as vigorously in public morality had Cato and the Gracchi never lived."[103] Bernard Bailyn, too, concludes that, though the classical heritage was universally evident in the writings of the Founding Fathers, their classical learning was superficial, randomly selective, limited in range, and "illustrative, not determinative, of thought."[104]

But this is decidedly a minority view, being more and more thrown into the shade by penetrating specialized studies, particularly by some of our colonial historians, of the uses of classical learning in the formative age of our country. To Gilbert Chinard, "the study of the classics was more than a luxury and a painful task. It was an essential part in the moral foundation of many of the men who framed the American institutions."[105] As Adrienne Koch put it, modern behavioral scientists "will have to consider how it was that men who were classical scholars, students of philosophy and science, and moralists, were also men in the key positions, defining and moulding institutions for the democratic republic."[106] Gordon S. Wood holds that "for Americans the mid-eighteenth century was truly a neo-classical age—the high point of their classical period. . . . Such classicism was not only a scholarly ornament of educated Americans, it helped to shape their values and their ideals of behavior."[107]

Two modern historians who are at home in English culture of the seventeenth and eighteenth centuries, as well as in the early American period, support this view. For Charles F. Mullett, classical authors are to be counted among the Founding Fathers. "Not less than the Washingtons and the Lees [the] ancient heroes helped to found the independent American commonwealth."[108] To Louis B. Wright, "Nothing in our modern world is so certain and unquestioned as the belief held by the men of 1787 in the wisdom of the ancients."[109]

During the Revolutionary period Charles Lee expressed the sentiments of many eighteenth-century Americans nurtured in the classical tradition: "I us'd to regret not being thrown into the world in the glamorous third or fourth century of the Romans; but now I am thoroughly reconcil'd to my lot";[110] "it is natural to a young person whose chief companions are the Greek and Roman Historians and Orators to be dazzled with the splendid picture."[111]

Notes

1. On early American aloofness from ancient art and archaeology see William B. Dinsmoor, "Early American Studies of Mediterranean Archaeology," *Proc. Amer. Philos. Soc.* 87 (1943–44), pp. 74–104; J. Hector St. John Crèvecoeur, *Letters from an American Farmer* (1782; Garden City, n.d.), letter I (written ca. 1774), p. 16: "[In Italy] they must amuse themselves in viewing the ruins of temples and other buildings which have very little affinity with those of the present age, and must therefore impart a knowledge which appears useless and trifling."
2. Noteworthy is the definition of the antiquities of America as ancient history by James Bowdoin in his address in 1780 as first president of the American Academy of Arts and Sciences: "Our ancient history is that of the European colonists who settled here." See James Bowdoin, *Mem. Amer. Acad. Arts & Sci.* 1 (1785), pp. 4–6.
3. John Edwin Sandys, *A History of Classical Scholarship* (Cambridge, 1908; rpt. 1967), vol. III, pp. 450–452. While in Germany in his student years abroad, George Ticknor, later professor at Harvard, wrote from Göttingen in 1815: "We Americans do not yet know what a Greek scholar is. We do not even know the process by which a man is to be made one" (Sandys, p. 453).
4. For the comparable French experience see Harold T. Parker, *The Cult of Antiquity and the French Revolutionaries* (Chicago, 1937; rpt. 1965).
5. Letter to Crèvecoeur, Jan. 15, 1787, *Papers of Thomas Jefferson*, ed. Julian P. Boyd (Princeton, 1950–), vol. XI, p. 44.
6. The extraordinary diffusion of classical learning in America in the eighteenth century is noted by Arthur D. Kahn, "Classics for the Seventies," *Class. World* 67 (1973), p. 343.
7. See the Bibliography, under the headings "John Adams" and "Thomas Jefferson."
8. *The Snare Broken*, 2nd ed. (Boston, 1766), p. 43.
9. Jonathan Boucher, "On American Education" (1773), in *A View of the Course and Consequences of the American Revolution, in Thirteen Discourses Preached in North America between the Years 1763 and 1775* (London, 1797; rpt. New York; 1967), p. 199. Boucher concluded that such Americans were "grovel[ing] in the darkness and filth of Heathenism." On Boucher cp. Richard M. Gummere, *The American Colonial Mind and the Classical Tradition: Essays in Comparative Culture* (Cambridge, Mass., 1963), pp. 161–172; Anne Y. Zimmer and Alfred H. Kelly, "Jonathan Boucher: Constitutional Conservative," *Journal of American History* 58 (1972), pp. 897–922.
10. See, e.g., Richard Boyd Ballou, "The Grammar Schools in Seventeenth Century Colonial America" (Ph.D. diss., Harvard, 1940), app. D ("Educational Background of the Signers of the Declaration of Independence"), pp. 388–396;

and the character sketches by William Pierce of the delegates to the Constitutional Convention, in Max Farrand, ed., *The Records of the Federal Convention of 1787*, rev. ed. (New Haven, 1937; rpt. 1966), vol. III, pp. 87–97, and in Jane Butzner, ed., *Constitutional Chaff* (New York, 1941), pp. 158–171.

11. Letter to Thomas Cooper, Oct. 7, 1814, in *Writings of Thomas Jefferson*, Memorial Edition (Washington, D.C., 1905), vol. XIV, pp. 200–201.

12. See, e.g., H. Trevor Colbourn, *The Lamp of Experience: Whig History and the Intellectual Origins of the American Revolution* (Chapel Hill, 1965), pp. 21–25.

13. Letter to James Madison, Oct. 17, 1774, in *Papers of James Madison*, ed. William T. Hutchinson and William M. E. Rachal (Chicago, 1962–), vol. I, p. 126 (Tyrtaeus, seventh century B.C., wrote martial poems for Sparta). Many decades earlier, Puritan Cotton Mather, in a remarkable confession, conceded to his son, while warning him against the allurements of poetry: "Poetry . . . has from the Beginning been in such Request, that I must needs recommend unto you some Acquaintance with it. . . . I can not wish you a Soul that shall be wholly Unpoetical" (*Manductio ad Ministerium. Dissertation for a Candidate of the Ministry* [Boston, 1726], pp. 38–42).

14. *Diary and Autobiography of John Adams*, ed. L. H. Butterfield (Cambridge, Mass., 1962), vol. I, p. 73. In his old age Adams once said, "Lord! Lord! what can I do with so much Greek?" (letter to Jefferson, July 9, 1813, in *The Works of John Adams* [Boston, 1850–56], vol. IX, p. 49).

15. As a youth Jefferson read and excerpted in his commonplace book passages from Homer, Herodotus, Euripides, Anacreon, Quintus of Smyrna, Cicero, Vergil, Ovid, Horace, Livy, Statius, Manilius, Seneca, and Catullus. In his early education he probably also read Xenophon, Thucydides, Plutarch's *Lives*, Caesar, Tacitus, Sophocles, Terence, Theocritus. See Karl Lehmann, *Thomas Jefferson, American Humanist* (New York, 1947), p. 36.

16. Jefferson, *Writings*, vol. X, p. 147.

17. J. Gardner Bartlett, "University Alumni Founders of New England," *Publ. Colon. Soc. Mass.*, vol. XXV (1925), *Transactions*, 1922–24, pp. 14–18; Mrs. P. W. Hiden, "Education and the Classics in the Life of Colonial Virginia," *Va. Mag. Hist. & Biog.* 41 (1941), p. 25.

18. Harvard was founded by early New Englanders who were concerned "to advance Learning and perpetuate it to Posterity: dreading to leave an illiterate Ministry to the Churches, when our present ministers shall lie in the Dust" ("New England's First Fruits" [1643], in *American Higher Education: A Documentary History*, ed. Richard Hofstadter and Wilson Smith [Chicago, 1962], vol. I, p. 6).

19. Edgar W. Knight, *A Documentary History of Education in the South Before 1860* (Chapel Hill, 1949–53), vol. I, p. 511.

20. There were, of course, some local variations, and revisions from time to time, and, especially in the South, private tutors were more flexible. John Quincy Adams enjoyed a highly individualized education. The correspondence between him and his father John Adams in the early 1780s is very instructive in this connection (*Adams Family Correspondence*, ed. L. H. Butterfield [Cambridge, Mass., 1963–73]). John Quincy was studying Cicero, Erasmus, Phaedrus, Nepos, Greek grammar, among other subjects (vol. III, pp. 307–308; vol. IV, pp. 113–114). But John Adams desired him to begin Sallust as soon as possible (vol. IV, p. 118). In 1780 John Adams wrote, "my Wish at present is that your principal Attention should be directed to the Latin and Greek Tongues, leaving the other studies to be hereafter attained, in your own Country. I hope soon to hear that you are in Virgil and Tully's orations, or Ovid or Horace or all of them" (vol. III, pp. 308–309). It is remarkable to find him advising his son also as follows: "Admidst your Ardour for Greek and Latin I hope you will not forget your mother Tongue. Read Somewhat in the English

Poets every day" (vol. IV, p. 114). For John Quincy Adams's attainments in classical authors see n. 27, below.

21. James Madison, letter to Jefferson, April 27, 1785, in *The Writings of James Madison*, ed. Gaillard Hunt (New York, 1901), vol. II, p. 134, Jefferson, *Papers*, vol. VIII, p. 111. For lists of "School Books" in eighteenth-century America see such typical booksellers' catalogues as: *Catalogue of Books Just Imported from London, And to be Sold by W. Bradford* (Philadelphia, 1760), pp. 12–14; *A Catalogue of Books, &c., Sold by Garrat Noel, Bookseller and Stationer from London* (New York, 1762), pp. 29–32; *A Catalogue of Books, Sold by Noel and Hazard* (New York, 1771), pp. 19–23; *A Catalogue of a Scarce and Valuable Collection of Books . . . Which are now Selling by William Prichard, Bookseller and Stationer* (Philadelphia, 1785), pp. 30–36; *Catalogue of Books to be Sold by Isaiah Thomas at his Book-Store in Worcester, Massachusetts* (Worcester, 1787), pp. 19–20 ("Classical and School Books"); *Mathew Carey's Catalogue of Books, &c. For Sale* (Philadelphia, 1794), pp. 57–59 ("Latin and Greek School-Books"); *Thomas and Andrews's Catalogue of Books* (Boston, 1793), pp. 50–53 ("Latin and Greek Classics").

22. *The Independent Reflector*, by William Livingston and Others, ed. Milton M. Klein (Cambridge, Mass., 1963), p. 424. On the aims, methods, and curriculum of the early American secondary (grammar) schools see the Bibliography, under "American Education and the Classics," as well as the following: Elmer E. Brown, *The Making of Our Middle Schools*, 2nd ed. (New York, 1905), pp. 31–59; Robert F. Seybolt, *The Public Schools of Boston, 1635–1775* (Cambridge, Mass., 1935); Thomas J. Wertenbaker, *The Puritan Oligarchy. The Founding of American Civilization* (New York, 1947), pp. 135–158; Samuel E. Morison, *The Intellectual Life of Colonial New England* (New York, 1956), pp. 4–23, 86–112.

23. The "College Enthusiasm" in colonial America noticed by Ezra Stiles, president of Yale, is revealed by the statistics. From 1715–45, 1,400 bachelor degrees were awarded by three colleges; from 1745–76, 3,100 by ten colleges. See Beverly McAnear, "College Founding in the American Colonies," *Mississippi Valley Historical Review* 42 (1955), pp. 24–44. But by 1776 only about one American in a thousand had been to college (Evarts B. Greene, *The Revolutionary Generation 1763–1790* [New York, 1943], pp. 122–123). In New England in the entire seventeenth century (1635–1700) there was a total of less than 600 college students (all at Harvard), of which only 450 received degrees (Morison, *Intellectual Life*, p. 57).

24. *Magnalia Christi Americana* (Hartford, 1820 [1st Amer. ed., from London ed. of 1702]), vol. II, p. 9.

25. Samuel Eliot Morison, *Harvard College in the Seventeenth Century* (Cambridge, Mass., 1936), vol. I, p. 81.

26. Hofstadter and Smith, *American Higher Education*, vol. I, pp. 54, 117; Edwin C. Broome, *A Historical and Critical Discussion of College Admission Requirements*, Columbia University Contributions to Philosophy, Psychology and Education, vol. XI, nos. 3–4 (New York, 1903), pp. 17–39.

27. On April 24, 1785, John Adams wrote Benjamin Waterhouse, professor of physics at Harvard, detailing the unusual reading program of John Quincy, about to enter the university: Vergil's *Aeneid*; Suetonius; Sallust; Tacitus' *Agricola, Germania,* and *Annals*; Horace; Ovid; Caesar; Cicero's orations; Aristotle's *Poetics*; Plutarch's *Lives*; Lucian; Homer's *Iliad*; and "the choice of Hercules, in Xenophon" (*The Selected Writings of John and John Quincy Adams*, ed. Adrienne Koch and William Peden [New York, 1946], pp. 71–73).

28. In addition to the books and articles in the Bibliography, under "American Education and the Classics," for early American higher education see Edward K. Rand, "Liberal Education in Seventeenth-Century Harvard," *New*

Engl. Quart. 6 (1933), pp. 525–551; Knight, *Documentary History*, vol. I, pp. 501–528; Francis L. Broderick, "Pulpits, Physics, and Politics: The Curriculum of the College of New Jersey, 1746–1794," *Wm. & Mary Quart.*, 3rd ser., 6 (1949), pp. 42–68; Richard Hofstadter and C. De Witt Hardy, *The Development and Scope of Higher Education in the United States* (New York, 1952), pp. 3–15; Morison, *Intellectual Life*, pp. 27–56; Louis B. Wright, *The Culture of the American Colonies 1607–1763* (New York, 1957), pp. 116–125; Daniel J. Boorstin, *The Americans: The Colonial Experience* (New York, 1958), pp. 178–184; Gummere, *American Colonial Mind*, pp. 63–75.

    Even in the seventeenth century, when the curriculum of Harvard was more heavily theological than later, among the textbooks and reference books used were the following: Cicero's orations and *De Officiis*, Vergil, Sallust, Terence, and Hesiod. See Arthur O. Norton, "Harvard Text-Books of the Seventeenth Century," *Publ. Colon. Soc. Mass.*, vol. XXXVIII (1934), *Transactions*, 1930–33, pp. 361–438. Note that "no seventeenth-century textbook on politics has been found" (p. 437).

29. Samuel Latham Mitchill, *The Present State of Learning in the College of New-York* (New York, 1794), pp. 6–7; John Clarke, *Letters to a Student in the University at Cambridge, Massachusetts* (Boston, 1795), pp. 36–39, 42–52; Samuel Miller, *A Brief Retrospect of the Eighteenth Century* (New York, 1803), vol. II, pp. 492–493, 498–499; Thomas J. Wertenbaker, *Princeton 1746–1896* (Princeton, 1946), pp. 92–93.

30. The stated purpose of this library was "the propagating of Virtue, Knowledge & useful Learning."

31. Edwin Wolf 2nd, "The Romance of James Logan's Books," *Wm. & Mary Quart.*, 3rd ser., 13 (1956), p. 342.

32. E.g., even Miles Standish of the Plymouth Colony had a little library of fifty books, several of which were on classical subjects.

33. Charles R. Hildeburn, *A Century of Printing. The Issues of the Press in Pennsylvania 1685–1784* (Philadelphia, 1885–86; rpt. 1968), vol. I, pp. 96, 121, 192, 328, 377; vol. II, pp. 166, 266, 271, 277, 279–280, 370.

34. Katherine H. Packer, *Early American School Books: A Bibliography Based on the Boston Booksellers' Catalogue of 1804* (Ann Arbor, 1954), p. 3. As late as 1840 Alexis de Tocqueville declared: "Almost all important English books are republished in the United States. The literary genius of Great Britain still darts its rays into the recesses of the forests of the New World" (*Democracy in America* [New York, 1945], vol. II, p. 58).

35. John Adams, *Works*, vol. X, p. 275 (letter of Adams, Jan. 14, 1818). In 1763 a *Latin Grammar for the College* was published in Philadelphia by the Steuart press. Francis Hopkinson found 151 errors in the volume, and wrote the satirical pamphlet *Errata, or the Art of Printing Incorrectly*. In retaliation the faculty of the College of Philadelphia censured the versatile and talented Hopkinson by preventing him from reading his ode to science prepared for the commencement exercises, and by excluding him from musical participation at the commencement. See Carl Bridenbaugh, "The Press and the Book in Eighteenth Century Philadelphia," *Pa. Mag. Hist. & Biog.* 65 (1941), p. 12.

36. E.g., the Library Company of Philadelphia had a library of the best-sellers of the eighteenth century that was intensely utilitarian, with a predominant interest in history (see catalogue of 1741). All its titles on classical subjects were in translation. See Edwin Wolf 2nd, "Franklin and his Close Friends Choose Their Books," *Pa. Mag. Hist. & Biog.* 80 (1956), pp. 11–36.

37. Even as early as 1638 the library of John Harvard, containing ca. 10 percent of books in classics, had translations of classical authors.

38. Jefferson, *Papers*, vol. I, pp. 76–77; Eleanor D. Berman, *Thomas Jefferson Among the Arts* (New York, 1947), pp. 268–272.

39. Donald G. Wing and Margaret L. Johnson, "The Books Given by Elihu Yale in 1718," *Yale University Library Gazette* 13 (1939), pp. 46–67.
40. Joe W. Kraus, "Book Collections of Five Colonial College Libraries: A Subject Analysis" (Ph.D. diss., University of Illinois, 1960), p. 284.
41. Wright, *Culture*, pp. 149–150. On the contents of American libraries as a clue to the reading tastes of Americans up to 1800, see, in addition to the books and articles in the Bibliography, under "Books and Libraries," the following: "The Bowdoin Library," *Proc. Mass. Hist. Soc.* 51 (1918), pp. 362–368; Thomas Goddard Wright, *Literary Culture in Early New England 1620–1730* (New Haven, 1920), pp. 25–61, 110–136, 174–196, 219–295; Austin K. Gray, *Benjamin Franklin's Library* (New York, 1937); Lehmann, *Thomas Jefferson*, pp. 17–23; E. Millicent Sowerby, ed., *Catalogue of the Library of Thomas Jefferson* (Washington, D.C., 1952–59); Morison, *Intellectual Life*, pp. 133–151; Edwin Wolf 2nd, "The Romance of James Logan's Books," pp. 342–353; Wright, *Culture*, pp. 126–153; Marcus A. McCorison, ed., *The 1764 Catalogue of the Redwood Library Company at Newport, Rhode Island* (New Haven, 1965); Joe W. Kraus, "Private Libraries in Colonial America," *Journal of Library History* 9 (1974), pp. 31–53; William Simpson, Jr., "A Comparison of the Libraries of Seven Colonial Virginians, 1754–1789," *Journal of Library History* 9 (1974), pp. 54–65; Louis B. Wright, "The Prestige of Learning in Early America," *Proc. Amer. Antiq. Soc.* 83 (1973), pp. 15–27.
42. E.g., letter of Timothy Pickering to his son John, student at Harvard, June 4, 1795: "Like me the greater part of the collegians, imprudently neglecting to read Latin daily, or at least weekly, after they leave college . . . forget the language" (Mary O. Pickering, *Life of John Pickering* [Boston, 1887], pp. 83–84). Even the vaunted facility of early Americans with classical quotations may be exaggerated. At the ratifying convention in Virginia in 1788, William Grayson, a lawyer with a good classical education, sat on guard against slips in classical quotations, which he would not allow to pass by without comment, and he even corrected errors of the speakers in pronunciation of Latin. "He was not surprised, he is reported to have said, that men who were, in his opinion, about to vote away the freedom of a living people, should take such liberties with a dead tongue." See *The History of the Virginia Federal Convention of 1788*, Collections of the Virginia Historical Society, n.s. pts IX–X, (Richmond, 1890), vol. I, p. 202.
43. E.g., letter to Peter Carr, Aug. 19, 1785, in Jefferson, *Papers*, vol. VIII, pp. 407–408; letter to Thomas Mann Randolph, Aug. 27, 1786, ibid., vol. X, pp. 305–309. Cp. Lehmann, *Thomas Jefferson*, pp. 16–17.
44. See Meyer Reinhold, *The Classick Pages: Classical Reading of Eighteenth-Century Americans* (University Park, Pa., 1975), pp. 39–47; and Chapter X, below.
45. *Independent Reflector*, p. 116.
46. Many Greek texts used in America had Latin translations in parallel columns, the fashion since the Renaissance.
47. Gummere, *Colonial Mind*, p. 174, deprecates the view that many early Americans relied on translations, "secondhand material."
48. *Remarks Upon Education, with Respect to the Learned Languages* (Philadelphia, 1795), pp. 20–21, p. 33.
49. On the preference for translations, see, e.g., Louis B. Wright, "The Classical Tradition in Colonial Virginia," *Papers of the Bibliographical Society of America* 33 (1939), pp. 89, 93; Colbourn, *The Lamp of Experience*, pp. 21–22.
50. "Proposals Relating to the Education of the Youth in Pennsylvania," in Thomas Woody, *Educational Views of Benjamin Franklin* (New York, 1931), p. 167.

51. Louis B. Wright and Marion Tinling, *The Secret Diary of William Byrd of Westover 1709–1712* (Richmond, 1941); Maude H. Woodfin and Marion Tinling, *Another Secret Diary of William Byrd of Westover, 1739–1741* (Richmond, 1942); Louis B. Wright and Marion Tinling, *William Byrd of Virginia: The London Diary (1717–1721)* (Oxford, 1958); Pierre Marambaud, *William Byrd of Westover 1674–1744* (Charlottesville, 1971), pp. 131–134, 148–150.

52. Miller, *Brief Retrospect*, vol. II, p. 273, n. y, 434–436. The American experience had parallels in Europe, and even in Latin America, where in the eighteenth century there was also a "veritable flood of classical translations," natively produced. See Tom B. Jones, "The Classics in Colonial Hispanic America," *Trans. Amer. Philolog. Assn.* 70 (1939), pp. 37–45.

53. Cary H. Conley, *The First English Translators of the Classics* (New Haven, 1927); Francis O. Matthiessen, *Translation, an Elizabethan Art* (Cambridge, Mass., 1931); Henry B. Lathrop, *Translations from the Classics into English from Caxton to Chapman 1477–1620*, University of Wisconsin Studies in Language & Literature, no. 35 (Madison, 1933); Eleanor Rosenberg, *Leicester, Patron of Letters* (New York, 1955), pp. 152–183. In general, on translations of Latin and Greek works during the Renaissance, see Gilbert Highet, *The Classical Tradition* (London, 1949), pp. 103–126.

54. "A Satyr on Modern Translators," in *The Literary Works of Matthew Prior*, ed. H. Bunker Wright and Monroe K. Spears (Oxford, 1939), vol. I, pp. 19–24.

55. John W. Draper, "The Theory of Translation in the Eighteenth Century," *Neophilologus* 6 (1921), pp. 241–254; William Frost, *Dryden and the Art of Translation*, Yale Studies in English, vol. 128 (New Haven, 1955). Cp. Flora Ross Amos, *Early Theories of Translation* (New York, 1920). James Logan, first American translator of the classics (see Reinhold, *The Classick Pages*, pp. 33–35, 60–63), expressed his view on translation thus: "I have ever thought that the best [versions] were such as kept closest to the original, expressing at the same time the thought in full propriety of the language translated into." Cited by Frederick B. Tolles, "Quaker Humanist: James Logan as a Classical Scholar," *Pa. Mag. Hist. & Biog.* 79 (1955), p. 428. Alexander Pope, in the preface to his translation of the *Iliad* (1715) expressed his conception thus: "It is the first grand duty of an interpreter to give his author entire and unmaimed . . . , above all things to keep alive the spirit and fire which make his chief character."

56. See "The Quest for Useful Knowledge in Eighteenth-Century America," Chapter II, below.

57. *Ars Poetica*, line 343.

58. Louis B. Wright, "Thomas Jefferson and the Classics," *Proc. Amer. Philos. Soc.* 87 (1943–44), pp. 223–226. On the pursuit of useful knowledge by Americans in the eighteenth century, including the utility of the classics, see also the volume by Charles Nisbet, first president of Dickinson College, *The Usefulness and Importance of Human Learning* (Carlisle, 1786); Wright, "The Classical Tradition in Colonial Virginia," pp. 95–97; idem, "The Purposeful Reading of Our Colonial Ancestors," *ELH: Journal of English Literary History* 4 (1937), pp. 85–111; Carl and Jessica Bridenbaugh, *Rebels and Gentlemen: Philadelphia in the Age of Franklin* (New York, 1942), p. 364; Daniel J. Boorstin, *The Lost World of Thomas Jefferson* (New York, 1948), pp. 213–225; Bernard Bailyn, *Education in the Forming of American Society* (Chapel Hill, 1960), pp. 33–36; Lawrence A. Cremin, *American Education: The Colonial Experience 1607–1783* (New York, 1970), pp. 357–412.

59. *An Oration on the Advantages of an Early Education* (Exeter, N.H., 1783), p. 16, note.

60. Letter to Marcomb in 1646, in Sir Henry Lyons, *The Royal Society 1660–1940* (Cambridge, 1944), pp. 9–10.

61. Letter to Mary Stevenson, ca. Nov., 1760, in *Papers of Benjamin Franklin*, ed. Leonard W. Labaree (New Haven, 1959–), vol. IX, p. 251. By "philosophy" Franklin meant "natural science."
62. *Virginia Gazette* (ed. Rind), April 14, 1774.
63. William Smith, *A General Idea of the College of Mirania* (New York, 1753), pp. 11, 19. Thirty years later, in connection with the founding of Washington College in Maryland, he offered the following *Prayer for Wisdom and Obedience:* "Holy and Merciful Father! . . . Give thy Blessing to this Seminary of Virtue and Useful Learning" (William Smith, *An Account of Washington College, in the State of Maryland* [Philadelphia, 1784], p. 46).
64. "Of the Sciences," *The Instructor*, April 24, 1755, p. 34.
65. Charter of the Society, dated March 15, 1780, *Trans. Amer. Philos. Soc.* 2 (1786), p. xi.
66. Letter to Abigail Adams, May, 1780, in *Adams Family Correspondence*, vol. III, p. 342. Cp. Miller, *Brief Retrospect:* "Pursuits of more immediate utility and profit have generally occupied the attention of our citizens, and must continue to occupy it, until their wealth and taste shall be greatly augmented" (vol. I, p. 428).
67. Sec. 44, Constitution of Pennsylvania, in *The Federal and State Constitutions*, ed. Francis N. Thorpe (Washington, D.C., 1909), vol. V, p. 3091; art. XLI, Constitution of North Carolina, vol. V, p. 2794. Cp. Knight, *Documentary History*, vol. III, p. 1.
68. Leman Thomas Rede, *Bibliotheca Americana* (London, 1789), pp. 9, 18. Cp. Brooke Hindle, *The Pursuit of Science in Revolutionary America 1735–1789* (Chapel Hill, 1956), pp. 353–354; Stuart C. Sherman, "Leman Thomas Rede's *Bibliotheca Americana,*" *Wm. & Mary Quart.*, 3rd ser., 4 (1947), pp. 332–349.
69. Daniel J. Pratt, *Annals of Public Education in the State of New York from 1626–1746* (Albany, 1872), p. 22.
70. Robert F. Seybolt, *The Private Schools of Colonial Boston* (Cambridge, Mass., 1935), p. 17.
71. Richard Peters, *A Sermon on Education, Wherein Some Account is Given of the Academy Established in the City of Philadelphia* (Philadelphia, 1751), p. 25.
72. *Adams Family Correspondence*, vol. III, p. 348.
73. *U. S. Chronicle* (Providence), Oct. 12, 1786.
74. Lecture in 1795 to medical students at the University of Pennsylvania, in Harry G. Good, *Benjamin Rush and His Services to American Education* (Berne, Ind., 1918), p. 237.
75. *Letters of Benjamin Rush*, ed. L. H. Butterfield (Princeton, 1951), vol. I, pp. 604–607. Cp. "Opponents of Classical Learning in America during the Revolutionary Period," Chapter IV, below.
76. Cited by Lehmann, *Thomas Jefferson*, p. 199.
77. Jefferson, *Writings*, vol. XV, pp. 209–211.
78. See "Opponents of Classical Learning," Chapter IV, below; A. Owen Aldridge, "Thomas Paine and the Classics," *Eighteenth Century Studies* 1 (1968), pp. 370–380; cp. Patrick Crutwell, "The Eighteenth Century: A Classical Age?," *Arion* 7 (Spring, 1968), pp. 110–131; Edwin A. Miles, "The Young American Nation and the Classical World," *Journal of the History of Ideas* 35 (1974), pp. 259–274; Linda K. Kerber, *Federalists in Dissent. Imagery and Ideology in Jeffersonian America* (Ithaca, 1970), pp. 95–134 ("Salvaging the Classical Tradition").
79. *A Letter to the Right Reverend Father in God, John, Bishop of Landaff* (New York, 1768), pp. 23–24; Rutherford E. Delmage, "The American Idea of Progress, 1750–1800," *Proc. Amer. Philos. Soc.* 91 (1947), p. 307.
80. *Independent Reflector*, p. 172.
81. *New Haven Gazette*, March 16, 1791.

82. Miller, *Brief Retrospect*, vol. II, pp. 36, 54.
83. James Russell Lowell, "Harvard Anniversary," in *Democracy and Other Addresses* (Boston, 1893), pp. 217–218.
84. Cp. Woody, *Educational Views of Benjamin Franklin*, p. 158.
85. Benjamin Henry Latrobe, *The Journal of Latrobe* (New York, 1905), pp. 72–74.
86. Gerald F. Else, "The Classics in the New World," *Newsletter of the American Council of Learned Societies*, vol. 16, no. 5 (May, 1965), p. 3.
87. Clarke, *Letters to a Student*, p. 45.
88. See further on this subject in Reinhold, *The Classick Pages*, pp. 81–98.
89. Henry Steele Commager, "Leadership in Eighteenth-Century and Today," *Daedalus* 90 (1961), pp. 659–671; idem, "The Future Belonged to America," *New York Times*, July 4, 1973, Op Ed Page.
90. Wharton, in *True Briton*, Sept. 9, 1723. Cited by R. N. Stromberg, "History in the Eighteenth Century," *Journal of the History of Ideas* 12 (1951), p. 302.
91. Smith, *Mirania*, pp. 27, 30, 76.
92. *Everyman His Own Historian* (New York, 1935), pp. 47–80, esp. p. 49. Cp. Smith, *Mirania*, p. 29: "Everything between Augustus and the beginning of the sixteenth century is past over."
93. Clarke, *Letters to a Student*, pp. 61–71 ("On History").
94. Letter to Thomas Mann Randolph, Aug. 27, 1786, in Jefferson, *Papers*, vol. X, pp. 305–309; *Crusade Against Ignorance: Thomas Jefferson on Education*, ed. Gordon C. Lee (New York, 1961), p. 141.
95. Cp. Kenneth B. Murdock, "Clio in the Wilderness: History and Biography in Puritan New England," *Church History* 24 (1955), pp. 221–238; Murdock cites Cotton Mather's remark about searching "the *Archives* of Antiquity for a *Parallel*" (p. 232).
96. On the study and influence of ancient history in early America see: Colyer Meriwether, *Our Colonial Curriculum 1607–1776* (Washington, D.C., 1907), pp. 145–147; Charles F. Mullett, "Classical Influences on the American Revolution," *Classical Journal* 35 (1939–40), pp. 92–104; Douglass Adair, "The Intellectual Origins of Jeffersonian Democracy" (Ph.D. diss., Yale, 1943); Herbert Butterfield, *The Whig Interpretation of History* (London, 1951), pp. 11, 24, 107–132; Adrienne Koch, "Pragmatic Wisdom and the American Enlightenment," *Wm. & Mary Quart.*, 3rd ser., 18 (1961), pp. 325–326; Colbourn, *The Lamp of Experience*, passim; Douglass Adair, "Experience Must be our Only Guide: History, Democratic Theory, and the United States Constitution," in *The Reinterpretation of Early American History: Essays in Honor of John Edwin Pomfret* (San Marino, 1966), pp. 129–148 (=Jack P. Greene, ed., *Reinterpretation of the American Revolution 1763–1789* [New York, 1968], pp. 396–416); Thomas Preston Peardon, *The Transition in English Historical Writing, 1760–1830*, Studies in History, Economics & Public Law, Columbia University, no. 390 (New York, 1966), pp. 10–11; Andrew Lossky, "On History in the Eighteenth Century," in *The Transformation of the Roman World: Gibbon's Problem After Two Centuries* (Berkeley, 1966), pp. 1–29; James William Johnson, *The Formation of English Neo-Classical Thought* (Princeton, 1967), pp. 31–105; Gordon S. Wood, *The Creation of the American Republic 1776–1787* (Chapel Hill, 1969), pp. 45–53; Kerber, *Federalists in Dissent*, pp. 123–134. Cp. also Henry Steele Commager, "The American Enlightenment and the Ancient World: A Study in Paradox," *Proc. Mass. Hist. Soc.* 83 (1971), pp. 3–15.
97. Aug. 19, 1785, Jefferson, *Papers*, vol. VIII, pp. 407–408.
98. Jefferson, *Writings*, vol. XVI, p. 124. Cp. Jefferson's letter to John Garland Jefferson, April 14, 1793, vol. XIX, p. 104; H. Trevor Colbourn, "Thomas Jefferson's Use of the Past," *Wm. & Mary Quart.*, 3rd ser., 15 (1958), pp. 56–70.

99. The evidence has been very usefully collected by Colbourn, *The Lamp of Experience*, app. II, pp. 199–232.

100. Richard G. Gummere has abundantly illustrated this in *The American Colonial Mind,* passim, and in his *Seven Wise Men of Colonial America* (Cambridge, Mass., 1967), passim.

101. As the contemporary use of classical allusions in parliamentary speeches and writing in England was called by Horace Walpole. See *Horace Walpole, Writer, Politician, and Connoisseur,* ed. Warren H. Smith (New Haven, 1967), p. 46.

102. *O Strange New World. American Culture: The Formative Years* (New York, 1964), pp. 240, 251, 427–428.

103. *Seedtime of the Republic* (New York, 1953), p. 357.

104. *The Ideological Origins of the American Revolution* (Cambridge, Mass., 1967), pp. 23–26; *Pamphlets of the American Revolution 1750–1766* (Cambridge, Mass., 1965), vol. I, pp. 20–22.

105. *The Literary Bible of Thomas Jefferson: His Commonplace Book of Philosophers and Poets,* ed. Gilbert Chinard (Baltimore, 1928), p. 4.

106. Koch, "Pragmatic Wisdom and the American Enlightenment," p. 326.

107. Wood, *The Creation of the American Republic,* p. 49.

108. Mullett, "Classical Influences on the American Revolution," p. 104.

109. Wright, "The Classical Tradition in Colonial Virginia," p. 97.

110. Letter to Patrick Henry, July 29, 1776, in *The Lee Papers,* vol. II, Collections of the New-York Historical Society for the Year 1872 (New York, 1873), p. 177.

111. Letter to Robert Morris, Aug. 15, 1782, ibid., vol. IV, Collections of the New-York Historical Society for the year 1874 (New York, 1875), p. 26.

II. The Quest for Useful Knowledge in Eighteenth-Century America

$\mathbf{O}$n May 1, 1783, the eloquent Reverend David M'Clure, at the inauguration ceremonies of Phillips Exeter Academy, of which he was a trustee, noted that "a growing taste for useful knowledge is an important characteristic of the people of this new world."[1] The Reverend Mr. M'Clure was surely aware of a great new surge of utilitarian energy in America unleashed by freedom from Britain and fed by egalitarian aspirations. But this was not the occasion to tell his distinguished audience in Exeter that everyone in America favored useful knowledge (even if few could formulate or agree to a precise definition), or that the concept was not a native product but a British transplant increasingly cultivated in the new country. He merely sought to place the newly founded academy in context, for, like many other such institutions established at this time, it was intended to serve educational ends different from and more practical than those of the conventional grammar schools with their traditional classical curriculum.[2]

As regards utility, however, it must be remembered that even the age-old training in the Latin and Greek classics, both in the grammar schools and the colleges, had utilitarian functions from the start, when they were first naturalized on American soil in the middle of the seventeenth century. Particularly in Puritan New England, classical learning was at first tolerated and then fostered as a useful means of teaching religious truth, inculcating morality, and

50

training professionals in the service of church and state.[3] This was also partly true even in Virginia, where the status value of classical learning as the hallmark of the gentleman was more esteemed as an elitist, ornamental cachet. Yet, on the whole, education in the first century of America, predominantly theological and classical, was mainly prized for its usefulness, through discipline and moral and religious instruction, in molding the inner order of man.

Meanwhile, on the other side of the Atlantic a new theory of useful knowledge was winning wide currency in the seventeenth century. The decisive impulse was Francis Bacon's imposition of a utilitarian end for knowledge: the public good and the relief of man's estate.[4] This Baconian doctrine of the practical usefulness of knowledge for social ends was fostered by the English Puritan and sectarian educational reformers of the seventeenth century, such as Samuel Hartlib, John Dury, and William Petty, who advocated experiential, experimental and utilitarian criteria.[5] This reform program involved not only a reordering of priorities in learning, and rejection of traditional school subjects, but also socially directed emphases.

For instance, William Walwyn, a prominent member of the Leveller party, wrote about 1650 that men must learn to become selective in what they study and "reject what is uselesse (as most of that which hath hitherto borne the name of learning, will upon impartiall examination prove to be) and esteeme that only which is evidently usefull to the people."[6] Accordingly, Latin, Greek, and Hebrew were demoted by some of the reformers to the subordinate role of tool subjects, useful only for understanding Scriptures and for increasing the knowledge of "immediately useful" and "profitable Arts and Sciences." John Dury's formulation was unmistakable: "Tongues are no further finally usefull than to enlarge Traditionall Learning; and without their subordination unto Arts and Sciences, they are worth nothing towards the advancement of our Happiness."[7] Thus there was emerging in educational thought, under the impact of the criterion of utility, a hierarchy of means and ends, with a resultant shift away from the study of the dead languages as unprofitable formal disciplines devoted only to "words, not things."[8]

Thus launched and popularized by the Baconian tradition, the concept of useful knowledge was to remain, however, imprecise and impressionable, a slippery slogan lying ready to be usurped by innovators and traditionalists, scientists and humanists, secularists and theologians, advocates of intellectual training and anti-intellectuals alike, both in Britain and America.

In the troubled times of the 1640s, when discussions were afoot regarding the feasibility of forming a scientific society in England, the great chemist Robert Boyle wrote in 1646 that he was applying himself to "other humane studies . . . [namely], natural philosophy, the mechanics and husbandry, according to our new philosophical college that values no knowledge but as it has a tendency to use."[9] When the Royal Society of London for the Promotion of Natural Knowledge was finally founded in the 1660s, Henry Oldenburg, charter member and first editor of its *Transactions*, spoke of "promoting the improvement of philosophical matters," of the "advancement of learning and profitable discoveries," of "solid and usefull knowledge," and of contributions to "the grand design of improving natural knowledge, and perfecting all philosophical arts and sciences."[10] Soon after, in 1668, it devolved upon Joseph Glanvill, another member of the Royal Society, to defend the concept of science as useful knowledge. He reviewed recent inventions of scientific instruments and extolled the Royal Society for its "noble purposes," as "a great ferment of useful and generous knowledge," and as "a bank of all useful knowledge," particularly practical and theoretical physics.[11]

Toward the end of the century the criterion of utility in the school curriculum was given a powerful new validity by John Locke, who stressed selecting for use in teaching only "what is most necessary," "of greatest consequence, and frequentest use, in the ordinary course and occurrences of that Life, the young Man is designed for."[12] This Lockian manifesto was to thrive as a continuing directive for practical vocational training in England and America. War had been declared against the absolute power of the classical curriculum enthroned in the Renaissance.

On this side of the Atlantic, there emerged an explicit concern for useful knowledge in the second half of the seventeenth century, particularly in the middle provinces, where the classical curriculum was least in vogue. As early as 1658 the people of New Amsterdam petitioned Peter Stuyvesant for permission to instruct their children "in the most useful languages, the chief of which is the Latin tongue."[13] It was in Pennsylvania, among the Quakers, that the first impulse toward a definition of useful knowledge in America was given. The utilitarian direction of Quaker thought was first charted by the founder of the Society of Friends, George Fox, who introduced the "guarded education" of the Quakers, and whom William Penn characterized as a man "ignorant of useless and sophistical science . . . [and who] had in him the grounds of useful and commendable knowledge, and cherished it everywhere."[14] Accordingly, Quaker education was from the beginning in America infused with an intense practicality, and was long opposed, on egalitarian grounds as well, to ornamental knowledge, and to the training of a cultured elite and a highly specialized ministry.

William Penn's well-known interest in the practical—for the prosperity and welfare of his people—took the form of special advocacy not only of religion and morality but of "fair writing," reading, "the most useful parts of Mathematics," and vocational training through "useful arts and sciences, suitable to their sex, age and degree."[15] Penn's most famous dictum on useful knowledge is to be found in his *Letter to Wife and Children:* "Let it be useful knowledge such as is consistent with truth and godliness, not cherishing a vain conversation or idle mind. . . . I recommend the useful parts of mathematics, as building houses, or ships, measuring, surveying, dialing, navigation; but agriculture especially is my eye. Let my children be husbandmen and housewives; it is industrious, healthy, honest, and of good example."[16] Penn condemned what he called "false knowledge," especially emphasis on words, grammar, rhetoric, and Latin and Greek ("that it is ten to one may never be useful to them"), and praised mechanical, physical, and natural knowledge, which would be useful to them for the rest of their lives.[17] In the Frame of 1682 for the government of the province Penn provided not only for public schools but also for premiums to "authors of useful sciences and laudable inventions."[18]

Shortly afterwards began the efforts of many Quakers to integrate themselves into the prevailing educational system, particularly since under the "guarded education" no effort was made to prepare Quaker youth for college. As early as 1685 Thomas Budd, a recent convert to the sect, presented an educational plan, generally utopian in character, which followed Penn's injunctions regarding public education of boys and girls in "all the most useful Arts and Sciences" but added to formal instruction in the English language "Latine and other useful Speeches and Languages," as well as arithmetic and bookkeeping. Boys were to be taught a trade, girls homemaking skills. But in general Budd appears to have been motivated by a special concern for fostering the commercial life of the province.[19]

Throughout the eighteenth century, numerous Quaker communities along the Atlantic seaboard reaffirmed the sect's utilitarian position regarding public schools, implementing the directive of useful knowledge in the form of religious and moral instruction, and training in basic skills and vocational subjects.[20] With growing affluence some Quakers, aspiring to college education for their sons, advocated an expanded curriculum and justified the inclusion of modern languages, as well as Latin, Greek, and Hebrew.[21]

In the 1780s, directly after the extraordinary Reform of the 1778 Yearly Meeting, which authorized a broader scope for the education of Quaker youth, many Quaker communities began to reassess their commitment to education. Many were content to reaffirm their obligation to provide instruction for the youth in "useful learning,"[22] which contented itself with practical subjects in the lower branches. Some, such as Moses Brown in Rhode Island, would allow the teaching of Latin, other learned languages, and also French, because they may be useful to a few scholars, even though "most Friends here think only a little knowledge of Reading, Writing, and Arithmetick necessary."[23] The most authoritative spokesman for the prevailing Quaker concept of useful knowledge was Anthony Benezet, who in 1783 advocated the teaching of English "& such other useful parts of learning as their respective situation may make necessary, to render them happy in themselves, & serviceable to others," including the living languages for some, but excluding the learned languages. At the end of his teaching career of forty years, Benezet outlined a curriculum that embraced writing, English grammar, the useful parts of arithmetic, mensuration, merchant accounts, mechanics, geography, astronomy, history, religion, anatomy, "these necessary parts of knowledge so useful in directing the youthfull mind in the path of virtue & wisdom."[24]

In England, the activities of the Society of Friends, of the educational reformers and sectaries, and of the scientists in promoting their special perceptions of useful knowledge generated a parallel movement on behalf of the Anglican Church. The lead in this was taken by the English divine Thomas Bray, founder of the influential Society for the Promotion of Christian Knowledge (SPCK) in 1699 and organizer of numerous public parish libraries in England, Wales, and North America. Bray's tract *An Essay towards Promoting all Necessary and Useful Knowledge, Both Divine and Human, in all Parts of His Majesty's Dominions, Both at Home and Abroad*[25] contains the first elaboration (even if still vague) of the notion of useful knowledge in the prevailing English acceptance. In the preface he wrote: "But especially a Man is Esteemed for his Knowledge, if his Understanding is Eminent in things laudable, and of great Weight and Moment, for whatever is greatly useful is highly valuable." His principal concern was for knowledge useful to men in the professions: clergymen, physicians, lawyers. But he included under the banner of "useful" also history, travel, humanity (classical literature), agriculture, mathematics, physick, and law, with a view to serving the needs of "young Gentle-Men, when removed from the Universities, those Fountains of useful and substantial Knowledge," and also to furnishing the youth of the gentry, "with that useful Knowledge in History, Travels, Humanity, Agriculture, and all such Noble Arts and Sciences, as will render 'em serviceable to their Families and Countries." Yet of the fifty-five titles Bray proposed for starting lending libraries, thirty-three were in theology, the rest being distributed among the areas of history (both ecclesiastical and civil), geography and travels, humanity (only Vergil, Horace, Juvenal, and Persius), anatomy and gardening.[26]

Bray's view of what was useful knowledge for the American colonies is to be found in his unpublished tract entitled "Bibliothecae Americanae Quadripartitae . . . or Catalogue of the Libraries Sent into the Severall Provinces of America." Bray wrote: "The Design of Writing and Reading Books is to Improve Knowledge. And the Tendency of good Books is to Advance necessary and usefull Knowledge. And Libraries, being a Collection of many Books written upon various Subjects, the end of them is to give Requisite Helps to Considerable Attainments in All the Parts of necessary and Usefull Knowledge." While his principal concern was for the clergy in the rude and unenlightened colonies, in his "Compleat Scheme of Severall Sciences or Parts of necessary and Usefull Knowledge," Bray embraced an astonishingly comprehensive range of fields: theology, the humane sciences (ethics, economics, politics, law, history, geography), natural philosophy (medicine, chemistry, pharmacology, anatomy, chirurgery), mathematics, trade and commerce, grammar, rhetoric, poetry, logic.[27] In thirty years at the beginning of the eighteenth century the Rev. Thomas Bray, through the SPCK, established thirty-nine libraries along the Atlantic coast, and sent over 34,000 books.[28]

There is ample and varied evidence of the steady growth of conscious utilitarian aims in acquiring information and systematic learning in America during the next century. For example, self-instructors were immensely popular for a century, such as *The Young Man's Companion; or The several Branches of Useful Learning made perfectly easy,* by the English Quaker William Mather (first edition published in London in 1681).[29] Numerous private libraries and booksellers' catalogues reveal that among the reading preferences of colonial Americans there was a high priority of practical books useful in a new country, especially such as provided self-help and self-improvement. Virginia gentry (as well as educated men in the other colonies) read classical literature not only for its ornamental value but also for its practical utility as a repository of secular wisdom providing moral and ethical guidance, models of literary taste and rhetoric, and lessons in statecraft and politics.

This penchant for the practical value of knowledge as useful for self-improvement was balanced by an operative conviction of the social function of knowledge.[30] This emergent American pragmatism, however, remained throughout the eighteenth century merely a national mood; it was never formally articulated in a systematic way.[31] One of the most popular mottoes of eighteenth-century Americans was Horace's utilitarian dictum: *Omne tulit punctum qui miscuit utile dulci*[32] ("The [author] who combines the useful with the pleasurable is the most successful"). Colonial education, at all levels, was dedicated to utility and directed to the needs of life: training of the youth in moral virtue and for specific roles in society. In this connection Robert F. Seybolt's researches have demonstrated the diffusion and importance of private schools and evening schools in colonial America, which arose in response to a growing demand for training in practical and vocational skills for a new country, including such subjects as bookkeeping, surveying, navigation, mensuration, shorthand, English, and modern foreign languages.[33]

As early as 1712 statutes of South Carolina provided for instruction "in useful and necessary learning" in free public schools in the parishes of the province.[34] In New England, Cotton Mather in 1713 was troubled by his laxness in instructing his family and domestics in piety and "enrich[ing] them with useful Knowledge," by which he meant religious instruction.[35] But near the end of his life, in 1724, he declared that "the most useful erudition is not what we are fondest of," voicing his own doubt that Harvard students would lend their support to the appointment of professors of mathematics and experimental philosophy (i.e., science).[36]

In the same year, 1724, a perceptive book was published on *The Present State of Virginia* by the Reverend Hugh Jones, professor of mathematics and natural philosophy at the College of William and Mary, in which he recommended discontinuing the traditional classical curriculum in Virginia—on practical grounds. The young gentlemen of the plantations would profit, he argued, from a course of education consisting of English, Christianity, mathematics (arithmetic, algebra, geometry), surveying, navigation. "These," he urged, "are the most useful branches of learning for them, and such as they willingly and readily master, if taught in a plain and short method, truly applicable to their genius."[37] That very same year a broader, publicly oriented significance to the concept of useful knowledge was provided in Philadelphia by Samuel Keimer (the maverick printer who once employed Benjamin Franklin) when he decided to reprint the radical Whig discourses of J. Trenchard and Thomas Gordon from the *Independent Whig* of London. These tracts, he announced in his preface, he intended to publish in the interests of promoting useful knowledge, to help dispel "Ignorance and Superstition" for "the publick Good." Similarly, in the prospectus of his new journal, the *Pennsylvania Gazette, or Universal Instructor*, first issued December 24, 1728, Keimer proposed to cover a great variety of subjects—mostly scientific—and so to provide the reader with "the richest Mine of useful Knowledge (of the Kind) ever discover'd" in America.[38] There is evidence of a sharp qualitative change in America toward the secularization of American society about the end of the first quarter of the eighteenth century. The new utilitarian mood appears to be both antitheological and anticlassical. This is perhaps what Benjamin Franklin's brother James Franklin (d. 1735) meant by "cobweb learning to catch flies," in his appeal for "the pursuits of true philosophy" and for "the study of things of solid use and benefit."[39]

About this same time a utilitarian, revolutionary approach to secondary education was penetrating American grammar schools, through the influence of a work of the progressive English teacher and classical scholar, John Clarke, long master of the grammar school at Gloucester. In 1720 he published an influential work entitled *An Essay upon the Education of Youth in Grammar Schools* that was to serve as a vade mecum for teachers of classics in America for generations.[40] Basing his views on John Locke's educational thought, Clarke, while acknowledging the study of Latin and Greek as indispensable and basic, assailed the exclusive concern with words and the study of the classical languages as ends in themselves. Clarke advocated that the youth be taught "a great deal of useful Knowledge . . . at the same time they learn the Languages," particularly history, geography (modern as well as ancient), chronology, divinity, and English style.[41]

In Philadelphia, in particular, discontent with the exclusive nature of the classical curriculum and with veneration of classical lit-

erature as a species of secular Scriptures found sympathetic support
in the Quaker advocacy of practical useful knowledge for the improvement of man's estate. The prohibition by the Friends of both
frivolous amusements and ornamental knowledge, their empirical,
rational approach to thought, and their positive attitude toward the
study of nature were all encouragements to the pursuit of science
among Quakers.[42] Stimulated by this atmosphere in Philadelphia of
utilitarianism, secularism, and scientific study, Benjamin Franklin
in 1743 issued *A Proposal for Promoting Useful Knowledge among
the British Plantations in America.* Franklin's concept of useful
knowledge was already unreservedly practical: he proposed the establishment of a society, "to be called *The American Philosophical
Society*," for the study of botany, medicine, mining and quarrying,
mathematics, chemistry, mechanical inventions, new arts, trades,
manufactures, geography, animal husbandry, agriculture, and for
the pursuit of "all philosophical experiments that let Light into the
Nature of Things, tend to increase the Power of Man over Matter,
and multiply the Conveniences or Pleasures of Life."[43] Under
Franklin's aegis the new society held some meetings but was dormant from 1745 to 1767.[44] In 1748, an informal Society for the Promotion of Useful Knowledge was founded also in New York by
William Livingston, William Smith, Jr., and John Morin Scott.[45]

Soon after, in connection with proposals then afoot for the establishment of a public academy in Philadelphia,[46] in 1749, Franklin
published his *Proposals Relating to the Education of the Youth in
Pennsylvania.* "As to their Studies," he recommended, "it would be
well if they could be taught *every Thing* that is useful, and *every
Thing* that is ornamental. But Art is long, and their Time is short. It
is therefore proposed that they learn those things that are likely to
be *most useful* and *most ornamental*, Regard being had to the several professions for which they are intended." He regarded as the
most useful for all to be able to "write a fair hand," to study drawing, arithmetic, accounts, geometry, astronomy, English, agriculture, and ancient history. Such history was to be taught not by the
study of Latin and Greek but through translations of ancient historians and through modern works on Greek and Roman history.
This study, he urged, would introduce the students advantageously
and pleasurably to "all kinds of useful knowledge," such as geography, chronology, ancient customs and monuments, morality, religion, and natural history.[47]

This preliminary overview by Franklin was followed in the same
year, with his active participation, by the *Constitutions of the Pub-*

lick Academy in the City of Philadelphia, in which was elaborated his antitraditionalist, socially oriented educational plan. "Nothing can more effectually contribute to the Cultivation and Improvement of a Country," he wrote, "the Wisdom, Riches, and Strength, Virtue and Piety, the Welfare and Happiness of a People, than a proper Education of Youth, by forming their Manners, imbuing their tender Minds with Principles of Rectitude and Morality, instructing them in the dead and living Languages, particularly their Mother Tongue, and all useful Branches of Liberal Arts and Science."[48] The wide array of subjects he proposed for the Academy of Philadelphia, to prepare the youth for an open, practical world, included: Latin, Greek, English, French, German, Spanish ("the most useful living foreign Languages"), history, geography, chronology, logic, rhetoric, writing, arithmetic, algebra, mathematics, natural and mechanic philosophy, drawing, "and every other useful Part of Learning and Knowledge."[49] The following year, 1750, an appropriation was made by the Philadelphia Council for the establishment of the Academy, "for instructing Youth in the several Branches of useful Learning," and the subjects offered at the opening of the Academy of Philadelphia included the subjects proposed by Franklin, except English (!) and Spanish, with the addition of merchants' accounts, surveying, gauging, navigation, and astronomy.[50]

Shortly afterwards the versatile Cadwallader Colden, also committed, like Franklin, to science and education for the public good, wrote a letter to Franklin commending his proposals, particularly the inclusion of agriculture as one of the sciences to be taught in the new Academy, "since it is truely the foundation of the Wealth and wellfare of the Country & it may be personally usefull to a greater number then of any of the other sciences." Colden urged greater concern for the English language and the study of English authors than for Latin and Greek, which for most (except those intended for the professions of divinity, law, and medicine) are of little value to those "who afterwards in their course of life perhaps may never make use of them." Merchants and those engaged in foreign commerce ought to have command of at least one foreign language—French.[51] But there was sharp division within the Board of Trustees of the Academy on the proper balance between the classical curriculum and the newer subjects. The dispute was resolved by the establishment of both an English school and a Latin school.

One of the first trustees of the Academy of Philadelphia was the pious, scholarly Richard Peters, president of the Board from 1756 to 1764. Even before the Academy opened its doors, Peters urged a thoroughgoing education in Latin and Greek as indispensable both for the professions and general education in "this Academy for the Instruction of Youth in Piety, Virtue, and Useful Knowledge." For, he argued, "there is an Abundance of useful Knowledge which can be acquired in no other Language."[52] It is noteworthy that, however much Franklin and Peters differed over the specifics of the curriculum, both were strong advocates of useful knowledge. The Reverend William Smith, later to become the first provost of the College and Academy of Philadelphia, composed "An Evening Prayer" for the Academy in 1753, which concluded with the following petition: "Help [the Trustees] to put it upon the best Foundation, and to form from Time to Time such Orders and Regulations in it, as will best promote thy Glory, and the Establishment of solid and useful Learning."[53] Franklin would readily have concurred in the need for divine guidance, for he counseled that "Most of the Learning in use is of no great Use."[54] Even as regards scientific knowledge and experiments, he expressed the famous dictum, "What signifies Philosophy that does not apply to some Use?"[55]

In 1750 some leading Philadelphians founded a society of which Franklin was a member, and which he later called the young Junto. In 1766 it called itself the American Society for Promoting and Propagating Useful Knowledge, Held at Philadelphia. In May, 1751, Franklin wrote his English friend Peter Collinson about the new society, which he hoped "would soon produce something agreeable to you and all Lovers of Useful Knowledge."[56] Near the end of his life, when he learned that the English School at the Academy in Philadelphia had been discontinued, through a combination of faculty neglect and parental and student disinterest, he issued an angry criticism of this development which gave the primacy to the Latin School, concluding that "learning the ancient [languages] for the purpose of acquiring Knowledge is become absolutely unnecessary."[57] In 1803 Samuel Miller, surveying the intellectual history of eighteenth-century America, offered due tribute of praise to Franklin for "his exertions for promoting useful knowledge."[58]

Franklin's dispute with the trustees of the Academy of Philadelphia in 1789 over the demise of the English School there is but one incident in the ever-widening debate over the kind of knowledge useful in a new country and in an atmosphere of increasing egalitarian aspirations. Beginning sporadically in the 1750s, and bursting forth with spectacular intensity from 1785 to 1800, a vigorous effort was made in America to dethrone the age-old sovereignty of Latin and Greek in the curriculum. The battle lines were drawn between defenders of classical learning and its aggressive opponents who assailed the dominance of the classics as elitist, impractical, and useless for most in America.[59] In New York, for instance, with its dominant commercial and business interests and lack of a tradition of a college and public schools, a fresh start without the ancient languages was favored by many. As early as 1752, in a discussion about public schools, it was affirmed by the *New-York Gazette* that Latin and Greek were in "no way necessary for the general education of Youth, in any thing necessary for useful knowledge," since they are not useful to most in life and business but only to those intended for the professions of divinity, law, and medicine. "Now we have Books in English sufficient for instruction, in every part of a genteel education, and generally useful Knowledge."[60] Similarly, in 1753, during the debate over the establishment of a college for New York, in the *Independent Reflector* William Livingston, its principal editor, adopted a reserved view of the usefulness of the classics. An exclusive education in Latin and Greek would be absurd, "for these Branches of Literature, however useful as preparatory to real and substantial Knowledge, are in themselves perfectly idle and insignificant. The true use of Education, is to qualify them for the different Employments of Life, to which it may please God to call them." In Livingston's view, a useful education should not only improve the inner man, but also inculcate public spirit, love of country, zeal for liberty and service to the commonwealth. "Whatever literary acquirements cannot be reduced to Practice, or exerted to the Benefit of Mankind, may perhaps procure its Possessor the Name of a Scholar, but is in Reality no more than a Specious Kind of Ignorance. . . . This therefore, I will venture to lay down for a capital Maxim, that unless the Education we propose be calculated to render our Youths better Members of Society, and useful to the Public, in Proportion to its Expence, we had better be without it."[61] In a later issue of the *Independent Reflector*, however, Livingston's associate, William Smith, Jr., set forth in detail the values of the study of Latin and Greek in the proposed college of New York, and held out high hopes for it as "the fountain of felicity to the province," and as a "seminary for the instruction of youth in useful knowledge."[62]

As a contribution to the widespread discussion regarding the founding of a college in the province of New York, the Reverend William Smith in 1753 set forth his views in the influential tract *A General Idea of the College of Mirania*, proposing two types of education: one for the learned professions, the other for the

"Mechanic" professions. For the former, knowledge of the learned languages was indispensable, not, however, as an end in itself, but "as a means of acquiring other useful Knowledge." The aim of education, Smith proclaimed, is to "make better Men and better Citizens." Otherwise, knowledge "is but a Knowledge of Trifles; it is not Learning but a specious and ingenious sort of Idleness," for "a Great stock of Learning, without knowing how to make it useful in the Conduct of Life, is of little Significancy." Logic, mathematics, physics, rhetoric, and philosophy were highly useful, Smith held, but priority was to be given to history, agriculture, and religion in a plan of education for a new country. "It is history that, by presenting those bright Patterns to the Eyes of Youth awakens Emulation, and calls them forth steady Patriots to fill the Offices of the State."[63]

When King's College (now Columbia University) was founded by royal charter in 1754, and soon entrusted to Samuel Johnson as its first president, the aims of the new college stressed religion and morality for the students, as well as "all such useful Knowledge as may render them creditable to their Families and Friends, Ornaments to their country, and useful to the public Weal in their generations," particularly "for the comfort, the convenience, and elegance of life." For the attainment of these aims the subjects to be taught were: the learned languages; the arts of reasoning, writing, speaking, numbering, and measuring; surveying; navigation; geography; history; husbandry; commerce; government; and sciences (pertaining to meteors, mines, minerals, plants, animals).[64] It is interesting to note how much more crassly utilitarian was the view of the British crown on the functions of such colleges as King's College and the College of Philadelphia. In 1762 the Royal Council granted letters patent to the two colleges authorizing collections of funds in Great Britain for their support. Both colleges, declared the document, were established, with a view "not so much at any high improvements in knowledge, as to guard against total ignorance, to instil into the minds of youth just principles of religion, loyalty, and love of our excellent constitution, to instruct them in such branches of knowledge and useful arts as are necessary to trade, agriculture, and a due improvement of our valuable colonies."[65]

This urgent utilitarianism in education and the quest for useful knowledge in the Province of New York in the pre-Revolutionary decades manifest themselves in other sources. In an article entitled "Of the Sciences," published in 1755,[66] the author divided the sciences into necessary (divinity and morality), useful, and hurtful.

Among the useful sciences he included geometry, natural philosophy, and agriculture, especially their practical applications. "Men should consider Study," he said, "not as an End, but as a Means to fit them for Business. . . . Use is the Soul of Study."[67] In 1760 Cadwallader Colden of New York wrote *An Introduction to the Study of Philosophy*[68] for young Peter De Lancey. Motivated in part by a vigorous anticlericalism and by hostility to the remnants of scholasticism (particularly in theology and the law), Colden urged upon his young relative the acquisition of knowledge useful for public and private life, and warned against the traditional education, which "serves only to fill young people's heads with useless notions and prejudices, which unfit them for the acquiring of real and useful knowledge. . . . This kind of learning, at first introduced into the popish schools, has of late obtained the name of *school learning*, in oppositon to the real knowledge of things," which Colden called the only "real and useful knowledge." The traditional "school learning is really a misapplication of time, in learning of things which exist nowhere but in the imaginations of idle, monkish, useless men, and serves no good purpose in life." The sciences are useful knowledge, for they serve to promote our well-being, life, health, pleasures, whether as private persons or as members of society. Indeed, more useful knowledge can be garnered from conversations than from books, and general practical knowledge is more worthy of respect than excessively learned specialization in one field.[69]

Was Colden guilty of incipient anti-intellectualism in his condemnation of the "mere scholar?"[70] Indeed, the emphasis on practical utility tended in this direction. William Livingston, that outspoken critic of established institutions, was deeply offended in 1768 by the bishop of Landaff's criticism of the inadequacy of American collegiate facilities for training ministers. In an outburst of patriotic fervor, he responded by expatiating on the practical priorities of a pioneering country. "We want hands, my lord, more than heads. The most intimate acquaintance with the classics, will not remove our oaks; nor a taste for the *Georgics* cultivate our lands. Many of our young people are knocking their heads against the Iliad, who should employ their hands in clearing our swamps and draining our marshes. Others are musing, in cogitation profound, on the arrangement of a syllogism, while they ought to be guiding the tail of a plow."[71]

It is clear that from about 1760 the quest for useful knowledge, however loosely this was defined, was in full swing in America. Many subscription lending libraries, modeled on the Library Company of Philadelphia, were established and flourished for the rest of the century. They offered "useful books" for the advancement of "useful knowledge."[72] The Juliana Library Company of Lancaster, Pennsylvania, for example, issued the following grandiloquent flourish: "Indeed, the World in general is now happily stored with Collections of choice and valuable Books in every Language, for the Advancement of Arts and Sciences; and the more of this *Treasure* any Community enjoys, the richer in useful Knowledge must she be" and "certain it is that the Promotion of useful Knowledge is an Undertaking truly virtuous and Praise-worthy, and such as flows from the generous Breast alone." But it is obvious that in their collection in Lancaster the members gave highest priorities to agriculture and the mechanic arts.[73] On the other hand, two decades earlier, useful knowledge in this connection had had a less utilitarian connotation. In 1747 Abraham Redwood at Newport, Rhode Island, gave £500 sterling for "a collection of useful Books suitable for a Public Library . . . having nothing in View but the Good of Mankind." The directors proceeded to draw up a list of books they deemed best suited for the purposes of such a library intended for "the propagating [of] Virtue, Knowledge & useful Learning," and it is noteworthy that of 1,500 books and pamphlets (866 titles) in the new library (officially opened March, 1750) there were numerous Greek and Latin texts, translations of classics, ancient histories, and books on Greek and Roman antiquities.[74] Near the end of the century Leman Thomas Rede, the perceptive Englishman who came to visit the United States to survey the book trade in this country, expressed scorn for scholarship in Europe, where learned parasites make "no addition to the real elegancies or conveniences of living," while America "may, however, claim the possession of all useful learning." Rede isolated the following interests of Americans: science, politics, animal husbandry, agriculture, manufactures, mechanics, navigation. "Whatever is useful, sells," he concluded.[75]

In Philadelphia the future of the College was under the guidance of Provost William Smith, who implemented Franklin's utilitarian view of education, with emphasis on things, not words; on the classical languages as tools, and on knowledge of "use for the conduct of life."[76] Despite the favorable atmosphere, the group later to be called the American Society for Promoting and Propagating Useful Knowledge, Held at Philadelphia languished and went out of existence in 1762 but was revived in 1766 by Charles Thomson. In September, 1768, it shortened its name to American Society Held at

Philadelphia, for Promoting Useful Knowledge. Meanwhile, Franklin's older American Philosophical Society was revived as a competing group in January of 1768. After months of tension and rivalry a union of the two societies was effected, to form on January 2, 1769, the American Philosophical Society Held at Philadelphia for Promoting Useful Knowledge,[77] which has had a continuous existence since.

From the start it was evident that, despite the adoption of guidelines for conducting discussions relating to "Philosophical and other usefull subjects," science and practical interests were to predominate in the society. Charles Thomson, the first secretary of the society and later to achieve fame as the permanent secretary of the Continental Congress, had been master of the Latin School in the Philadelphia Academy but left to go into mercantile trade in 1760. One of his first duties as secretary of the earlier American Society was to outline the purposes of the society, and he did so on September 18, 1767, when he proposed as priorities for discussion for "promoting Knowledge really useful," agriculture, manufactures, and commerce. On January 1, 1768, he read a formal paper on the proposed society in which he declared: "Knowledge is of little Use when confined to mere Speculation: But when Speculative Truths are reduced to Practice, when Theories, grounded upon Experiments, are applied to common Purposes of Life, and when, by these, Agriculture is improved, Trade enlarged, and the Arts of Living made more easy and comfortable, and of course, the Increase and Happiness of Mankind promoted, Knowledge them becomes really useful."

Moreover, he urged the society "to encourage and direct Enquiries and experiments, collect and digest discoveries and inventions made, and unite the labour of many to attain one grand End, namely the Advancement of useful Knowledge and Improvement of our Country." The directives are unmistakable: special attention was to be given to agriculture, trade, living conditions, roads, bridges, physics, mechanics, astronomy, mathematics, etc.[78]

As Brooke Hindle has pointed out, "This utilitarian emphasis was particularly welcome in America where youth and necessity gave added prestige to all that was useful. Praise of useful science echoed and re-echoed through the colonies."[79] Elsewhere in America societies similar to the American Philosophical Society were founded in the next three decades. The Virginian Society for the Promotion of Useful Knowledge,[80] founded in Williamsburg in 1772 or 1773, was ambitious but short-lived (it disbanded in 1774) and not very influential. The design of the society, which may have been launched as an aid to the troubled economy of the province, was set forth as the "Study of Nature, with a View of multiplying the Advantages that may result from this Source of Improvement." Discourses and experiments that benefit mankind were to be fostered, especially in climate, soils, minerals, springs, vegetables, animals, as "may conduce to the Purposes of Commerce and the Comforts of Life." One of the members of the society wrote under the pseudonym Academicus that "in the Commencement of Literature in any Country we are not to expect voluminous and finished Works in History, Philosophy, or the fine Arts; it is rather to be supposed that the first efforts of its Members will appear in detached Facts and Improvements," in experimental knowledge, especially commerce, nagivation, astronomy, geometry, agriculture, mechanics, chemistry, natural history, natural philosophy. The aim was to be "the public good." Landon Carter wrote when he was elected to the society in 1774, "With me the very idea of useful knowledge must animate every endeavor; so very evident does the real emolument of it appear to every community."[81]

Other equally ineffectual and short-lived societies of this type, established during the last fifteen years of the eighteenth century, were: The New York Society for Promoting Useful Knowledge (founded 1784); The Pennsylvania Society for Encouragement of Manufactures and Useful Arts (1787); The Kentucky Society for Promoting Useful Knowledge (1787); Society for the Promotion of Useful Arts (Albany, N.Y., 1792); The Trenton Society for Improvement in Useful Knowledge; New Jersey Society for Promoting Agriculture, Commerce and Arts (the last two between 1781 and 1789); Alexandria Society for the Promotion of Useful Knowledge (after the war); Society for the Attainment of Useful Knowledge (Philadelphia, 1794).[82]

The first great commitment to the advancement of useful knowledge in this country came from the activities of the American Philosophical Society and the American Academy of Arts and Sciences, both formally chartered in 1780. In anticipation, David Ramsay (physician, political leader, historian of the Revolution), in the first great Fourth of July oration, delivered in Charleston in 1778, lauded the foundation of the Royal Society in England and urged a similar concern in America for "promoting useful knowledge."[83] The charter of the American Philosophical Society, dated March 15, 1780, proclaims a utilitarian goal: the "cultivation of useful knowledge," and the "advancement of all useful branches of knowledge," for "the improvement of agriculture, the enlargement of trade, the ease and comfort of life, the ornament of society," and, in general, "the happiness of the country and of mankind."[84] The preface to the first volume of the *Transactions* of the Society (published in 1771), reiterating the statement of purpose of Charles Thomson on January 1, 1768, added "that this Society, therefore, may, in some degree, answer the ends of its institution, the members propose to confine their disquisitions, principally, to such subjects as tend to the improvement of their country, and advancement of its interest and prosperity." It is not surprising that, though the charter refers to the "advancement of the liberal arts and sciences," when the committees of the Society were announced in the Laws and Regulations, the humanities were not represented! The six committees were: (1) Geography, Mathematics, Natural Philosophy, and Astronomy; (2) Medicine and Anatomy; (3) Natural History and Chemistry; (4) Trade and Commerce; (5) Mechanics and Architecture; (6) Husbandry and American Improvements.[85] Indeed, even Francis Hopkinson, liberally educated in the humanities and the sciences, statesman, musician, poet, lawyer, patriot, could proclaim prospectively in an address to the American Philosophical Society on January 16, 1784: "[Foreign nations] look towards us as a country that may be a great nursery of arts and sciences—As a country affording an extensive field of improvements in agriculture, natural history, and other branches of useful knowledge."[86]

Similarly, the charter of the American Academy of Arts and Sciences, established in Boston, promulgated May 4, 1780, announced as the aims of the new society the improvement of agriculture, manufactures, and commerce; the promotion of knowledge, specifically the antiquities of America, natural history, medicine, mathematics, philosophy, experiments, astronomy, meteorology, geography; "and in fine, to cultivate every art and science, which may tend to advance the honor, dignity and happiness of a free, independent and virtuous people."[87] The preface to the first volume (1785) of the *Memoirs* of the society stressed the promotion of useful knowledge advantageous to society through the advancement of "the sciences, the arts, agriculture, manufactures and commerce." The para-academic mission of such societies is indicated by the praise accorded the work of many such societies in Europe through whose contributions "knowledge of various kinds, and greatly useful to mankind, has taken the place of the dry and uninteresting speculations of schoolmen." James Bowdoin, first president of the American Academy of Arts and Sciences, rich merchant, devotee of science and literature, governor of Massachusetts 1785–87, in his presidential address on November 8, 1780, on the ends and designs of the Academy, defined "antiquities of America" as the ancient history of the European colonists, investigation of which is advantageous for "political and other useful knowledge," and he lauded the publications of the Royal Society as "a noble collection of useful knowledge."[88]

Thus many forces and institutions in America at the end of the eighteenth century not only accelerated the quest for useful knowledge but also gave a heightened new prestige to practicality as the criterion of utility. Besides the influence of the American Philosophical Society and the American Academy of Arts and Sciences, the practical needs in the development of a new country, and the founding of many societies after 1785 for promoting agriculture and manufacturing, other factors such as the expansion of vocational opportunities and the remarkable spread of literacy[89] may have contributed to this transformation in the valuation of knowledge. The American aversion to metaphysics, the mounting criticism of the aridity of "school learning" with its emphasis on words as useless knowledge, tended to elevate practical pursuits and mechanical ingenuity to a new pride of place in the pursuit of useful knowledge in America, especially when applied to the "common concerns of life."[90] The common traditional use of "science" in the Latin sense of "knowledge" was giving way at the end of the century to a more limited connotation closer to the modern concept of science. The tenor of American utilitarianism is reflected in verses which appeared in 1789:

> Bright Science too, beneath our sacred dome,
> Shall find a last retreat, a fav'rite home,
> And, freed from schoolmen's trammels, shall impart
> Her cheering influence to each useful art,
> Diffuse her blessings, to humblest cell,
> And with the lowliest peasant deign to dwell.[91]

Characteristically utilitarian were the views, e.g., of Benjamin Smith Barton, physician and naturalist, who lamented the dominance of the classical languages as "studies which are useless and ignoble," and who asked for priority for the study of the physical universe and for the practical applications of medical discoveries in the cure of disease.[92] Similarly circumscribed was the perspective of the Philadelphia Society for Promoting Agriculture, which advocated education that is "practicable and most useful for the great body of citizens" through a combination of "other useful knowledge suitable for the Agricultural Citizens of the State" with "Knowledge of that most important Art," agriculture.[93] Noteworthy is the fact that the constitutions of North Carolina and Pennsylvania, both promulgated in 1776, contained articles in identical language providing, in most general terms, that "all useful learning shall be duly encouraged and promoted in one or more universities."[94] At the Constitutional Convention in 1787 Madison proposed the following provision: "It should be provided that the government have the power to encourage by premiums and provisions the advancement of useful knowledge and discoveries."[95] But the wording passed by the Convention, and still the national directive reads (art. I, sec. 8 of the Constitution): "The Congress shall have the power. . . . To promote the progress of science and useful arts, by securing for limited times to authors and inventors the exclusive right to their respective writings and discoveries."

In 1800 Dr. George Logan sensed the mood of the country when he wrote from Lancaster regarding the founding of an association for promoting agriculture, manufactures, and useful arts: "In an age . . . when Philosophical Inquiries have universally pervaded the civilized World, and when human researches have been directed to the attainment of useful knowledge; the Arts and Sciences have arrived to a degree of improvement, that justly distinguishes the present Century. . . . Perseverance in the investigation of the nature, properties, and the uses of things must necessarily lead to further attainments in useful knowledge.[96]

The continued dominance of the classical curriculum in the grammar schools and the colleges, despite the growing demand for and pursuit of useful knowledge in new forms, led to a vigorous debate between the defenders of the classics and the advocates of educational reform and modern subjects. In 1762 the Reverend James Maury questioned the usefulness of Latin and Greek for wealthy Virginia youths who were destined for business and would therefore profit more from history, geography, chronology, laws, constitutions, interests, and religion.[97] In 1772–73 John Trumbull, barely out of Yale, wrote his satirical poem *The Progress of Dulness*, in which he held up to ridicule contemporary education, on the grounds that "the meer knowledge of antient languages, of the abstruser parts of mathematics, and the dark researches of metaphysics, is of little advantage in any business or profession in life."[98] When the "fopperies of learning" are eradicated, Trumbull declared, and the classics demoted to a tool for improving the beauties of English, then will American students

> From schools dismiss'd, with lib'ral hand,
> Spread useful learning o'er the land,[99]

by which he meant specifically oratory and knowledge of English. In 1773 the Reverend Jonathan Boucher in Virginia argued that not all boys should study Greek and Latin, and that "it is much to be wished some discrimination could be made, and that boys hereafter might be taught, not words only, but such things as they are best qualified to learn, and such as are likely to be of most use to them in the part they are hereafter to act in the great drama of life."[100] In 1774 Philip Vickers Fithian, tutoring at Nomini Hall, recorded the doubts of his employer Robert Carter whether his children could obtain a useful education at William and Mary.[101] About 1774 St. John Crèvecoeur, a Frenchman who had settled in America, wrote about European obsession with classical antiquities: "[In Italy] they must amuse themselves in viewing the ruins of temples and other buildings which have very little affinity with those of the present age, and must therefore impart a knowledge which appears useless and trifling."[102]

After the Revolution the debate on the meaning of "useful knowledge" was resumed with renewed intensity. John Gardiner, native of Boston, lawyer, Whig activist, and reformer, in a famous July Fourth oration in Boston declared that "in no part of the habitable globe is learning and truly *useful* knowledge so universally disseminated as in *our native country*." But by useful knowledge Gardiner meant only letters (i.e., writing and reading, especially the Bible), practical arithmetics, and politics.[103] In answer to a defense of the study of Latin and Greek as useful knowledge in the highest degree, an anonymous writer (probably a Quaker), writing in the *U. S. Chronicle* in October, 1786, replied with a vigorous assault on the dead languages. "[Our youth] ought rather to be acquiring useful knowledge," which he specified as mathematics, spelling, reading, English grammar, geography, music, religion and morality, science, literature. "Among the *fine arts*," he maintained, "none is more useful or ornamental than an elegant hand-writing."[104] Among the burst of items in American magazines from 1787–1800 attacking the classics as useless and advocating practical subjects is a vigorous letter by Dr. Hugh Williamson to William Samuel Johnson, president of Columbia College, entitled "On the Study of the

Dead Languages." Williamson urged a utilitarian education based on "improvements in useful knowledge" then in progress, and advocated the teaching of science, English, and history.[105] At the end of the century Benjamin Henry Latrobe, naturalist, engineer, Jefferson's favorite architect, assailed "pretended knowledge" through the dead languages, the excessive emphasis on language study, and urged knowledge of science for the improvement of the enjoyment of American society. "No one ever learned a single useful fact" from Terence, Phaedrus, Ovid. "Homer conveys no information which can ever be practically useful."[106] In 1796 in an attack on the dead languages "Philenos" advocated an education for "real utility." "Which *one* of [the] *Sciences* is not more noble . . . than the *smattering* of dead languages which is usually acquired under the present system of education?"[107]

American educators, locked into the traditional classical curriculum and confronted with the demand for practical knowledge, had to face up to the dilemma. Yet by the end of the century the traditional grammar schools and the colleges remained virtually unchanged. In 1789 a bizarre proposal was made by the Reverend William Nixon for integrating the study of Latin and science in America. Since, he urged, "the study of the elements of the sciences contributes more than any other, to enlarge and strengthen the faculties of the human minds . . . , it would contribute much to the advancement of solid and useful knowledge" if in place of the usual Latin and Greek books studied in the schools ("as teach nothing materially useful but mere words") books on the sciences written in Latin were studied. In this manner students would acquire, in addition to the useful classics, also logic, geometry, astronomy, natural philosophy, and moral philosophy. This compromise should, he declared, satisfy both the traditionalists and the innovators, for "the advancement of literature and of useful knowledge yields advantages which pervade the whole mass of civilized society. . . . The improvement of the liberal, and of all the useful arts yield advantages, which extend to every member of civilized society."[108]

In 1799 the Reverend Ebenezer Fitch, president of Williams College, in a discourse to the students on *Useful Knowledge and Religion* defined useful knowledge as service, through the professions of medicine, law, and religion, to country, mankind, and God. Such knowledge, which includes philology, oratory, geography, cultural history, and natural science, becomes useful when applied to the improvement, convenience, and happiness of man. "The mere scholar, the man of idle speculation, who pursues his researches in

science solely for the purpose of gratifying his taste or curiosity . . .
is a useless drone in society."[109]

This scorn for pure scholarship, a pervading utilitarian perspective, and a low priority assigned to ornamental knowledge are to be
found in much of the thinking about education in the last decades
of the eighteenth century. "Useful knowledge" is everywhere employed with approbation, often merely in a vague general sense, but
most often associated with public usefulness, moral virtue, and natural science.[110]

Except in the education of his sons, John Adams did not concern
himself with the content and role of schooling in America. Though
a charter member of the utilitarian American Academy of Arts and
Sciences, he was early in life a devotee of the classics, and remained
cautiously (at times ambiguously) faithful to his love of classical
learning to the end of his life.[111] When he was abroad in 1780, he
fussed about the education of his sons, who were studying in Europe. On one occasion he wrote John Quincy that geography, geometry, and fractions were "useful sciences," and that all branches of
mathematics were "the most profitable and most satisfactory of all
human knowledge," but that he desired his sons to direct their principal attention to Latin and Greek, together with French, "which
will be . . . useful and necessary for them in their own country,
where they are to spend their Lives."[112] At about the same time he
was writing his wife Abigail (May, 1780) the impassioned and justly
famous words:

> It is not indeed the fine Arts which our Country requires. The Use-
> full, the Mechanic Arts, are those which We have occasion for in a
> young Country. . . . I must study Politicks and War that my sons
> may have liberty to study Mathematicks and Philosophy. My sons
> ought to study Mathematics, and Philosophy, Geography, natural
> History, Naval Architecture, Navigation, Commerce and Agricul-
> ture, in order to give their children a right to study Painting, Poetry,
> Music, Architecture, Statuary, Tapestry, and Porcelaine.[113]

One of Adams's good friends, Benjamin Rush, became, on the
other hand, the principal opponent of classical learning as useless
knowledge for America. Distinguished physician and teacher,
signer of the Declaration of Independence, founder of Dickinson
College, he conducted an unrelenting campaign from 1788 until his
death in 1813 to eradicate the classics from American education.[114]
In 1765, when he was about twenty, he called the reading and writing of Latin "that useful branch of improvement,"[115] and as late as

1786 he still advocated the study of the classics "as the best foundation for a correct and extensive knowledge of the language of our country."[116] At this time, when he was immersed in rethinking the type of education for a republic, one that would inculcate both virtue and political understanding, he advocated above all the study of the Bible in public schools as the greatest repository of "useful knowledge."[117]

Shortly after, in October, 1788, in his tentative "Plan for a Federal University," he turned against Greek, Latin, and Hebrew as not needed to "prepare our youth for civil and public life." His proposed curriculum included government, history, chronology, agriculture, manufactures, commerce, mathematics, natural philosophy, chemistry, natural history, philosophy, rhetoric, criticism, English, German, French, and athletics. Rush's aim—and here he provided a comprehensive definition of "useful knowledge"—was to train the youth of America to acquire "those branches of knowledge which increase the conveniences of life, lessen human misery, improve our country, promote population, exalt the human understanding, and establish domestic, social, and political happiness."[118] Swept along by the momentum of his thinking about useful knowledge for a republic, he issued in June of 1789 a full-scale assault on the teaching of Greek and Latin as obstructive of the practical needs of a new country, and of private happiness and public usefulness. "Many sprightly boys of excellent capacities for useful knowledge," he wrote, "have been so disgusted with the dead languages, as to retreat from the drudgery of the schools." Autodidacts like Rittenhouse by their contributions to the nation prove "the superiority of practical useful knowledge above technical and speculative learning." Latin and Greek as branches of liberal education have produced useless snobs. "Useful knowledge generally humbles the mind, but learning, like fine clothes, feeds pride, and thereby hardens the human heart." Besides being elitist, the study of the classical languages is a great obstacle to the cultivation of the English language in America. There is too much to be done in this country; there are higher priorities on the energies of the people.

> Here the opportunity of acquiring knowledge and of advancing private and public interest are so numerous . . . , that not a particle of time should be mis-spent or lost. We occupy a new country. Our principal business ought to be to explore and apply its resources, all of which press us to enterprize and haste. Under the circumstances,

to spend four or five years in learning two dead languages, is to turn our backs upon a gold mine, in order to amuse ourselves in catching butterflies.

Useful knowledge in Rush's plan of education, in order to qualify "for public usefulness or private happiness," should embrace English, agriculture, manufacture, commerce, philosophy, chemistry, medicine, geography, French, German, arithmetic, grammar, oratory, mathematics, philosophy, logic, chronology, history, government, and Christian religion.[119] In particular, for a new national ideal, Rush came to distrust the dead languages as fetters on the expansion of science,[120] on the viability of democratic institutions, and on the material development of the country. He conceived of education as an agent of social progress and wanted above all to inculcate religious commitment, love of virtue, patriotism, and dedication to republican government.[121]

In 1791 Rush was delighted to learn from James Muir, principal of the Alexandria Academy in Virginia, that only a few of the students there were studying Latin. He approved of Muir's elevation of this small statistic into a national trend, and exulted in this as "proof of the taste of Americans in the present day, who prefer the *useful* to the ornamental"; and he commended the good sense of the young men in the academy for preferring "*useful* to *useless*, or at best, ornamental literature."[122] In 1795 Rush, in a lecture to a class of medical students at the College of Philadelphia, again assailed the uselessness of the study of classical languages for "the time, the country, and the government in which we live," though he mitigated this general condemnation by allowing that the ancient historians and philosophers "contain much useful knowledge, capable of being applied to many useful purposes in life."[123]

Rush continued his assault on the dead languages on many fronts. In his correspondence with John Adams in 1810–11 on this subject, Rush assailed Latin as useless and harmful. "The human intellects," he charged, "are brutalized by being stuffed in early life with such offal learning. It is the more necessary to banish it from our schools since the late wonderful increase of knowledge in all useful arts and sciences."[124] He called it "monkish learning," and declared: "Were every Greek and Latin book (the New Testament excepted) consumed in a bonfire, the world would be the wiser and better for it." They were suitable for the idle and the rich, but not for the needs of the modern world. "*Delenda, delenda est lingua Romana* should be the voice of reason and liberty and humanity in every part of the world."[125] Rush died unrepent, in 1813. Adams wrote Jefferson shortly after: "Classics, in spite of our friend Rush, I must think indispensable."[126]

Jefferson, while he retained an active and committed love of the classics to the end of his life, was the leading advocate of a balanced knowledge of the humanities and the sciences. In 1821 he recalled retrospectively that when he was at William and Mary from 1760–62 the greatest single influence upon him was that of Dr. William Small, professor of mathematics, "a man profound in most of the useful branches of science."[127] Despite his own attachment to the classics, Jefferson scorned the view of the unbending classicist who held that "nothing can be useful but the learned lumber of Greek and Roman reading with which his head is stored," in the course of suggesting a catalogue of books for general reading to Robert Skipwith in 1771. Even fiction he regarded as not without utility, and commented that "everything is useful which contributes to fix in the principles and practices of virtue."[128]

While Jefferson was not unresponsive to aesthetic enjoyment, he frowned on intellectualism in isolation for purely private contemplation or inner enrichment. A strong utilitarian conviction directed his own uses and promotion of knowledge. He measured the value of knowledge by its utility to mankind when directed to the conquest of nature, the increase in material comforts, and civil and social happiness.[129] "I am not fond," he once said, "of reading what is merely abstract and unapplied to some useful science."[130] In this context the Latin and Greek classics were for Jefferson highly utilitarian, a practical preparation for the professions, civic life, and intelligent living, for they provided a wealth of useful information, sound moral principles of living, even "delight."[131] But while he himself delighted in the classics all his life, in the famous letter to John Brazier of August 24, 1819, on the usefulness of Greek and Latin studies, he demurred as to their general utility. After outlining many specific uses of the classics as supportive of various fields of study, he concluded, "To sum the whole . . . it may truly be said that the classical languages are a solid basis for most, and an ornament to all the sciences." But he conceded that these studies were not useful to all: "There are conditions of life to which they must be forever estranged, and there are epochs of life too, after which the endeavor to attain them would be a misemployment of time."[132]

As early as 1782, in his *Notes on Virginia* that dealt with plans for education in Virginia, he provided for "all the useful sciences" at William and Mary, and proposed teaching "the most useful lan-

guages, ancient and modern," to boys between eight and sixteen.[133]
In 1785, writing to John Banister, after objecting to sending American youth to Europe for education, he specified as the objects of
"an useful American education" the following subjects: classical
knowledge, modern languages (especially French, Spanish, and Italian), mathematics, civil history, ethics, natural philosophy, and
natural history, including chemistry, agriculture, and botany.[134]

As the years passed and his plans for the University of Virginia
were being clarified, he wrote Joseph Priestley, January 18, 1800,
that "in an institution meant chiefly for use, some branches of science, formerly esteemed, may now be omitted; so may others now
valued in Europe, but useless to us for ages to come." In his admittedly hastily devised incomplete list of subjects useful to America
he included botany, chemistry, zoology, anatomy, surgery, medicine, natural philosophy, agriculture, mathematics, astronomy, geography, politics, commerce, history, ethics, law, arts, and fine
arts.[135] These were among the useful sciences which would be
taught at the University "in their highest degree, . . . the particular
sciences of real use in human affairs."[136] In 1818 in the famous
"Report of the Commissioners Appointed to Fix the Site of the
University of Virginia" (Rockfish Gap Report), which was written
by Jefferson himself, he deplored the fact that "some good men,
and even of respectable information, consider the learned sciences
as useless acquirements; some think they do not better the condition of man." Jefferson himself advocated popular support for "an
establishment embracing all the sciences which may be useful and
even necessary in the various vocations of life."[137]

Jefferson's utilitarian view of the sciences in the building of a
new nation was crudely expressed as early as 1803: "Our citizens
almost all follow some industrious occupation, and, therefore have
little time to devote to abstract science."[138] Shortly before his death,
he wrote in 1825: "I revolt against metaphysical reading . . . the
business of life is with matter that gives us tangible results. han-
dling that, we arrive at the knolege of the axe, the plough, the
steam-boat, and every thing useful in life. but, from metaphical
speculations, I have never seen one useful result."[139] Jefferson once
received what he termed a "charming treatise on manures," and
wrote the author that "science never appears so beautiful as when
applied to the uses of human life."[140]

Shortly after the death of Jefferson and John Adams, both on
July 4, 1826, Daniel Webster, delivering a joint eulogy in Boston,
declared: "Men have seen that [classical learning] might exist with-

out mental superiority, without vigor, without good taste, and without utility. . . . Those whose memories we honor were learned men; but their learning was kept in its proper place and made subservient to the uses and objects of life."[141]

In Jefferson, American humanist, the quest for useful knowledge in Early America attained its highest consummation, the happy marriage of the humanities and the sciences—for the good of the nation and mankind. Others of lesser vision advocated, with varying degrees of fervor, more limited views of the utility of learning. The concept of useful knowledge, arising in a pluralistic culture and evolving in turbulent times, emerged at the end of the century with pluralistic nuances of interpretation. Though not rich in definitive resolutions, it bequeathed to the nation a solid legacy of utilitarianism.

But Jefferson's ideals were not the then current practice or the future fulfillment. At the very beginning of the nineteenth century, when Samuel Miller in 1803 took stock of the intellectual life of America during the preceding century, he noted that the classics, because of the disproportionate demands on the time of students, the excessive emphasis on language, and the treatment of the classics as ends in themselves, had by his time "come to be regarded by a large portion of the literary world, as among the most useless objects of pursuit."[142] The pressures for immediate practical utility in a new country were bringing to the center of the stage, in place of Latin and Greek, the physical sciences, modern belles lettres, modern languages, history, geography. Scientific knowledge, in particular, was being fostered and "rendered subservient to practical utility." The time is coming, he prophesied, "when we shall be able to make some return to our transatlantic brethren, for the rich stores of useful knowledge, which they have been pouring upon us for nearly two centuries."[143]

Moreover, the favorable overtones of the phrase "useful knowledge" had not yet spent themselves, and it survived far into the nineteenth century, though largely as a slogan. As early as 1809 De Witt Clinton championed free schools for poor children in New York City on the Lancastrian Plan, with emphasis on reading, writing, arithmetic, and Scriptures as the basic elements of useful knowledge preliminary to vocational training.[144] In the decade 1802–12 Noah Webster published four volumes of *Elements of Useful Knowledge*, intended as school textbooks in American, European, Asiatic, and African history and geography, and in the science of biology; and in 1810 there appeared a large work on natural history entitled *Useful Knowledge; a Familiar Account of the Various Productions of Nature*.[145] Two new periodicals sought to attract readers to useful knowledge. The *New-York Magazine and General Repository of Useful Knowledge*, founded 1814, in its prospectus offered the public an array of subjects as general as possible (including poetry) for "the general good of the community," to enable readers of all stations of life "to treasure up useful knowledge."[146] In Boston the *American Magazine of Useful and Entertaining Knowledge*, of which Hawthorne was editor briefly, had a short life in the mid-1830s.[147] In the second half of that decade Alexis de Tocqueville was struck by the "purely practical objects" of Americans, their requiring "nothing of science but its special applications to the useful arts and the means of rendering life comfortable." Across the Atlantic, he observed, the "permanent inequality of conditions lead men to confine themselves to the arrogant and sterile research for abstract truths, while the social conditions and the institutions of democracy prepare them to seek the immediate and useful practical results of the sciences."[148] An inscription on the façade of the New York Public Library still preserves the eighteenth- and early nineteenth-century slogan:

THE ASTOR LIBRARY
FOUNDED BY
JOHN JACOB ASTOR
FOR THE
ADVANCEMENT OF USEFUL KNOWLEDGE
MDCCCXLVIII

On the other side of the Atlantic the diffusion of useful knowledge was promoted early in the nineteenth century by an American loyalist, Benjamin Thompson, who fled to Europe and, after an extraordinary career on the continent, became Sir Benjamin Thompson, Count Rumford. In particular, he was the founder of the Royal Institution in Great Britain in 1799–1800 (it is still in existence), whose charter defines its aims as "a Public Institution for diffusing the knowledge and facilitating the general introduction of Useful Mechanical Inventions and Improvements; and for teaching, by courses of Philosophical Lectures and Experiments, the Application of Science to the common Purposes of Life." Among the specific aims, as defined in the Act of Parliament of 1800, are "the promotion of chemical science by experiments and lectures, improving arts and manufactures, discovering the use of mineral and natural products of this country, and the diffusion and extension of useful knowledge in general."[149]

Not to be outdone, the Whigs and other groups in Britain committed to the betterment of the lot of the workers, advocated and promoted the "diffusion of useful knowledge" as widely as possible. In 1816 Jeremy Bentham published his *Chrestomathia*,[150] a term meaning "useful learning" which he coined from the Greek words *chrestos* and *mathia*.[151] This work was Bentham's educational handbook for a projected school conducive to useful learning. In the Benthamite view, inherited from James Mill, the usefulness of knowledge was its application to the business of life for the public welfare.[152] A decade later (in 1827) Lord Brougham launched an extensive program of popular adult education for the working classes of Britain with the foundation of the Society for the Diffusion of Useful Knowledge (SDUK). Besides its lectures for adults, the Society published under its auspices the inexpensive *Penny Magazine of the Society for the Diffusion of Useful Knowledge*,[153] the *Library of Useful Knowledge*, and the *Library of Entertaining Knowledge*, to provide elementary treatises on scientific, literary, historical, and ethical subjects.[154]

By the middle of the nineteenth century, the concept of useful knowledge in America had been narrowed to mean applied science and vocational training, as the result of the institution of the public high school, the industrial revolution, and the separation of academic learning from social utility. Thus Thomas Bulfinch in 1855 in the preface to his *Age of Fable* could concede that the study of mythology was not useful knowledge in the contemporary sense, for it did not help "to enlarge our possessions or to raise our station in society," though as a handmaid of literature it helps to promote virtue and happiness. So also Heinrich Schliemann, when he was in the United States in 1869, noted that in this country "useful knowledge goes beyond every other consideration," so that support would be forthcoming for a proposed expedition to the North Pole.[155]

At about this time, as a reaction against the narrow cult of applied science and the dominance of material interests, an effort was made to isolate and elevate some branches of knowledge for their special value as being "useless." In particular, classicists in both Britain and the United States, have, since the 1860s, often defended their discipline against the competition of science and other practical fields precisely on the ground that the study of classical languages and literatures provides no direct utilitarian value.[156] James Russell Lowell in an oration on the 250th anniversary of Harvard reminisced that about 1860 he had defined a university as "a place where nothing useful is taught."[157]

The current ferment in American higher education, with its quest for "relevance" (read "useful knowledge") is, in some measure, a return to the origins. Daniel Boorstin reminds us that "the most distinctive feature of our system is not a system, but a quest, not a neat arrangement of men and institutions, but a flux."[158]

Notes

1. *An Oration on the Advantages of An Early Education* (Exeter, N.H., 1783), p. 16. The "quest of useful knowledge" in America was lauded by President Charles Nisbet of Dickinson College in *An Address to the Students of Dickinson College* (Carlisle, 1786), p. 13.
2. Elmer E. Brown, *The Making of Our Middle Schools*, 2nd ed. (New York, 1903), pp. 155–203, 228–257; Homer H. Young, "Theory of American Education during the Revolutionary Period 1743–1809" (Ph.D. diss., University of Texas, 1949), pp. 170, 260, 289; Harriet W. Marr, *The Old New England Academies Founded Before 1826* (New York, 1959), pp. 168–169, 178; Robert Middlekauff, *Ancients and Axioms: Secondary Education in Eighteenth-Century New England* (New Haven, 1963), pp. 138–153.
3. Richard M. Gummere, *The American Colonial Mind and the Classical Tradition* (Cambridge, Mass., 1963), pp. 37–38; Kenneth B. Murdock, *Literature and Theology in Colonial New England* (Cambridge, Mass., 1949), p. 96; Samuel E. Morison, *The Intellectual Life of Colonial New England*, 2nd ed. (New York, 1956), p. 17; Middlekauff, *Ancients and Axioms*, pp. 3, 195.
4. Richard F. Jones, *Ancients and Moderns: A Study of the Rise of the Scientific Movement in Seventeenth-Century England*, 2nd ed. (St. Louis, 1961), pp. 59–60, 99, 116, 120.
5. Richard L. Greaves, *The Puritan Revolution and Educational Thought: Background for Reform* (New Brunswick, 1969), pp. 26–47.
6. *The Compassionate Samaritaine*, pp. 36–37, cited by Greaves, *Puritan Revolution*, p. 42.
7. John Dury, *The Reformed School* (1650), in Charles Webster, *Samuel Hartlib and the Advancement of Learning* (Cambridge, 1970), pp. 155–156. Cp. Greaves, *Puritan Revolution*, pp. 93, 95.
8. R. M. Ogilvie would have us believe that the principal aim of the English educational reformers was to redirect classical learning toward factual knowledge, moral training, and practical subjects (e.g., farming, warfare, architecture, and politics) (*Latin and Greek: A History of the Influence of the Classics on English Life from 1600–1918 [London, 1964], p. 38).
9. In Sir Henry Lyons, *The Royal Society 1660–1940* (Cambridge, 1944), pp. 9–10.
10. In the introduction to the first issue of the *Philosophical Transactions* of the Royal Society, March 6, 1664. Cp. Martha Ornstein, *The Role of Scientific Societies in the Seventeenth Century*, 3rd ed. (Chicago, 1938; rpt. 1963), pp. 125–127.
11. *Plus Ultra: or, The Progress and Advancement of Knowledge since the Days of Aristotle. In an Account of Some of the most Remarkable late Improvements of Practical, Useful Learning: To Encourage Philosophical Endeavours occasioned by a Conference with one of the Notional Way* (Robert Crosse is meant). Cp. Ornstein, *Scientific Societies*, pp. 131–132.

12. *Some Thoughts Concerning Education* (first published 1693), ed. F. W. Garforth (New York, 1964), pp. 107, 115, 122. Text also edited by Peter Gay, in Teachers College, Classics in Education, no. 20 (New York, 1964); James L. Axtell, *The Educational Writings of John Locke* (Cambridge, 1968), pp. 109–325.

13. Daniel J. Pratt, *Annals of Public Education in the State of New York, from 1626–1746* (Albany, 1872), p. 22.

14. *The Witness of William Penn*, ed. Frederick B. Tolles and E. Gordon Alderfer (New York, 1957), pp. 42–43. Cp. Greaves, *Puritan Revolution*, p. 43; Howard H. Brinton, "The Quaker Contribution to Higher Education in Colonial America," *Pennsylvania History* 25 (1958), pp. 234–250. On Quaker utilitarianism see Richard B. Ballou, "The Grammar Schools in Seventeenth Century Colonial America" (Ph.D. diss., Harvard, 1940), pp. 236–251; and on Quaker educational policy, Thomas Woody, *Quaker Education in the Colony and State of New Jersey* (New York, 1923; rpt. 1969), pp. 8–37.

15. "The Advice of William Penn to His Children Relating to Their Civil and Religious Conduct," in *The Fruits of Solitude and Other Writings* (London, 1915), p. 103; Thomas Woody, *Quaker Education in Pennsylvania*, Teachers College, Columbia University Contributions to Education, no. 105 (New York, 1920), p. 30; Edward C. O. Beatty, *William Penn as Social Philosopher* (New York, 1939), pp. 257–265.

16. Woody, *Quaker Education, Pennsylvania*, p. 29; Ballou, *Grammar Schools*, p. 240.

17. From "Some Fruits of Solitude" (1693), in *The Witness of William Penn* (see n. 14, above), pp. 167–169.

18. Article XII of the Frame, in *Minutes of the Provincial Council of Pennsylvania* (Philadelphia, 1852), vol. I, p. 34.

19. Thomas Budd, *Good Order Established* (Philadelphia, 1685). Cp. Woody, *Quaker Education, Pennsylvania*, pp. 36–38; Ballou, *Grammar Schools*, p. 241.

20. See, e.g., Frederick B. Tolles, *Meeting House and Counting House: The Quaker Merchants of Colonial Philadelphia 1682–1763* (Chapel Hill, 1948), pp. 149, 207; Woody, *Quaker Education, Pennsylvania*, pp. 47–48, 101, 136; Woody, *Quaker Education, New Jersey*, pp. 22–23; George S. Brookes, *Friend Anthony Benezet* (Philadelphia, 1937), p. 492.

21. Woody, *Quaker Education, Pennsylvania*, p. 190; *New Jersey*, pp. 315–316.

22. William C. Dunlap, *Quaker Education in Baltimore and Virginia Yearly Meetings* (Philadelphia, 1936), pp. 28, 177, 183, 288; Zora Klain, *Educational Activities of New England Quakers: A Source Book* (Philadelphia, 1928).

23. Letter of Moses Brown to Anthony Benezet, 1780, in Klain, *New England Quakers*, pp. 10–11; letter of Moses Brown to Samuel Neal, 1787, ibid., p. 71 (cp. p. 201).

24. Brookes, *Benezet*, pp. 360, 389–391.

25. London, 1697. Cp. Bernard C. Steiner, "Rev. Thomas Bray and His American Libraries," *American Historical Review* 2 (1896–97), pp. 63–64. Bray crossed the Atlantic and was in Maryland from March, 1700, to the summer of 1701. For Bray's career see Steiner, pp. 59–75; *Dictionary of National Biography*, vol. II, pp. 1147–1149; *Dictionary of American Biography*, vol. II, pp. 610–611.

26. Bray, *An Essay*, pp. 12, 17–22 ("The Catalogue of Books Design'd to lay the Foundations of Lending-Libraries").

27. Steiner, "Rev. Thomas Bray," p. 64.

28. Jesse H. Shera, *Foundations of the Public Library: The Origins of the Public Library Movement in New England 1629–1855* (Chicago, 1949; rpt. 1965), pp. 26–29; William D. Houlette, "Parish Libraries and the Work of the Reverend Thomas Bray," *Library Quarterly* 4 (1934), pp. 588–609.

29. This book, the principal work of William Mather, reached its 24th edition in 1775 and was widely sold in the colonies. It was a sort of miniature encyclopedia, containing information on many practical subjects. Almost as popular was George Fisher's *The Instructor; or, Young Man's Best Companion*, 25th ed. (London, 1789). It was reprinted in Philadelphia in 1760 by the press of Steuart. Cp. Rena L. Vassar, "Elementary and Latin Grammar School Education in the American Colonies, 1607–1700" (Ph.D. diss., University of California, Berkeley, 1958), p. 286.

30. Carl and Jessica Bridenbaugh, *Rebels and Gentlemen: Philadelphia in the Age of Franklin* (New York, 1942), p. 364; Louis B. Wright, "The Purposeful Reading of Our Colonial Ancestors," *ELH: American Journal of English Literary History* 4 (1937), pp. 85–111; idem, "The Classical Tradition of Colonial Virginia," *Papers of the Bibliographical Society of America* 33 (1939), pp. 95–97; Merle Curti, *The Growth of American Thought*, 3rd ed. (New York, 1964), p. 55; Bernard Bailyn, *Education in the Formation of American Society: Needs and Opportunities for Study* (Chapel Hill, 1960), p. 19.

31. Max Savelle, *The Colonial Origins of American Thought* (Princeton, 1964), pp. 58–60.

32. *Ars Poetica*, line 343.

33. Lawrence A. Cremin, *American Education: The Colonial Experience 1607–1783* (New York, 1970), pp. 357–412; Charles A. Barker, *American Convictions: Cycles of Political Thought, 1600–1850* (Philadelphia, 1970), pp. 210–213; Robert F. Seybolt, *The Evening School in Colonial America*, Bureau of Educational Research, College of Education, University of Illinois, no. 24 (Urbana, 1925); idem, *The Private Schools of Colonial Boston* (Cambridge, Mass., 1935); Middlekauff, *Ancients and Axioms*, pp. 63–70, 120–127, 136–139; Frank Klassen, "Persistence and Change in Eighteenth Century Colonial Education," *History of Education Quarterly* 2 (1962), pp. 92–96.

    In the announcements in colonial newspapers these private schools stress "the most useful parts of Mathematicks." In the case of a Boston boarding school opened in 1727, which included instruction in Latin, French, and English, the claim was made that "it is also intended, That in Three Languages they shall Read such Books, in which they may Learn Sciences and Useful things, besides the Language" (Seybolt, *Private Schools*, p. 17). Cp. Pratt, *Annals of Public Education*, p. 93.

34. John B. Dillon, *Oddities of Colonial Legislation in America* (Indianapolis, 1879), pp. 114–115.

35. *Diary of Cotton Mather* (New York, n.d.), vol. II, pp. 228–229, 405.

36. Letter to Isaac Greenwood, July 16, 1724, in *Selected Letters of Cotton Mather*, ed. Kenneth Silverman (Baton Rouge, 1971), p. 389.

37. Hugh Jones, *The Present State of Virginia* (London, 1724), ed. Richard L. Morton (Chapel Hill, 1956), p. 81. Cp. Richard M. Gummere, *Seven Wise Men of Colonial America* (Cambridge, Mass., 1967), pp. 1–11.

38. C. Lennart Carlson, "Samuel Keimer: A Study in the Transit of English Culture to Colonial Pennsylvania," *Pa. Mag. Hist. & Biog.* 61 (1937), p. 376; *Pennsylvania Gazette*, vol. I, no. 1 (Dec. 24, 1728).

39. Cremin, *American Education*, p. 387.

40. The second, revised edition (London, 1730) became the standard and was reprinted in numerous editions. The text is in Wilson Smith, ed., *Theories of Education in Early America 1655–1819* (Indianapolis, 1973), pp. 61–97. Cp. George E. Littlefield, *Early Schools and School-Books of New England* (Boston, 1904), p. 96. Clarke edited many Latin and Greek school texts, which were the most popular ones used in America to the end of the eighteenth century. They presented the Latin or Greek text with English translation on parallel pages, and this method was employed in the American grammar schools throughout most of the century.

41. Smith, *Theories of Education*, p. 66.
42. Brooke Hindle, "The Quaker Background and Science in Colonial Philadelphia," *Isis* 46 (1955), pp. 243–250; Roy N. Lokken, "The Scientific Papers of James Logan," *Trans. Amer. Philos. Soc.*, vol. 62, no. 6 (1972). See, e.g., p. 27, Logan's tribute to the autodidact Thomas Godfrey, who invented the mariner's quadrant ca. 1730: "Nor is it to be wondered that mankind should be so generally eager in this respect, since nothing redounds more to the honor of any state than to have it said that some science of general utility to mankind was invented or improved by them." Logan was also one of the best classical scholars of his time; he translated two ancient texts which were published by Franklin, and he possessed the largest classical library in America in the first half of eighteenth century (now the Loganian Library in Philadelphia).
43. *Papers of Benjamin Franklin*, ed. Leonard W. Labaree (New Haven, 1959–), vol. II, pp. 378–383. Cp. Thomas Woody, *Educational Views of Benjamin Franklin* (New York, 1931), pp. 58–62.
44. Peter Collinson, English businessman, naturalist, botanist, antiquary, fellow of the Royal Society, in a letter of Aug. 23, 1744, to Cadwallader Colden, hastened to commend "the Authors & promoters of a Society for Improvement of Natural knowledge" (in Carl Van Doren, "Beginnings of the American Philosophical Society," *Proc. Amer. Philos. Soc.* 87 [1943], p. 283).
45. Cremin, *American Education*, pp. 410, 428–429. These were the forerunners of numerous societies of this type established in America in the second half of the eighteenth century.
46. As early as 1740 a decision was made in Philadelphia to establish a charity school with emphasis on "useful Literature and the Knowledge of Christian Religion." But the plan was not implemented at that time (see Edward Potts Cheney, *History of the University of Pennsylvania 1740–1940* [Philadelphia, 1940], p. 23).
47. Text in Woody, *Educational Views of Benjamin Franklin*, pp. 149–181, esp. 158, 167, 176; John Hardin Best, *Benjamin Franklin on Education*, Teachers College Classics in Education, no. 14 (New York, 1962), pp. 133–134. M. Roberta Warf Keiter insists on making the distinction that Franklin's concept of education was not primarily practical and utilitarian but "purposeful" ("Benjamin Franklin as an Educator" [Ph.D. diss., University of Maryland, 1957], pp. ii, 223, 236–237).
48. Best, *Franklin on Education*, pp. 152–153; Thomas H. Montgomery, *A History of the University of Pennsylvania from its Foundation to A.D. 1770* (Philadelphia, 1900), pp. 46–47; Bailyn, *Education*, pp. 33–36; Cremin, *American Education*, pp. 374–378.
49. Montgomery, *University of Pennsylvania*, p. 47.
50. Ibid., pp. 139, 501.
51. *The Letters and Papers of Cadwallader Colden, 1748–1754*, vol. IV, Collections of the New-York Historical Society for the Year 1920 (New York, 1921), pp. 157–158. On Colden see Alice M. Keys, *Cadwallader Colden, A Representative Eighteenth Century Official* (New York, 1906); *Dictionary of American Biography*, vol. IV, pp. 286–287; I. Woodbridge Riley, *American Philosophy: The Early Schools* (New York, n.d.), pp. 329–372.
52. Richard Peters, *A Sermon on Education. Wherein Some Account is given of the Academy Established in the City of Philadelphia* (Philadelphia, 1751), esp. pp. 1, 25; *Dictionary of American Biography*, vol. XIV, pp. 508–509.
53. *Prayers for the Use of the Philadelphia Academy* (Philadelphia, 1753). Cp. Montgomery, *University of Pennsylvania*, p. 197.
54. Franklin, *Papers*, vol. III, p. 347 (*Poor Richard*, 1749).
55. Letter to Mary Stevenson, ca. Nov., 1760, Franklin, *Papers*, vol. IX, pp. 247–252.

56. Brooke Hindle, *The Pursuit of Science in Revolutionary America 1735–1789* (Chapel Hill, 1956), pp. 121–122; Franklin, *Papers*, vol. IV, p. 135.
57. *Observations Relative to the Intentions of the Original Founders of the Academy of Philadelphia* (Philadelphia, 1789). In his autobiography, written in 1788, Franklin recommended that French and Italian as first foreign languages for students "might be serviceable in common Life." (*Autobiography*, ed. Leonard W. Labaree et al. [New Haven, 1964], p. 169).
58. Samuel Miller, *A Brief Retrospect of the Eighteenth Century* (New York, 1803), vol. II, pp. 346–358.
59. See "Opponents of Classical Learning in America during the Revolutionary Period," Chapter IV, below. A. Owen Aldrige, "Thomas Paine and the Classics," *Eighteenth Century Studies* 1 (1968), pp. 370–380; Edwin L. Miles, "The Young American Nation and the Classical World," *Journal of the History of Ideas* 35 (1974), pp. 259–274; Patrick Crutwell, "The Eighteenth Century: A Classical Age?" *Arion* 7 (Spring, 1968), pp. 110–131. Lawrence Stone holds that it is methodologically wrong to view this dispute as a renewal of the debate between the Ancients and the Moderns in the earlier Battle of the Books in Europe, or as a contest between conservatives and liberals (*New York Review of Books* 16 [January 28, 1971], p. 23). But see Chapter VI, below.
60. *New-York Gazette, or Weekly Post-Boy,* Dec. 11, 1752.
61. *The Independent Reflector,* by William Livingston and others, ed. Milton M. Klein (Cambridge, Mass., 1963), no. XVII, Mar. 22, 1753, p. 172. Cp. Howard Mumford Jones, *O Strange New World. American Culture: The Formative Years* (New York, 1964), p. 245.
62. *Independent Reflector,* no. L, Nov. 8, 1753, pp. 421–424. Characteristically, private schools in New York emphasized useful knowledge, especially practical subjects. E.g., *The New-York Gazette,* Apr. 29, 1765, carried an item headed "For promoting Useful Education in New York" that announced the establishment of an academy for teaching writing, ciphering, bookkeeping, navigation, geography, surveying "and other useful branches of Mathematicks," as well as Greek! Seybolt's *Private Schools* contains the announcement in 1755 in New York City of the English Grammar School of Thomas Byerley and Josiah Day, who offered, besides English, "every useful branch of Knowledge: Writing, Mathematics, Reading, Bookkeeping, Mensuration, Gauging, Trigonometry, Surveying, Navigation, Gunnery, Fortification, Optics, Geography, Cosmography, Dialing, Astronomy, Natural Philosophy, Algebra, Fluxions" (pp. 96–97).
63. William Smith, *A General Idea of the College of Mirania* (New York, 1753), pp. 11, 14, 19, 27–28, 76. Cp. Albert F. Gegenheimer, *William Smith, Educator and Churchman 1727–1803* (Philadelphia, 1943), pp. 14–42; Cremin, *American Education,* pp. 378–384, 641–642. See also [William Smith], *Some Thoughts on Education* (New York, 1752). On the uses of history, particularly ancient history, in the eighteenth century, see R. N. Stromberg, "History in the Eighteenth Century," *Journal of the History of Ideas* 12 (1951), pp. 295–304; Carl Becker, "The Spirit of '76," in *Everyman His Own Historian* (New York, 1935), pp. 47–80; H. Trevor Colbourn, *The Lamp of Experience: Whig History and the Intellectual Origins of the American Revolution* (Chapel Hill, 1965); Douglass Adair, "Experience Must be our Only Guide: History, Democratic Theory, and the United States Constitution," in *The Reinterpretation of Early American History: Essays in Honor of John Edwin Pomfret* (San Marino, 1966), pp. 129–148 (=Jack P. Greene, ed., *The Reinterpretation of the American Revolution 1763–1789* [New York, 1968], pp. 396–416); James Wilson Johnson, *The Formation of English Neo-Classical Thought* (Princeton, 1967), pp. 31–105; Gordon S. Wood, *The Creation of the American Republic 1776–1787* (Chapel Hill, 1969), pp. 46–53.

64. Herbert and Carol Schneider, *Samuel Johnson, President of King's College: His Career and Writings* (New York, 1929), vol. IV, pp. 222–224; Montgomery, *University of Pennsylvania*, p. 417. Writing shortly after 1763, Johnson stressed the mathematical sciences as the proper means for the practice and improvement of all useful arts, and in general all knowledge useful for the public welfare of their own country and of mankind, so that students will be made "useful to their country in public stations when they come forth to act their parts upon the stage of life" ("Raphael, or the Genius of English America: A Rhapsody," in Schneider, *Samuel Johnson*, vol. II, pp. 567, 571).

65. Schneider, *Samuel Johnson*, vol. IV, pp. 231–233; Montgomery, *Univeristy of Pennsylvania*, pp. 402–403. On Dec. 15, 1761, the trustees of the College of Philadelphia issued an appeal for financial support to "All Charitable Persons, Patrons of Literature, and Friends of Useful Knowledge." Shortly after, in London, William Smith and James Jay, representing the College of Philadelphia and King's College, respectively, appealed, when writing to the clergy, for funds "for the advancement of Religion and useful Knowledge," while to the general public their appeal was "to all Charitable Persons and Patrons of Useful Knowledge" (Montgomery, *University of Pennsylvania*, pp. 382–383, 387, 406).

66. *The Instructor*, April 24–May 1, 1755, pp. 32–34.

67. Rhetoric he considered hurtful knowledge, and Greek and Latin as not indispensable for acquiring useful knowledge. The author preferred the practical Romans to the speculative Greeks: "Rome was never wiser or more virtuous than when moderately learned and meddled with none but the useful sciences. Athens was never more foolish than when it swarmed with Philosophers" (p. 34).

68. The text of Colden's tract, *An Introduction to the Study of Philosophy. Wrote in America for the Use of a Young Gentleman* (New York, 1760), is given in Joseph L. Blau, ed., *American Philosophical Addresses, 1700–1900* (New York, 1946), pp. 289–311; and (in part) in Herbert W. Schneider, *A History of American Philosophy*, 2nd ed. (New York, 1963), pp. 66–67.

69. Blau, *American Philosophical Addresses*, pp. 288–292, 295–296, 301–311.

70. See Colden in Blau, *American Philosophical Addresses*, p. 311: "The mere Scholar, the mere Physician, the mere Lawyer, Musician, or Painter, take them out of their own way, and they are often more insipid than the mere plowman."

71. William Livingston, *A Letter to the Right Reverend Father in God, John, Lord Bishop of Landaff* (New York, 1768), pp. 23–24. Cp. Rutherford E. Delmage, "The American Idea of Progress, 1750–1800," *Proc. Amer. Philos. Soc.* 91 (1947), p. 307.

72. See, e.g., *A Catalogue of Books Belonging to the Union-Library Company of Philadelphia* (Philadelphia, 1754), p. 3; *The Charter, Laws, and Catalogue of Books, of the Library Company of Philadelphia* (Philadelphia, 1764), p. 4; *A Catalogue of Books Belonging to the Association Library Company of Philadelphia* (Philadelphia, 1765), p. 3; *The Charter, Laws, and Catalogue of Books of the Library Company of Burlington* [N.J.] (Philadelphia, 1758); *The Charter, Laws, and Catalogue of Books in the Union Library Company of Hartborough* [Pa.] (Philadelphia, 1768), Preamble; *A Catalogue of Books Belonging to the Gloucester United Library* (Providence, 1796), Introduction; *A Catalogue of Books Belonging to the Frederickstown Library Company* (Washington, Pa., 1797).

73. *The Charter, Laws, Catalogue of Books . . . of the Juliana Library-Company in Lancaster* (Philadelphia, 1766), pp. vii–ix, 16. Conversely, the library of the College of New Jersey, "intended for the Advancement of Religion and useful Learning," had a very large number of texts of Greek and Latin authors. See *A*

Catalogue of Books in the Library of the College of New-Jersey (Woodbridge, N.J., 1760), pp. iii–iv.

74. Marcus A. McCorison, ed., *The Catalogue of the Redwood Library Company at Newport, Rhode Island* (New Haven, 1965), pp. ix–x. As early as 1733, the Book Company of Durham, Connecticut, a lending library, had expressed as their purpose "to improve our leisure hours in enriching our minds with useful and profitable knowledge by reading." See Jesse H. Shera, *Foundations of the Public Library: The Origins of the Public Library Movement in New England 1629–1855* (Chicago, 1949; rpt. 1965), p. 248.

75. Leman Thomas Rede, *Biblioteca Americana* (London, 1789), pp. 9, 18. Cp. Stuart C. Sherman, "Leman Thomas Rede's *Biblioteca Americana*," *Wm. & Mary Quart.*, 3rd ser., 4 (1947), pp. 332–349; Hindle, *Pursuit of Science*, pp. 353–354.

76. William Smith, *Account of the College, Academy and Charitable School of Philadelphia in Pennsylvania* (first published 1759; rev. ed. 1762), ed. Thomas R. Adams (Philadelphia, 1951), pp. 16–17. At the commencement of May 30, 1765, there was a "Prayer for the King, the Royal Family, the Benefactors of the College, for the whole Church of Christ and the Propagation of the Gospel and useful Science" (Montgomery, *University of Pennsylvania*, p. 452). See also Francis Hopkinson's poem *Science* (Philadelphia, 1762), a tribute by the college's first graduate to its combined program of classics and modern subjects.

In 1758 an honorary degree was awarded by the University of Glasgow to Dr. Francis Alison, long a famous teacher in the Latin School of the Academy of Philadelphia, for his "pious and faithful labour for the propagation of useful knowledge in these untutored parts" (*American Magazine*, Oct., 1758). Francis Alison was the founder of the New London (Pa.) Academy in 1743, and later became vice-provost of the College of Philadelphia in 1755. Benjamin Franklin in 1775 lauded the range of his knowledge, which included agriculture, philosophy, and theology; and the Reverend Jacob Duché remarked, regarding the recognition of his services to useful knowledge, that "he has the honor of being among the first that introduced science into this heretofore untutored wilderness." See Thomas Clinton Pears, "Francis Alison, Colonial Educator," *Delaware Notes* 17 (1944), pp. 9–22; *Dictionary of American Biography*, vol. I, pp. 181–182.

77. *Early Proceedings of the American Philosophical Society for Useful Knowledge* (Philadelphia, 1884), pp. 1–29; Edwin G. Conklin, "A Brief History of the American Philosophical Society," *Year Book of the American Philosophical Society*, 1959, pp. 36–46; Hindle, *Pursuit of Science*, pp. 122–136; Ralph S. Bates, *Scientific Societies in the United States*, 3rd ed. (Cambridge, Mass., 1965), pp. 7–8.

78. Hindle, *Pursuit of Science*, pp. 123–125; *Pennsylvania Chronicle*, Feb. 29–Mar. 7, 1768; *Dictionary of American Biography*, vol. XVIII, pp. 481–482; William E. Lingelbach, "B. Franklin and the Scientific Societies," *Journal of the Franklin Institute* 26 (1956), pp. 9–31; George H. Daniels, *Science in American Society: A Social History* (New York, 1971), pp. 47–68, 101–125.

79. Hindle, *Pursuit of Science*, p. 191.

80. It was also referred to variously as the Philosophical Society for the Advancement of Useful Knowledge in Williamsburgh; Society for the Advancement of Useful Knowledge; and Society for Propagating Useful Knowledge in Virginia.

81. *Virginia Gazette* (Purdie and Dixon), May 13, July 22, Aug. 5, Oct. 22, Nov. 11, 1773; Apr. 2, May 19, June 9, June 16, 1774; *Virginia Register* (Rind), Apr. 14, 1774; *Virginia Hisorical Register* 6 (1853), pp. 216, 218; *Wm. & Mary Quart.*, 1st ser., 4 (1895), pp. 200–201; *Wm. & Mary Quart.*, 1st ser., 16 (1907–08), pp. 37–38; Lyon G. Tyler, "Virginia's Contribution to Science," *Wm. & Mary Quart.*, 1st ser., 24 (1915–16), p. 222; Hindle, *Pursuit of Science*,

pp. 29, 213–215, 275; Richard M. Jellison, "Scientific Enquiry in Eighteenth Century America," *The Historian* 25 (1962–63), pp. 305–311; Robert and B. Katherine Brown, *Virginia 1705–1786: Democracy or Aristocracy?* (East Lansing, 1964), pp. 278–279.

82. Lewis C. Gray, *History of Agriculture in the Southern United States to 1860* (Gloucester, 1932), vol. II, p. 783; Richard P. McCormick, *Experiment in Independence: New Jersey in the Critical Period 1781–1789* (New Brunswick, 1950), p. 62; Hindle, *Pursuit of Science*, pp. 274–275; Bates, *Scientific Societies*, p. 26; *Society for the Attainment of Useful Knowledge* (Philadelphia, 1794); *The Diary of Elihu Hubbard Smith (1771–1798),* ed. James E. Cronin, *Memoirs of the American Philosophical Society*, vol. 95 (Philadelphia, 1973), p. 126 [Smith deplores that efforts to establish a society in New York City "friendly to literature & useful knowledge" have all failed]; *American Museum* 8 (Aug. 1790), p. 85. For the Mississippi Society for the Acquirement and Dissemination of Useful Knowledge, ca. 1805, see Whitfield J. Bell, Jr., "As Others Saw Us: Notes on the Reputation of the American Philosophical Society," *Proc. Amer. Philos. Soc.* 116 (1972), p. 271.

    In 1792 when David Ramsay, distinguished physician and political leader of Charleston, author of historical works on South Carolina and the American Revolution, was elected corresponding member of the newly founded Massachusetts Historical Society, he wrote Jeremy Belknap to offer best wishes for the success of the society "& particularly of your own labor for diffusing useful knowledge." See *David Ramsay, 1749–1815: Selections from his Writings,* ed. Robert L. Brunhouse, *Trans. Amer. Philos. Soc.*, vol. 55, pt. 4 (Philadelphia, 1965), pp. 132–133.

83. *An Oration on the Advantages of American Independence, Spoken Before a Public Assembly of the Inhabitants of Charlestown, in South-Carolina, on the Second Anniversary of that Glorious Era* (Charleston, 1778); text also in Smith, *Theories of Education*, p. 225.

84. *Trans. Amer. Philos. Soc.* 2 (1786), pp. xi–xii.

85. Ibid., p. x. These committees already existed under the Laws of the American Philosophical Society promulgated in 1768–69. A seventh committee, for History, Moral Science, and General Literature, was established in 1815.

86. *The Miscellaneous Essays and Occasional Writings* (Philadelphia, 1792), vol. I, p. 361.

87. *Mem. Amer. Acad. Arts & Sci.* 1 (1785), p. vii.

88. Ibid., pp. 4–6, 19.

89. See, e.g., Kenneth A. Lockridge, *Literacy in Colonial New England* (New York, 1974).

90. Daniels, *Science in American Society*, pp. 104–105, 153–155; Hindle, *Pursuit of Science*, p. 354; Whitfield J. Bell, Jr., "The Scientific Environment of Philadelphia, 1775–1790," *Proc. Amer. Philos. Soc.* 92 (1948), pp. 6–14; A. Crocker, "Essay on Raising Apple Trees, and Making Cider," *Mem. Amer. Acad. of Arts & Sci.* 2 (1793), p. 100.

    Cp. the book published in England in 1785 by John Imison, a clock and watchmaker and optician, *The School of Arts; or, An Introduction to Useful Knowledge,* cited in A. E. Musson and Eric Robinson, *Science and Technology in the Industrial Revolution* (Toronto, 1969), p. 110. Imison's subjects were: mechanics, electricity, optics, astronomy, instrument making, watchmaking, and other crafts. In the second edition, of 1794, he added pneumatics, hydrostatics, and hydraulics.

91. *American Museum* 5 (1789), p. 207, by W. I. Cp. the advertisement of an evening school in New York City in 1782 by a Mr. Davis, who announced "practical subjects" (reading, arithmetic, bookkeeping, geometry, navigation, surveying, mensuration, and algebra), and added:

These lively fields pure pleasure do impart,
The fruit of science, and each useful art,
Which forms the mind and clears the cloudy sense,
By truth's powerful pleasing eloquence.

See Seybolt, *Evening School*, p. 64.

92. Benjamin Smith Barton, *Collections for an Essay Towards a Materia Medica* (Philadelphia, 1798), pp. 40, 43–44; cp. Daniel J. Boorstin, *The Lost World of Thomas Jefferson* (New York, 1948), pp. 215, 221.

93. *Outline for Establishing a Society of Agriculture in Pennsylvania* (Philadelphia, 1794), pp. 1–2.

94. Ben Perley Poore, comp., *The Federal and State Constitutions, Colonial Charters, and Other Organic Laws of the United States* (Washington, D.C., 1877), p. 1414 (art. XLI of Constitution of North Carolina); p. 1547 (sec. 44 of Constitution of Pennsylvania). The University of North Carolina was not established until 1789. The intensification in the middle of the century of American concern for useful knowledge can be seen, e.g., in the difference between the charters of the College of New Jersey (Princeton), given in 1746, and that of Queen's College (Rutgers), promulgated twenty years later, in 1766. Both provided, in virtually identical language for "the Education of Youth in the Learned Languages and in the Liberal Arts and Sciences," but the latter added "and Useful" after "Liberal." See George P. Schmidt, *Princeton and Rutgers: Two Colonial Colleges of New Jersey* (Princeton, 1960), p. 10.

95. Jane Butzner, ed., *Constitutional Chaff: Rejected Suggestions of the Constitutional Convention of 1787* (New York, 1941), p. 64.

96. *A Letter to the Citizens of Pennsylvania on the Necessity of Promoting Agriculture, Manufactures, and the Useful Arts* (Lancaster, 1800). Cp., in the same year, John Vaughan's *Valedictory Lecture Delivered Before the Philosophical Society of Delaware* (Wilmington, 1800), pp. 33–34, which extols the zeal evinced in America "in the pursuit of useful knowledge," which Vaughan equates with science as distinct from "scholastic vices."

97. Brown, *Virginia*, pp. 277–278. The *Virginia Gazette* of Sept. 26, 1777, carried an advertisement of the opening of a private school at Glebe in Sussex, England, which offered Latin and Greek to sons of colonials but assured that, since these were of little use to boys designed for trade, business, or mechanical arts, students would also be taught English and practical subjects.

98. *The Satiric Poems of John Trumbull: The Progress of Dulness and M'Fingal*, ed. Edwin T. Bowden (Austin, 1962), p. 30 (Trumbull's preface).

99. *Progress of Dulness*, pt. I, lines 223–224.

100. Discourse IV ("On American Education"), in Jonathan Boucher, *A View of the Causes and Consequences of the American Revolution; in Thirteen Discourses Preached in North America between the Years 1763 and 1775* (London, 1797; rpt. 1967), pp. 196, 199.

101. Philip Vickers Fithian, *Journal and Letters, 1767–1774*, ed. John Rogers Williams (Princeton, 1900), pp. 80, 160.

102. J. Hector St. John Crèvecoeur, *Letters from an American Farmer* (1782; Garden City, n.d.), letter I, p. 16. Cp. William B. Dinsmoor on early American aloofness from ancient art and archaeology ("Early American Studies of Mediterranean Archaeology," *Proc. Amer. Philos. Soc.* 87 (1943), pp. 74–104).

103. *An Oration, delivered July 4, 1785* (Boston, 1785), pp. 21–22; Hindle, *Pursuit of Science*, pp. 254–255.

104. *U. S. Chronicle* (Providence), Oct. 12, 1786; Feb. 8, 1787 ("Thoughts on Education").

105. *Massachusetts Magazine*, Dec., 1789, pp. 746–749; also in *American Museum* 7 (Jan. and Feb., 1790), pp. 33–35, 103–105. See also *New Haven Gazette*, June

12, 1788, by "A Countryman" (perhaps Roger Sherman), who rejected the dead languages and advocated agriculture, clothing, trades, commerce; *American Magazine*, Feb., 1788, p. 160 (English, mathematics, agriculture); *Massachusetts Magazine*, June, 1789 (for useful knowledge, such as English, but not Greek and Latin).

Thomas Paine in 1794–96 attacked the learned languages as useless, and supported scientific knowledge and the living languages ("The Age of Reason," in *Complete Writings of Thomas Paine*, ed. Philip S. Foner [New York, 1945], pp. 491–492). Francis Hopkinson advocated modern languages as "the most useful to be known" ("On the Learned Languages," in *Miscellaneous Essays and Occasional Writings* [Philadelphia, 1792], vol. II, p. 48). One of the pupils of Robert Proud, master of Greek and Latin and mathematics at the Friends School, Philadelphia, from 1761–70 and 1780–90, remembered him a generation later as "a zealous advocate for useful learning." See Charles W. Thomson, "Notices of the Life and Character of Robert Proud," *Memoirs of the Historical Society of Pennsylvania* 1 (1826), p. 435. Robert Proud, author of the first *History of Pennsylvania* (1797–98), was a man of broad learning and interests. It is relevant to note that when on Jan. 25, 1786, he reported to the overseers of the school on the library of the school, he made a distinction between the classics and other books "such as are best adapted for the Instruction & Improvement of youths in the most necessary & useful Branches of Science." See Jean S. Straub, "Teaching in the Friends Latin School of Philadelphia in the Eighteenth Century," *Pa. Mag. Hist. & Biog.* 91 (1967), p. 453.

On the campaign for useful knowledge other than Latin and Greek see, e.g., Homer H. Young, "Theory of American Education during the Revolutionary Period, 1743–1809," (Ph.D. diss., Texas University, 1949), pp. 5, 159, 284–285, 415, 421; Middlekauff, *Ancients and Axioms*, p. 120; Jackson Turner Main, *The Social Structure of Revolutionary America* (New York, 1965), pp. 245–252.

106. Letter of Benjamin Latrobe to Ferdinand Fairfax, May 28, 1798, in *The Journal of Latrobe* (New York, 1905), pp. 67–74.

107. *Massachusetts Magazine*, Dec., 1796.

108. Reverend William Nixon, *Specimen of a Plan, for Facilitating the Acquisition of the Latin Language, and the Elements of the Sciences usually taught in the Universities* (Charleston, 1789). Nixon's proposal actually received the support of a number of distinguished Charlestonians, including Dr. David Ramsay. See Ramsay, *Writings*, p. 33, n. 14.

109. Ebenezer Fitch, *Useful Knowledge and Religion, Recommended to the Pursuits and Improvement of the Young* (Pittsfield, 1799).

110. Cp., e.g., Varnum Lansing Collins, *President Witherspoon: A Biography* (Princeton, 1925), pp. 184, 204–205; Douglas Sloan, *The Scottish Enlightenment and the American College Ideal* (New York, 1971), pp. 126–127; Reverend David M'Clure, *An Oration on the Advantages of an Early Education* (Exeter, N.H., 1783), pp. 3, 12, 16; William Smith, *An Account of Washington College in the State of Maryland* (Philadelphia, 1784), pp. 15, 46 (Prayer for Wisdom and Obedience: "Holy and merciful Father! Give thy Blessing to this Seminary of Virtue and useful Learning"); Reverend Enos Hitchcock, *A Discourse on Education* (Providence, 1785), p. 14; Charles Nisbet, *The Usefulness and Importance of Human Learning* (Carlisle, 1786); Pauline Holmes, *Tercentenary History of the Boston Latin School 1635–1935* (Cambridge, Mass., 1935), pp. 423–429; Edgar W. Knight, *A Documentary History of Education in the South Before 1860* (Chapel Hill, 1949–53), vol. III, p. 20 (charter of Blount College, near Nashville, Tennessee, 1794, named after William Blount, territorial governor of Tennessee: to train youth in virtuous conduct and "the various branches of useful science, and in the principles of the ancient and

modern languages"); Samuel Harrison Smith, *Remarks on Education* [awarded prize in contest for best essay on a national system of education offered by the American Philosophical Society] (Philadelphia, 1798), reprinted in Frederick Rudolph, ed., *Essays on Education in the Early Republic* (Cambridge, Mass., 1965), pp. 198, 213, 217, 223 ("Let us, then, with rapture anticipate the era when the triumph of peace and the prevalance of virtue shall be rendered secure by the diffusion of useful knowledge"); Reverend Samuel Knox, *An Essay on the Best System of Liberal Education Adapted to the Genius of the Government of the United States* (Philadelphia, 1799), reprinted in Rudolph, *Essays on Education*, pp. 271–372; anonymous paper submitted in competition to the American Philosophical Society, 1797, for which see Merle M. Odgers, "Education and the American Philosophical Society," *Proc. Amer. Philos. Soc.* 87 (1943), p. 14; Sloan, *Scottish Enlightenment*, p. 175, on Samuel Stanhope Smith, president of Princeton from 1795 to 1805, who advocated useful knowledge for virtue and national progress through the sciences and the humanities.

Magazines in the United States now began to speak of themselves as "repositories of useful knowledge." See, e.g., *Boston Magazine*, Apr., 1784, p. 238; *The New-York Magazine; Or, Literary Repository* 1 (Jan., 1790), p. viii (Preface).

111. Richard M. Gummere, "The Classical Politics of John Adams," *Boston Public Library Quarterly* 9 (1957), pp. 167–182; idem, *The American Colonial Mind and the Classical Tradition* (Cambridge, Mass., 1963), pp. 191–197; Alfred Iacuzzi, *John Adams, Scholar* (New York, 1952); Dorothy M. Robathan, "John Adams and the Classics," *New England Quarterly* 19 (1946), pp. 91–98; Susan Ford [Wiltshire], "Thomas Jefferson and John Adams on the Classics," *Arion* 6 (Spring, 1967), pp. 116–132.

112. *Adams Family Correspondence*, ed. L. H. Butterfield and Marc Friedlaender (Cambridge, Mass., 1973), vol. III, pp. 308–309, 348. It is curious to compare John Quincy Adams's own evaluation of his student years twenty-five years later (Dec. 31, 1805): "My studies were assiduous and seldom interrupted. I meant to give them such a direction as should be useful in its tendency. Yet on looking back, and comparing the time consumed with the knowledge acquired, I have no occasion to take pride in the result of my application. . . . An immense proportion of the time I have dedicated to the search of knowledge has been wasted upon subjects which can never be profitable to myself or useful to others" (*The Diary of John Quincy Adams, 1794–1845*, ed. Allan Nevins [New York, 1951], p. 27).

113. *Adams Family Correspondence*, vol. III, p. 342.

114. On Rush as enemy of the classics see especially "Opponents of Classical Learning in America during the Revolutionary Period," Chapter IV, below; Richard M. Gummere, *Seven Wise Men of Colonial America* (Cambridge, Mass., 1967), pp. 64–80.

115. Letter to Ebenezer Hazard, Nov. 8, 1765, in *Letters of Benjamin Rush*, ed. L. H. Butterfield, *Memoirs of the American Philosophical Society*, no. 30 (Philadelphia, 1951), vol. I, p. 18.

116. *A Plan for the Establishment of Public Schools and the Diffusion of Knowledge in Pennsylvania; to Which are Added, Thoughts upon the Mode of Education Proper to a Republic. Addressed to the Legislature and Citizens of the State* (Philadelphia, 1786); Smith, *Theories of Education*, pp. 240–256; Rudolph, *Essays on Education*, pp. 1–23. Curiously, as late as 1792, he advised his son Richard to continue his study of Latin (*Letters*, vol. I, p. 619).

117. *A Plan*, p. 10 (=Smith, *Theories of Education*, p. 246).

118. "To Friends of the Federal Government: A Plan for a Federal University," Oct. 29, 1783, in *Letters*, vol. I, pp. 491–494.

119. "An Enquiry into the Utility of a Knowledge of the Latin and Greek Languages as a Branch of Liberal Studies, with Hints of a Plan of Liberal Instruction,

Without Them, Accommodated to the Present State of Society, Manners, and Government in the United States," *American Museum* 5 (1789), pp. 525–535; also in Benjamin Rush, *Essays, Literary, Moral & Philosophical* (Philadelphia, 1798), pp. 21–56.

120. See Lyman H. Butterfield, "Benjamin Rush as a Promoter of Useful Knowledge," *Proc. Amer. Philos. Soc.* 92 (1948), pp. 26–36; Sloan, *Scottish Enlightenment,* pp. 203–208.

121. Sloan, *Scottish Enlightenment,* pp. 185–224; David Freeman Hawke, *Benjamin Rush, Revolutionary Gadfly* (Indianapolis, 1971), pp. 284–298.

122. *Letters,* vol. I, pp. 604, 607.

123. Harry S. Good, *Benjamin Rush and His Services to American Education* (Berne, Indiana, 1918), pp. 235–236.

124. *The Spur of Fame, Dialogues of John Adams and Benjamin Rush 1805–1813,* ed. John A. Schutz and Douglass Adair (San Marino, 1960), pp. 169, 178; Rush, *Letters,* vol. II, pp. 1066, 1080–1081, 1114.

125. Rush, *Letters,* vol. II, pp. 1066–1067.

126. *The Works of John Adams* (Boston, 1850–56), vol. X, p. 105.

127. *Autobiography,* in *The Complete Jefferson,* ed. Saul K. Padover (New York, 1943), p. 1120.

128. Letter to Skipwith, Aug. 3, 1771, in *Papers of Thomas Jefferson,* ed. Julian P. Boyd (Princeton, 1950–), vol. I, pp. 76–77. That the study of the classical languages was being subjected about this time to the criterion of usefulness is evident, e.g., from a forensic debate topic at the commencement in Princeton in 1770: "The Study of the dead Languages is for the Emolument of Science, even in a State where every useful and ornamental Branch of Learning is copiously treated in the Language proper to that State." See David Potter, *Debating in Colonial Chartered Colleges: An Historical Survey, 1642–1900,* Teachers College, Columbia University Contributions to Education, no. 899 (New York, 1944), p. 45.

129. Daniel J. Boorstin, *The Lost World of Thomas Jefferson* (New York, 1948), pp. 3–4, 213–225; Richard Beale Davis, *Literature and Society in Early Virginia 1608–1804* (Baton Rouge, 1973), p. 232; Eleanor Davidson Berman, *Thomas Jefferson Among the Arts* (New York, 1947), p. 10.

130. *Crusade Against Ignorance: Thomas Jefferson on Education,* ed. Gordon C. Lee, Teachers College, Columbia University Classics in Education, no. 6 (New York, 1961), p. 20.

131. Louis B. Wright, "Thomas Jefferson and the Classics," *Proc. Amer. Philos. Soc.* 87 (1943), pp. 223–233; Richard Beale Davis, *Intellectual Life in Jefferson's Virginia 1790–1830* (Chapel Hill, 1964), p. 29; Karl Lehmann, *Thomas Jefferson, American Humanist* (New York, 1947), passim.

132. *Writings of Thomas Jefferson,* Memorial Edition (Washington, D.C., 1905), vol. XV, pp. 209–211.

133. Ibid., vol. II, pp. 203–206. The *Notes on Virginia* was written in 1782, printed in Paris 1784 (rev. ed. 1787).

134. Jefferson, *Papers,* vol. VIII, p. 636; Jefferson, *Crusade Against Ignorance,* pp. 104–138 ("The Useful Sciences in their Highest Degree"). On July 19, 1788, Jefferson deprecated Buffon's scorn for chemistry, declaring, "I think it on the contrary among the most useful sciences, and big with future discoveries for the utility and safety of the human race" (Jefferson, *Papers,* vol. XIII, p. 381). On Jefferson's view of mathematics, natural history, botany, and physics as useful sciences, see letter to Thomas Mann Randolph, Aug. 27, 1786, in *Papers,* vol. X, p. 306; *Crusade Against Ignorance,* pp. 140–144.

135. Jefferson, *Writings,* vol. X, pp. 140–142; Roy J. Honeywell, *The Educational Work of Thomas Jefferson* (Cambridge, Mass., 1931), p. 215.

136. In letters to John Adams in 1812–1813, *Writings of Thomas Jefferson*, ed. Paul Leicester Ford (New York, 1892–99), vol. IX, pp. 427, 464–465; letter to J. Correa da Serra, 1817, Jefferson, *Writings*, Memorial Edition, vol. X, pp. 94–96; Jefferson, *Crusade Against Ignorance*, pp. 112–114; Honeywell, *Educational Work*, pp. 40–41, 146.

137. Honeywell, *Educational Work*, p. 250. In 1820, writing to his grandson Francis Wayles Eppes, he advised him to learn "those useful branches which cannot well be acquired without the aids of the college." "It is, or ought to be," he declared, "the rule of every collegiate institution to teach to every particular student the branches of science which those who direct him think will be useful in the pursuits proposed to him, and to waste his time on nothing which they think will not be useful to him" (*To the Girls and Boys, Being the Delightful Little-Known Letters of Thomas Jefferson to and from his Children and Grandchildren*, ed. Edward Boykin [New York, 1964], pp. 201–202).

138. Cited by Edwin T. Martin, *Thomas Jefferson: Scientist* (New York, 1952), p. 37.

139. Ibid., p. 36.

140. Ibid., p. 38; Daniels, *Science in American Society*, p. 102.

141. *The Works of Daniel Webster*, 4th ed. (Boston, 1853), vol. I, p. 143.

142. Samuel Miller, *A Brief Retrospect of the Eighteenth Century* (New York, 1803), vol. II, pp. 36, 54.

143. Ibid., pp. 272, 409–410. On Miller's brilliant survey see Gilbert Chinard, "Progress and Perfectability in Samuel Miller's Intellectual History," *Studies in Intellectual History* (Baltimore, 1953), pp. 94–122; idem, "A Landmark in American Intellectual History: Samuel Miller's *A Brief Retrospect of the Eighteenth Century*," *Princeton University Library Chronicle* 14 (1953), pp. 55–71; Jacob L. Susskind, "Samuel Miller's Intellectual History of the Eighteenth Century," *Journal of Presbyterian History* 49 (1941), pp. 15–37.

144. Address to the Free School Society, in Smith, *Theories of Education*, pp. 345–360.

145. Noah Webster, *Elements of Useful Knowledge*, vol. I (Hartford, 1802); vol. II (New Haven, 1804); vol. III (Boston, 1806); vol. IV (New Haven, 1812). A similar work by the English miscellany writer William Bingley, in three volumes, was also published in Philadelphia (1810). A second edition (1818) bore the title *Useful Knowledge: or, A Familiar and Explanatory Account of the Various Productions of Nature, Mineral, Vegetable, and Animal*.

146. Vol. I (1814), pp. 1–2, 9.

147. Sept., 1834–Sept., 1837. Cp. *Hawthorne as Editor*, ed. Arlin Turner (University, La., 1941). The magazine was imitative of the *Penny Magazine* published by the Society for the Diffusion of Useful Knowledge in England, but it was largely American in content.

148. *Democracy in America* (New York, 1945), vol. II, pp. 37–38, 45, 47. The work was first published 1835–40.

149. Henry S. Williams and Edward H. Williams, *A History of Science* (New York, 1914), vol. V, pp. 29–33; A. Wolf, *A History of Science, Technology & Philosophy in the 18th Century*, 2nd ed. (New York, 1952), vol. I, pp. 42–44; W. J. Sparrow, *Knight of the White Eagle: A Biography of Sir Benjamin Thompson, Count Rumford (1753–1814)* (London, 1964), pp. 107–140; K. D. C. Vernon, "The Foundation and Early Years of the Royal Institution," *Proceedings of the Royal Institution* 179 (1963); J. A. Thompson, *Count Rumford of Massachusetts* (New York, 1935).

150. *The Works of Jeremy Bentham* (New York, 1962), vol. VIII, pp. 5–191.

151. Did Bentham know Aristotle, *Politics* 8.3.1 (1338a)? Aristotle indeed was the first to try to define useful knowledge in world thought. He distinguished in the education of children between what is useful in itself (*to chresimon*), such as

learning (*mathesis*) to read, which is useful as a means of acquiring other branches of knowledge.

152. John W. Adamson, *English Education 1789-1902* (Cambridge, 1964), pp. 102-105; Nicholas Hans, *New Trends in Education in the Eighteenth Century* (London, 1951), p. 209; Ian Cumming, *Useful Learning: Bentham's "Chrestomathia"* (Auckland, 1961); Southwood Smith, *Westminster Review* 4 (July, 1825), p. 149.

153. Vol. I (1832). Also published in New York and Boston.

154. Arthur Aspinall, *Lord Brougham and the Whig Party* (Manchester, 1927), pp. 232-235; Chester W. New, *The Life of Henry Brougham to 1830* (Oxford, 1961), pp. 347-357. The Society became bankrupt in 1844. It could hardly have escaped the attention of Englishmen that Brougham's society was in competition for public attention with the still operative Society for Promoting Christian Knowledge (SPCK) founded over a century before.

155. Letter to Charles Parsons, July 16, 1869, in Eli Lilly, *Schliemann in Indianapolis* (Indianapolis, 1961). I owe this reference to Professor Carol Thomas of the University of Washington.

156. Cp. John W. Adamson, *English Education*, p. 311.

157. James Russell Lowell, "Harvard Anniversary," in *Democracy and Other Addresses* (Boston, 1893), pp. 217-218; cp. William Lyon Phelps's approval in *Teaching in School and College* (New York, 1912), pp. 167-168. In 1839 Lowell wrote: "Our stout Yankee national would swap all the poems that ever were penned for a treatise on ventilation" (Martin Duberman, *James Russell Lowell* [Boston, 1966], p. 30).

158. *Democracy and its Discontents: Reflections on Everyday America* (New York, 1974), p. 122. In a curious little book, *Useful Knowledge* (New York, 1928), Gertrude Stein, just before the long agony of the Great Depression, optimistically, in her preface, defined useful knowledge as "every little that helps to be American. . . . Romance is Useful Knowledge."

III. Classical Influences and Eighteenth-Century American Political Thought

$\mathbf{H}$ow strangely is antiquity treated!" wrote Thomas Paine in 1792, repudiating the doctrine of precedents. "To answer some purposes, it is spoken of as the times of darkness and ignorance, and to answer others, it is put for the light of the world."[1] In eighteenth-century America during the formative time of the new nation (ca. 1750–90) reading of the classics and uses of knowledge of antiquity were indeed grossly selective, complacently antiquarian, instrumental.[2] The prize of knowledge for the leaders of the Revolutionary generation—politicians, pamphleteers, patriots—was not systematic learning and the truth but freedom from the mother country and establishment and management of a stable and durable multi-state republic, with the guidance of what John Adams called "the divine science of politics."

Typical of the centrality of political thought for the Founding Fathers is Josiah Quincy's provision in his will (1774): "I give to my son, when he shall arrive at the age of fifteen years, Algernon Sidney's works,—John Locke's works,—Lord Bacon's works,—Gordon's Tacitus,—and Cato's Letters. May the Spirit of Liberty rest upon him!"[3] The almost reverential appeal to classical political theory and practice as the absolute standard for inspiration, guidance, and testing of governmental innovation through comparative process was endemic. This leap into the classical past for political precedents gleaned from the "perfect Models of Antiquity"[4] is in full view, for example, in the grandiloquent flourish of the remarkable Hugh Henry Brackenridge, in 1779, in a "Letter to the Poets, Philosophers, Orators, Statesmen and Heroes of Antiquity":

> It is indeed high time [for you] to abandon [the British] and to turn your attention to the free people of America. Here your correspondence will be much courted, and your observations very generally attended to. . . . History and politics . . . will be more to the taste of the present times; and for that reason I am particularly anxious to interest in our behalf those great legislators [of antiquity]. . . . The sentiments of these great men upon Government, will be of great service at the present day. . . . It would much oblige us, if Solon and some others, of your best politicians would send up a few observations on the nature of Government in general, which we may use as a compass to steer our opinions in this wide waste of argument.[5]

The late Hannah Arendt concluded that "without the classical example . . . none of the men of the revolutions on either side of the Atlantic would have possessed the courage for what then turned out to be unprecedented action." American classicists would like to agree with her; few American intellectual historians do.[6]

No one may doubt, however, that there occurred in the Revolutionary Age—the Golden Age of the classical tradition in America —the greatest outpouring of lessons from antiquity in the public arena that America was ever again to witness. The Founding Fathers ransacked the ancient world as a usable past for guidelines, parallels, analogies to present political problems, and indeed for partisan politics. They frequently scoured ancient history and political theory and institutions as "the lamp of experience" in search of authoritative precedents to legitimate and validate conclusions already arrived at through wide reading in contemporary literature and through the exercise of reason.[7] For the Founding Fathers instinctively associated liberty and republicanism with the ancient commonwealths, "those free Governments of old, whose History we so much admire, and whose Example we think it an Honour to imitate."[8] And it was preeminently the Roman republic that was their exemplar, serving as a timeless model in which the civic virtues as well as corrupting vices stood out with classical clarity. In their quest for good government many among the Revolutionary generation were inspired by this comparative method, this almost ritualistic communion with ancient thought, with high optimism and confidence in the viability of a *novus ordo saeclorum.*

Yet for the most part this aggregation of classical knowledge was extracted not from the original texts but from such shortcuts as traitorous translations, modern histories of the ancient world, handbooks of antiquities, and encyclopaedias.[9] Ezra Stiles, president of Yale College, could write to Jefferson in 1790 in response to a scholarly inquiry: "We too much content ourselves with perusing the modern and inaccurate and injudicious Retailers of ancient History neglecting the original Historians, whether in the original Languages or their Translations. . . . [Students] read only the modern Writers or Compilers of antient History."[10] More significantly, the understanding of ancient republicanism and of classical political theory that reached the Founding Fathers was a filtered and refracted one, derived from the works of selected contemporary transatlantic political theorists and publicists assiduously read by early Americans.[11] And it was especially from the ideology of the English radical Whigs that Americans imported and naturalized their model of antiquity. Throughout the eighteenth century the *Independent Whig* and *Cato's Letters* of John Trenchard and Thomas Gordon, as well as Gordon's political discourses prefixed to his best-seller translations of Tacitus and Sallust were required reading for American libertarians. These disquisitions equipped them with an ideological code, with classical political vocabulary and with political models. Gordon taught Americans that the Roman republic especially was "the standard and Pattern . . . and useful Instruction . . . , an Example to us." In line with the prevailing deterministic "uniformitarian" theory of history, the ancient prototypes were deemed highly instructive because "mankind will always be the same, will always act within one Circle; and when we know what they did a Thousand Years ago in any Circumstance, we shall know what they will do a Thousand Years hence in the same. This is what is called Experience."[12]

As early as 1765 John Adams outlined, in part, the blend of experience that was to guide the Founding Fathers: "Let us study the law of nature; search into the spirit of the British Constitution; read the histories of the ancient ages; contemplate the great examples of Greece and Rome; set before us the conduct of our British ancestors, who have defended for us the inherent rights of mankind against foreign and domestic tyrants and usurpers. . . . Let every sluice of knowledge be opened and set a-flowing."[13] Indeed, the classical doctrine of *ius naturale* enjoyed immense prestige in eighteenth-century America, as counterclaim overriding repugnant enactments of the crown and Parliament. But though the classical roots of the American appeal to inalienable rights and the higher law were known and cited (Aristotle, the Stoics, notably Cicero *De Legibus* 3.4.10), Americans ardently espoused this concept less from direct knowledge of the ancient sources than from the English heritage of law and government, especially as mediated through Milton, Coke, Algernon Sidney, and Locke, and from the continental jurists de Vattel, Pufendorf, and Burlamaqui.[14] These sources were superficially summarized by John Adams in 1774, when he asserted that American revolutionary rights were founded on "the principles of Aristotle and Plato, of Livy and Cicero, and Sidney, Harrington and Locke; the principles of nature and eternal reason."[15]

Now the models of antiquity which Americans perceived, and were content with, were largely simplistic stereotypes, and these tended to fall into polarised patterns. For example, in the 1760s James Otis formulated the prevailing American view that Greece was a better mother of colonies than Rome, which dominated hers overbearingly and brutally.[16] The founders of the first modern republic, on the crest of utopian aspirations and from a need for both instant history and historical legitimation, tended to idealize extravagantly the ancient republics. John Adams, while acknowledging the general progress of mankind, maintained that "the knowledge of the principles and construction of free governments . . . have remained at a full stand for two or three thousand years." Hence he turned his political sights to "the ancient seats of liberty, the Republics of Greece and Rome"; and in 1782 he wrote to Lafayette: "I [am] . . . a republican on principle. . . . Almost every thing that is estimable in civil life has originated under such governments. Two republican powers, Athens and Rome, have done more honor to our species than all the rest of it. A new country can be planted only by such a government."[17]

Yet among the Greek states it was not Athens, suspect because of its turbulent history, direct democracy, factionalism, and demagogues, that was venerated by Americans,[18] but rather Sparta. From Plutarch's *Lycurgus* and contemporary European celebration of Sparta, notably by Montesquieu, American leaders judged Sparta to be a model of freedom and order, a stable, long-lived commonwealth, its people distinguished by virtue, simple life-style, patriotism, vigor. As "brave and as free a people as ever existed" John Dickinson called the Spartans.[19] While the republic of Carthage was also studied as model because of its longevity, it was above all Rome that Americans turned to as republican archetype. This appeal of the Roman republic to Americans lay in its pluralistic culture, its perdurability, flexibility in policy, balanced constitution, agricultural economy, religious toleration, the vaunted purity of its great men, and its Roman virtues (especially patriotism, self-sacrifice, and frugality).[20] For Alexander Hamilton Rome was "the nurse of freedom"; and "the Roman republic attained to the utmost height of human greatness."[21] John Adams was unrestrained: "The Roman constitution formed the noblest people and the greatest power that has ever existed."[22]

As counterthrust to the image of a decadent and corrupt England exported to America mostly by the radical Whigs, Americans envisaged the New World as the land of virtue par excellence. The incantation of virtue swelled to a crescendo in eighteenth-century America,[23] taking secular form about 1730, and then being redirected into politico-ethical channels in the crisis atmosphere of the Revolutionary Age. True, this American cult of virtue at its height—civic virtue as public spirit for the public good—had its subterranean roots in the ancient preoccupation with virtue and moral knowledge and in the classical republics and heroes idealized by Americans. But the quest for republican virtue in America was fired to an intense glow by the teachings of the Whig tracts, Lord Bolingbroke's "Letters on the study and use of history," published in 1752, and Montesquieu's *Esprit des Lois*.[24] A few examples from a virtual flood of exhortations to virtue will illustrate. John Adams wrote in 1776, "Politicks . . . is the Science of human Happiness and human Happiness is clearly best promoted by Virtue"; and "Public Virtue is the only Foundation of Republics. There must be a positive Passion for the public good, the public Interest."[25] Robert Livingston of New York proclaimed, "More virtue is expected from our People than any People ever had"; and an anonymous slogan said, "No virtue, no commonwealth."[26]

Among the numerous classical role models in America, mostly from Plutarch's republican saints and martyrs, pride of place was given above all to Cicero and hardly less to Cato Uticensis. Indeed, the Catonic model in America long served as a clarion call to dedication to virtue, civic duty, and freedom. The high popularity of Addison's tragedy *Cato* in eighteenth-century America—there were numerous performances from New Hampshire to South Carolina and at least eight American editions before 1800—is proof enough.[27] Particularly cultivated also was the cautionary model of Cincinnatus, who epitomized the early American deprecation of lengthy holds on the reins of power. Among the many Americans who imitated or recalled Cincinnatus were Washington, John Adams, Jefferson, Israel Putnam, John Jay, and even the suspect Order of the Cincinnati, the association of retired army officers of the Revolutionary army founded immediately after the peace with Britain, in 1783. In that year, too, long before Washington was elected first president of the United States, Charles Wilson Peale's victory arch depicted him as Cincinnatus, and he was greeted in Philadelphia on December 8, 1783, with the following lines:

> So HE who Rome's proud legions sway'd,
> Return'd and sought his native shade.[28]

This paradigmatic return to the plough, to the ancestral estate in America was more than a symbolic gesture; it was a response to a mix of impulses: the gentleman's Sabine Farm ideal of the eighteenth century; English country ideology; the value of frugality espoused by the British commonwealthmen; the moral exaltation of agriculture in the eighteenth century; the devaluation of trades as banausic, and of cities and commerce as corruptive, encouraging luxury and political ambition; traditional American "primitivism" (up to 1800 about 90 percent of the American people were engaged in some form of agriculture); and the legacy of classical political theory of a free agricultural commonwealth composed of self-sufficient, economically independent farmer-soldier-citizens.[29] American agrarianism was, like its classical antecedents, politico-ethical in nature: an agricultural base for the republic with availability of freehold land was deemed by most of the Founding Fathers to be a prime safeguard for liberty and stability. The virtuous farmer, the purity and simplicity of his life, were widely invoked, a model conjured up from a classical past simpler than the English and French present. The American poet of the Revolution Philip Freneau wrote in 1775 in his "American liberty, a poem":

> like the ancient Romans, you
> At once are soldiers, and are farmers too.[30]

While invoking classical republican models, the Founding Fathers were fully aware of the classical cyclical theory of political change with its admonition of the impermanence of political systems, the decay and death of states, and rotation of governments. The classical component, however, was but one of the many streams that flowed into American political thought: English, continental, American colonial. In addition to the theory of cycles, the doctrine of mixed government, separation of powers, country ideology, natural law—these were all vigorously debated in England in the late seventeenth and early eighteenth centuries. Notably, regarding the doctrine of balanced government, there was already a vast literature in England during the constitutional discussions preceding the civil wars of the seventeenth century, and this literature was available to Americans in the Revolutionary Age, as was Montesquieu's *Esprit des Lois*, whose roots reach back to Machiavelli. Moreover, separation of powers in America (among colonial governor, council, and colonial assembly) were already in practice as far back as the Virginia Charter of 1624, so that Americans were receptive to such a principle from their own institutional history in colonial times.[31]

Why then, it may be asked, did the Americans in the Revolutionary Age so often have recourse to the "pure fountains" of antiquity? Since the only precedents for republican government were to be found in the ancient states, "they were *obliged* to study Greece and Rome, if they would gain 'experimental' wisdom in the dangers and potentialities of the republican form."[32] Moreover, there were no precedents in English history for a league of states. Thus ancient political theory and experience served Americans as an empirical laboratory for exploring and testing the political options. And, deeply troubled by the fact that the republics of antiquity were all in the graveyard of history, Americans were also practicing what a contemporary called "political pathology," performing, as it were, autopsies on the dead republics with a view to discovering how to retard the process of inevitable decay through proper safeguards for the first modern republic.[33]

The prime safeguard was deemed to be the balance inherent in the mixed constitution of classical derivation, with its blending of monarchic, aristocratic, and democratic elements. The ideal of balance was indeed one of the dominant metaphors of the Revolutionary Age, responsive to a highly pluralistic society in thirteen colonies. As early as 1772 John Adams declared that "the best Governments of the world have been mixed. The Republics of Greece, Rome, Carthage were all mixed Governments."[34] In his massive *Defence of the Constitutions of Government of the United States of America* (1787–88), he applauded Cicero's advocacy of the mixed constitution of three elements as "founded on a reason that is unchangeable."[35] The constitutional practices of Sparta, Carthage, and Rome were thus carefully studied by the Founding Fathers, and the ancient sources for balanced government (Plato *Laws* 3; Aristotle *Politics*, e.g., 1265b, 1269a–b, 1294b, 1316a–b; Cicero; Polybius 6; Plutarch *Lycurgus*) were ransacked as unimpeachable authorites. Adams was fully aware of the mortality of ancient republics despite their balanced constitutions, and of Tacitus' gloomy hindsight comment (*Ann.* 4.33.1) on the impossibility or evanescent character of a balanced constitution.[36] Yet he argued that "a Balance, with all its difficulty, must be preserved, or liberty is lost forever. Perhaps a perfect balance, if it ever existed, has not been long maintained in its perfection; yet, such a balance as has been sufficient to liberty, has been supported in some nations for many centuries together."[37] Despite this, he could not refrain from such rhetoric as "the institutions now made in America will not wholly wear out for thousands of years."[38]

The paramount model for the Founding Fathers of a constitution structured to retard political decay and assure at the same time freedom and stability was the constitution of Rome of the end of the third-early second centuries B.C.—as analyzed by Polybius in book 6, the vaunted prototype of a commonwealth since the Renaissance, the favorite source for classical republicanism in the seventeenth and eighteenth centuries. John Adams[39] was aware that the blessings of the Roman constitution did not long survive Polybius' analysis and proceeded to assess the weaknesses of the Roman government, attributing the fall of the republic—with the advantages of hindsight—to imperfect, "ineffectual balance" and prescribing stronger negative votes, separated powers, and checks and counterchecks. As it turned out, indeed, rather than a melting pot of a mixed constitution, the Constitution of the United States, put together in Philadelphia in 1787, was a document of numerous compromises, based on the principles of a broadly pluralistic balance and separation of powers, despite the confidence placed by the Founding Fathers in the Polybian mixed constitution of Rome. It is not uninstructive for an understanding of the eighteenth-century uncritical use of antiquity to compare their reliance on Polybius with our own view of his treatment of Rome's constitution as a tendentious and theoretical analysis of Roman government prepared in support of the Roman nobility. Moreover, Polybius' method is vitiated by his schematic application of Greek political categories and vocabulary to Rome, and his treatment is highly selective and glosses over the actual domination of the Senate and the Roman nobility.[40] We may add other cautions regarding the American appeal to the ancient mixed constitutions and to Polybius: Carthage,

Sparta, and Rome were imperial states striving for internal balance
so as to present a posture of strength toward their subjects and foreign states; that such categories as monarchic, aristocratic, and
democratic were unsuitable for America; and that the Greek political theory of the *mikte* identified ideal balance with unchangeable,
immobile perfection, a goal incompatible with the dynamism of
America.

It was the Constitutional Convention of 1787, at the various state
ratifying conventions, and in the pamphlet literature and political
tracts spun off in great numbers to influence the structure of the
new government, that the appeal to classical political theory and
practice reached its peak. John Adams, in Europe at the time as
American representative, in writing his *Defence* ransacked ancient
sources and modern works for classical constitutions and leagues.[41]
Many of the delegates to the Convention in Philadelphia did their
classical homework diligently, especially Madison, Hamilton, and
James Wilson. William Pierce (delegate from Georgia) said of Madison, for example, that he "ran through the whole Scheme of the
Government,—pointed out the beauties and defects of ancient Republics; compared their situation with ours wherever it appeared to
bear any analogy."[42] It is clear that the precedents, analogies, and
lessons Madison and others quarried from antiquity were not mere
window dressing or "pedantry in politics," but solemn exercises in
comparative politicial institutions and history. The records of the
Federal Convention, and *The Federalist* papers, written by Madison, Hamilton and John Jay (notably nos. 6, 9, 18, 38, 63, 70) are
dotted with classical parallels and lessons. It is discernible that
some of these were extracted from translations of Plato, Aristotle,
Demosthenes, Polybius, Livy, Cicero, Sallust, Strabo, Tacitus, and
Plutarch, but most were from contemporary works on ancient political theory and history, such as Rollin, Vertot, Edward Montagu,
Adam Ferguson, Walter Moyle, Conyers Middleton, Mably, Millot,
Mitford, and Gillies.[43]

One of the prime lessons adduced from antiquity by the Founding Fathers was the unsuitability of direct assembly government
because of the instances known of instability and capriciousness of
decisions in ancient republics. Further, such direct participation of
citizens was incompatible with a republic possessing a large terri-
tory. Hence the Founding Fathers introduced into the Constitution
the principle of representative government, repeatedly proclaiming
that the secret of representation was invented by them, and that
this innovation constituted a major advance over the governments

of the ancient republics.[44] But, aside from the term "senate," it is to be noted that not a single direct adaptation from ancient institutions was incorporated into the Constitution;[45] and that the principle and practice of separation of powers already existed in both colonial governments and in state constitutions before 1787.[46]

Great attention was directed at the time of the Convention to the theoretical and practical aspects of federalism, and in this connection the debates and polemical literature analyzed the merits and failures of Greek leagues. Of all classical political models ancient federalism was the most extensively studied because there were no precedents in the English experience or in colonial America.[47] The best informed about Greek leagues were Adams, Madison, and James Wilson, yet their knowledge was limited; for the most part they repeated similar information on Greek leagues found in secondary works.[48] The confederation most frequently cited by the Founding Fathers was the Amphictyonic Council, because it was the one most commonly instanced in handbooks and histories. For example, in the frequently used work of Abbé Mably on Greek institutions they found the Amphictyonic Council elevated to "une république fédérative" and "les états généraux de la Grèce."[49] James Wilson's vacillation is instructive. In 1790–91, in support of the United States Constitution, he lectured that the Amphictyonic Council was "the Congress of the United States of Greece"; that "the general intention and invariable aim of all its modellers and directors was, to form a complete representation of all Greece"; and that "the establishment of the Amphictyons should be admired, as a great master-piece in human politicks."[50] But earlier at the Constitutional Convention Wilson had said: "If a proper model were not to be found in other Confederacies it is not to be wondered at. The number of them was small and the duration of some at least short. The Amphyctionic and Achaean were formed in the infancy of political science; and appear by their History & fate, to have contained radical defects. . . . They soon fell victims to the inefficacy of their organization. . . . There is no reason to adopt their Example."[51] We may ourselves object to their adducing of the Amphictyonic Council as a flawed analogy, for it was neither a political body nor a federative league, but a religious organization of twelve tribal groupings. In general, the lessons drawn from the Greek leagues were the deficiencies of the Amphictyonic, Achaean, Aetolian, and Lycian leagues: their short duration, the tyranny of the larger states over the smaller, and the destruction of the ancient leagues by foreign intervention (Macedon, Rome).[52] The Lycian

Confederacy was especially admired by some, for Montesquieu's endorsement of it as the "model of an excellent confederate republic" carried great weight because it embodied the principle of proportional representation. Madison went so far as to call the Achaean League "the last hope of ancient liberty."[53]

Yet the Founding Fathers were not unaware of the limitations and slipperiness of their knowledge of Greek leagues and of the unsuitability of such precedents for the United States. As early as 1776 Stephen Hopkins of Rhode Island, best known as signer of the Declaration of Independence, cautioned that "too little is known of the antient confederations to say what was their practice."[54] James Madison, who spoke and wrote most on the Greek leagues (especially in "Federalist," no. 18), acknowledged reliance on imperfect monuments a "very imperfect account."[55] James Wilson pointed out at the Pennsylvania Ratifying Convention how defective their knowledge of the ancient leagues was: "Ancient history discloses, and barely discloses to our view, confederate republicks—the Achaean league, the Lycian confederacy, and the Amphityonick council. . . . Besides, the situation and dimensions of these confederacies, and the state of society, manners, and habits in them, were so different from those of the United States, that the most correct description could have supplied but a very small fund of applicable remarks."[56]

Wilson also reported that he had endeavored to learn more about the Lycian League, with little success.[57] In short, the Founding Fathers' knowledge of Greek leagues was superficial and refracted at best, their application of lessons therefrom generally partisan and opportunistic. Edward Freeman, Larsen's great predecessor in the study of federal government in antiquity, summed this up as follows: the American Founding Fathers "instinctively saw the intrinsic interest and practical importance of the history of Federal Greece, and they made what use they could of the little light they enjoyed on the subject." But, Freeman reminds us, the founders of the American union were not scholars, but practical politicians.[58]

The constant appeal to historical examples ("the lamp of experience," Patrick Henry; "Experience must be our only guide," John Dickinson at the Convention arguing that "reason may mislead us") clashed with the uneasiness on the part of many that history might mislead, and that ultimately reason must be the guide.[59] Madison leaned more and more to the latter view, advising "quitting the dim light of historical research, attaching ourselves purely to the dictates of reason and good sense"; and he concluded that "as far as antiquity can instruct us on this subject, its examples support the reasoning we have employed."[60] And it was Madison who neatly summed up the prevailing compromise between ancient thought, reason, and present needs, the operative mix of empiricism and rationalism: "Is it not the glory of the people of America that, whilst they have paid a decent regard to the opinions of former times and other nations, they have not suffered a blind veneration for antiquity . . . to overrule the suggestions of their good sense . . . and the lessons of their own experience."[61] The aged Benjamin Franklin at the Convention unequivocally deplored the appeal to ancient models: "We indeed seem to feel our own want of political wisdom, since we have been running about in search of it. We have gone back to ancient history for models of government and examined the different forms of those Republics which having been formed with the seeds of their own destruction now no longer exist."[62] Some, like the pragmatic Gouverneur Morris, deplored the hunt for classical precedents as an academic futility improper in the practical science of government, and as productive of "the same pedantry with our young scholars just fresh from the university who would fain bring everything to a Roman standard."[63]

Still others urged emancipation from the ancient models on the grounds of the great advances made in political knowledge since antiquity. Hamilton, for example, declared: "The science of politics . . . , like most other sciences, has received great improvement. The efficacy of various principles is now well understood, which were either not known at all, or imperfectly known to the ancients."[64] Dissociation from ancient political models was also urged because of their unsuitability for American national character and the uniqueness of the American experience. Hamilton wrote: "There is a total dissimulation in the circumstances, as well as the manners, of society among us; and it is as ridiculous to seek models in the simple ages of Greece and Rome, as it would be to go in quest of them among the Hottentots and Laplanders"; and "Neither the manners nor the genius of Rome are suited to the republic or the age we live in. All her maxims and habits were military, her government was constituted for war. Ours is unfit for it, and our Situation still less than our constitution, invites us to emulate the conduct of Rome."[65]

Similarly, Thomas Paine uncompromisingly rejected "the complimentary references" to antiquity. "The wisdom, civil governments, and sense of honor of the states of Greece and Rome, are frequently held up as objects of excellence and imitation." But why, he wrote, do we need to go "two or three thousand years back for lessons and examples." "We do great injustice to ourselves by placing them in a superior line. . . . I have no notion of yielding the palm of the United States to any Grecians or Romans that were ever born. We have equalled the bravest in times of danger, and excelled the wisest in construction of civil governments."[66] At the Constitutional Convention the thoughts of Charles Pinckney of South Carolina raised the most serious doubts about analogies from antiquity: "The people of this country are not only very different from the inhabitants of any state we are acquainted with in the modern world; but I assert that their situation is distinct . . . from the people of Greece or Rome, or of any state we are acquainted with among the antients. . . . Can we copy from Greece or Rome? Can this apply to the free yeomanry of America? We surely differ from the whole. Our situation is unexampled."[67]

More important, this breaking away from the comparative historico-political method and the concept of uniformitarianism was accompanied by critical analysis and rejection of analogy in constitution making and governmental practice. Though Madison acknowledged that "there are many points of similitude which render these examples not unworthy of our attention," he recommended caution: "I am not unaware of the circumstances which distinguish the American from other popular governments, as well ancient as modern; and which render extreme circumspection necessary, in reasoning from one case to the other."[68] James Wilson was even more circumspect: "I know that much and pleasing ingenuity has been exerted, in modern times, in drawing entertaining parallels between some of the ancient constitutions and some of the mixed governments that have since existed in Europe. But I suspect that on strict examination, the instances of resemblance will be found to be few and weak . . . and not to be drawn immediately from the ancient constitutions themselves, as they were intended and understood by those who framed them."[69]

The most incisive critique of the use of analogies for the American government from ancient political theory and practice was made in 1785 by a young Marylander, William Vans Murray, then a law student in London. In a brilliant essay Murray assailed the idealization of antiquity as unhistorical, rejecting the excessive use of classical parallels to America, which he considered to be a unique society. He also explicitly rejected Montesquieu's doctrine that civic virtue combined with frugality was essential to sustain republics. All classically based views, Murray declared, are "argue-

ments derived from the falsely imagined character of antiquity."
He wrote: "It is impossible to say that ancient republics were models . . . the picture of ancient governments, except freedom, could
furnish but a slight resemblance to the American democracies. . . .
From such precedents Americans can learn little more than the
contagion of enthusiasm. From antiquity they could gain little." In
sum, such comparisons were to Murray "fancied analogy," misguided admiration, "phantasms of scientifical superstition."[70]

In this connection the debate between John Adams and John
Taylor of Virginia (planter, lawyer, political leader, friend of Jefferson and Madison) is particularly significant. Though Taylor's *Inquiry into the Principles and Policy of the Government of the United
States* appeared in 1814, it was twenty years in the writing and reflects eighteenth-century polemics in transition to the nineteenth
century. Taylor sharply criticized Adams's political philosophy in
the *Defence* for "following the analysis of antiquity" and for his reliance on three generic constitutional forms—monarchic, aristocratic, and democratic. The United States, maintained Taylor, was
something new and unique. Taylor rejected Adams's praise of Sparta's mixed constitution and its longevity; Sparta, Taylor argued,
had no democratic balance, its government was in the hands of a
minority, and "duration [is not] evidence of political perfection."
Greek governments were based on fraud; in the Roman republic
the artistocracy ruled by fraud to preserve its power. Therefore,
searching "among the relicks of antiquity" is irrelevant to America.
"Instead of diving after wisdom into the gloom of antiquity," we
must start from the knowledge that in America "human character
has undergone a moral change." "The history of ancient times is
hardly more weighty, when opposed to living evidence, than the
wanderings of fancy; it is invariably treacherous in some degree,
and comes, like an oracle, from a place into which light cannot penetrate. We are to determine, whether we will be intimidated by apparitions of departed time . . . to shut our eyes, lest we should see
the superiority of our policy, not in theory, but in practice, not in
history, but in sight."[71]

Adams's reply was the timeworn formula: there is one eternal,
unchangeable truth—that all men are the same everywhere, and
that therefore antiquity is relevant to modern problems.[72]

Henry Steele Commager has given us a provocative analysis of
the tension between the old and the new, between antiquity and the
young republic in Revolutionary America. The classical world to
which the Founding Fathers had appealed for guidance was a ste-

reotype, an abstraction, a rational model outside historical time. But America was in fact a unique, dynamic, revolutionary, pluralistic, progressive nation and could not be forced into the classical mold.[73] Indeed, after peace with Britain in 1783 there rapidly emerged a sense of national pride, self-confidence in government and resultant conviction of superiority over the ancient republics, rampant materialism, growth of democratic forms, anti-intellectualism, and deterioration of the quality of and respect for the traditional classical education, as well as rampant luxury, factionalism, and abuses of power. Belief in a morally better society after the classical pattern, which had no deep roots in America, began to wither rapidly after 1789.[74] The classical models and classical political theory had served useful purposes in the crisis of the independence movement and the forging of the Constitution. They were now to be jettisoned. The retreat from antiquity and disenchantment with the ancient guidelines were in full swing in the early national period. The ancient world was losing its bloom as absolute standard for testing modern political innovations.

There can be no more decisive evidence of the loss of reverence for the ancient republics and classical political theory than the profound revisionism in the thinking of Jefferson and Adams, both long advocates of the classical tradition, both now retired from the educative rigors of the American presidency. In 1816 Jefferson wrote to Isaac Tiffany: "But so different was the style of society then, and with those people, from what it is now and with us, that I think little edification can be obtained from their writings on the subject of government. . . . The introduction of this new principle of representative democracy has rendered useless almost everything written before on the structure of government; and, in a great measure, relieves our regret, if the political writings of Aristotle, or of any other ancient, have been lost, or are unfaithfully rendered or explained to us."[75] A few years later, in an exchange with Adams in 1819, Jefferson wrote: "When the enthusiasm . . . subsides into cool reflection, I ask myself, what was that government which the virtues of Cicero were so zealous to restore, and the ambitions of Caesar to subvert? . . . they never had [good government], from the rape of the Sabines to the ravages of the Caesars. . . . Steeped in corruption, vice and venality, as the whole nation was . . . , what could even Cicero, Cato, Brutus have done, had it been referred to them, to establish a good government for their country?"[76] Adams's reply shortly after was: "I never could discover that [the Romans] possessed much virtue, or real liberty."[77]

Most Americans would now have agreed with Jefferson when he said in 1816: "I like the dreams of the future better than the history of the past."[78] Two decades later Alexis de Tocqueville came to one of his solemn, quotable conclusions: "When I compare the Greek and Roman republics with these American states; . . . when I think of all the attempts that are made to judge the modern by the aid of those of antiquity, and to foresee what will happen in our time by what happened two thousand years ago, I am tempted to burn my books in order to apply only new ideas to so new a condition of society."[79]

Notes

1. *The Rights of Man*, in *The Complete Writings of Thomas Paine*, ed. Philip S. Foner (New York, 1945), vol. I, p. 387. Cp. Howard Mumford Jones, *Revolution & Romanticism* (Cambridge, Mass., 1974), pp. 151–187.
2. Louis B. Wright, "The Purposeful Reading of Our Colonial Ancestors," *Journal of English Literary History* 4 (1937), pp. 85–111; Charles F. Mullett, "Classical Influences in the American Revolution," *Classical Journal* 35 (1939–40), pp. 92–104; Bernard Bailyn, *Education in the Forming of American Society* (Chapel Hill, 1960), pp. 33–36; "The Cult of Antiquity in America," Chapter I, above; "The Quest for Useful Knowledge in Eighteenth-Century America," Chapter II, above. The absence of systematic classical scholarship in America's first two centuries is documented by the silence of John E. Sandys, *A History of Classical Scholarship* (Cambridge, 1908; rpt. 1967), vol. III, pp. 450–452; Rudolf Pfeiffer, *History of Classical Scholarship from 1300–1850* (Oxford, 1976).
3. Josiah Quincy, *Memoir of the Life of Josiah Quincy Jun.* (Boston, 1825), p. 330. Cp. Reverend Jonathan Mayhew in 1766 in his thanksgiving sermon on the repeal of the Stamp Act: "Having been initiated, in youth, in the doctrines of civil liberty, as they were taught by such men as Plato, Demosthenes, and Cicero, and other renowned persons among the ancients, and such as Sidney, Milton, Locke and Hoadley among the moderns; I liked them; they seemed rational!" (*The Snare Broken* [Boston, 1766], p. 43).
4. Richard Peters, *A Sermon on Education, Wherein Some Account is Given of the Academy Established in the City of Philadelphia* (Philadelphia, 1751).
5. *United States Magazine*, Jan., 1779, pp. 11–14; or Hugh Henry Brackenridge, *Gazette Publications* (Carlisle, Pa., 1806), pp. 221–223. Cp. James Madison in a letter to Jefferson, June 30, 1789: "We are in a wilderness without a single footstep to guide us. Our successors will have an easier task" (*Papers of Thomas Jefferson*, ed. Julian P. Boyd [Princeton, 1950–], vol. XV, pp. 224–225).
6. *On Revolution* (New York, 1963), p. 197. For Arendt on the classical sources and the impact of ancient political theory on the American Revolution see also pp. 13–14, 20, 119, 139–215. Clinton Rossiter, e.g., *Seedtime of the Republic* (New York, 1953), p. 357, held that the ancient authors taught the Founding Fathers nothing new.
7. This is why Bernard Bailyn concluded that the classics were "illustrative, not determinative of thought." See *The Ideological Origins of the American Revolution* (Cambridge, Mass., 1967), pp.23–26.
8. William Livingston in *The Independent Reflector*, by William Livingston and Others (1753), ed. Milton M. Klein (Cambridge, Mass., 1963), p. 279.

9. Meyer Reinhold, *The Classick Pages: Classical Reading of Eighteenth-Century Americans* (University Park, Pa., 1975), passim; H. Trevor Colbourn, *The Lamp of Experience: Whig History and the Intellectual Origins of the American Revolution* (Chapel Hill, 1965), app. II, pp. 199–232, for popular books on ancient history and politics in numerous eighteenth-century American libraries.

10. Letter to Jefferson, Aug. 27, 1790, in Jefferson, *Papers*, vol. XVII, p. 443.

11. See, e.g., James W. Johnson, *The Formation of English Neo-Classical Thought* (Princeton, 1967), pp. 31–105; Charles F. Mullett, "Ancient Historians and 'Enlightened' Reviewers," *The Review of Politics* 21 (1959), pp. 550–565; Michael Kraus, "Literary Relations between Europe and America in the Eighteenth Century," *Wm. & Mary Quart.*, 3rd ser., 1 (1944), pp. 210–234; R. N. Stromberg, "History in the Eighteenth Century," *Journal of the History of Ideas* 12 (1951), pp. 295–304; Zera S. Fink, *The Classical Republicans: An Essay in the Recovery of a Pattern of Thought in Seventeenth Century England* (Evanston, 1945); Caroline Robbins, *The Eighteenth-Century Commonwealthman* (Cambridge, Mass., 1959); Gerald Stourzh, *Alexander Hamilton and the Idea of Republican Government* (Stanford, 1970), chap. II; Edwin A. Miles, "The Young American Nation and the Classical World," *Journal of the History of Ideas* 35 (1974), pp. 259–274.

12. From *Cato's Letters*, no. 18 (Feb. 25, 1720), in David L. Jacobson, *The English Libertarian Heritage* (Indianapolis, 1965), pp. 57–61. Cp. Colbourn, *The Lamp of Experience*; Gordon S. Wood, *The Creation of the American Republic 1776–1787* (Chapel Hill, 1969), pp. 45–53 ("The Appeal of Antiquity"). Pope mocked Gordon's "Whigizing" of Tacitus: "There's honest Tacitus once talked as big, / But is he now an independent Whig?" (unpublished MS reading after verse 26 in "Epilogue to the Satires," dialogue I).

13. *Dissertation on the Canon Law and Feudal Law* (1765), in *The Works of John Adams* (Boston, 1850–56), vol. III, p. 462.

14. Carl Becker, *The Declaration of Independence: A Study in the History of Political Ideas* (New York, 1922), pp. 24–79; Edward S. Corwin, *The "Higher Law" Background of American Constitutional Law* (Ithaca, 1955); Charles G. Haines, *The Revival of Natural Law Concepts* (Cambridge, Mass., 1931); Cornelia G. LeBoutillier, *American Democracy and Natural Law* (New York, 1950); H. Trevor Colbourn, "Thomas Jefferson's Use of the Past," *Wm. & Mary Quart.*, 3rd ser., 15 (1958), pp. 56–70; Stourzh, *Alexander Hamilton*, pp. 1–37; Paul K. Conkin, *Self-Evident Truths* (Bloomington, 1974).

15. *Novanglus*, in *Works*, vol. IV, p. 15. Similarly, Jefferson recalled in 1825 (in a letter to Henry Lee) that the Declaration of Independence "was intended to be an expression of the American mind. . . . All its authority rests then on the harmonizing sentiments of the day, whether expressed in conversation, in letters, in printed essays, or in the elementary books of public right, as Aristotle, Cicero, Locke, Sidney, etc." (*Writings of Thomas Jefferson*, Memorial Edition [Washington, D.C., 1905], vol. XVI, pp. 118–119).

16. Richard M. Gummere, *The American Colonial Mind and the Classical Tradition* (Cambridge, Mass., 1963), pp. 97–119. Jefferson, for example, excerpted passages from Stanyan's *Grecian History* based on Thucydides that dealt with how Greek colonies freed themselves from mother countries. See *The Commonplace Book of Thomas Jefferson: A Repertory of his Ideas of Government*, ed. Gilbert Chinard (Baltimore, 1926), pp. 181–185.

17. *On the Canon Law and Feudal Law*, in *Works*, vol. III, p. 454; vol. VII, p. 593. On classical models of republicanism in America see, e.g., Edward McNall Burns, "The Philosophy of History of the Founding Fathers," *The Historian* 16 (1954), pp. 143–147, 162–163; Miles, "The Young American Nation"; Gordon S. Wood, "Republicanism as a Revolutionary Ideology," in *The Role of Ideology in the American Revolution*, ed. John H. Howe, Jr. (New York, 1970), pp. 83–97.

18. See the criticism of Greek factionalism, for example, by John Adams in his *Defence of the Constitutions of Government of the United States of America* (1787–88), in *Works*, vol. IV, p. 287: "In the name of human and divine benevolence, is such a system as this to be recommended to Americans, in this age of the world?"; by Alexander Hamilton, "The Continentalist no. I" (July, 1781), in *Papers of Alexander Hamilton*, ed. Harold C. Syrett (New York, 1961), vol. II, p. 657: "No friend to order or to rational liberty, can read without pain and disgust the history of the commonwealths of Greece"; by Fisher Ames of Massachusetts, in *Debates in the Several Conventions on the Adoption of the Federal Constitution* (Philadelphia, 1891), vol. II, p. 8: "Such were the paltry democracies of Greece and Asia Minor, so much extolled, and so often proposed as a model for our imitation."

19. *Letters from a Farmer in Pennsylvania* (New York, 1903), letter III (written 1767 or 1768), p. 30. Charles Pinckney of South Carolina rejected the militarism of Sparta (Max Farrand, ed., *Records of the Federal Convention of 1787*, rev. ed. [New Haven, 1937; rpt. 1966], vol. I, p. 401); Hamilton ridiculed Sparta's severe lifestyle (*Papers*, vol. III, p. 102). Elizabeth Rawson's comments in *The Spartan Tradition in European Thought* (Oxford, 1969), p. 368 ("Note on the United States"), that Sparta was generally thought irrelevant to the United States, are incorrect for the Revolutionary Age.

20. Documentation in Johnson, *Formation of English Neo-Classical Thought*; Fink, *Classical Republicans*; Robbins, *Eighteenth-Century Commonwealthman*.

21. In *A Full Vindication of the Measures of Congress* (1774), in *Papers*, vol. I, p. 53; "Federalist," no. 34, *The Federalist*, by Alexander Hamilton, James Madison, and John Jay, ed. Benjamin F. Wright (Cambridge, Mass., 1961), p. 249.

22. *Works*, vol. IV, p. 439.

23. Norman S. Fiering, "President Samuel Johnson and the Circle of Knowledge," *Wm. & Mary Quart.*, 3rd ser., 28 (1971), pp. 233–234.

24. Lawrence M. Levin, *The Political Doctrine of Montesquieu's "Esprit des Lois"*: *Its Classical Background* (New York, 1936), pp. 68–70; Paul M. Spurlin, *Montesquieu in America, 1760–1801* (Baton Rouge, 1940); Stourzh, *Alexander Hamilton*, pp. 63–75 ("Virtue as the Principle of Republican Government"); Henry F. May, *The American Enlightenment* (New York, 1976), pp. 155–156; Kenneth Silverman, *A Cultural History of the American Revolution* (New York, 1976), pp. 505–506; Eric Foner, *Tom Paine and Revolutionary America* (New York, 1976), pp. 158–160; "The Classics and the Quest for Virtue in Eighteenth-Century America," Chapter V, below.

25. *Warren-Adams Letters* (Boston, 1917–25; rpt. 1972), vol. I, pp. 202, 222 (both in 1776).

26. Livingston, cited by Wood, *Creation of the American Republic*, p. 95; Anon., cited by Silverman, *Cultural History of the American Revolution*, p. 505.

27. Reinhold, *The Classick Pages*, pp. 147–151; Frederic M. Litto, "Addison's *Cato* in the Colonies," *Wm. & Mary Quart.*, 3rd ser., 23 (1966), pp. 431–439. On Cato as a symbol of republicanism in the eighteenth century see Johnson, *Formation of English Neo-Classical Thought*, pp. 95–105.

28. Silverman, *Cultural History*, pp. 425, 434.

29. J. Hector St. John Crèvecoeur, *Letters from an American Farmer* (1782; Garden City, n.d.); Douglass G. Adair, "The Intellectual Origins of Jeffersonian Democracy: Republicanism, the Class Struggle, and the Virtuous Farmer," ("Ph.D. diss., Yale, 1943), pp. i–ii, 27–30, 65–95, 272–295; A Whitney Griswold, *Farming and Democracy* (New York, 1948), pp. 18–46; J. G. A. Pocock, "Civic Humanism and its Role in Anglo-American Thought," *Il Pensiero Politico* 1 (1968), pp. 172–189; idem, *Politics, Language and Time: Essays on Political Thought* (New York, 1971), pp. 80–103.

30. *The Poems of Philip Freneau*, ed. Fred L. Pattee (Princeton, 1902), vol. I, p. 150.
31. The principal classical sources Americans knew, analyzed, and cited are: Thucydides 3.81–83; Plato *Republic* 8; Aristotle *Politics* 5; Polybius 6.3–9; Sallust *Catiline* 5–9, 9–10; Livy 1 (*Praefatio*); Tacitus *Annals* 3.26–28. On the mix of American political theory see: Benjamin F. Wright, "The Origins of Separation of Powers in America," *Economica* 13 (1933), pp. 169–185; Stanley Pargellis, "The Theory of Balanced Government," in *The Constitution Reconsidered*, ed. Conyers Read (New York, 1938), pp. 37–49; Stow Persons, "The Cyclical Theory of History in Eighteenth Century America," *American Quarterly* 6 (1954), pp. 147–163; Edward M. Burns, "The Philosophy of History of the Founding Fathers," *The Historian* 16 (1954), pp. 142–168; Stanley N. Katz, "The Origins of American Constitutional Thought," *Perspectives in American History* 3 (1969), pp. 474–490; Bernard Bailyn, *The Origins of American Politics* (New York, 1968); John Ellis, "Habits of Mind and an American Enlightenment," *American Quarterly* 28 (1976), p. 164.
32. Douglass G. Adair, "Experience Must Be Our Only Guide: History, Democratic Theory, and the United States Constitution," in *Reinterpretation of the American Revolution, 1763–1789*, ed. Jack P. Greene (New York, 1968), p. 405 (rpt. in *Fame and the Founding Fathers: Essays by Douglass Adair*, ed. Trevor Colbourn [Williamsburg, 1974]).
33. See, e.g., Wood, "Republicanism as a Revolutionary Ideology."
34. John Adams, *Diary and Autobiography*, ed. L. H. Butterfield (Cambridge, Mass., 1962), vol. II, p. 58. Note Adams's rejection of Athens in his *Defence*: "We shall learn to prize the checks and balances of a free government, . . . if we recollect the miseries of Greece, which arose from its ignorance of them" (*Works*, vol., IV, p. 285).
35. *Works*, vol. IV, pp. 294–295.
36. In *Defence*, in *Works*, vol. IV, pp. 294, 297–298.
37. *Discourses on Davila* (1790), in *Works*, vol. VI, p. 399. On Adams's excerpts from Polybius 6, and his comments on the "balanced constitution" of Rome see *Works*, vol. IV, pp. 435–443, 540–541.
38. *Defence*, in *Works*, vol. IV, p. 298.
39. *Works*, vol. IV, pp. 540–541.
40. On Polybius' methods, the nature and weakness of his analysis of the Roman constitution, and the American preoccupation with "mixed government" and appeal to classical sources, see: Adair, "Intellectual Origins of Jeffersonian Democracy," pp. 152–186; Kurt von Fritz, *The Theory of the Mixed Constitution in Antiquity* (New York, 1954); F. W. Walbank, *A Historical Commentary on Polybius* (Oxford, 1954), vol. I, pp. 635–746; Paul Pédech, *La méthode historique de Polybe* (Paris, 1964), pp. 303–330; Thomas Cole, "The Sources and Composition of Polybius VI," *Historia* 13 (1964), pp. 478–482; Frank W. Walbank, "Polybius and the Roman State," *Greek, Roman and Byzantine Studies* 5 (1964), pp. 239–260; E. Graeber, *Die Lehre von der Mischverfassung bei Polybius* (Bonn, 1968); Frank W. Walbank, *Polybius*, Sather Classical Lectures, no. 42 (Berkeley, 1972), pp. 130–156; Arnaldo Momigliano, "Polybius' Reappearance in Western Europe," in *Polybe*, Fondation Hardt, Entretiens, vol. XX (Vandoeuvres, 1973), pp. 343–372; Claude Nicolet, "Polybe et les institutions romaines," ibid., pp. 209–258.
41. *Works*, vols. IV–VI.
42. *Records of the Federal Convention*, vol. I, p. 110. See also William Pierce's comments on the classical knowledge of other delegates to the Convention, ibid., vol. III, pp. 87–97. For example, Luther Martin, from the small state of Maryland, cited Rollin's *Ancient History*, chapter and verse, in support of two senators from each state on the grounds that in the Amphictyonic Council there

were two representatives from each of the Greek cities "who were notwithstanding the disposition of the Towns equal" (ibid., vol. I, p. 459).

43. Richard M. Gummere, "John Adams, Togatus," *Philological Quarterly* 13 (1934), 203–210; *Records of the Federal Convention*, passim; R. A. Ames and H. C. Montgomery, "The Influence of Rome on the American Constitution," *Classical Journal* 30 (1934–35), pp. 19–27; Mullett, "Classical Influences"; Gilbert Chinard, "Polybius and the American Constitution," *Journal of the History of Ideas* 1 (1940), 38–58; Adair, "Intellectual Origins of Jeffersonian Democracy," pp. 24–25, 82, 113; Adair, "Experience Must be Our Only Guide," pp. 129–131; Dorothy M. Robathan, "John Adams and the Classics," *New Engl. Quart.* 19 (1946), pp. 91–98; Epaminondas P. Panagopoulos, "Classicism and the Framers of the Constitution" (Ph.D. diss., Chicago, 1952); Raoul S. Naroll, "Clio and the Constitution: The Influence of the Study of History on the Federal Convention of 1787" (Ph.D. diss., University of California, Los Angeles, 1953), pp. 11–12, 14–16, 35–36; Burns, "Philosophy of History of the Founding Fathers," pp. 143–147, 162–165; Richard M. Gummere, "The Classical Politics of John Adams," *Boston Public Library Quarterly* 9 (1957), pp. 167–182; Winton U. Solberg, *The Federal Convention and the Union of American States* (New York, 1958), pp. xix–xxiii; *Notes of Debates in the Federal Convention of 1787*, Reported by James Madison (Athens, Ohio, 1966), passim; Richard M. Gummere, "The Classical Ancestry of the United States Constitution," *American Quarterly* 14 (1961), pp. 3–18; idem, *The American Colonial Mind*, pp. 173–190; *The Federalist*; William Gribbin, "Rollin's Histories and American Republicanism," *Wm. & Mary Quart.*, 3rd ser., 29 (1972), pp. 611–622; George Kennedy, "Classical Influences on *The Federalist*," in *Classical Traditions in Early America*, ed. John W. Eadie (Ann Arbor, 1976), pp. 119–138.

44. E.g., Alexander Hamilton in Jonathan Elliott, ed., *Debates in the Several State Conventions on the Adoption of the Federal Constitution* (Philadelphia, 1891), vol. II, pp. 352–353; James Wilson, *The Works of James Wilson*, ed. Robert G. McCloskey (Cambridge, Mass., 1967), vol. I, p. 763; David Ramsay of South Carolina, speech on July 4, 1778, in Alden T. Vaughan, ed., *Chronicles of the American Revolution* (New York, 1965), p. 321. Cp. W. Neil Franklin, "Some Aspects of Representation in the American Colonies," *North Carolina Historical Review* 6 (1929), pp. 38–68; Gordon S. Wood, *Representation in the American Revolution* (Charlottesville, 1969).

45. E.g., Madison, "Federalist," no. 63, in *The Federalist*, pp. 414–417; Wilson, *Works*, vol. I, p. 186.

46. E.g., Adair, "Intellectual Origins of Jeffersonian Democracy," pp. 82, 113; Panagopoulos, "Classicism and the Framers of the Constitution," pp. 176–197, 208–210; Wright, "Origins of Separation of Powers in America," pp. 169–185.

47. Cp. Walter H. Bennett, *American Theories of Federalism* (University, Alabama, 1964), pp. 54, 68–69.

48. See, e.g., Madison's sources on Greek leagues in *Letters and Other Writings of James Madison* (Philadelphia, 1865), vol. I, pp. 293–298 ("Notes on Ancient and Modern Confederacies Preparatory to the Federal Convention of 1787"). On the wide range of secondary works on ancient political institutions consulted by Madison see Marvin Meyers, ed., *The Mind of the Founder: Sources of the Political Thought of James Madison* (Indianapolis, 1973), pp. 69–73; on those used by John Adams see Alfred Iacuzzi, *John Adams, Scholar* (New York, 1952). Americans were, of course ignorant of epigraphic evidence and critical research on Greek leagues. For the present state of this knowledge see Jakob A. O. Larsen, *Representative Government in Greek and Roman History*, Sather Classical Lectures, no. 28 (Berkeley, 1955); idem, *Greek Federal States* (Oxford, 1968); idem, "Amphictionies," *Oxford Classical Dictionary*, 2nd ed., p. 54.

49. *Observations sur l'histoire de la Grèce* (Paris, 1766), pp. 9–10.

50. "Of Man, as a Member of a Confederation," Wilson, *Works*, vol. I, p. 247–248.
51. *Notes of Debates in the Federal Convention*, p. 161; *Records of the Federal Convention*, vol. I, p. 350.
52. Hamilton, *Papers*, vol. II, pp. 655–656 (from "The Continentalist, no. 2," July, 1781); *Records of the Federal Convention*, vol. I, pp. 143, 343, 348, 350, 473 (by James Wilson); vol. I, pp. 317–320, 326 (by Madison); 285; 296 (by Hamilton); 441, 454 (by Luther Martin); Madison, "Federalist," no. 18, in *The Federalist*, pp. 171–176; *Debates in the Several State Conventions*, vol. III, pp. 129–130; *The Writings of James Madison*, ed. Gaillard Hunt (New York, 1904), vol. V, pp. 139–140 (at Virginia Ratifying Convention); James Wilson, "Of Man, as a Member of a Confederation," *Works*, vol. I, pp. 249–250, 265–266.
53. "Federalist," no. 18, in *The Federalist*, p. 176.
54. *Journals of the Continental Congress, 1774–1789* (Washington, D.C., 1906), vol. VI, p. 1105 (August, 1776).
55. *The Federalist*, p. 174; *Notes of Debates in the Federal Convention*, p. 3.
56. *Works*, vol. II, p. 762.
57. *Debates in the Several State Conventions*, vol. II, p. 483: "I have endeavored, in all the books that I have access to, to acquire some information relative to the *Lycian republic*, but its history is not to be found; the few facts that relate to it are mentioned only by Strabo; and however excellent the model it might present, we are reduced to the necessity of working without it."
58. Edward A. Freeman, *History of Federal Government in Greece and Italy*, 2nd ed., J. B. Bury, ed. (London, 1893), pp. 95–111, 243–251, esp. 250.
59. *Notes of Debates in the Federal Convention*, p. 447.
60. *The Federalist*, pp. 419, 453.
61. "Federalist," no. 14, in *The Federalist*, p. 154.
62. *Records of the Federal Convention*, vol. I, p. 457.
63. *Diary and Letters of Gouverneur Morris*, ed. Anne C. Morris (New York, 1888), vol. I, p. 114.
64. "Federalist," no. 9, in *The Federalist*, p. 125.
65. "The Continentalist, no. 6" (July, 1782), in *Papers*, vol. III, p. 103; vol. IV, p. 140 (1787).
66. *Complete Writings*, vol. I, pp. 123–124 (*The Crisis*, no. 5, 1778).
67. *Secret Proceedings and Debates of the Convention* (Richmond, 1839), p. 175; cp. *Records of the Federal Convention*, vol. I, p. 401; *Notes of Debates in the Federal Convention*, p. 185.
68. "Federalist," no. 63, in *The Federalist*, p. 416.
69. *Works*, vol. II, pp. 762–763 (1790–91). Cp. p. 774 (July 4, 1788) for an instance of the growing pejorative assessment of antiquity: "You have heard of Sparta, of Athens, and of Rome; you have heard of their admired constitutions, and of their high-prized freedom," but they were inferior to America because their constitutions were imposed by lawgivers without the consent of the people.
70. William Vans Murray, *Political Sketches* (London, 1787), published also in *American Museum* 2 (Sept., 1787), pp. 228–235. Cp. Alexander de Conde, "William Vans Murray's *Political Sketches*: A Defence of the American Experiment," *Mississippi Valley Historical Review* 41 (1954–55), pp. 623–640.
71. *An Inquiry into the Principles and Policy of the Government of the United States*, ed. Leon Baritz (Indianapolis, 1969), esp. pp. 11–13, 19–25, 121–122, 171–172, 345.
72. *Works*, vol. VI, pp. 443–522, esp. letters VIII, XIII, XVIII.
73. "The American Enlightenment and the Ancient World: A Study in Paradox," *Proc. Mass. Hist. Soc.* 83 (1971), pp. 3–15; reprinted in Commager, *Jefferson, Nationalism, and the Enlightenment* (New York, 1975), pp. 125–139. Cp. J. G. A. Pocock, "On the Non-Revolutionary Character of Paradigms," in *Politics, Language and Time: Papers on Political Thought and History* (New York, 1971), pp. 273–291.

74. D. H. Meyer, *The Instructed Conscience: The Shaping of the American National Ethic* (Philadelphia, 1972), p. 142; Miles, "The Young American Nation"; Henry F. May, *The Enlightenment in America* (New York, 1976), pp. 223, 359; "The Silver Age of Classical Studies in America, 1790–1830," Chapter VI, below.

75. *Writings of Thomas Jefferson*, vol. IV, pp. 65–66.

76. Ibid., vol. XV, p. 233.

77. Ibid., p. 237.

78. Ibid., p. 59.

79. *De la Democratie en Amérique* (Paris, 1835), vol. II, p. 243. The translation is mine.

IV. Opponents of Classical Learning in America during the Revolutionary Period

$\mathbf{R}$ecently we have had the pleasure of being conducted by Richard M. Gummere on an illuminating and inspiriting, albeit nostalgic, pilgrimage through *The American Colonial Mind and the Classical Tradition*,[1] a study which has been called "the best statement in print for the relevance of classics to the U.S.A."[2] In his analysis and description of the dominant educational passion of the American colonial psyche, Mr. Gummere neglected to report in detail the views and activities of a hostile minority that sought to dethrone the classical curriculum in this country. Beginning in the middle of the eighteenth century, and mounting in intensity through the Revolutionary period to the end of the century, a clamorous campaign was conducted to eliminate classical learning entirely from the curriculum, or, failing that, to demote it to a subordinate status. Supported or initiated often by persons of high position and influence in molding the new society, the campaign of the militant anticlassicists was persistent and vociferous, even if never effectively concerted.[3]

It was inevitable that the early colonists in America should have brought with them the educational model of the traditional classical curriculum. Yet, from their English beginnings, the attitude of the Puritans toward the classics—like that of some of the early Christian fathers—was ambivalent. Many Puritans, both English and American, were suspicious of the classics on the ground that trafficking with pagan writers constituted a mortal danger to morality and the true religion, as well as to the primacy of the Scriptures. Nor should we forget that prejudice against classical studies—*paganica studia*—has existed among Christians in every epoch, from Tertullian to the end of the nineteenth century. In the attacks against the classics in the seventeenth and eighteenth centuries there often lurks the recurrent theme of the paganism and immorality of the classics in the educational curriculum. New England Puritans had to come to terms with the problem before there could be general acceptance of the classics in their schools. After a struggle, the dominant and future tone was established in colonial New England, and, in general, elsewhere in the colonies, when in the 1650s a reconciliation between the classics and theology was effected.[4] From that time the traditional classical education remained entrenched in colonial education, providing a general education in the liberal arts for the professions and serving as a distinctive badge for an educated elite. The dominance of classical education was preserved by the force of tradition, the influence of clergymen in the governance of schools and colleges, and the social status attaching to classical education, despite the pressures for useful studies and vocational training in a pragmatic society with a continent to conquer and not enough hands or time for all there was to be done.[5] Most of the Founding Fathers, it is well known, were trained in and devoted to the classics.[6]

Yet the Quaker communities, with their "guarded education," remained outside the classical tradition for a long time, preferring an emphasis on practical subjects and the study of the English language.[7] Characteristic are William Penn's objections that, though he did not want foreign languages to be despised or neglected, "we press [children's] memory too soon, and puzzle, strain, and load them with words and rules; to know grammer and rhetoric, and a strange tongue or two, that it is ten to one may never be useful to them."[8] With their basic pietistic views and practicality the Quakers were also hostile to university education and its curriculum, though in time they began to include in their schools the traditional curriculum of Greek and Latin side by side with the useful arts.[9]

Despite the continuity and strength of the classical tradition in colonial America, the widespread faith in education among all classes of the population raised questions about the value of a classical education for all students. The pressure of time needed to accomplish the building of a new world generated demands for vocational training for those not destined for the ministry or other professions.[10] There must have been criticism in many quarters both of the harsh methods and of the uniform curriculum. The earliest instance known to me of open rebellion against the classical curriculum occurred at a town meeting in Boston in 1711, when a group of parents ("Some innovators, restless spirits who were not satisfied to leave things as they were. . . ."[11]) petitioned the townsmen to change the curriculum in the Boston Latin School. The recalcitrant parents particularly criticized—with all due respect—the tyrannical methods, but they were also concerned that "very many hundreds of boys in this town, who by their parents were never designed for a more liberal education, have spent two, three, and four years or more of their early days at the Latin School, which hath proved of very little or no benefit to their after accomplishment." The petition "was referred to Committees in the good old way, and came to nothing then."[12] This mild petition of Bostonians for varied educational curricula and utilitarian subjects was to be followed by more vociferous demands for change in the colonies.

Utilitarianism in education, and the accompanying assaults on the primacy of the classical curriculum with a view to opening up room for other subjects, began in Europe over a hundred years before. Indeed, the dazzling preeminence of the classics from Petrarch to the end of the nineteenth century has served to blind us to the fact that determined and outspoken enemies were constantly hurling challenges during that domain of over half a millennium when the classics occupied the central role in the educational curriculum created by the humanists. The intellectual history of Europe and this country is dotted with assaults against the classics, and every century and country have had to mount defenses against the opponents,[13] who have been indefatigable in marshalling new arguments and attacks against the primacy of the classics. Especially beginning with the "century of genius" from Galileo to Newton, the awesome breakthroughs in science in the seventeenth century fomented attacks upon the classics as impediments to progress and generated demands for the teaching of science and other utilitarian subjects. Moreover, by 1600 almost the entire classical heritage could be read in English translations, and, what is more, the rising status of the vernaculars and their literatures began to crowd the classics, particularly in France and England. Inevitably, the phenomenal increase in knowledge, the diffusion of knowledge through printing, the prestige of the scientists, and the spread of the idea of progress produced a vigorous demand in Europe for scientific and utilitarian education, with instruction in useful trades for specific vocations, and due place for modern subjects. One phase of this utilitarian movement in education was a de-emphasis on language study and a respect for "things, not words." This utilitarianism had a strong influence in America, where the vast material and social opportunities and the increasing egalitarianism tended to produce tensions between the social, political, and economic evolution and the traditional educational system.[14]

The advocates of the study of the vernaculars, utilitarianism and vocationalism in education, and the dethronement of Latin and Greek from their regal position had included Comenius, the "father of modern pedagogy," and his reformist followers in England (notably John Durie, Noah Biggs, John Webster, William Petty, and Samuel Hartlib), John Locke, Thomas Hobbes, and the moderns in the Battle of the Books in France and England. In the eighteenth century the *philosophes* of the Enlightenment, though most of them were passionately attached to antiquity, stirred the intellectual life of Europe and America with their devotion to science; their faith in progress, reason (rather than tradition), and natural law; their hostility to institutionalized religion; and their enthusiasm for the vernaculars. If Joseph Priestley was mild in his criticism of a classical education for "civil and active life" and in his proposals for the introduction of utilitarian subjects,[15] in France Diderot, and, later, the French liberal revolutionaries Brissot and Condorcet, the champion of popular education and the forerunner of Herbert Spencer in raising the issue of science versus the classics, fulminated against the traditional classical education.[16] These influences, which touched many in eighteenth-century America, were greatly strengthened on this side of the Atlantic by nationalistic and patriotic feelings and egalitarian ideals, thus deepening the natural, pragmatic tendencies toward utilitarianism in education in a pioneering society. If England, to use Montmorency's phrase, slumbered in "a century of educational sleep," despite efforts to rouse it,[17] a complex of political, economic, and social conditions in this country produced greater ferment among the "New Americans."

Outspoken critics of classical learning, many anonymous, took their case to the public in pamphlets, newspapers, and magazines.[18] Such an attack, a rather early one, appeared in 1735 in an anonymous article in the *American Weekly Mercury*, published in Philadelphia.[19] The writer argued that there was a need for better methods of teaching and for other subjects than those in the classical curriculum, to suit different vocations and qualifications; that too little attention was devoted to the study of English; that those destined for trades and business soon forgot all they had learned of Latin, could not read Latin, and, what was worse, could not read or write English properly; that the study of grammar should be conducted in the English language, not in Latin; that those designed for trades should not study Latin at all but English and other practical subjects; that the study of Latin for the understanding of English words was unnecessary. "Latin being a dead Language, and spoke nowhere as a Mother Tongue, renders it unnecesary to most People." It is not in accord with reason to continue the traditional curriculum.[20]

Benjamin Franklin, the American apostle of utilitarianism in education, as early as 1749 proposed liberalization of the curriculum, so that all students would not be required to learn Latin, Greek, or even modern foreign languages. He would permit students who have an "ardent desire" to learn these languages to do so, provided they did not thereby neglect English, arithmetic, and other absolutely necessary subjects.[21] Though Franklin was bitterly attacked for utilitarianism in education and for his desire to see the base of education broadened along democratic lines,[22] his proposals were heartily endorsed by the brilliant scientist, later lieutenant governor of New York, Cadwallader Colden, who proposed the abolition of foreign languages as prerequisites for admission to college. English, Colden wrote to Franklin, should be "our principal care." For most students the study of the great English poets and prose writers was more desirable "than to have the learned languages taught to them, who afterwards in their course of life perhaps may never make use of them."[23] In his *Autobiography* (written 1771–89) Franklin offered "to the Consideration of those who superintend the Education of our Youth" the suggestion that, since many students devote years to the study of Latin without attaining proficiency—and so waste their time—it would be preferable for them to learn French or other modern language first before they undertake the study of Latin. In this way, even if they abandoned foreign-language study before they reached the study of Latin, they would at least have acquired another language or two, practical ones at that.[24]

Not only did Franklin not approve of idolatry of the classics, which he considered largely ornamental, but because of his utilitarianism he was motivated occasionally to heap flippant scorn upon antiquarianism and the value of the classics. "It is better," he once said, "to bring back from Italian travel a receipt for Parmesan cheese than copies of ancient historical inscriptions."[25] Nor did he hesitate to call classical learning the "quackery of literature."[26]

The principal doctrine of Franklin's program of democratic educational reform was the use of the vernacular: he desired instruction to be entirely in English. The charter of the Academy of Philadelphia, founded in 1749 (later the University of Pennsylvania) had provided for both Latin and English schools, the latter for vernacular and more practical education. But the preferences of parents and students, as well as the partiality of the trustees of the Academy for the Latin School had resulted in the decline and virtual extinction of the English School, whose curriculum of utilitarian subjects was not generally as valued as mastery of the ancient languages. Accordingly, in 1789 Franklin, as trustee of the Academy, felt impelled to issue a statement of "Observations Relative to the Intentions of the Original Founders of the Academy."[27] The charter, Franklin insisted, required the Academy to provide opportunity for complete English education. Learning Latin and Greek "for the purpose of acquiring Knowledge is become absolutely unnecessary." Everything worthwhile in the classics is available in translation; many subjects of study are now being presented in the vernacular; through printing, books are relatively inexpensive and accessible to all; there is rising literacy and a demand for books in English. "But," regrets Franklin, "there is in Mankind an unaccountable Prejudice in favor of ancient Customs and Habitudes, which inclines to a Continuance of them after the Circumstances, which formerly made them useful, ceased to exist." "Thus the Time spent in that Study might, it seems, be much better employ'd in the Education for such a country as ours." He concluded that "the still prevailing Custom of having Schools for teaching generally our Children, in these days, the Latin and Greek languages, I consider therefore in no other light than as the *chapeau bras*[28] of modern Literature."

The pejorative tag "quackery of literature" may have been borrowed by Franklin from the popular American poem *The Progress of Dulness*, by John Trumbull. It is memorable that both Trumbull and Philip Freneau, the two most celebrated American poets of the eighteenth century, were hostile to the classical curriculum. In Trumbull's preface to the poem, a satire on contemporary collegiate education, published in 1772–73, he objected that "the meer knowledge of antient languages, of the abstruser parts of mathematics, and the dark researches of metaphysics, is of little advantage in any business or profession in life." The English language demands the attention of all places of public education. While Trumbull did not desire the study of the classics to be abolished, he condemned the education of the times in which students "plodding on in one dull tone, / Gain antient tongues and lose their own."

> Oh! might I live to see that day,
> When sense shall point to youth their way;
> Through every maze of science guide;
> O'er education's laws preside;
> The good retain; with just discerning
> Explode the quackeries of learning;
> Give antient arts their real due,
> Explain their faults, and beauties too;
> . . . .
> From antient languages well known
> Transfuse new beauties to our own.[29]

During the Revolutionary period the Quakers were deeply concerned with educational reform. They had begun to extend the scope of their guarded education in the early '70s in response to the changing educational needs of the growing nation. In general, the Friends schools had rejected as superfluous subjects which were solely for adornment. Some Quaker schools did teach Latin, Greek, and Hebrew as practical subjects, to prepare Quaker missionaries. Not all agreed with this trend. For instance, in 1780 Moses Brown, the New England Quaker leader, in a letter to Anthony Benezet, the distinguished teacher of the Friends English School of Philadelphia (later William Penn Charter School), declared that a correct understanding of English could be had without knowledge of Latin or other learned languages. But, since Latin might be useful to some geniuses, there ought to be a school capable of teaching the learned languages. However, since Latin would be useful only to a few, Brown wondered whether French or some other modern language ought not to be encouraged. In the same year Benezet, in a letter to Robert Pleasants, expressed the fear that the study of Latin and Greek tended to create "a natural tendency to wed to the world, and beget an enmity to the cross." In general, the authors studied in the schools (Ovid, Vergil, Horace) contained sentiments "opposed to our Religious Profession." Therefore, declared Benezet, "I much desire to see such a knowledge of the English Language taught in our Schools, as may make the use of the learned Languages unnecessary."[30]

Educational reform was in the air in America throughout the eighteenth century. The assertion of Middlekauff that "the classical curriculum remained unexamined" until 1784[31] is manifestly an error. While Middlekauff has gathered some interesting material on challenges to the relevance of the traditional classical curriculum in New England in this period, and on the utilitarianism, vocationalism, and nationalism of the anticlassicists, he erroneously describes the disputants as polarized into formal groupings of "ancients" and "moderns," as in the Battle of the Books of the seventeenth century. Further, though he recognizes properly that the classics were considered by many to be of limited utility, because of their impatient desire to build a new, unique nation rapidly, Middlekauff is misleading when he labels the period from 1784 to 1800 "The Tradition Altered."[32]

The impatient yearning of American patriots to overturn tradition and launch out in new directions, while the systems of government and education were still in process of formation, is apparent in the efforts of Noah Webster to reorientate American education.[33] The basic tenets of Noah Webster's educational thinking were: the importance of science in education; distrust of classical education; utilitarianism and practical education for specific careers; universal education; nationalistic emphasis; primacy of the English language and English grammar.[34] In *A Grammatical Institute of the English Language*, part I, first published in 1783, Webster, in setting forth a course of study in English, declared by way of preface:

> This ridiculous practice [of neglecting the study of English] has found its way to America; and so violent have been the prejudices in support of it, that the whispers of common sense, in favor of our native tongue, have been silenced amid the clamour of pedantry in favour of Greek and Latin. . . . Such material alterations of the old system of education, will undoubtedly alarm the rigid friends of antiquity; but in vindication of the work, the author assures the public, that it has the approbation and patronage of many of the principal literary characters of America.

Webster, impassioned by strong national feeling, dedicated himself to the restoration of a pure English language. He rejected as a "stupid opinion"[35] the view that a knowledge of Latin helped the student to understand English.

In an article "On the Education of Youth in America," published in the *American Magazine* in 1788,[36] Noah Webster propounded his views on American education. Systems of instruction should be adopted which diffuse knowledge of the sciences. "The first error that I would mention, is, a too general attention to the dead languages, with a neglect of our own."[37] The English language is now a perfected medium, and the most important works in Latin and Greek have been adequately translated into English, thereby communicating all the ideas of the originals. Moreover, "What advantage does a merchant, a mechanic, a farmer, derive from an acquaintance with the Greek and Roman tongues?"[38] The many years of study required to master the dead languages were not compensated by the advantages to be derived from them. Other subjects, especially English and vocational studies, have high priorities. Though parents desired a classical education for their children, the inutility of the classical languages was evident. "This absurdity is the subject of common complaint; men see and feel the impropriety of the usual practice; and yet no arguments that have hitherto been used, have been sufficient to change the system; or to place an English school on a footing with a Latin one, in point of reputation."[39] While the study of the dead languages was useful for young men preparing for the learned professions, they are not necessary for future businessmen, merchants, mechanics, farmers, etc. Experience proves that a prior knowledge of Latin and Greek is not required for the study of English. Finally, place must be made in the curriculum for the study of modern foreign languages.

Websterian pragmatism is reflected in Robert Coram's *Plan for the General Establishment of Schools Throughout the United States*, published in 1791.[40] In this proposal for a national system of education Coram asserts that "no modes of faith, systems of manners, or foreign or dead languages should be taught in those schools. As none of them are necessary to obtain a knowledge of the obligations of society, the government is not bound to instruct the citizens in anything of the kind."[41]

It is well known that Thomas Jefferson, despite his warm attachment to the classics, desired that American education embrace the sciences, as well as the study of English and modern languages. In 1779 Jefferson proposed to discontinue the teaching of Latin and Greek at William and Mary College, not because he opposed them, but because the essentials of the classical languages were expected to be taught in the grammar schools of Virginia, and because the income was needed to provide instructors of scientific and other subjects. Jefferson proposed to substitute oriental languages, Gothic, Anglo-Saxon, and Icelandic for Greek and Latin at William and Mary. This latter proposal had to be dropped, but Jefferson succeeded in establishing the first professorship of modern languages in America.[42]

An outright opponent of the classics was Francis Hopkinson, American statesman, composer, satirist, founding member of the American Philosophical Society, and signer of the Declaration of Independence. His essay "On a Learned Education" is a mild satire on the study of Latin. While studying a dead language, Hopkinson complained, "the student remains a stranger to his own," and instead of useful and practical history he consumes his time reading such books as the *Aeneid*.[43] In 1786 he delivered a talk which purports to be a debate on the value of the classics. Actually it is a one-sided presentation of arguments against the Latin and Greek languages. In the first part, "On the Learned Languages," a criticism of the dead languages is presented. Study of Latin and Greek authors was useless because all their works have been translated into the vernacular, and, moreover, French had become a universal language displacing Latin. Further, the study of Latin, Greek, and Hebrew did not, as claimed by their proponents, polish the manners or enrich the mind any more than other subjects. The classical languages were not of so much worth as to warrant the time required to master them. "To what purpose then are so many years spent in acquiring these obsolete languages?" Then, in "A Reply to the Foregoing Speech," Hopkinson's arguments for the defense were turned into an ironical assault on the classics. Even translations, he commented, were inadequate because scholars could not ascertain the precise meaning of the original; the learned languages afforded scholars an inexhaustible source of controversy; and the technical terms in the arts and sciences derived from the learned languages bestowed on them an air of obscurity and mystery.[44]

That passionate democrat Philip Freneau, the poet of the American Revolution, also vented his spleen on the classics. With his usual sarcasm, he affirmed he was publishing some of his letters "that may at least amuse the ignorant, whose brains, like my own, are not able to bear deep reasoning, because they have never learned Latin."[45]

Much more blatantly outspoken on the traditional curriculum was Thomas Paine, apostle of the Enlightenment. He had read much of the classics in translation but had no knowledge of Latin because the Quakers objected to the books in which the language was taught. He admired the achievements of the ancients but was convinced of the superiority of the modern world. "We do great injustice to ourselves" by supposing "ourselves inferior" to Greece and Rome. "I have no notion of yielding the palm of the United States to any Grecians or Romans that were ever born."[46] But it was in *The Age of Reason*, published in 1794–95, that Paine opened all stops. Learning, he maintained, consists not in knowledge of languages but of the material world, not in words but things. Language study is barren drudgery, kills the student's genius, destroys the philosopher in him. Since all the most useful ancient books have been translated, "there is now nothing new to be learned from the dead languages"; "the languages are become useless and the time expended in teaching and learning them is wasted." Only the living languages contain new knowledge; "and certain it is that, in general, a youth will learn more of a living language in one year than of a dead language in seven, and it is but seldom that the teacher knows much of it himself." "It would therefore be advantageous to the state of learning to abolish the study of dead languages, and to make learning consist, as it originally did, in scientific knowledge."[47]

In the colonial newspapers and magazines, beginning in the late 1780s, a lively, usually anonymous, debate was conducted on the value of the classics. Of course, there were many defenders of the classics: their arguments were the conventional ones. The opponents were the more daring, more passionate, more clamorous. The earliest attack in this period known to me appeared in the *New-Haven Gazette* in June, 1788. Here "A Countryman" assailed the proposal to introduce the study of Greek as being as impractical as the study of Latin and Hebrew. He argued that they were dead languages of dead civilizations; there were translations of classical writers; the art of printing had diffused knowledge of antiquity in the vernaculars; and the study of Latin and Greek was not related to real life. In the *Massachusetts Magazine* of June, 1789, appeared a plea by "Friend of Liberty" for education in English instead of Latin. Later that same year, in December, another attack was published in the *Massachusetts Magazine* deploring the neglect of English while years were spent on the study of Latin and Greek. It was an absurdity and folly, the writer declared, that parents throughout the country gave preference to those languages. "Is it not a waste of time? Could not our youth treasure up much useful knowledge in the time which they now spend in puzzling their heads with this dry and unfruitful study?"

In the same issue of the *Massachusetts Magazine* (December, 1789) was printed an extract from a letter, dated September 14, 1789, addressed to William Samuel Johnson, president of Columbia College, New York, by Hugh Williamson, M.D., statesman and scientist, friend of Benjamin Franklin. In this communication Williamson assailed the study of the classics as "useless subjects," "the murder of time," "this grievous servitude," "the tyranny of Greek and Latin." He saw no need for learning Latin, since all useful books have been translated. Teachers of Latin and Greek were numerous and influential, and so were able to deceive and lead astray the rising generation. Conceding that his "ideas concerning the education of youth are extremely different from those which are commonly received," he urged that science, history, and English be substituted for Greek and Latin. "Whether you are disposed to retain the dead languages, to give them up entirely, or to have them taught to a particular class of students," with respect to the introduction of utilitarian subjects, urged Dr. Williamson, "we had better adopt the measure ourselves than recommend it to posterity."

The role of the American Philosophical Society, founded in 1769, on the model of the Royal Society in England, was ambivalent in regard to classical learning. A leading force in molding American thought, it fostered science, and, at the same time, was conservative as regards changes in the traditional curriculum. This dualism reflected division of opinion among the members of the society. Among the proponents of change was Francis Hopkinson, one of its leading members. In an address to the Society on January 16, 1784, he castigated the Society for its lethargy in failing to take a more active part in fostering science and experimentation. "The door to knowledge," he affirmed, "seems to be wider open than ever it was." Knowledge of the learned languages was not absolutely necessary any longer, yet because of the strength of tradition many scholars were lost to "experimental pursuits." But "the language of Nature is not written in Hebrew or Greek."[48] Some years later, in 1797, the American Philosophical Society sponsored a national competition for essays regarding the organization of education in America. Two prizes were awarded, one to Samuel Harrison Smith, journalist and author, the other to Samuel Knox, then principal of the Frederick Academy in Virginia. Smith, who was well versed in the classics and quoted them with ease, expressing no hostility to classical learning, revealed an amalgam of respect for tradition, utilitarianism, nationalism, and democratic idealism. His principal contribution was an emphasis on the study of English and modern languages.[49] Taking a less modern stance, Samuel Knox defended the study of the Latin and Greek languages against proposals by "some even of the most enlightened" to exclude them entirely from the curriculum of liberal education. These persons, he objected, citing the cases of isolated scientific geniuses, such as David Rittenhouse and Benjamin Franklin, who achieved international distinction without formal academic education, derogated the traditional education and proposed a new educational system whereby students were to be introduced at once to the "study of the sciences, without the usual attention . . . to the classics and ancient languages." They proposed this because devotion to the Greek and Latin languages "has a tendency to damp natural genius [and] pervert its powers and misapply its attention." Knox rejected as a hackneyed argument against a classical education the existence of good translations. If, he emphasized, parents would see to it that their children were exposed to Latin and Greek early enough, "there could not be so much objection made as there commonly is against the acquisition of the Greek and Latin classics."[50]

Another member of the American Philosophical Society, Benjamin Rush, physician, scientist, patriot, signer of the Declaration of Independence, became the most outspoken, determined, and passionate enemy of classical education in this country. Fired with republican enthusiasm, utilitarian in outlook, deeply influenced by the Enlightenment, he came to distrust the study of ancient languages as a fetter on development of science, the material development of the country, and the expansion of democratic institutions.[51] Rush emerged as one of the focal points of aggressive efforts to reconstruct radically the educational patterns of the young country. With almost missionary fervor he marshalled every criticism and argument against classical learning formulated from the Renaissance to the end of the eighteenth century in his efforts to eliminate Greek and Latin from its preeminence in American education. The influences that molded the mind and personality of Rush were American and European, nationalistic, utilitarian, cosmopolitan, scientific. A friend of Franklin, Rush, as a medical student in Edinburgh, knew David Hume and William Robertson and, when he was in Paris, became acquainted, for example, with Diderot, an outspoken anticlassicist.[52] Rush had an excellent classical education, and in his youth maintained an active interest in the classics ("I take great pleasure in reading Latin authors . . . that useful branch of improvement [Latin]").[53] As late as 1786, when he was about forty, Rush supported the traditional place of the classics in the curriculum: "I do not wish the Learned or Dead Languages, as they are commonly called, to be reduced below their present just rank in the universities of Europe, especially as I consider an acquaintance with them as the best foundation for a correct and extensive knowledge of the language of our country."[54]

But in 1789, for reasons we can no longer discover, he turned vigorously against the classics, declaring himself its implacable enemy. In June of that year he published in the *American Museum* a full-scale blast against the ancient languages.[55] In this unrestrained denunciation Rush assailed "the strong and universal prejudice in favour of the Latin and Greek languages, as a necessary branch of liberal education," and proclaimed the necessity of "combating this formidable enemy of human reason . . . , this tyrant." An inordinate amount of time (four to five years) was needed to acquire competence in the Latin and Greek languages, which were difficult and, moreover, afforded little pleasure to young students ("How few boys relish Latin and Greek lessons!"). Indeed, Rush attributed large numbers of school dropouts to the required study of the dead languages. "Many sprightly young boys of excellent capacities for useful knowledge, have been so disgusted with the dead languages, as to retreat from the drudgery of schools, to low company, whereby they have become bad members of society, and entailed misery upon all who have been connected with them." Moreover, the study of some of the classics is deleterious to morals and religion, because of the vices, paganism, and other undesirable concepts contained in them, including glorified murders and militarism. Above all, "the study of these languages is improper in a peculiar manner in the United States," because it tends to confine education to the few, whereas universal education is necessary for the very preservation of the republican form of government. "The cultivation of the Latin and Greek languages is a great obstacle to the cultivation and perfection of the English language. . . . It is likewise one of the greatest obstructions that has ever been thrown in the way of propagating useful knowledge," because it leads to slavish imitation of wrongly supposed perfect models and checks originality and invention, and its study has greatly obstructed the spread of useful knowledge because the study of English has been neglected. The passion for and servile attachment to ancient writers have caused a great lack of originality in modern times, though "the late improvements in the English language [are due] chiefly to the neglect of the Latin and Greek languages," and "we shall never equal the sublime and original authors of antiquity unless we cease to study them." The practice of teaching English grammar and vocabulary through th medium of the dead languages Rush considered absurd. In addition, the study of the ancient classics was "hurtful to morals." To those who argued that a knowledge of Greek and Latin was needed to understand allusions to mythology, he answered that "the less we know of this subject the better," for mythology exposes boys to immorality and paganism. The rapidly growing new knowledge of modern times, particularly in science and inventions, was available in English. Any justification of the use of Latin in Europe should carry no weight in America, which "is like a new planet." This existence of translations into English of all the most useful books destroys the argument that Latin is necessary for the learned professions—law, medicine, divinity. "I see no use at the present time for a knowledge of the Latin and Greek languages for a lawyer, a physician, or a divine, in the United States, except it be to facilitate the remembrance of a few technical terms which may be retained without it." It was not even necessary to learn Greek to understand the New Testament, which was available in good English translations. The art of printing, the diffusion of knowledge, the rise of modern literatures have made the vernaculars of great importance. The world has changed materially and socially since the fifteenth century, so that Greek and Latin were no longer useful for the advancement of agriculture, manufacture, and commerce. There was so much to be done in this new country and society, and there were high priorities on the energies of the people.

> Under the circumstances to spend four or five years in learning two dead languages, is to turn our backs upon a gold mine, in order to amuse ourselves in catching butterflies. . . . The next ray of truth that irradiates human reason upon this subject, I hope will teach us to reject the Latin and Greek languages altogether, as branches of liberal education. . . . The generations which are to follow us, will probably view our partiality for the Classic ground of Greece and Rome with [pity and horror]; . . . future ages will treat our superstitious veneration for the ancient poets and orators with the same ridicule.

Posterity will be astonished that in the period of the American Revolution, with all its glorious exploits, "the human understanding was fettered by prejudice in favour of the Latin and Greek languages. . . . But I hope with the history of this folly, some historian will convey to future generations, that many of the most active and useful characters in accomplishing this revolution, were strangers to the formalities of a Latin and Greek education." As a fact, Rush did not desire to make Latin and Greek extinct in the world, but rather to reserve its study for specialists, a distinct profession of

classicists (linguists and translators). The advantages of removing
Latin and Greek from liberal education, to Rush's new conviction,
were many. Importantly, it would improve the English language
and its purity and vigor. "The rejection of the Latin and Greek languages from our schools would produce a revolution in science, and
in human affairs. That nation which shall first shake off the fetters
of these ancient languages, will advance further in knowledge, and
in happiness, in twenty years, than any nation in Europe has done,
in a hundred." This would tend to destroy the prejudice of the common people against schools and colleges, would spread knowledge,
increase the number of students in colleges, and remove the immense disparity which existed between the sexes in educational opportunity and achievement.

In the same year, Rush conducted his campaign against the classics in his private letters. On June 15, 1789, he wrote to John
Adams: "Let us try the effect of banishing the Latin and Greek languages from our country. They consume the flower of human life,
and by enabling us to read agreeable histories of ancient crimes often lead us to imitate or tolerate them."[56] In reply to John Adams's
defense of the study of Latin and Greek, Rush sent him a "small essay" (probably the article in the *American Museum*), adding: "I
shall class them [Greek and Latin] hereafter with Negro slavery and
spiritous liquors, and consider them as, though in a less degree, un-
friendly to the progress of morals, knowledge, and religion in the
United States."[57] On July 13 he wrote Jeremy Belknap, clergyman
and author, about "the inutility of the Latin and Greek languages."[58] On July 21 he wrote Adams again about his current bête
noire, the classics. "Who are guilty of the greatest absurdity—the
Chinese who press the feet into deformity by small shoes, or the
Europeans and Americans who press the brain into the obliquity of
Greek and Latin?" He berated those who favored the classical languages as undemocratic and advocates of an elite. "I often look
back," he declared, "upon the four years I spent . . . in learning the
Latin and Greek languages. . . . I should wish the memory of those
years blotted out of my mind forever," asserting that he owed nothing to the classics "but the turgid and affected style of my youthful
compositions and a neglect of English grammar." Rush's confidence in the success of his campaign was very great. "I expect to
prevail in the United States in my attempt to bring the dead languages in disrepute, for my next attack upon them shall be addressed to our American ladies."[59] The emphasis in the schools on
Greek and Roman mythology, he warned, had led to infidelity,

immorality, and bad government. "Men love wars, royalty, titles, and the Latin and Greek languages. They make wars, enslave their fellow-creatures, distill and drink rum, all because they are not formed by Reason."[60] In another letter to John Adams, dated February 2, 1790, Rush expressed his present partiality for modern langages, particularly French, Italian, and Spanish, conceding that this was one of the reasons for his quarrel with the dead languages.[61]

Among the thoughts recorded by Benjamin Rush about this time in his *Commonplace Book* are his views *On the Latin and Greek Languages*.[62] The claims that learning, scholarship, and "humanity" belonged exclusively to the curriculum of the Latin grammar schools he dubbed "All wrong!" The classics fostered immorality and paganism, and since monuments of idolatry have been destroyed, why not destroy the languages? Besides, all that was valuable in the writings of the dead languages had been diffused through modern works. If the study of the classical languages is to be continued, it should be confined to specialists in the field, he insisted.

In July, 1791, Rush received a letter from James Muir, principal of the Alexandria Academy in Virginia, which spurred him to renewed attacks on the classics, in an article published in the *American Museum* in August of that year.[63] James Muir had written Rush that there was little interest in the learned languages in the Alexandria Academy. Of ninety students enrolled only nineteen were studying Latin and Greek. Moreover, Muir was convinced that the taste of Americans of the time was for the useful, not the ornamental. Publishing an extract from Muir's letter with glee, Rush again attacked "the present state of the prejudices of our countrymen" in favor of Latin and Greek. As a concession, if Latin continued to be taught, only the reading of Latin should be emphasized. This plan would at least enable students to read more of the classics, for the sake of their contents, since, as things were, "very few boys ever carry away with them any thing but a smattering of the classics." It was quite absurd to demand a knowledge of the Latin and Greek languages as an introduction to the study of English, and equally absurd to spend years teaching students to speak and write Latin, skills they rarely required in later life. "Much more, in my opinion, might be said in favour of teaching our young men to speak the Indian language of our country, than to speak or write Latin," because of the utilitarian value in communicating with and civilizing the American Indians.

> Is it not high time to wrest the power over the education of our youth, out of the hands of ignorant or prejudiced schoolmasters, and place it in the hands of men of more knowledge and experience in the affairs of the world? We talk much of our being an enlightened people; but I know not with what reason, while we tolerate a system of education in our schools, which is as disgraceful to the human understanding as the most corrupt tenets or practices of the pagan religion, or of the Turkish government.

Rush also wrote a long letter to James Muir on August 24, 1791,[64] in which he repeated and elaborated upon the views expounded in his recent article. He gave, first, a summary of the many replies sent him by supporters of the classics in answer to his article in the *American Museum* in 1789. Rush ridiculed the view that a knowledge of the dead languages conferred taste and elegance in use of the English language, as well as in the amenities of good breeding. He set forth in greater detail his proposal to teach boys only the reading of Greek and Latin works, for their content, as a concession "accommodated to the present state of the prejudices of our countrymen" in favor of the classical languages. This would enable them to read whole works, instead of "a smattering of the classics," and thus put an end to "the present indiscriminate and preposterous mode of teaching the dead languages" through grammar and the writing of Latin versions.

It comes, therefore, as a distinct surprise to find Rush in 1792 writing his young son Richard (then almost twelve), no doubt in response to a request for parental guidance concerning his studies: "Go on with your class in learning Latin."[65]

A few years later, in 1796, on the occasion of the death of David Rittenhouse, president of the American Philosophical Society, patriot and signer of the Declaration of Independence, self-educated but internationally renowned scientist, Rush delivered a eulogy in which he ascribed Rittenhouse's extensive knowledge and splendid character "to his having escaped the pernicious influence of monkish learning upon his mind in early life." The usual classical education, Rush orated, "would probably have consumed the force of his genius. . . . Rittenhouse the Philosopher, and one of the luminaries of the eighteenth century, might have spent his hours of study in composing syllogisms, or in measuring the feet of Greek and Latin poetry."[66]

In the last decade of the century attacks against the classics continued to be published in contemporary magazines and newspapers. In the *Massachusetts Magazine* of July, 1795,[67] pity and indignation were expressed for the many years spent by boys in learning the rules of a dead language for which they would have no use the rest of their lives. Though the author expressed partiality for the classics, he asserted that he was not blind to the absurdity of teaching them to boys who would never use them in adult life and did not, moreover, possess the ability to learn them. A practical, vocational education suited to the future of each student was required. The benefit of "what is foolishly enough called a liberal education" has not prepared tradesmen and merchants for their futures, for they have not only forgotten the little Latin and Greek they were taught but are totally ignorant of many branches of knowledge that are absolutely necessary for them. "We are in general deceived into the most absurd notion, that the acquisition of the learned languages is the great point to be aimed at in the education of the youth," whereas the classics, prejudices aside, should be made subordinate to the more practical subjects. In October and December, 1796, there appeared in the *Massachusetts Magazine* an article "The Living Languages" by "Philenos,"[68] in reply to a defense of "The Dead Languages" by "Onkelos" in that magazine published in August of that year. Philenos argued that the dead languages monopolized more time in the schools than their real utility warranted. The living tongues have more to offer in less time. A Christian people, what is more, should have no traffic with the idolatrous, pagan, immoral writings of the ancients. We are vastly different from the ancient peoples. Philenos was fully aware that "The strong current of prejudice bears against me. . . . Official and interested motives have engulfed many to support the credit of the dead languages," though there exist people in the United States of independent judgment who distinguish between real utility and what is fashionable in education. "Which *one* of [the] *Sciences* is not more noble in itself, and more useful in the sphere of social life, than the *smattering* of dead languages which is usually acquired under the present system of education?"

In the same year, 1797, William Godwin, writing "Of the Study of the Classics,"[69] discussed the contemporary debate over the place of the classics in the education of the youth. It was a time when "inquisitive and active spirits are little inclined to take anything upon trust." Two weighty arguments presented by the opponents of the study of Greek and Latin, he set forth, were that they may be read in translation, and that a superficial acquaintance with Latin is ridiculous for children destined not for literary study but for more ordinary occupations. About the same time, Louis Hue Girardin, a professor of modern languages, pointed out that in Europe "writers of transcending genius," particularly in countries with high levels of commerceand agriculture, had declared the study of the dead languages "pedantic, and of no immediate use."[70]

But by the year 1800, when the revolutionary ardor had subsided (cooled, in part, by time, and, in part, by the excesses of the French Revolution), the animated debate over the place of the classics in the curriculum of American schools and colleges was virtually over[71]—with a victory for tradition.[72] Despite the Franklins, the Paines, and the Rushes, despite the theorizing, heat, agitation, and despite the efforts to sweep along the schools in the momentum of revolutionary change, most people remained unmoved, and few aspects of American education were altered. True, the Boston Latin School in 1789 reduced its course from seven to four years; English grammar, under Noah Webster's influence, appeared in more curricula; and science began to make inroads in higher education, for example, at Harvard.[73] But the classical tradition, as the vehicle of liberal education for leadership and the professions, remained unshaken.[74] The reforming zeal of the latter part of the eighteenth century was to lie dormant for a generation (as it did in England, in an interesting parallel),[75] until the 1820s, when population growth, industrialization, and the upsurge of a strong middle class brought into being the free, utilitarian public high schools, the first serious institutionalized challenge to the classical curriculum.[76] It is noteworthy, for example, that after 1800 Noah Webster became increasingly more conservative, recanting and abandoning many of his earlier views as hastily conceived youthful enthusiasms of the Revolutionary Age.[77]

But Benjamin Rush remained an unreconstructed die-hard, continuing for over a decade his tirades against the classical languages —the last of the revolutionary anticlassicists, a lone voice shouting into the wind. In May, 1807, for example, in a letter addresssed probably to Ashbel Green,[78] eminent clergyman and educator, regarding the curriculum of theological schools, he urged that Latin and Greek poets and historians be excluded from these schools so as to shield students from the "crimes of heathen gods and men" and "heathen mythology." But it was John Adams who bore the brunt of Rush's continuous fulminations against the classics and reiterations of his arguments against Latin and Greek in the curriculum. It is "folly and madness," he wrote Adams in 1810, to waste four or five years in teaching boys Latin and Greek and the classical authors, when they should be reading English and French writers.

"Were every Greek and Latin book (the New Testament excepted) consumed in a bonfire, the world would be the wiser and better for it." They were suitable for the idle and the rich but not for the needs of the modern world. *"Delenda, delenda est lingua Romana* should be the voice of reason and liberty and humanity in every part of the world."[79] Adams rebuked Rush's "fanaticism against Greek and Latin," but Rush summarily rejected his arguments in their favor.[80] When Adams commented that the study of Greek and Latin had had a revival in Europe, Rush attributed this to sinister motives on the part of Napoleon, "the head of the junto confederated to restore and establish them," in order to divert attention from his tyranny, one of his many acts "to bring back the darkness and ignorance of the 14th and 15th centuries," using the classics for the same purpose as had George III.[81] Rush would not object to the *reading* of the dead languages for the content of the classics, but he continued to fulminate against what he called "offal learning," which should be banished from the schools because the great increase in knowledge of the useful arts and sciences had destroyed the value of "monkish learning."[82] Rush's intransigeance finally evoked from Adams the rebuke: "I do most cordially hate you for writing against Latin, Greek, and Hebrew. I will never forgive you until you repent, retract, and reform. No! Never! It is impossible!"[83] Rush died in 1813, an unrepentant prophet. John Adams wrote Jefferson on July 16, 1814: "Classics, in spite of our friend Rush, I must think indispensable."[84]

It is an instructive paradox that in the third quarter of the eighteenth century there emerged in this country the most vigorous effort before the twentieth century to topple the classics from its regal position, at a time when, as Mr. Gummere has told us, "America, like England, was at the height of her classical period . . . , when statesmen, poets, and painters most deliberately and successfully imitated the example of the ancients."[85] The classics continued to perform a significant educational function in the nineteenth century, partly because of tradition, but largely because of their vitality and flexibility in serving important social needs. And they will continue to serve a significant purpose if their champions, now without the comforting support of tradition, continue to display even greater resilience in adapting the teaching of the classics to today's urgencies. We must take warning, comfort, and a challenge from Paul Oskar Kristeller's words:

The situation is such that many responsible scholars are rightly worried. Yet I am inclined to hope and to expect that the interest in the Classics and in historical learning will be continued and even revived, for I am firmly convinced of their intrinsic merit, and believe that it cannot fail to impose itself again, although perhaps in a form different from the one in which we are accustomed, and more in accordance with the needs of our time and society.[86]

Notes

1. Cambridge, Mass., 1963.
2. William Calder III, *Gnomon* 38 (1966), p. 638.
3. Colyer Meriwether, *Our Colonial Curriculum, 1607–1776* (Washington, D.C., 1907), pp. 87–91.
4. Gummere, *American Colonial Mind*, pp. 1–8; Samuel E. Morison, *The Intellectual Life of Colonial New England*, 2nd ed. (New York, 1956), p. 17; cp. Perry Miller, *The New England Mind: The Seventeenth Century* (Cambridge, Mass., 1954), p. 98, on the caution with which the classical heritage was used.
5. Harvey Wish, *Society and Thought in Early America: A Social and Intellectual History of the American People through 1865* (New York, 1950), pp. 160, 283–284; Gummere, *American Colonial Mind*, passim; R. Freeman Butts, *A Cultural History of Western Education* (New York, 1955), pp. 260–263; H. G. Good, *A History of American Education*, 2nd ed. (New York, 1962), pp. 48–58; Agatho Zimmer, *Changing Concepts of Higher Education in America Since 1700* (Washington, D.C., 1938), pp. 1–5; Robert F. Seybolt, *Source Studies in American Colonial Education: The Private School*, Bureau of Educational Research, College of Education, University of Illinois, Bulletin no. 28 (Urbana, 1925), p. 95. The ambivalent guarded attitude to the classics is evident, for example, in the Statutes of William and Mary (1727) in which, though Latin and Greek were to be taught by "the same books which by law or custom are used in the schools of England," yet "the Master [is to] take special care, that if the author is never so well approved on other accounts, he teach no such part of him to his scholars, as insinuates anything against religion and good morals." See Richard Hofstadter and Wilson Smith, *American Higher Education: A Documentary History* (Chicago, 1961), vol. I, p. 43.
6. See, e.g., Gummere, *American Colonial Mind*, passim; Charles F. Mullett, "Classical Influences on the American Revolution," *Classical Journal* 35 (1939), pp. 92–104; Johannes Urzidil, *Amerika und die Antike* (Zurich, 1964), p. 16.
7. Thomas Woody, *Early Quaker Education in Pennsylvania*, Teachers College, Columbia University, Contributions to Education, no. 105 (New York, 1928), p. 11.
8. *The Fruits of Solitude and Other Writings* (London, 1915), p. 28, quoting, in part, maxims 6 and 7 of pt. I.
9. Louis B. Wright, *The Colonial Civilisation of North America, 1607–1763* (London, 1949), p. 195; Wish, *Society and Thought*, pp. 160–161.
10. See, e.g., Seybolt, *Private School*, for the growth, in response to popular demand, of English grammar schools in colonial America, as well as evening schools offering modern foreign languages and practical, vocational subjects (pp. 96–99). Cp. Robert F. Seybolt, *The Evening School in Colonial America*, Bureau of Educational Research, College of Education, University of Illinois, Bulletin no. 24 (Urbana, 1925).
11. Phillips Brooks, *Essays and Addressses, Religious, Literary, and Social* (New York, 1894), p. 409.

12. Ibid., p. 410.
13. If we do not neglect the Catos among the Romans themselves, the early Christian Fathers, Jewish opponents of the classics, and the anti-humanists in the Middle Ages and even during the Renaissance, the history of the opposition is indeed a long one.
14. See, e.g., Russel B. Nye, *The Cultural Life of the New Nation* (New York, 1960), pp. 152–153; Theodore R. Crane, *The College and the Public, 1782–1862*, Teachers College, Columbia University, Classics in Education, no. 15 (New York, 1963), p. 3.
15. "An Essay on a Course of Liberal Education, for Civil and Active Life" (published 1764), in *Lectures on History and General Policy* (Dublin, 1788), pp. xvii–xxxvii; *Joseph Priestley: Selections from His Writings*, ed. Ira V. Brown (University Park, Pa., 1962), pp. 78–100.
16. See, e.g., Peter Gay, *The Enlightenment: An Interpretation. The Rise of Modern Paganism* (New York, 1967), pp. 279–321; R. Freeman Butts, *The College Charts its Course: Historical Conceptions and Current Proposals* (New York, 1939), pp. 49–57; Kenneth Urwin, *A Century of Freedom: A Survey of the French "Philosophers"* (London, 1946).
17. Nicholas Hans, *New Trends in Education in the Eighteenth Century* (London, 1951), pp. 5, 13–15.
18. It would be desirable to collect and study all this occasional criticism published in colonial newspapers and magazines.
19. Dec. 31–Jan. 7; Jan 7–14: "Some Thoughts of Education to render the Education of Youth more Easy and Effectual in respect to their Studies at School."
20. The text is also given in Seybolt, *Private School*, pp. 103–107.
21. "Proposals Relating to the Education of the Youth in Pennsylvania," in *The Papers of Benjamin Franklin*, ed. Leonard W. Labaree and Whitfield J. Bell, Jr. (New Haven, 1961), vol. III, p. 415; Thomas H. Montgomery, *A History of the University of Pennsylvania from its Foundation to 1770* (Philadelphia, 1900), p. 499.
22. See, e.g., Frederick Mayer, *American Ideas and Education* (Columbus, 1964), pp. 5, 88–89.
23. Letter to Benjamin Franklin, Nov., 1749. See *The Works of Benjamin Franklin*, ed. Jared Sparks (Boston, 1840), vol. VII, pp. 46–47. Cp Mayer, *American Ideas*, pp. 96–97.
24. *Autobiography of Benjamin Franklin*, ed. Leonard W. Labaree et al. (New Haven, 1964), pp. 168–169.
25. Gummere, *American Colonial Mind*, p. 128.
26. "Excerpts from the Papers of Dr. Benjamin Rush," *Pa. Mag. Hist. & Biog.* 29 (1905), p. 27: "Had a long conversation with him [Franklin] on the Latin and Greek languages. He called them the 'quackery of literature.'" The date is June 12, 1789.
27. Text in Thomas Woody, *The Educational Views of Benjamin Franklin* (New York, 1931), pp. 220–227 (cp. pp. 191–192); *The Writings of Benjamin Franklin*, ed. Albert H. Smyth (New York, 1905–07), vol. X, pp. 28–32; John H. Best, *Benjamin Franklin on Education*, Bureau of Publications, Teachers College, Classics in Education, no. 14 (New York, 1962), pp. 173–174 (cp. pp. 13–14).
28. That is, purely ornamental, like the hats carried by elegant European gentlemen, never worn, to avoid disarrangement of the wig, but carried uselessly under the arm.
29. John Trumbull, *The Progress of Dulness, Part First*, 2nd ed. (New Haven, 1773). See also Alexander Cowie, *John Trumbull, Connecticut Wit* (Chapel Hill, 1936), pp. 94–124; Moses C. Tyler, *The Literary History of the American Revolution* (New York, 1907), vol. I, pp. 215–221.

30. George S. Brookes, *Friend Anthony Benezet* (Philadelphia, 1937), pp. 27, 86, 351–352, 433–434; Zora Klain, *Educational Activities of New England Quakers: A Source Book* (Philadelphia, 1928), pp. 10–11, 201; Howard H. Brinton, *Quaker Education in Theory and Practice* (Wallingford, Pa., 1940), pp. 96–97.
31. Robert Middlekauff, *Ancients and Axioms: Secondary Education in Eighteenth-Century New England* (New Haven, 1963), pp. 30, 119–120.
32. Ibid., pp. 111–127. On the influence of French and English liberalism and the Enlightenment on the educational thinking of many American intellectuals in the Revolutionary and post-Revolutionary generations, see especially Allen O. Hansen, *Liberalism and American Education in the Eighteenth Century* (New York, 1926).
33. Cp. Webster's "Now is the time and *this* the country, in which we may expect success, in attempting changes favorable to language, science, and government. . . . Let us seize the present moment, and establish a *national* language, as well as a national government." Cited by Harry R. Warfel, *Noah Webster, Schoolmaster to America* (New York, 1936), p. 129.
34. Ervin C. Shoemaker, *Noah Webster: Pioneer of Learning* (New York, 1936), pp. 44–47, 54–55; Wish, *Society and Thought*, p. 284.
35. Middlekauff, *Ancients and Axioms*, pp. 164–165.
36. Text in Noah Webster, *A Collection of Essays and Fugitiv Writings on Moral, Historical, Political and Literary Subjects* (Boston, 1790), pp. 1–35.
37. Ibid., p. 3.
38. Ibid., p. 4.
39. Ibid., p. 5.
40. Wilmington, 1791. Text also in Frederick Rudolph, *Essays on Education in the Early Republic* (Cambridge, Mass., 1965), pp. 79–145.
41. Coram, *Plan for the General Establishment of Schools*, p. 101.
42. Roy J. Honeywell, *The Educational Work of Thomas Jefferson* (Cambridge, Mass., 1931), pp. 56, 112–113. For Jefferson's knowledge and love of the classics see Karl Lehmann, *Thomas Jefferson, American Humanist* (New York, 1947).
43. Francis Hopkinson, *The Miscellaneous Essays, and Occasional Writings* (Philadelphia, 1792), vol. II, pp. 1–12.
44. Ibid., pp. 41–57. Cp. George E. Hastings, *The Life and Works of Francis Hopkinson* (Chicago, 1926), pp. 412–416.
45. Philip Freneau, *Letters on Various Interesting and Important Subjects* (New York, 1943), Preface. Cp. Lewis Leary, *That Rascal Freneau* (New Brunswick, 1941); Mary S. Austin, *Philip Freneau, the Poet of the Revolution* (New York, 1901).
46. Quoted in Harry Hayden Clark, *Thomas Paine* (New York, 1944), p. civ. See also *The Writings of Thomas Paine*, ed. M. D. Conway (New York, 1894–96), vol. IV, pp. 62–63.
47. *The Life and Major Writings of Thomas Paine*, ed. Philip S. Foner (New York, 1945), pp. 491–492. On Paine's views on education, see Clark, *Thomas Paine*, pp. c–cviii.
48. Hopkinson, *Miscellaneous Essays*, vol. I, pp. 364–365.
49. Samuel Harrison Smith, *Remarks on Education* (Philadelphia, 1798), pp. 68–69. The text of the pamphlet is also available in Rudolph, *Essays on Education*, pp. 167–223.
50. Samuel Knox, *An Essay on the Best System of Liberal Education, Adapted to the Genius of the Government of the United States* (Baltimore, 1799), pp. 18–21. Text also in Rudolph, *Essays on Education*, pp. 271–372.
51. See, e.g., Hansen, *Liberalism and American Education*, pp. 43, 50–54, 61; Harry G. Good, *Benjamin Rush and His Services to American Education* (Berne, Ind., 1918), pp. 171–254.

52. See the instructive summary of some of the intellectual influences on Benjamin Rush in David B. Davis, *The Problem of Slavery in Western Culture* (Ithaca, 1966), p. 486.

53. In letters to his classmate, later postmaster general, Ebenezer Hazard, in June and November of 1765. See *Letters of Benjamin Rush*, ed. L. H. Butterfield, *Memoirs of the American Philosophical Society*, no. 30 (Philadelphia, 1951), vol. I, pp. lxvii, 17–18. Rush also informed Hazard that he intended to begin reading Hippocrates "in the original Greek, in which I find myself lamentably deficient." On Rush's love of the classics see also a letter of his to John Adams, in *Letters*, vol. I, p. 524: "the delight with which I once read the Roman poets and historians."

54. "A Plan for the Establishment of Public Schools and the Diffusion of Knowledge in Pennsylvania; to Which Are Added, Thoughts upon the Mode of Education, Proper in a Republic. Addressed to the Legislature and Citizens of the State." See also Rudolph, *Essays on Education*, p. 18.

55. "An enquiry into the Utility of a knowledge of the Latin and Greek languages as a branch of liberal Studies, with hints of a plan of liberal instruction, without them, accommodated to the present state of society, manners, and government in the United States," published in *American Museum* 5 (1789), pp. 525–535, and signed "By a citizen of Philadelphia." Published also in Benjamin Rush, *Essays, Literary, Moral & Philosophical* (Philadelphia, 1798), pp. 21–56, with slightly altered title: "Observations Upon the Study of the Latin and Greek Languages, as a Branch of Liberal Education, with Hints of a Plan of Liberal Instruction without them, Accommodated to the Present State of Society, Manners, and Government in the United States."

56. Rush, *Letters*, vol. I, p. 516.

57. Ibid., pp. 517–518. Adams in his reply on June 19 declared: "I should as soon think of closing all my window shutters, to enable me to see, as of banishing the Classicks, to improve Republican ideas" (*Old Family Letters* [Philadelphia, 1892], vol. I, p. 40). Cited by Butterfield in Rush, *Letters*, vol. I, p. 518, n. 1.

58. Rush, *Letters*, p. 520.

59. Rush did not carry out this plan. It may be assumed that he intended to use the tack that American women were being shortchanged in educational opportunities by the exclusive emphasis on the classics.

60. Rush, *Letters*, vol. I, p. 525.

61. Ibid., pp. 531–532.

62. *The Autobiography of Benjamin Rush*, ed. George W. Corner, *Memoirs of the American Philosophical Society*, no. 25 (Philadelphia, 1948), pp. 345–347.

63. *American Museum* 10 (1791), pp. 61–63; reprinted in his *Essays* (1798), p. 50.

64. Rush, *Letters*, vol. I, pp. 604–607.

65. Ibid., p. 619.

66. Benjamin Rush, *An Eulogium Intended to Perpetuate the Memory of David Rittenhouse* (Philadelphia, 1796).

67. "On Education," *Massachusetts Magazine*, July, 1795, pp. 202–205.

68. "The Living Languages," *Massachusetts Magazine*, Oct., 1796, pp. 529–535; Dec., 1796, pp. 657–660.

69. William Godwin, *The Enquirer: Reflections on Education, Manners and Literature* (Philadelphia, 1797), pp. 29–44.

70. Louis Hue Girardin, *Education: Circular Relating to the Formation of a School at Dumfries, Virginia, for Teaching Languages and Other Subjects Belonging to a Course of Liberal Education* (Richmond, 1798), pp. 1–2.

71. Rudolph is in error in declaring Pierre Samuel Du Pont de Nemours second to none in scathing denunciation of the standard classical studies, citing Du Pont's statement, "All our great men have overcome the misfortune of having gone through these studies" (*Essays on Education*, p. xviii). Cp. [Pierre Samuel] Du

Pont de Nemours, *National Education in the United States of America*, translated from the second French edition by B. G. Du Pont (Newark, Del., 1923), p. 124 (this was an essay written in 1800 at the request of Thomas Jefferson). But Du Pont was, at that point, writing about European universities and criticizing their methods. Earlier Du Pont defended and specified the teaching of Greek and Latin in secondary school, more especially Greek (pp. 59–61).

72. R. Freeman Butts, *The College Charts its Course*, pp. 84–86; Hansen, *Liberalism and American Education*, p. 47; Middlekauff, *Ancients and Axioms*, p. 124.

73. Middlekauff, *Ancients and Axioms*, pp. 154–171.

74. Butts, *The College*, pp. 62–63; Butts, *Cultural History*, pp. 325–326; Gummere, *American Colonial Mind*, p. 56.

75. Nicholas Hans, *New Trends*, p. 212.

76. See, e.g., Wish, *Society and Thought*, pp. 284–287; Howard Mumford Jones, *America and French Culture, 1750-1848* (Chapel Hill, 1927), pp. 66–67, 473–474, 480.

77. Shoemaker, *Noah Webster*, pp. 58–59, 63; Wish, *Society and Thought*, p. 285.

78. Rush, *Letters*, vol. II, p. 946.

79. Ibid., pp. 1066–1067.

80. Adams, *Old Family Letters*, pp. 265–268 (letter to Rush, Oct. 13, 1810, cited by Butterfield in Rush, *Letters*, vol. II, p. 1073, n. 1); ibid., vol. II, p. 1073 (letter of John Adams, Dec. 21, 1810).

81. Rush, *Letters*, vol. II, p. 1077 (letter to John Adams, Jan. 10, 1811).

82. Letters to John Adams, Feb. 4, 1811, and Dec. 26, 1811.

83. Letter to Benjamin Rush in 1810. See Page Smith, *John Adams* (Garden City, 1962), vol. II, pp. 1085–1086.

84. *Works of John Adams* (Boston, 1850–56), vol. X, p. 105.

85. Gummere, *American Colonial Mind*, pp. 1–2, quoting Stuart P. Sherman.

86. Paul O. Kristeller, *Renaissance Thought. The Classic, Scholastic, and Humanist Strains* (New York, 1961), p. 89. My study was completed before the publication of Richard M. Gummere's *Seven Wise Men of Colonial America* (Cambridge, Mass., 1967). In this book Gummere devotes only minor attention to the attacks of "protestants or abolitionists" against the classical curriculum, though it is his intent that "the historical critic should have his inning no less than the classicist" (p. vi). In his chapter on Benjamin Rush (pp. 64–80: "A Classical Doctor's Dilemma") Gummere attributes Rush's hostility to the classics to his argumentative nature but sharply underemphasizes his criticism, offers us the paradox of the sceptic toward the classical curriculum who used numerous classical allusions in his writings, and believes that Rush desired not the abolition of the classical curriculum in America but a new humanistic method of teaching the classics. Similarly, in his chapter on Thomas Paine (pp. 81–96: "Was He Really Anti-Classical?"), we are presented with a Paine who used classical tags and was a "reformer in the field of the classics"!

V. The Classics and the Quest for Virtue in Eighteenth-Century America

The leaders of American society in the second half of the eighteenth century would, for the most part, have readily subscribed to the words of Gilbert Tennent and Samuel Davies, written in 1754, that the aim of education was "to advance the Happiness and Glory of a Community" by training up the youth in "useful Knowledge and Virtue."[1] About 1730, with the growing secularization of American society, the previous predominantly theological considerations gave way to the theory and practice of morality for civic ends.[2] Thus, in Norman Fiering's words, moral philosophy became for Americans the "semisecular way station" between theology and objective science, "the one subject of common and universal understanding among American intellectuals from ca. 1730–1800 and beyond." Hence "the almost mysterious incantaton of *virtue*" in eighteenth-century America.[3]

The fervor for "virtue" was not transplanted from the well-known European "courtesy" books for molding gentlemen; nor did Americans pursue it in order to promote the merit principle as a counterthrust to the privileges of hereditary aristocracy.[4] In its most characteristic form in eighteenth-century America virtue, particularly with the onset of the Revolutionary period, was predominantly civic virtue, public spirit, concern for the common good,[5] though recognition of the claims of private virtue was not uncommon. Benjamin Franklin, for instance, in his classic enumeration of

142

the moral virtues in 1784 catalogued thirteen virtues (a synthesis of Christian and classical virtues) without specifically relating them to the public good.[6] And in 1797 Samuel Harrison Smith, proposing a national plan of education, offered a comprehensive interpretation: "Without attempting precise definition, it may be sufficiently correct . . . to style VIRTUE that active exertion of our faculties, which, in the highest degree promotes our own happiness and that of our fellow-men." Caught up in the rhetorical fervor of national aspirations, Smith concluded his essay as follows: "Let us . . . with rapture anticipate the era, when the triumph of peace and the prevalence of virtue shall be rendered secure by the diffusion of useful knowledge."[7]

More than a generation earlier, however, the civic content of virtue was more dominant. A striking, but typical, example is the view of William Livingston in 1753 in his comments on the goals of the proposed college in New York: "The true Use of Education," he wrote, "is . . . to infuse a public Spirit and Love of their Country, to inspire them with the Principles of Honour and Probity, with a fervent Zeal for Liberty, and a diffusive Benevolence of Mankind; and in a Word, to make them the more extensively serviceable in the Common-wealth. . . . This, therefore, I will venture to lay down for a capital Maxim, that unless the Education we propose, be calculated to render our Youth better Members of Society, and useful to the Public in Proportion to its Expence, we had better be without it."[8] The Constitution of Massachusetts, promulgated in the intensity of the War of Independence, is explicit: "Wisdom and knowledge, as well as virtue, diffused generlly among the body of the people [are] necessary for the preservation of their rights and liberties."[9]

Indeed the "incantation of virtue" was most fervent during the uncertainties of the war and the ensuing polemics over the Constitution. The *New-Jersey Magazine* proclaimed in 1787, "Now it is virtue alone, that qualifies a man for the discharge of . . . important offices. . . . It is virtue, that gives him a true taste of glory, that inspires him with zeal for his country, and with proper motives to serve it to the utmost of his power. . . . The end of all study, therefore, is to make men virtuous."[10] In Boston the Reverend Jonathan Mason declared during the war "that the greatness and prosperity of a people depend upon the proportion of public spirit and the love of virtue which is found to exist among them, seems to be a maxim established by the universal consent, and I may say, experience of all ages. . . . Patriotism is essential to the preservation and well being of every form of government. . . . A constitution, built upon such principles, and put in execution by men possessed with the love of virtue and their fellow-men, must always insure happiness to it's members."[11] The American cult of virtue was summed up by Clinton Rossiter as follows: "Few people in history have been more given to public moralizing, to proclaiming a catalogue of virtues and exhorting one another to exhibit them, than the American colonists. . . . It seems safe to say that no people in history was more dedicated to the notion that free government rests upon public and private morality. For our colonial ancestors human liberty was a problem in ethics rather than economics."[12]

Americans were indeed committed to the pursuit of virtue as the bulwark of freedom under a republic. Samuel Adams maintained to the end of his life, without ever losing faith, that virtue was the keystone of liberty. "Virtue," he wrote in 1774, "is our best Security. It is not possible that any state sh[oul]d long remain free, when Virtue is not supremely honored." Therefore, education is essential for diffusing "the Principles of Morality, so essentially necessary to the Preservation of publick Liberty. There are Virtues & Vices which are properly called *political*. . . . For no people will timidly surrender their Liberties, nor can any be easily subdued, when Knowledge is diffused and Virtue is preserved."[13] Similarly, in 1779 he declared, "If Virtue & Knowledge are diffused among the People, they will never be enslaved. This will be their great Security. Virtue & Knowledge will forever be an even Balance for Power & Riches";[14] in 1776, "You will justly observe that the Soul or Spirit of Democracy is Virtue";[15] in 1778, "*Esto perpetua*! is my most ardent Prayer for the rising Republick. That will depend upon the Principles and Manners of the People. Publick Liberty will not long survive the loss of Public Virtue."[16] In 1790, when John Adams's advocacy of public virtue had turned to pessimism, Samuel Adams remained unshaken in his confidence in the efficacy of virtue: "This Constitution [of the state of Massachusetts]," he wrote John Adams, "was evidently founded in the expectation of further progress, and extraordinary degrees of virtue. It injoyns the encouragement of all Seminaries of Literature, which are the nurseries of Virtue depending upon these for the support of Government, rather than Titles, Splendor, or Force."[17]

Indeed, until the 1790s, John Adams's enthusiasm for public virtue had been equally warm. As early as 1765 he excerpted in his commonplace book a passage from Joseph Butler's analysis of public virtue as a source of strength in society.[18] "Politicks," he wrote in 1776, "is the Science of human Happiness and human Happiness is clearly best promoted by Virtue."[19] To his wife, Abigail, he wrote, "Public Virtues, and political Qualities therefore should be incessantly cherished in our Children."[20] During the Revolutionary period the key to liberty for Adams was virtue as social responsibility, concern for the public good. "Public Virtue," he declared, "is the only Foundation of Republics. There must be a positive Passion for the public good, the public Interest . . . and this public Passion, must be Superiour to all private Passions. . . . Is there in the World a Nation, which deserves this Character? There have been several, but they are no more."[21] Adams's views were identical with those of Alexander Hamilton,[22] and of Jefferson, who wrote in 1771, "everything is useful which contributes to fix in the principles and practice of virtue," even the reading of fiction.[23] Jefferson once said, "Self-love is the sole antagonist of virtue, leading us constantly by our propensities to self-gratification in violation of our moral duties to others."[24]

When Washington in his *Farewell Address* declared, "It is substantially true that virtue or morality is a necessary spring of popular government,"[25] he was summing up the eighteenth-century conviction that a republic cannot be sustained without inner-directed virtue, that is, zeal for the public good, as opposed to the motives of fear and private aggrandizement.[26] Robert Livingston of New York put it this way: "More virtue is expected from our People than any People ever had."[27]

The primacy of virtue in a republic had the support also of Madison, who said in the debate on the Constitution at the Virginia ratifying convention: "No theoretical checks, no form of government can render us secure. To suppose that any form of government will secure liberty or happiness without any virtue in a people, is a chimerical idea."[28] The philosophical underpinning and authentication of the principle of virtue in a people as the key to success of a republic came from the works of the French *philosophes*, particularly from Montesquieu's *Spirit of Laws*, which was avidly studied by Americans. From this work they imbibed the definition of republican virtue as patriotism, public spirit, self-sacrifice, frugality —as exemplified in the ancient republics, Rome especially, but also Crete and Sparta, which Montesquieu cited as models of virtue. "*Virtue*, in a republic," Montesquieu wrote, "is love of one's country, that is, love of equality. It is not a moral virtue, nor a Christian, but a political *virtue*."[29]

It was, accordingly, generally agreed among American leaders during the second half of the eighteenth century that the content and emphases of education should be structured to teach useful knowledge and inculcate virtue. The concept of virtue as civic commitment indispensable for winning freedom from England and to sustain a republic was a central theme in the educational theorizing and the political sermons of the Revolutionary period.[30] Samuel Adams reiterated this;[31] Noah Webster set it as the focal point of his plans for national education.[32] It was also central to John Clarke's famous work on grammar school education, which for a century remained a vade mecum for American secondary school teachers. Clarke's dictum, "the great End of Education . . . is to instill into the Minds of Youth a Love of Virtue and Knowledge,"[33] remained the general directive in instruction. Also in the hands of many Americans since its publication in 1748 was a kind of self-instructor, Robert Dodsley's *The Preceptor*. The frontispiece of this book displayed an engraving representing a boy led by Athena who points to a Temple of Virtue, above which is a Temple of Honour. Accompanying this allegory were the following verses:

> The Youth, who led by WISDOM'S guiding Hand,
>   Seeks VIRTUE'S Temple and her Law Reveres:
> He, he alone, in HONOUR'S Dome shall stand,
>   Crown'd with Rewards, & rais'd above his Peers:
> Recording Annals shall preserve his Name;
>   And give his Virtues to immortal Fame.[34]

The two major emphases in American education during the second half of the eighteenth century were instruction in morality and history. William Livingston, writing in 1754, declared: "the Education of Youth hath been the peculiar Care of all the wise Legislators of Antiquity, who thought it impossible to aggrandize the State without imbuing the minds of its members with Virtue and Knowledge."[35] His associate as editor of the *Independent Reflector* in New York, William Smith, Jr., wrote shortly after: "Boys in the study of Languages [i.e., Latin and Greek], are employed in a Manner best suited to their Capacities. Plain Rules of Morality and History are generally the Subjects of the Books put in their Hands."[36] In 1793, in an appeal for funds to support the University of North Carolina, "A Friend to the University" wrote: "Ye that love virtue, liberty and good laws! *give*. Friends to a republican government! *give*. A republican government is founded on *virtue*."[37] No wonder that *abeunt studia in mores*[38] was a popular motto of the eighteenth century! Characteristically, in the iconography of the Phi Beta Kappa key, designed in 1776 at William and Mary College, one of the three stars on the obverse symbolizes morality (the other two stand for literature, i.e., knowledge, and for friendship), morality in the sense of responsibility for the use of knowledge for the public good.

It is abundantly evident that "eighteenth-century education with its emphasis on the classics and on history was designed to instill in the youth an avid sense of duty and of civic virtue."[39] The principles that determined the selection of the classical authors studied in the schools and colleges were intended to assure what Moses Coit Tyler called "the study of sublime antique models of virtue and greatness."[40] Henry "Light-Horse Harry" Lee of Virginia (graduate of Princeton, class of '73), in his declining years advised his son at Harvard, "Dwell on the virtues. . . . Adhere to history & ethical authors of universal character."[41] Similarly, John Adams wrote John Quincy Adams when he was abroad as a student, "In Company with Sallust, Cicero, Tacitus, and Livy, you will learn Wisdom and Virtue. You will see them represented with all the Charms which Language and Imagination can exhibit, and Vice and Folly painted in all their Deformity and Horror. You will ever remember that all the End of Study is to make you a good Man and a useful Citizen."[42]

The same themes were orchestrated by lesser personalities. For instance, an anonymous article in the *New-Jersey Magazine* in 1787 presented an elaborate rationale for the study of the classics as mentors of "the love of virtue and abhorrence of vices" through "the writings of the most approved authors." Thus, through the "opinions and examples of the great men of antiquity . . . our youth are taught to have a taste . . . for virtue, and to fix their attention on real merit." In short, the "perusal of the best authors . . . forms a kind of relation betwixt us and the greatest men of the ancients."[43] In the *New-York Magazine* in 1790 T. Q. C., writing in defense of classical learning, epitomized the appeal of antiquity for many Americans thus: "The ancient classics contain . . . the struggles of a virtuous people for liberty, the expulsion of tyrants, the almost incredible exertions of states, and even of individuals, in defence of their liberty, examples of the most ardent patriotism, accurate observations upon nature, wise reflections upon laws and government, sound criticism, irresistible oratory, sublime poetry, and many pure precepts of morality."[44]

The value of the classics as an instrument for inculcating moral
truths was advocated by Puritans and Virginians alike. As early as
1665 Charles Chauncy, president of Harvard, in defense of a selective study of the classics wrote: "And who can deny that there are
found many excellent & divine morall truths in *Plato, Aristotle,
Plutarch, Seneca, etc.*: and to condemn all pel-mel, will be an hard
censure, especially to call universities Antichrists for reading
them."[45] Regarding the Virginia plantation gentry Louis B. Wright
concludes that "morals and ethics were subtly affected by Aristotle,
Plutarch, Seneca, Epictetus, and Epicurus cannot be denied."[46] In
Philadelphia Francis Hopkinson, first graduate of the College of
Philadelphia, extolled its classical reading program in his tribute to
his alma mater, *Science. A Poem*, composed in 1762. With respect
to Vergil's *Aeneid* he penned the following lines:

> Thro' ev'ry page engaging virtues shine
> And frequent precepts grace each moral line.[47]

In 1763 when Benjamin Prat (Harvard, class of '37), chief justice of
the province of New York, died, his eulogy contained a tribute to
his classical learning in a short poem ending as follows:

> In him tho' science did it's ray unite,
> And shed around him a distinguish'd light,
> 'Twas but a second merit.—Virtue more
> Adorn'd the man than all his learning's store.[48]

Thomas Jefferson's plundering of the classics for moral lessons
led Gilbert Chinard, one of the first modern colonial historians to
recognize the significance of the classical tradition in early America,
to declare that "in those remote days the study of the classics was
more than a luxury or a painful task. It was an essential part of the
moral foundation of many of the men who framed the American
institutions."[49] Indeed, Thomas Jefferson, turning away from traditional Christian morality, constructed out of the "ancient heathen
moralists" a working system of ethics that combined classical and
Christian ideals, in order to provide himself with a "moral shelter
in which he could find refuge for the rest of his days."[50] In his
youth, in the years from about 1764 to 1772, he excerpted 150 passages embodying moral generalizations from thirteen Greek and
Latin authors, mostly from Euripides, Homer, Cicero, and Horace.[51] Almost half of these excerpts (70 passages) were taken from

five plays of Euripides, *Hecuba, Orestes, Phoenissae, Medea,* and *Hippolytus.* There is no reason for concluding that these plays were favorites of Jefferson; they were simply in the order of plays in the first volume of a text of Euripides, the traditional arrangement of Euripidean tragedies since the Middle Ages. "Whether he felt the charm and human tenderness of the drama can only be surmised, but all in all, he copied only those passages which contained moral teachings from which he could draw a lesson."[52] In 1785, when outlining a reading program for young Peter Carr, he advised: "In morality read Epictetus, Zenophontis memorabilia, Plato's Socratic dialogues, Cicero's philosophies."[53] Near the end of his life, in his famous letter to John Brazier in 1819 on the value of classical education, Jefferson was somewhat reserved: "To the moralist they [classical authors] are valuable, because they furnish ethics writings highly and justly esteemed: although in my opinion, the moderns are far advanced beyond them in this line of science."[54]

The specific classical authors early Americans read for moral instruction and edification are well known. The most readily available and most quotable material came from books of Latin moral maxims, often arranged by topics and even provided with translations.[55] Thesauruses of Greek maxims were less popular, and indeed less accessible until the publication of Richard François Phillipe Brunck's *Ēthikē Poiēsis, sive Gnomici Poetae Graeci,* in 1784.[56] John Adams owned a copy of this book in 1813, when he gave it to his grandson George Washington Adams as he went off to school.[57] Moral and ethical principles were, of course, stressed in the books used in Latin grammar schools as exercise books or readers.[58]

Among the classical authors the ancient moralists occupied a leading place as favorites of early Americans.[59] As early as 1759 John Adams exhorted himself to "study Seneca, Cicero, and all other good moral Writers."[60] It was customary for young people to be exposed very early to *Aesop's Fables,* many versions of which were available. That of the English translator, poet, miscellany writer, Samuel Croxall, *Fables of Aesop and Others* (first edition 1722), popular for many generations, explains that "these Fables abound in a Variety of Instruction, Moral and Political. They furnish us with Rules for every Station of Life. They mark out a proper Behaviour for us . . . and demonstrate to us, by a Kind of Example, every Virtue which claims our best Regards, and every Vice which we are most concerned to avoid."[61] Immensely popular as first Latin reader was the *Disticha Catonis,* a collection of moral aphorisms of the third or fourth centuries A.D., written in dactylic hexameter couplets. This collection was popular enough among the general reading public for Benjamin Franklin to bring out a verse translation by the famous Philadelphia Quaker James Logan.[62]

In the admiration of early Americans Cicero took pride of place as orator, political theorist, stylist, and moralist. Especially popular for moral teaching was *Tully's Offices (De Officiis)*, which subsumed the essence of the moral heritage and humanistic values of the ancient world. This comprehensive compendium of moral instruction, useful to both young and mature readers, offered enlightenment and guidance for both private and civic virtue.[63] Many Americans would have agreed also with Erasmus's judgment of Cicero's *Tusculan Disputations*, widely read, too, in eighteenth-century America, that the work "inspired my soul and made me feel myself a better man."[64] Josiah Quincy owned three editions of Cicero's *Tusculans*, which he employed to inculcate virtue in his family, and which he liked because of its "noble patterns of behavior."[65]

Among the Greek moralists John Adams studied the Golden Verses of Pythagoras, perhaps in the Greek-Latin edition of Brunck,[66] although we do know that he used the French translation of André Dacier. While he approved of most of the moral injunctions in the Golden Verses (yet next to one he wrote "Mad!"), at the end he demurred: "How dark, mean and meagre are those golden verses, however celebrated and really curious in comparison with the Sermon on the Mount, and the Psalms of David or the Decalogue!"[67] A high favorite with early Americans was Xenophon's intellectual biography of Socrates, the *Memorabilia*, which they valued not for its philosophic views but for moral instruction. Particularly popular was that portion (2.1.22–23) known as the Choice of Hercules, one of the most enduring classical allegorical themes since the Renaissance. It was John Adams's favorite classical myth, because it encapsulated, through the choice faced by the young Hercules between virtue and pleasure, the central theme of American moral philosophy and education.[68] As for Isocrates' speeches, it is true that they were studied as models of Attic prose, but it was his moral tone and gnomic oratory in the 370s in Athens, particularly his speech "To Demonicus" (an avalanche of moral maxims) that gave him a special vogue in eighteenth-century America.[69]

Despite Jefferson's early interest in Euripides, the only classical dramatist widely read in early America was Terence (his plays were a secondary school textbook). Thus in 1781 John Adams advised his son John Quincy to read him, for "Terence is remarkable, for good Morals, good Taste, and good Latin."[70] Later, when he was in retirement in 1816, John Adams read through the six plays of Terence in Latin and excerpted about 140 passages for his grandchildren. "The six Plays of Terence," he commented, "are valuable [for a number of reasons, including] . . . the Maxims and Proverbs, which are now and have been for 2000 Years common place expressions of all civilized nations." Yet, he concluded, "I have great doubts whether Terence's Plays are proper for the Instruction of Youth," for "this is not Christian Morality."[71]

Horace, too, was valued by early Americans, not as belles lettres, but as a repository of quotable moral commonplaces and practical maxims for living.[72] John Adams, in one of his early commonplace books copied down the eighth and ninth stanzas of *Odes* 4.4 (To Drusus). It was surely not for the eighth stanza, which expresses Horace's respect for hereditary potential from noble ancestors, but the emphasis on nurture in the ninth stanza:

> Instruction develops inborn potential, and
> upright training strengthens the heart, and
> when once moral precepts fail, faults mar
> what is good by nature.

Then Adams added this comment: "Horace in the 6th Satyr of the 1st Book inculcates the Lesson that true Nobility is to be measured by Virtue, and purity of Morals—A very clear and certain as well as very precious and important Truth."[73] Horace was the favorite Roman poet of William Ellery of Rhode Island (Harvard, class of '47, signer of the Declaration of Independence). Even in his nineties Ellery was busy translating part of Horace's *Epistles*. Ellery's qualified admiration of Horace is revealed in a letter he wrote to his grandson at school: "Horace whom you are . . . now studying, and who, though justly reprehensible for his obscenities, hath liberally disseminated . . . [the] most excellent maxims, the rules of life."[74]

The Stoic writers—Seneca, Epictetus, Marcus Aurelius—attracted readers among early Americans, even though the doctrines of the Stoics were indefensible from the Christian viewpoint. Despite repugnance to the extravagant, rigoristic views of the Stoics on human nature, Americans were drawn to them by their many fine moral rules of conduct, their advocacy of virtue, frugality, civic duty, reason, natural law, opposition to tyranny, and the concepts of "freedom" and the "brotherhood of man." Jefferson, for instance, wrote of Seneca: "Seneca is indeed a fine moralist, disfiguring his work at time with some Stoicisms, and affecting too much of antithesis and point, yet giving us on the whole a great deal of sound and practical morality."[75] The *Meditations* of Marcus Aurelius, sometimes to be found in American libraries, was far less read because of its obscurity and idiosyncratic nature. Much more satisfactory and popular as a breviary of moral wisdom was Epictetus' *Enchiridion*, many English versions of which were in circulation, the best being that of Elizabeth Carter (1758), a friend of Samuel Johnson. Though she cautioned the reader that "the Stoic Philosophy insults human nature," she concluded that "even now their Compositions may be read with great Advantage, as containing rules of Self-Government, and of social Behaviour."[76]

By far the most popular classical author in the seventeenth and eighteenth centuries in America was Plutarch, read as a repository of historical *exempla* and moral lessons. Early in the seventeenth century in England Henry Peacham in his famous *Compleat Gentleman* signalled the usefulness of Plutarch. "For Morality and rules of well being, delivered with such sententious gravity, weight of reason, so sweetened with lively and apt similitudes, entertaine *Plutarch*."[77] In the eighteenth century "the incomparable Plutarch" also served republicans as a "revolutionists' handbook" (in George Bernard Shaw's words), a gallery of republican "saints and martyrs," and a vast storehouse of memorable historical *exempla* of virtues and vices. Many an American would have applauded the famous words of Mme. Roland, French Girondist leader, "Plutarch had disposed me to become a republican; he had awakened in me that force and pride which gives republicanism its character; he had inspired in me a veritable enthusiasm for the public virtues and for liberty."[78]

Plutarch himself tells us, "Using history as a mirror, I try somehow to improve my life by modeling it upon the virtues of the men I write about." It was Plutarch's memorable portrayal of virtues and vices in his heroes, together with his charming style and vivid narrative talent, that made him the most popular classical author in early America. Almost every American library had a copy of Plutarch's *Lives*, in North's translation (1579), or the "Dryden" version (1683), or that of John and William Langhorne (1770).[79] Plutarch's *Moralia* was less available; it is unusual to find anyone, like John Quincy Adams as a youth, excerpting commonplace passages from his work.[80]

In 1804 the remarkable Hugh Henry Brackenridge wrote in the second part of his prolix satirical novel-miscellany *Modern Chivalry:* "Political studies ought to be the great object with the generous youth of a republic; not for the sake of place or profit, but for the sake of judging right and preserving the constitution inviolate. *Plutarch's lives is an admirable book for this purpose.* I should like to see an edition of 10,000 volumes bought up in every state. Plutarch was a lover of virtue, and his reflections are favourable to all that is great and good amongst men."[81] So Emerson the moralist could pontificate a few decades later, "I must think we are more deeply indebted to [Plutarch] than to all ancient writers."[82]

Among the ancient historians Sallust was read in school, as model of oratorical style, for his treatment of historical crises as moral issues, and as a quarry of sententious maxims.[83] But it was Tacitus who stirred Americans deeply, for his political realism, his hostility to tyranny, his unrelenting moral posture, and his pithy apothegms.[84] In December 1808 Jefferson wrote his beloved granddaughter Anne Cary Bankhead the famous lines: "Tacitus I consider as the first writer in the world without a single exception. His book is a compound of history and morality of which we have no other example."[85] In 1816 Adams wrote Jefferson, "The Morality of Tacitus, is the Morality of Patriotism."[86] And Tacitus was the favorite author even of that inveterate enemy of classical learning, Benjamin Rush, if we can trust his eulogist.[87]

We should be prepared to find that even the *Iliad, Odyssey,* and *Aeneid,* school and college texts, were read with an eye for moral commonplaces. Indeed, John Adams and John Quincy Adams excerpted numerous passages of this kind from the great classical epics.[88] John Quincy Adams similarly culled numerous excerpts (166 passages) from Juvenal's *Satires.*[89]

Like John Quincy Adams, many other Americans of the first generation of the nineteenth century were still convinced of the utility and efficacy of the classics for inculcating virtue.[90] George Bancroft, destined to become one of the great American historians, will serve as a striking example. When he established the Round Hill School at Northampton, he declared that it was the aim of the new school to develop "the moral and intellectual maturity of the mind of each boy we take charge of, and the means are to be first and foremost instruction in the classics."[91]

Even into the nineteenth century the Choice of Hercules remained a popular allegory. It had been John Adams's favorite classical theme. As early as 1759 he was first deeply impressed in the story by the symbol of the necessity for personal moral choice, writing: "the Choice of Hercules came into my mind, and left impressions there which I hope will never be effaced nor long unheeded."[92] Indeed, in 1776, when he served with Jefferson and Franklin as the first committee to select a theme for the Great Seal of the United States, Adams proposed the Choice of Hercules, which he had seen in an engraving by Gribelin. The proposal, however, was not accepted as being too complicated and unoriginal.[93] In 1780 Adams saw a book on mythology in Paris which he was tempted to buy for his sons, but did not because it was too expensive. Writing to Abigail, he singled out the Choice of Hercules among his comments on the values and dangers of the study of mythology: "There is every Thing here that can inform the Understanding, or refine the Taste, and indeed one would think that could purify the Heart. Yet it must be remembered that there is every thing here too, which can seduce, betray, deceive, deprave, corrupt, debauch it. Hercules marches here in full View of the Steeps of Virtue on the one hand, and the flowery Paths of Pleasure on the other—and there are few who make the Choice of Hercules. That my Children may follow his Example, is my earnest Prayer."[94] John Adams's ambivalence may be seen also in his attitude to the visual arts: "the fine arts," he once wrote, ". . . promote virtue while virtue is in fashion. After that they promote luxury, corruption, prostitution."[95] John Quincy Adams had apparently been indoctrinated with his father's obsession with the Choice of Hercules. In September 1780, as he tells us in his early diary, he copied out two versions of the allegory, one from the *Spectator*, the other from the *Tatler*.[96] In 1782, when he was in St. Petersburg, he copied down a long poem retelling the Choice of Hercules, which he found in Robert Dodsley's *Preceptor*.[97]

American college students of the early Federal period were inheritors of the quest for virtue. In 1799–1800 the Whig Society at Princeton adopted as its symbol the goddess Minerva guiding a youth who holds a book to a Temple of Virtue on a mountain; nearby is a tablet on which are engraved the names of Demosthenes, Xenophon, Homer, Cicero, Tacitus, and Vergil. In January, 1819, the Whig Society changed its symbol to the Choice of Hercules, painted for the society by Thomas Scully and engraved by John Neagle.[98] Similarly, at the University of North Carolina, student societies proclaimed their aspiration for virtue: the Dialectic Society adopted as its motto "Love of Virtue and Science"; the Philanthropic Society "Virtue, Liberty, Science."[99]

For students, citizens, and leaders, history constituted the highest order of social knowledge, a "school of private and public virtue," in Bolingbroke's words. "No study is so useful to mankind as History," wrote an Englishman in 1723, "where, as in a glass, men may see the virtues and vices of great persons in former ages, and be taught to pursue the one, and avoid the others."[100] In America in 1745 there appeared an item in the *Maryland Gazette* advocating the study of ancient history to foster virtue and the defense of liberty. Among other advantages, wrote the anonymous Marylander, history has "a Tendency, if we have any Regard for honest Fame and Reputation, to inspire us with a noble Esteem of Virtue, and a just Contempt of Vice. . . . Probably a Man is more or less fond of Historical Reading, according to the Degrees of Virtue and Vice he possesses." The ancient heroes who sought to promote the public good deserve our emulation. We learn also from the deeds of those possessed of boundless ambition (such as Caesar and Catiline) how the liberties of a free people are infringed and destroyed. "Such Writings tend to inspire us with generous Sentiments, worthy of our happy Constitution, and instill into us Principles, which will on every proper Occasion discover themselves in Defense of it; and enable us to secure our valuable Liberties and Privileges."[101]

As early as 1749 in Philadelphia, Benjamin Franklin urged the study of Greek and Roman history, which, he believed, would have the tendency "to fix in the minds of youth deep impressions of the beauty and usefulness of virtue of all kinds, public spirit, fortitude, etc."[102] But it was Lord Bolingbroke's famous "Letters on the Study and Use of History," published in 1752, that taught Americans the "exemplary theory of history," as providing lessons for moral and political instruction. "The true and proper object of this application [the study of history]," wrote Bolingbroke, "is a constant improvement in private and public virtue." It was especially the classical authors, particularly Sallust, Livy, Cicero, and Tacitus, who were "a school of private and public virtue." "History," he wrote, in what was to become one of the most quoted sentences in the eighteenth century, "is philosophy teaching by examples,"[103] a concept he borrowed admittedly from Dionysius of Halicarnassus (Bk. XI, 1.4–5). For Bolingbroke, as for most Englishmen, both Whigs and Tories, the examples of Roman virtue were the most instructive.

Of Bolingbroke John Adams said in 1813: "I have read him through, fifty years ago, and more than five times in my life, and once within five years past."[104] His views were at once transplanted to America, and immediately appropriated by William Smith (soon to be provost of the College of Philadelphia). In 1753 Smith wrote that history is "a Lesson of *Ethics* and *Politics*—an useful Rule of Conduct and Manners thro' Life . . . the History of *Greece* and *Rome*, which may be justly called the History of *Heroism, Virtue*, and *Patriotism*" and that history gives the youth "a previous acquaintance with the World, and makes them behold Virtue and Vice and all their Consequences painted in genuine colors by Historians. . . . It is History that, by presenting those bright Patterns to the eyes of Youth, awakes Emulation and calls them forth steady Patriots to fill the Offices of State."[105]

It was especially from the beginning of the Revolutionary period to the end of the eighteenth century that the moral lessons of ancient history were in men's minds and on their pens and tongues. In 1778 Jonathan Austin urged upon Americans the lesson that the ancient republics reached heights of greatness "when actuated by the principles of liberty, virtue and honor."[106] In 1780 Jonathan Mason also praised the virtue of the ancient heroes, such as Timoleon, and warned that the waning of patriotic virtue ruined Greece and Rome: "We have the experience of ages to copy from," he declared.[107] Thomas Dawes, Jr., praising the great ancient republics, proclaimed, "*America*! fairest copy of such great originals! be virtuous."[108] John Warren in 1783 expatiated on the civic virtues, which were "the means of elevating to the highest pitch of glory, those famed Republics of antiquity, which later ages have considered as the models of political perfection."[109] John Gardiner in 1785 warned that, after public virtue had raised the ancient states to greatness, luxury caused their decay.[110] In 1786 Jonathan Austin reviewed the virtues of Sparta, Athens, and Rome, and declared, "Virtues like these have shown conspicuous in America."[111] Finally, in 1798 David Tappan observed that history proves the need for moral behavior. "It is a well known fact," he declared, "that the most celebrated states and kingdoms of the earth have risen by virtue and fallen by vice. . . . The history of the ancient Republics of Greece and Rome is, in this view, peculiarly instructive to the people of America. The prosperity, declension and ruin of those states, experimentally show that virtue is the soul of republican freedom, that luxury tends to extinguish both sound morality and piety."[112]

Sparta stood high in American estimate as a virtuous, free, stable republic, characterized by frugality, public spirit, and an agricultural economy. John Dickinson and others idealized Sparta as a "brave and . . . free people."[113] Samuel Adams extolled his ideal of

Boston as a "Christian Sparta."[114] But it was Rome that was the true exemplar to Americans of virtues—and vices. Roman virtue was constantly the model held up to their eyes for imitation and inspiration,[115] and Roman vices were reiterated as the supreme warning of the dangers of excess luxury and political ambition.[116]

Particularly conducive to the inculcation of virtue was thought to be the emulation of the great men of antiquity, whose virtues were spread on the glorious pages of Plutarch's *Lives*, the most widely read classical work. In 1768, for example, the *Virginia Gazette* enlarged on the virtues of ancient heroes who fought for liberty, especially the Romans. "That we may secure this valuable blessing, and learn the greatness of its worth, let me, with all respect earnestly beg leave to recommend to my countrymen, especially the younger part of it, a thorough acquaintance with these records of illustrious liberty, the histories of *Greece* and *Rome*; from whence they will imbibe a just hatred of tyranny and zeal for freedom. Let them study well the godlike actions of those heroes and patriots, whose lives are delivered down to us by Plutarch, that they may be inspired with a glorious emulation of those virtues, which have immortalized their names."[117] "Light-Horse Harry" Lee at the end of the century advised his son Carter at Harvard to "dwell on the virtues, & imitate, so far as lies in your power, the great & good men whom history presents to your view—Lycurgus, Solon, Numa, Hannibal."[118] Samuel Adams, too, had his Roman heroes—among them Brutus and Cincinnatus, "that Roman Hero and Patriot."[119] Alexander Hamilton had his models, using the names of some of them as his pseudonyms from 1784 to 1803: Phocion, Cicero, Camillus, Pericles. The use of these four reveals Hamilton's own estimate of his destiny at various times: all were men of heroic virtue, and all four were misjudged and persecuted by their people.[120]

Side by side with this dominant view in the early national period, that the classical authors and the study of Roman and Greek history were exemplary vehicles for cultivating virtue, voices were heard assailing the classical curriculum. Fears were expressed that Americans were being exposed to pagan thought to the detriment of Christian morality. For example, in 1773 Jonathan Boucher, that arch-Tory, deplored the fact that many educated Americans had been "lost and undone by the habit, first acquired at school, of reading only Classics: instead of loving Christian verity and purity, they have been contented to grope and grovel in the darkness and filth of Heathenism."[121] In 1769 a Latin teacher, John Wilson, in the Friends Academy in Philadelphia (now William Penn Charter

School), resigned his post because of disaffection with the exclusive curriculum in dead languages and with the content of the classical authors read in school—Ovid, Horace, Juvenal, Vergil. These, he thundered, are not fit for the youth, for they "promote Ignorance, Lewdness & Profanity in our Youth . . . and are shocking to every system of Morality."[122] Many Quakers were never reconciled to the study of the learned languages and the classical authors. That gentle schoolmaster of Philadelphia, Anthony Benezet, opposed their study as corruptive of the morals of the youth. A "prodigious hurt" is done by the "Heathen Authors" studied at school, especially Ovid, Vergil, Homer, for these nourish "mad notions of heroism" and the spirit of war. "Their chief tendency," he anguished, "is to find the corrupt passions of the Human heart by raising a desire so contrary to what we as a people in divine favour have been called."[123]

For other Americans the general absorption with the "Pagan moralists" was at the heart of Deism, which many distrusted. To Benjamin Rush, for example, "Deism [is] derived from partiality to Greek and Roman writers—morality enough supposed to be found in them."[124] Rush also assailed the study of some of the classical authors as "unfavorable to morals," and the study of classical mythology, too, whose stories "shock the moral faculty."[125]

The epics of Homer and Vergil especially drew impassioned fire. As early as 1726 Cotton Mather denounced Homer's treatment of the gods as opening "the Floodgates for a prodigious Inundation of Wickedness to break in upon the Nations. . . . [Homer] was one of the *greatest Apostles* the *Devil* ever had in the World."[126] Thomas Paine, too, assailed "the morality of Homer" as "a book of false glory, tending to inspire immoral and mischieveous notions of honor."[127] In 1793 Richard Beresford of Charleston rejected the *Iliad* and the *Aeneid* as vehicles for inculcating virtue in a republic, asserting that "the morals of the two great epic poems of antiquity, are bad in essentials." In our enlightened age, "no longer are the Iliad and the Aeneid perused as exemplars in moral, but in poetic, excellence."[128] At the end of the century Benjamin Latrobe, Jefferson's favorite architect, condemned the *Iliad*'s use as a school text. "It poisons the minds of young men," he wrote, "fills them with a rage for military murder and glory, and conveys no information which can ever be practically useful."[129]

In the first decade of the nineteenth century, Joel Barlow, advocate of a new original national literature with a didactic-moral-political content, devoted part of the preface of his epic, *The Col-*

umbiad (published 1807), to a critique of the ancient epics. He rejected both the moral and political tendencies of the *Iliad* and the *Aeneid*, however great they are as works of poetic genius. In particular, the *Iliad*, he objected, inflames the youth with ardor for military fame, inculcates the doctrine of the divine right of kings, and glorifies plunder and conquest, violence and war. "How much of the fatal policy of states and of the miseries and degradations of social man have been occasioned by the false notions of honor inspired by the works of Homer, it is not easy to ascertain. . . . [Homer's] existence has really proved one of the signal misfortunes of mankind." "The moral tendency of the Eneid of Virgil is nearly as pernicious as that of the works of Homer."[130]

The most perceptive criticism of the incantation of ancient virtue in America was made by a young American in 1787, William Vans Murray. In his essay "On Virtue," he assailed the idealization of antiquity as unhistorical, and rejected the excessive use of classical analogues to America, which he considered to be a unique society. Murray explicitly rejected Montesquieu's doctrine that civic virtue, combined with frugality, is essential to sustain republics. All these concepts, Murray declared, with youthful daring but indisputable accuracy, are "arguments derived from the falsely imagined character of antiquity."[131] Murray would doubtless have agreed with David Ramsay, who, in writing the history of the Revolutionary period in 1789, rejected nurture for nature in concluding that "in these times of action, classical education was found of less service than good natural parts, guided by common sense and sound judgment."[132]

The high hopes of many of the Founding Fathers that virtue could be taught through the classics and other forms of "useful knowledge," that is, that a moral community with shared values could be created, were dealt a severe blow in the turmoil of the early Federal period. The ideal—the myth, if you want—that Americans could be "republicans by nature," predisposed to and educable in the civic virtues requisite to sustain a republic, was shattered by reality. When Revolutionary ardor had cooled, to take one example, Presbyterian leaders, among others, conceding that Americans were no more blessed with virtue than other peoples, resigned themselves to social discord as inevitable in America, and accordingly made the necessary institutional adjustments in their church.[133]

John Adams's hopes for Americans as a virtuous people waned into chastened pessimism. In 1785 he wrote Elbridge Gerry on the subject of republicanism. "Our countrymen may be the nearest," he said, "but there is so much wealth among them, and such a universal rage of avarice, that I often fear they . . . will become like the rest of the world. If this appears to be their determination, it will be not worth the while of you and me to die martyrs." Later, in 1790, disillusioned by the disharmony visible in American society, he wrote to the eternally optimistic Samuel Adams: "All projects of government founded in the supposition or expectation of extraordinary degrees of Virtue are . . . chimerical."[134] Even Jefferson gradually revised his idealization of the virtues of the ancient republics. In 1819 he wrote John Adams: "When the enthusiasm . . . subsides in cool reflection, I ask myself, what was that government which the virtues of Cicero were so zealous to restore, and the ambition of Caesar to subvert. . . . Steeped in corruption, vice, and venality, as the whole nation was . . . , what could even Cicero, Cato, Brutus have done." A week or so later came Adams's reply: "I could never discover that they [the Romans] possessed much virtue, or real liberty."[135]

As Federalist thought matured, the conception of the American people as possessing, or capable of, virtue in the classical sense faded away into the books from which the dream of a nation "bottomed" on classical virtue had been drawn. As J. G. A. Pocock has expressed it, "The partial withdrawal from citizenship to pursue commerce appeared as a rebellion against virtue and its repressive demands; the republic asked too much of the individual in the form of austerity . . . and virtue, and the diversification of life by commerce and the arts offered him the world of Pericles in place of that of Lycurgus, a choice worth paying for with a little corruption."[136] It is no accident that John Quincy Adams in the first decade of the nineteenth century offered Americans his translations of two satires of Juvenal—the seventh and the thirteenth—by a classical author previously neglected by Americans.[137] In 1805 Thomas Green Fessenden wrote in his merciless satire "The Jeffersoniad":

> The character of this our nation
> 'Tis time to place on some foundation,
> Which may without deceit declare
> To all mankind just what we are.
> And if Americans are Jockies,
> If public virtue but a mock is,
> Then—"Hail Columbia! happy land!"
> Where scoundrels have the upper hand.[138]

In 1811 R. S., writing in the *Port Folio* magazine in Philadelphia, declared: "The admirer of ancient glory, who tells us with enthusiasm of the virtues of Rome, is deceived by an empty name."[139] A decade later, in 1821, the aged Gouverneur Morris, speaking before the New York Historical Society, proclaimed that Roman virtue was no longer useful for Americans.[140]

But the ideal of Americans as a virtuous people along classical lines did not die. Charles Nisbet, president of Dickinson College at the end of the eighteenth century, had written defensively: "The moral sentences with which all the works of the Classick Poets abound, make them justly valuable to all the friends of Virtue and Mankind."[141] A decade or so later, John Jay, the Cincinnatus of New York, in retirement on his farm, appreciated his own "Roman virtue" and that of Washington. Writing about Washington's *Farewell Address*, he spoke a kind of valedictory on the ideal of a virtuous people: "There have been in the world but two systems of schools of policy, the one founded on the great principles of wisdom and virtue, the other on cunning, and its various artifices. In the first belonged Washington and all the other worthies of every country who ascended to the temple of Honour through the temple of Virtue. The doctrines, maxims, and precepts of this school have been explained and inculcated by the ablest writers, ancient and modern."[142] The words of the valedictorian of the class of 1805 at the University of Pennsylvania, for all its youthful rhetoric, expressed the still widely held view that the prevailing classical education should lead to imitation of "the bright examples of virtue which these illustrious models exhibit: a liberal education would fail, indeed, if this most essential part, that of making us feel that we are subject to moral obligation, and only great if virtuous [for the public good]. Without it [i.e., virtue], who will prefer the public good to his own private interest? . . . To the false reigning principles and corrupt examples [of today], let us therefore oppose the opinions of illustrious examples of antiquity. . . . Heroes of Greece and Rome, I hail you in my country's name, here offer to you the incense arising from that noble flame which your illustrious examples have enkindled in our country."[143] And in the second decade of the century another, lesser known, American Cincinnatus, in retirement on his farm in New York State, Judge Henry Sanford, was still sanguine that "virtue is the soul of the body politic. . . . It was upon such a basis . . . , and not upon financial supports, that ancient legislators founded their admirable policy," and he was proud, it is recorded, of "this *moral rust of antiquity*."[144]

Myths do not die, especially if they validate even the most fugitive dreams of a society. Long after our many lapses from national innocence, the myth of America as a virtuous nation, conjured up in the eighteenth century from the glorified ghosts of the ancient republican "perfect models," has survived—and continues to haunt us.

This is one of our legacies from the classical world and the American Revolutionary generation. In the first century of American culture, however heterogeneous the concept of virtue may have been in a highly pluralistic religious, social, and economic environment, the struggle for independence tended to channel it unmistakably into political directions. From the Renaissance, Machiavelli had bequeathed the principle that virtue (i.e., service for the common good) was the source of the greatness of the Romans and Greeks, and that the body politic and its freedom are undermined by private interests, luxury, and corruption. This doctrine was a commonplace of seventeenth- and eighteenth-century English political philosophy, in books and periodicals readily available to Americans.[145]

From the writings of the British commonwealthmen and radical Whigs American leaders had acquired the image of the mother country as corrupt—degenerating through luxury, factionalism, political decay. Their own simpler life-style appeared as a mark of their own virtue, and the risks and high stakes in the challenge to England demanded the sacrifice of private interests for the common purpose. Thus a mix of cultural debris from the vaunted Roman republican virtues, the theory of republicanism imported from Whig political thought, and traditional Puritan ideas of regeneration produced in the political language of the Revolutionary leaders an intense concern for civic virtue and social morality.[146] The importance of virtue in the ideology of the Founding Fathers was reinforced by the teaching of Montesquieu and the Encyclopedists, that civic virtue taking precedence over private interests is essential in a modern republic, as it was in the ancient states.[147] "No virtue, no commonwealth," wrote an anonymous American.[148]

This political-ethical conception of virtue in the Revolutionary Age was proclaimed in the face of deep-seated American pragmatism and aspirations for personal advancement, a growing laissez-faire commercial ethos, the profit motive,[149] and political factionalism—all of which were destined in the early national period to replace the Revolutionary ideal of civic virtue. The changing pattern of virtue in America is reflected in the evangelical fervor and theological polemics of the early nineteenth century, and later in the middle of the century by the middle-class virtues taught in the McGuffey readers.[150]

Notes

1. Gilbert Tennent and Samuel Davies, *A General Account of the Rise and State of the College, Lately Established in the Province of New-Jersey in America* (London, 1754), cited in *American Higher Education: A Documentary History*, ed. Richard Hofstadter and Wilson Smith (Chicago, 1961), vol. I, p. 91. Tennent and Davies, leaders of the Great Awakening, were then trustees of the College of New Jersey (later Princeton); Davies became the college's fourth president, 1759–61. See *Dictionary of American Biography*, vol. V, p. 102; vol. XVIII, pp. 366–368. Similar formulations of the interdependence of virtue and knowledge for the good of the commonwealth are to be found in "Frame of Government of William Penn" ("Virtue and useful knowledge and arts" [1682]), and in a bill introduced in the Governor's Council of Maryland in 1671 ("Learning and Virtue"), in Elsie W. Clews, *Educational Legislation and Administration of the Colonial Governments*, Columbia University Contributions to Philosophy, Psychology, and Education, no. 6 (New York, 1899), pp. 278–279, 410; John Clarke, *An Essay Upon the Education of Youth in Grammar Schools*, 2nd ed. (London, 1730) ("Virtue and Knowledge"); in Wilson Smith, ed., *Theories of Education in Early America 1655–1819* (Indianapolis, 1973), p. 93; William Livingston, "Remarks on Our Intended College" [King's College, New York], in *The Independent Reflector*, by William Livingston and Others, ed. Milton M. Klein (Cambridge, Mass., 1963), p. 172 ("Virtue and Knowledge"); advertisement of the opening of King's College, 1754, in Herbert W. and Carol Schneider, *Samuel Johnson, President of King's College; His Career and Writings* (New York, 1929), vol. IV, p. 223 ("all virtuous habits and all . . . useful knowlege"). Cp. a Carolinian, *South-Carolina Gazette*, Dec. 21, 1769 ("love of virtue and abhorrence of vice"; "love of useful knowledge"); Simeon Howard, *A Sermon . . . May 31, 1780* (Boston, 1780), in *The Pulpit of the American Revolution; or, The Political Sermons of the Period of 1776*, ed. John Wingate Thornton (Boston, 1860), p. 392 ("the principles of virtue, . . . all useful knowledge"); Phillips Payson, *A Sermon . . . , May 27, 1778*, in Thornton, pp. 336–337 ("knowledge and virtue"). For the complex problem of a definition of useful knowledge in eighteenth-century America see "The Quest for Useful Knowledge in Eighteenth-Century America," Chapter II, above.
2. See, e.g., Homer H. Young, "Theory of American Education during the Revolutionary Period, 1743–1809" (Ph.D. diss., University of Texas, 1949), pp. 109–117; J. G. A. Pocock, "Civic Humanism and its Role in Anglo-American Thought," *Il Pensiero Politico* 1 (1968), pp. 180–184; Henry Steele Commager, *Jefferson, Nationalism, and the Enlightenment* (New York, 1975), p. xi ("how the eighteenth century rejoiced in 'virtue'"); J. G. A. Pocock, *The Machiavellian Moment: Florentine Political Thought and the Atlantic Republican Tradition* (Princeton, 1975), pp. 506–522 ("The Americanization of Virtue").
3. Norman S. Fiering, "President Samuel Johnson and the Circle of Knowledge," *Wm. & Mary Quart.*, 3rd ser., 28 (1971), pp. 233–234.
4. These are the views of Edwin H. Cady, *The Gentleman in America: A Literary Study in American Culture* (Syracuse, 1949), pp. 5, 12; Michael V. Belok, "The Courtesy Tradition and Early Schoolbooks," *History of Education Quarterly* 8 (1968), pp. 306–311.

5. E.g., Gordon S. Wood, *The Creation of the American Republic, 1776–1787* (Chapel Hill, 1969), pp. 53–70.
6. *Autobiography of Benjamin Franklin*, ed. Leonard W. Labaree et al. (New Haven, 1964), pp. 148–160: Temperance, Silence, Order, Resolution, Frugality, Industry, Sincerity, Justice, Moderation, Cleanliness, Tranquillity, Chastity, Humility.
7. Samuel Harrison Smith, *Remarks on Education: Illustrating the Connection between Virtue and Wisdom* (Philadelphia, 1798), in W. Smith, *Theories of Education*, pp. 292, 305.
8. *Independent Reflector*, p. 172.
9. Ben Perley Poore, comp., *The Federal and State Constitutions, Colonial Charters, and Other Organic Laws of the United States* (Washington, D.C., 1877), p. 970.
10. "Curious Dissertation on the Valuable Advantages of a Liberal Education," *New-Jersey Magazine and Monthly Advertiser*, Jan., 1787, pp. 52–53.
11. Jonathan Mason, *An Oration, Delivered at Boston, March 6, 1780* (Boston, 1780), pp. 1, 8. Cp. H[ezekiah] Niles, *Principles and Acts of the Revolution in America* (Baltimore, 1822), pp. 41–42.
12. Clinton Rossiter, *Seedtime of the Republic* (New York, 1953), pp. 137–139, 144–146, 429–437. Cp. Stow Persons, *American Minds: A History of Ideas* (New York, 1958), pp. 80, 122.
13. *The Writings of Samuel Adams*, ed. Harry Alonzo Cushing (New York, 1904–08), vol. III, pp. 235–237 (letter to Warren, Nov. 4, 1775); similarly, vol. III, pp. 245–246 (letter to Warren, Dec. 26, 1775).
14. S. Adams, *Writings*, vol. IV, pp. 124–125 (letter to Warren, Feb. 12, 1779).
15. S. Adams, *Writings*, vol. III, p. 305 (letter to Benjamin Kent, July 27, 1776).
16. S. Adams, *Writings*, vol. IV, p. 108 (letter to Samuel Cooper, Dec. 25, 1778); cp. vol. III, p. 286.
17. S. Adams, *Writings*, vol. IV, p. 347 (letter to John Adams, Nov. 25, 1790).
18. Adams Family Papers, microfilm reel 187, Massachusetts Historical Society, Boston, from Joseph Butler, *The Analogy of Religion* (London, 1736; 3rd ed., 1740). Cp. John R. Howe, Jr., *The Changing Political Thought of John Adams* (Princeton, 1966), Frontispiece and p. 31.
19. Letter to Mercy Warren, Jan. 8, 1776, in *Warren-Adams Letters*, Massachusetts Historical Society Collections, nos. 72–73 (Boston, 1917–25), vol. I, p. 202. Cp. "Discourses on Davila," in which he expressed the view that all hopes of liberty depend on both public virtue and balanced government (*The Works of John Adams* [Boston, 1850–56], vol. VI, p. 399).
20. *Adams Family Correspondence*, ed. L. H. Butterfield (Cambridge, Mass., 1963–70), vol. I, p. 317 (letter dated Oct. 29, 1775).
21. *Warren-Adams Letters*, vol. I, p. 222 (letter to Mercy Warren, Apr. 16, 1776). Cp. Howe, *Thought of John Adams*, pp. 28–58 ("A Virtuous People"), p. 88.
22. Gerald Stourzh, *Alexander Hamilton and the Idea of Republican Government* (Stanford, 1970), pp. 63–75, esp. pp. 63–65.
23. Letter to Robert Skipwith, Aug. 3, 1771, in *Papers of Thomas Jefferson*, ed. Julian P. Boyd (Princeton, 1950–), vol. I, pp. 76–77.
24. Cited by Cady, *Gentleman in America*, p. 93.
25. *Washington's Farewell Address: The View from the Twentieth Century*, ed. Burton I. Kaufman (Chicago, 1969), p. 25.
26. Wood, *American Republic*, pp. 65–70 ("The Need for Virtue"); Stourzh, *Alexander Hamilton*, pp. 63–75 ("Virtue as the Principle of Republican Government"); [Richard Beresford], *A Plea for Literature, More Especially Literature of Free States* (Charleston, 1795), pp. 1–2.
27. Cited by Wood, *American Republic*, p. 95.

28. Cited by Paul M. Spurlin, *Montesquieu in America 1760–1801* (University, La., 1940), pp. 261–262.
29. Montesquieu, *The Spirit of the Laws*, trans. Thomas Nugent (Cincinnati, 1873), vol. I, pp. xxx, 23–24, 29–41, 47; Thomas L. Pangle, *Montesquieu's Philosophy of Liberalism: A Commentary on the Spirit of the Laws* (Chicago, 1973), pp. 57–59, 65, 85–86; Howard Mumford Jones, *O Strange New World: American Culture: The Formative Years* (New York, 1952), pp. 255–258; Spurlin, *Montesquieu in America*, pp. 223–257, 261.
30. See, e.g., Young, "Theory of American Education," pp. 109–117; Guy H. Miller, "A Contracting Community: American Presbyterian Social Conflict and Higher Education 1730–1830" (Ph.D. diss, University of Michigan, 1970; *Diss. Abstr.* XXXI [1971], p. 6513); Wood, *American Republic*, p. 426; Margaret W. Masson, "The Premises and Purposes of Higher Education in American Society, 1745–1770" (Ph.D. diss., University of Washington, 1971; *Diss. Abstr.* XXXII [1972], p. 6346); Kate M. Rowland, *The Life of Charles Carroll of Carrollton 1737–1832* (New York, 1898), vol. I, pp. 20–22 (letter of Oct. 10, 1753, from his father, with encouragement to excellence in virtue and learning); Michael V. Belok, "Forming the American Character: Essayists and Schoolbooks," *Social Science* 43 (1968), pp. 12–21. Typical sermons with advocacy of political virtue: Simeon Howard, *A Sermon . . . at Boston, May 31, 1780* (Boston, 1780), who declared, "Youth is the time to plant the mind with the principles of virtue, truth and honor, the love of liberty and of their country, and to furnish it with all useful knowledge"; Phillips Payson, *A Sermon . . . at Boston, May 27, 1778* (Boston, 1778), both in Thornton, *Pulpit of American Revolution*, pp. 336–337, 392.
31. Letters to James Warren, in S. Adams, *Writings*, vol. III, pp. 235–237 (Nov. 4, 1775); vol. III, pp. 245–246 (Dec. 26, 1775); vol. IV, pp. 124–125 (Feb. 12, 1779).
32. Noah Webster, "Education," *American Magazine*, Dec., 1787, pp. 232–236; also in *A Collection of Essays and Fugitiv Writings. On Moral, Historical, Political and Literary Subjects* (Boston, 1780), pp. 1–37; and in Frederick Rudolph, ed., *Essays on Education in the Early Republic* (Cambridge, Mass., 1965), pp. 41–77.
33. John Clarke, *An Essay Upon the Education of Youth in Grammar Schools*, 2nd ed. (London, 1730), in W. Smith, *Theories of Education*, pp. 63–64, 92–93.
34. [Robert Dodsley], *The Preceptor*, 7th ed. (London, 1783; 1st ed. 1748). The Preface, vol. I, pp. ii–v, addressed to Prince George, concludes: "may YOUR ROYAL HIGHNESS employ this early Years and most proper Season of your Life in adorning your Mind with useful Knowledge, in warming your Heart with the Love of Virtue." On Dodsley see n. 97, below.
35. *Independent Reflector*, p. 172. The date is March 22, 1753.
36. *Independent Reflector*, p. 424. Cp. the similar statement in Noah Webster, *Elements of Useful Knowledge, I* (Hartford, 1802), Preface.
37. R. D. W. Connor, Louis R. Wilson, and Hugh T. Lefler, eds., *A Documentary History of the University of North Carolina, 1776–1799* (Chapel Hill, 1953), vol. I, p. 218.
38. [Ovid], *Epist. Sapph., Heroides* 15.83. It was used, e.g., by John Witherspoon, famous president of the College of New Jersey (1768–94). See Richard M. Gummere, "A Scottish Classicist in Colonial America," *Publ. Colon. Soc. Mass.,* vol. XXXV (1947), *Transactions,* 1942–46, p. 157.
39. Henry Steele Commager, "Leadership in Eighteenth-Century America and Today," *Daedalus* 90 (1961), p. 670.
40. *A History of American Literature During the Colonial Time* (New York, 1897), vol. II, p. 310.

41. Cited by Thomas H. Boyd, *Light-Horse Harry Lee* (New York, 1931), pp. 336–337.
42. *Adams Family Correspondence*, vol. IV, p. 117 (May 18, 1781). Cp. Oliver Goldsmith, *Miscellaneous Essays* (London, 1764), no. 13 ("Cultivation of Taste," 1762). Goldsmith expatiates on the value of the study of the classics, as the result of which through "striking instances of superior virtue . . . culled for the perusal of the young pupil, who will read them with eagerness, and revolve them with pleasure . . . the young mind becomes enamoured of moral beauty. . . . In reading Cornelius Nepos and Plutarch's *Lives*, even with a view to grammatical improvement only, he will insensibly imbibe, and learn to compare, ideas of great importance. He will become enamoured of virtue and patriotism, and acquire a detestation of vice, cruelty, and corruption." In the last years of his life Goldsmith produced a *Roman History* (1769) and a *Grecian History* (1774), both of which were well received and studied by Americans. These "pot boilers" were embellished with moral reflections, particularly on the evils of luxury, overexpansion, and commercial enterprise. See Meyer Reinhold, *The Classick Pages: Classical Reading of Eighteenth-Century Americans* (University Park, Pa., 1975), pp. 184–186. See further on the role of the classics in fostering virtue in American education: Gummere, "A Scottish Classicist," p. 152; Wood, *American Republic*, pp. 48–53 ("The Appeal of Antiquity"); Joseph J. Ellis, *The New England Mind in Transition: Samuel Johnson of Connecticut, 1696-1772* (New Haven, 1973), p. 239; Henry Steele Commager, "The American Enlightenment and the Ancient World: A Study in Paradox," *Proc. Mass. Hist. Soc.* 83 (1971), pp. 9–10, 15 (=*Jefferson, Nationalism, and the Enlightenment* [New York, 1975], pp. 123–129).
43. "Curious Dissertation" (see n. 10, above), pp. 52–54.
44. "Observations on the Utility of the Latin and Greek Languages, *in a Series of Letters*," *New-York Magazine* 1 (1790), pp. 510–512 (see also pp. 276–277, 347–359, 396–398, 467–469, 585–588, 634–646). Cp. "The Dead Languages," by Onkelos in *Massachusetts Magazine* 8 (1796), p. 420 ("all these brilliant virtues, which have rendered the ancients the admiration of the world"); *South-Carolina Gazette*, Dec. 21, 1796 (the study of the classics instills "the first principles of honour and equity," and "love of virtue and abhorrence of Vice," as well as "love of useful knowledge"); *Independent Reflector*, p. 425 ("The Books [i.e., classics] read at School are full of incitements to Virtue, and Discouragements from Vice," quoting Jonathan Swift).
45. Charles Chauncy, *God's Mercy, Shewed to his People, In Giving Them a Faithfull Ministry and Schooles of Learning, for the Continued Suppleys Thereof* (Cambridge, Mass., 1665), in W. Smith, *Theories of Education*, pp. 5–6. Cp. Kenneth B. Murdock, *Literature and Theology in Colonial New England* (Cambridge, Mass., 1949), p. 68.
46. "The Classical Tradition in Colonial Virginia," *Papers of the Bibliographical Society of America* 33 (1939), p. 96. "But," Wright adds, "no one in this day can say how great was this influence." Cp. Richard Beale Davis, *Intellectual Life of Jefferson's Virginia, 1790-1830* (Chapel Hill, 1964), p. 6. Henri Peyre, *L'Influence des littératures antiques sur le littérature française moderne: États des Travaux* (New Haven, 1941), pp. 13–14, finds the moral influence of classical writers on moderns to have been profound: "C'est peut-être le cas le plus frappant que l'histoire ait jamais enregistré de l'action de la littérature sur la vie" ("It is perhaps the most striking case that history has ever recorded of the impact of literature on life").
47. Francis Hopkinson, *Science. A Poem* (Philadelphia, 1762), in *The Miscellaneous Essays and Occasional Writings* (Philadelphia, 1792), vol. III, pp. 92–101, lines 67–68. Hopkinson in his dedication quotes Horace *Odes* 4.4: *Doctrina sed vim promovet insitam, / Rectique cultus pectora roborant* ("But

education enhances inborn ability, and proper training strengthens the heart").
Cp. John Adams's interest in these lines, p. 151, above.

48. John L. Sibley and Clifford K. Shipton, *Biographical Sketches of Graduates of Harvard University* (Cambridge, Mass., 1873–), vol. X, p. 238.

49. *The Literary Bible of Thomas Jefferson: His Commonplace Book of Philosophers and Poets* (Baltimore, 1928), p. 4.

50. Gilbert Chinard, *Thomas Jefferson: The Apostle of Americanism*, 2nd ed. (Boston, 1939; rpt. 1949), pp. 24–25.

51. Chinard, *Literary Bible*. Jefferson also recorded passages from Herodotus, Livy, Vergil, Terence, Ovid, Anacreon, Statius, Manilius, Quintus of Smyrna. Cp. Gilbert Chinard, "Thomas Jefferson as a Classical Scholar," *American Scholar* 1 (1932), pp. 139–140; Louis B. Wright, "Thomas Jefferson and the Classics," *Proc. Amer. Philos. Soc.* 87 (1943–44), p. 228.

52. Chinard, *Literary Bible*, p. 11. Cp. Reinhold, *The Classick Pages*, pp. 143–144.

53. Letter to Peter Carr, Aug. 19, 1785, in *Papers of Thomas Jefferson*, ed. Julian P. Boyd (Princeton, 1950–), vol. VIII, pp. 407–408. Later in life he was passionately hostile to Plato's thought (cp. Reinhold, *The Classick Pages*, pp. 114–115).

54. *Writings of Thomas Jefferson*, Memorial Edition (Washington, D.C., 1905), vol. XV, p. 209.

55. Cp. the widely used children's book, *Sententiae Pueriles*, by Leonard Colman (Boston, 1723), with English translations by Charles Hoole.

56. Strasburg, 1784 (new ed., Leipzig, 1817). This book contained selections (with Latin verse translations) of Theognis, Callinus, Tyrtaeus, Mimnermus, Solon, Phocylides, Simonides, Pythagoras' Golden Verses, Callimachus, Hesiod's *Works and Days*, Cleanthes' *Hymn to Zeus*, the *Gnomae Monostichoi* (one-line maxims), as well as a number of minor gnomic poets. In 1813 John Adams quoted with enthusiasm four lines of Theognis, probably from this collection, and commented, "Has Science or Morals, or Philosophy, or Criticism, or Christianity, advanced or improved [on Theognis' concept]?" See *The Adams-Jefferson Letters*, ed. Lester J. Cappon (Chapel Hill, 1959), vol. II, p. 352; Susan Ford [Wiltshire], "Thomas Jefferson and John Adams on the Classics," *Arion* 6 (Spring 1967), pp. 122–123.

57. *Adams-Jefferson Letters*, vol. II, p. 352; Ford [Wiltshire], "Thomas Jefferson and John Adams," p. 119.

58. Cp. Adrian A. Holtz, *A Study of the Moral and Religious Elements in American Secondary Education up to 1800* (Menasha, 1917), pp. 48, 69–70; Howard Mumford Jones, *Revolution & Romanticism* (Cambridge, Mass., 1974), p. 124.

59. See Reinhold, *The Classick Pages*, pp. 65–80.

60. *Diary and Autobiography of John Adams*, ed. L. H. Butterfield (Cambridge, Mass., 1962), vol. I, p. 73 (entry of Jan., 1759). See also Adams's youthful literary commonplace book, which contains excerpts from Sallust, Cicero, Horace, Vergil (Adams Family Papers, microfilm reel 187).

61. 13th ed. (London, 1786), Dedication. Cp. Reinhold, *The Classick Pages*, pp. 31–33. Another popular version was that of Sir Roger L'Estrange, *Fables of Aesop and Other Eminent Mythologists: with Morals and Reflections*, 7th ed. (London, 1724), Preface: "the Foundations of Knowledge and Virtue are laid in our Childhood. [Fables help] toward the forming of an honourable and virtuous Life." See also Adams Family Papers, microfilm reel 218, which contains John Quincy Adams's French translation of the fables of Phaedrus in 1781.

62. *Cato's Moral Distichs, Englished in Couplets* (Philadelphia, 1735); Cp. Reinhold, *The Classick Pages*, pp. 33–35. Franklin also published Logan's translation of Cicero's *Cato Major*, in 1733 (Reinhold, pp. 60–62).

63. Cp. Reinhold, *The Classick Pages*, pp. 54–58; the popular translation of the eighteenth century by Thomas Cockman, *Tully's Three Books of Offices*, 5th ed. (London, 1732); Ellis, *The New England Mind*, p. 226.

64. Cp. Reinhold, *The Classick Pages*, pp. 58–60.

65. Cited by Richard M. Gummere, "Classical Precedents in the Writings of James Wilson," *Publ. Colon. Soc. Mass.*, vol. XXXII (1938), *Transactions*, 1933–37, p. 526.

66. See n. 56, above.

67. "The Golden Verses of Pythagoras: More Marginal Notes of John Adams," *More Books*, Bulletin of the Boston Public Library, 6th ser., 1 (1926), pp. 106–110; Zoltán Haraszti, *John Adams and the Prophets of Progress* (Cambridge, Mass., 1952), p. 302.

68. See Reinhold, *The Classick Pages*, pp. 65–68. For the importance of the Choice of Hercules in American moral thought see pp. 153–154 above.

69. Cp. Reinhold, *The Classick Pages*, pp. 68–70.

70. *Adams Family Correspondence*, vol. IV, p. 80 (letter to John Quincy Adams, Feb. 12, 1781).

71. Adams Family Papers, microfilm reel 188.

72. Cp. Reinhold, *The Classick Pages*, pp. 70–73.

73. Adams Family Papers, microfilm reel 188.

74. Cited by Robert Middlekauff, *Ancients and Axioms: Secondary Education in Eighteenth Century New England* (New Haven, 1963), p. 192.

75. Letter to William Short, Oct. 31, 1819, in Jefferson, *Writings*, vol. XV, p. 220. Especially popular was Sir Roger L'Estrange's *Seneca's Morals*, an adaptation of the pagan philosopher's thought "by way of abstract." Cp. Reinhold, *The Classick Pages*, pp. 73–76.

76. See Reinhold, *The Classick Pages*, pp. 76–79. In 1783 Ezra Stiles, president of Yale, in an "Election Sermon" declared: "How much soever we may admire the morals of Plato and Epictetus, they are not to be compared with those taught by Moses and the divine Jesus." (Thornton, *Pulpit of American Revolution*, p. 502). It was the moral message of Epictetus that enthralled Walt Whitman a few generations later. He said of the *Enchiridion* of Epictetus, "I have carried this [book] with me for years . . . Epictetus . . . is a universe in himself. He sets me free in a flood of light." Cited by Richard M. Gummere, "Walt Whitman and his Reaction to the Classics," *Harvard Studies in Classical Philology* 60 (1951), pp. 275–276.

77. Henry Peacham, *The Compleat Gentleman* (1st ed. 1622; London, 1637), p. 72.

78. *Mémoires de Madame Roland*, new ed. (Paris, 1905), vol. II, p. 185. (The translation is mine.)

79. See Reinhold, *The Classick Pages*, pp. 39–47. Cp. Harold T. Parker, *The Cult of Antiquity and the French Revolutionaries* (Chicago, 1937; rpt. 1965), pp. 3, 39, 63; Commager, "American Enlightenment," pp. 9–10.

80. Adams Family Papers, microfilm reel 222.

81. Claude M. Newlin, ed., *Modern Chivalry* (New York, 1962), p. 433.

82. From his essay "Heroism," in *Essays and Poems of Emerson*, ed. Stuart P. Sherman (New York, 1921), p. 199.

83. See Reinhold, *The Classick Pages*, pp. 98–106.

84. Reinhold, *The Classick Pages*, pp. 99–101, 106–111.

85. Jefferson, *Writings*, vol. XVIII, p. 255.

86. *Adams-Jefferson Letters*, vol. II, p. 462; Ford [Wiltshire], "Thomas Jefferson and John Adams," p. 117.

87. William Staughton, *An Eulogium in Memory of the Late Dr. Benjamin Rush* (Philadelphia, 1813), p. 14.

88. Adams Family Papers, microfilm reels 188, 220, 230.

89. Ibid., reel 238.

90. *The Monthly Anthology* 1 (1804), 225–227, quoting at length William Barrow, *Essays on Education* (London, 1802); [George Tucker, the future American historian], "On Classical Education," in *Essays on Various Subjects of Taste, Morals, and National Policy*, By a Citizen of Virginia (Georgetown, 1822), p. 106 (written in 1813); John Bristead, *America and Her Resources* (London, 1818), p. 347; Henry Wheaton, "Life of William Pinkney," in *Library of American Biography*, ed. Jared Sparks, 1st ser., vol. VI (Boston, 1835), p. 76.

91. Joseph G. Cogswell and George Bancroft, *Prospectus of a School to be Established at Round Hill, Northampton, Massachusetts* (Cambridge, Mass., 1823); idem, *Some Account of the School for Liberal Education of Boys Established in Round Hill, Northampton, Massachusetts* (Northampton, 1826): "Here is the reason, why the ancient orators, poets, and philosophers are still read. Moral truths are eternal ones." Cp. James McLachlan, *American Boarding Schools: A Historical Study* (New York, 1970), pp. 71–101, on Cogswell and Bancroft's famous school.

92. *Diary and Autobiography of John Adams*, vol. I, p. 72. Cp. vol. II, p. 75 (Dec. 31, 1772); *Defence of the Constitutions of Government of the United States of America*, in John Adams, *Works*, vol. VI, pp. 206–207.

93. *Adams Family Correspondence*, vol. II, pp. 96–97 (letter by Abigail Adams, Aug. 14, 1776). Cp. Butterfield, Introduction to vol. II, pp. ix–x, for detailed description of the engraving, and pl. 5. Adams saw the engraving in Anthony A. Cooper, Earl of Shaftesbury, *Characteristicks of Men, Manner, Opinions, Times,* 5th ed. (Birmingham, 1773), vol. III, p. 347.

94. *Adams Family Correspondence*, vol. III, p. 333 (letter from John Adams to Abigail, from Paris, April–May, 1780). The favorite Humanist theme the Choice of Hercules, or Hercules at the Crossroads, had been treated in many works of literature, music, and art since 1515. It was especially popular in the eighteenth century. See, e.g., Metastasio's opera *Alcide al Bivio* (1760); Handel's *Hercules* (1745); Wieland's *Die Wahl des Herkules* (1773). There were many representations in art, from the *Stultifera Navis* (1497) of Sebastian Brand on, including paintings by Lucas Cranach, Rubens, Veronese, Carracci, and more than a few in the eighteenth century. See Erwin Panofsky, *Hercules am Scheidewege*, Studien der Bibliothek Warburg, vol. XVIII (Leipzig, 1930), pp. vii, 39, 134–137, and pls. 30–97 (pl. 77 is the engraving of Gribelin, after Paolo de Matteis); C. Karl Galinsky, *The Herakles Theme* (Totowa, N.J., 1972), pp. 101–113, 198–200.

95. Cited by Neil Harris, *The Artist in American Society: The Formative Years 1796–1860* (New York, 1966), p. 36 (cp. p. 28). On the pervasive didacticism and moralism of John Adams's philosophy of the fine arts and literature see Wendell D. Garrett, "John Adams and the Limited Role of the Fine Arts," *Winterthur Portfolio* 1 (1964), pp. 243–255. Cp. James Thomas Flexner, "George Washington as an Art Collector," *American Art Journal* 4, no. 1 (1972), pp. 24–35; Fiske Kimball, "Jefferson Among the Arts," *Proc. Amer. Philos. Soc.* 87 (1943–44), pp. 238–245, in which Jefferson's choice of many classical subjects to adorn Monticello, picked for their moralizing character, is discussed. A striking example of the contemporary caution regarding the arts as luxuries dangerous to republicanism is the experience of Josiah Quincy, Jr. When he was in England in 1774–75, he visited a Colonel Barré, who showed him engravings of the ruins of Herculaneum, and said about such books: "let them get aboard and you are ruined. They will infuse a taste for buildings and sculpture, and when a people get a taste for the fine arts, they are ruined." See Sibley, *Harvard Graduates* (n. 48, above), vol. XV, p. 490; "Diary of Josiah Quincy, Jr., *Proc. Mass. Hist. Soc.* 50 (1916–17), p. 451 (entry of Jan 2, 1775); Josiah Quincy, *Memoir of the Life of Josiah Quincy, Jun. of Massachusetts* (Boston, 1825), pp. 289–290.

96. Adams Family Papers, microfilm reel 6.
97. Ibid., reel 219 (*Poetical Commonplace Book*), pp. 8–22. See "The Choice of *Hercules*," in 27 stanzas, preceded by an engraving of the allegory in [Robert Dodsley], *The Preceptor*, 7th ed. (1st ed. 1748; London, 1783), vol. II, pp. 534–555. Dodsley reports that this version is "here cloathed in a New Dress by a very eminent Hand" (p. 544). On Dodsley, English poet, dramatist, bookseller, see *Dictionary of National Biography*, vol. V, pp. 1075–1079.
98. James McLachlan, "*The Choice of Hercules*: American Student Societies in the Early 19th Century," in *The University in Society*, ed. Lawrence Stone (Princeton, 1974), vol. II, pp. 449–450, 488–492. The American-born painter Benjamin West, who turned to classical themes (historical and mythological) when he went abroad, painted *The Choice of Hercules* in 1764. See Grose Evans, *Benjamin West and the Taste of His Times* (Carbondale, 1959), pp. 424–427. Cp. James T. Flexner, "Benjamin West's American Neo-Classicism," *N.Y. Historical Society Quarterly* 36 (1952), pp. 5–41.
99. Henry D. Sheldon, *Student Life and Customs* (New York, 1901), p. 132.
100. Philip Wharton, in *True Briton*, Sept. 9, 1723, cited by Roland N. Stromberg, "History in the Eighteenth Century," *Journal of the History of Ideas* 12 (1951), pp. 295–304, esp. p. 302. Cp. Edward Manwaring, *An Historical and Critical Account of the Most Eminent Classic Authors* (London, 1737), pp. 357–365 ("History"); Carl L. Becker, *The Heavenly City of the Eighteenth-Century Philosophers* (New Haven, 1932), pp. 92–93; James W. Johnson, *The Formation of English Neo-Classical Thought* (Princeton, 1967), pp. 3–105 (the roles of historiography, Greece, Rome). For the eighteenth-century best-sellers among modern works on Roman and Greek history and their dominant emphases, see Reinhold, *The Classick Pages*, pp. 16–18, 155–214. Enormously popular in America for a century were the works of Charles Rollin, *Ancient History* and *Roman History*, which, besides recounting political events, emphasized history as providing exemplary lessons of virtue and vice.
101. Phil-Eleutherus, in *Maryland Gazette*, June 7, 1745.
102. Benjamin Franklin, "Proposals Relating to the Education of Youth in Pennsylvania" (1749), in Thomas Woody, *The Educational Views of Benjamin Franklin* (New York, 1931), p. 167.
103. Lord Bolingbroke, *Historical Writings*, ed. Isaac Kramnick (Chicago, 1972), pp. xvi, xxiii, 8; George H. Nadel, "Philosophy of History Before Historicism," in *Studies in the Philosophy of History: Selected Essays from History and Theory*, ed. George H. Nadel (New York, 1965), pp. 51, 65, 70.
104. John Adams, *Works*, vol. X, p. 82 (letter to Jefferson).
105. William Smith, *A General Idea of the College of Mirania* (New York, 1753), pp. 27–29, 76. Smith also borrowed from Bolingbroke, without so indicating, the famous words: "the Knowledge of what tends neither directly nor indirectly to make better Men and better Citizens, is but a Knowledge of Trifles, it is not learning but a specious and ingenious sort of Idleness" (p. 11). See Bolingbroke, *Historical Writings*, p. 8, where he attributes the last phrase ("specious . . . Idleness") to Tillotson.
106. *Oration, Delivered at Boston, March 5, 1778*, in Niles, *Principles and Acts*, p. 32.
107. *Oration Delivered at Boston, March 6, 1780* (Boston, 1780), pp. 8–9, 13–14, 21; Niles, *Principles and Acts*, pp. 42–44.
108. *Oration Delivered at Boston, March 5, 1781*, Niles, *Principles and Acts*, p. 55.
109. *An Oration Delivered July 4th, 1783* (Boston, 1783), pp. 6–8.
110. *An Oration Delivered July 4th, 1785* (Boston, 1785), pp. 8–9.
111. *An Oration Delivered July 4th, 1786* (Boston, 1786), p. 17.
112. *A Discourse Delivered to the Religious Society in Brattle Street, Boston*, 2nd ed. (Boston, 1798), pp. 18–19. Cp. also the early nineteenth-century emphases on

virtue and republicanism in Abijah Bigelow, *The Voters' Guide* (Leominster, Mass., 1803), pp. 13, 149; William Tudor, "A Discourse Intended to Have Been Delivered Before the Society of Phi Beta Kappa., Aug. 30, 1810)," *Monthly Anthology* 9 (1810), p. 152 ("The history of ancient nations may be made . . . useful to inculcate lessons of morality in youthful minds").

113. E.g., R. T. Halsey, ed., *Letters from a Farmer of Pennsylvania* (New York, 1903), p. 30. The date is 1768.

114. Cited by Wood, *American Republic*, p. 118. Cp. Howard Mumford Jones, *Revolution & Romanticism* (Cambridge, Mass., 1974), pp. 136–137. Elizabeth Rawson, *The Spartan Tradition in European Thought* (Oxford, 1969), p. 368 ("Note on the United States"), is superficial.

115. E.g., by Onkelos, "The Dead Languages," *Masssachusetts Magazine* 8 (1796), 475; Howard Mumford Jones, *O Strange New World. American Culture: The Formative Years* (New York, 1964), pp. 227–272 ("Roman Virtues"); Clinton Rossiter, *Seedtime of the Republic* (New York, 1953), pp. 138, 276, 430; Donald C. Earl, "Virtue and Politics: Rome and the Renaissance," in *Valeurs antiques et temps modernes. Classical Values and the Modern World*, ed. Étienne Gareau (Ottawa, 1972), pp. 141–180; Werner Eisenhut, *Virtus Romana* (Munich, 1973).

116. E.g., *Adams Family Correspondence*, vol. III, p. 26 (Abigail Adams to John Thaxter, May 21, 1778); *The Works of James Wilson*, ed. Robert C. McCloskey (Cambridge, Mass., 1967), vol. II, p. 777; S. Adams, *Writings*, vol. III, p. 286 (letter to John Scollay, April 30, 1776).

117. *Virginia Gazette* (Rind), March 3, 1768.

118. Boyd, *Light-Horse Harry Lee*, p. 336.

119. S. Adams, *Writings*, vol. II, p. 251; vol. IV, pp. 213–214 (letter to James Warren, Oct. 24, 1780). On George Washington, "the Cincinnatus of the West," as a classical hero, cp. Marcus Cunliffe, *George Washington, Man and Monument* (Boston, 1958), pp. 190–197 ("The Classical Code").

120. [Douglass Adair], "A Note on Certain of Hamilton's Pseudonyms," *Wm. & Mary Quart.*, 3d ser., 12 (1955), pp. 282–297.

121. "On American Education" (1773), in Jonathan Boucher, *A View of the Causes and Consequences of the American Revolution, in Thirteen Discourses, Preached in North America between the Years 1763 and 1775* (London, 1797; rpt. 1967), p. 199.

122. Wilson's letter of resignation, Dec. 28, 1769, in James Mulhern, *A History of Secondary Education in Pennsylvania* (Philadelphia, 1933), p. 44.

123. George S. Brookes, *Friend Anthony Benezet* (Philadelphia, 1937), pp. 389–390 (letter of Benezet to John Pemberton, May 29, 1783).

124. *Autobiography of Benjamin Rush*, ed. George W. Corner, *Mem. Amer. Philos. Soc.*, vol. XXV (Philadelphia, 1948), p. 347. Cp. *Letters of Benjamin Rush*, ed. L. H. Butterfield (Princeton, 1951), vol. I, p. 518; Charles Backus, *A Sermon Preached in Long-Meadow at the Public Fast, April 17th, 1788* (Springfield, 1788), pp. 14–15.

125. Benjamin Rush, "An Enquiry into the Utility of a Knowledge of the Latin and Greek Languages," *American Museum* 5 (June 1789), pp. 525–533 (=*Essays, Literary, Moral and Philosophical* [Philadelphia, 1798]), pp. 21–56; "Opponents of Classical Learning in America during the Revolutionary Period," Chapter IV, above. "The Quest for Useful Knowledge in Eighteenth-Century America," Chapter II, above; David Freeman Hawke, *Benjamin Rush, Revolutionary Gadfly* (Indianapolis, 1971), pp. 358–380 ("Reforms in the Cause of Virtue").

126. *Manductio ad Ministerium. Dissertation for a Candidate of the Ministry.* (Boston, 1726), p. 39.

127. From "The Age of Reason" (1794), in *The Complete Writings of Thomas Paine*, ed. Philip Foner (New York, 1945), vol. I, p. 543. Paine here also questions even the use of Aesop's fables to teach children moral truths, because, he said, "the cruelty of the fables does more injury to the heart, especially in a child, than the moral does good to the judgment."

128. [Richard Beresford], *A Plea for Literature, More Especially the Literature of Free States* (Charleston, 1793), pp. 29–30.

129. Benjamin Henry Latrobe, *The Journal of Latrobe* (New York, 1905), p. 74.

130. Joel Barlow, *The Columbiad* (Philadelphia, 1809), vol. I, pp. v–vii; vol. II, pp. 194–195. The transformation of Barlow's thought in the two decades from 1787–1807 into a Jeffersonian Deist and passionate American nationalist colored his view of his mission as American poet and his attitude toward the classics. In the original version of his poem, *The Vision of Columbus* (1787) there was no assault on Homer and Vergil. On Barlow's thought and *The Columbiad* see Arthur L. Ford, *Joel Barlow* (New York, 1971), pp. 74–84; James Woodress, *A Yankee's Odyssey: The Life of Joel Barlow* (Philadelphia, 1958), pp. 245–250.

131. William Vans Murray, "On Virtue," in *Political Sketches* (London, 1787), printed also in *American Museum* 2 (Sept. 1787), pp. 228–235. Cp. Alexander de Conde, "William Vans Murray's *Political Sketches:* A Defense of the American Experiment," *Mississippi Valley Historical Review* 41 (1954–55), pp. 623–640; *Dictionary of American Biography*, vol. XIII, pp. 368–369.

132. David Ramsay, *The History of the American Revolution* (Philadelphia, 1789), vol. II, p. 316. On Ramsay, see *Dictionary of American Biography*, vol. XV, pp. 338–339; *David Ramsay, 1749–1815: Selections from his Writings*, ed. Robert L. Brunhouse, *Trans. Amer. Philos. Soc.*, n.s., vol. LV, pt. 4 (Philadelphia, 1965).

133. Guy H. Miller, "Contracting Community."

134. *North American Review* 28 (1829), p. 57; John R. Howe, Jr., *The Changing Political Thought of John Adams* (Princeton, 1966), p. 164; see also pp. 28–58, 136, 156–161.

135. Jefferson, *Writings*, vol. XV, pp. 232, 237.

136. Pocock, *The Machiavellian Moment*, pp. 551–552. Cp. William Biglow, *Education: A Poem, Spoken at Cambridge at the Request of Phi Beta Kappa, July 18th, 1799* (Salem, 1799), p. 11: "But wealth increas'd and Luxury was bred, / And virtue, knowledge and religion fled."

137. *Port Folio* 1 (1801), pp. 6–8; 5 (1805), pp. 150–152. See Linda K. Kerber and Walter J. Morris, "Politics and Literature: The Adams Family and the *Port Folio*," *Wm. & Mary Quart.*, 3rd ser., 23 (1966), pp. 450–476.

138. Christopher Caustic [Thomas Green Fessenden], *Democracy Unveiled, or Tyranny Stripped of the Garb of Patriotism*, 2nd ed. (Boston, 1805), p. 121.

139. *Port Folio*, 3rd ser., 5 (1811), p. 486.

140. "An Inaugural Discourse, Delivered before the New York Historical Society," *Collections of the New York Historical Society* 3 (1821), pp. 34, 37.

141. "Classical Learning," in *Port Folio*, new ser., 5 (1808), p. 20.

142. Letter to Richard Peters, March 29, 1811, in *Port Folio*, 6th ser., 1 (1826), p. 452.

143. *Port Folio* 5 (1805), pp. 205, 241.

144. *Port Folio* 12 (1822), pp. 249–250.

145. Stourzh, *Alexander Hamilton*, pp. 35–36, 132.

146. Kenneth Silverman, *A Cultural History of the American Revolution* (New York, 1976), pp. 73, 504–505.

147. Lawrence M. Levin, *The Political Doctrine of Montesquieu's Esprit des Lois: Its Classical Background* (New York, 1936), pp. 68–70; *Encyclopédie*, new ed. (Geneva, 1777), vol. XI, pp. 815–818, s.v. "Economie (Morale & Politique),"

by Rousseau; *Encyclopédie*, vol. XXXV, pp. 261–262, s.v. "Vertu," by Romilly; Eric Foner, *Tom Paine and Revolutionary America* (New York, 1976), pp. 158–159.

148. Cited by Silverman, *Cultural History*, p. 150.
149. Foner, *Tom Paine*, p. 159; Royall Tyler's *The Contrast. A Comedy* (1787; rpt. New York, 1970), pp. 63–64, on the sapping of virtue by luxury and corruption; Silverman, pp. 558–563.
150. Richard D. Mosier, *Making the American Mind: Social and Moral Ideas in the McGuffey Readers* (New York, 1947).

VI. The Silver Age of Classical Studies in America, 1790–1830

The Golden Age of classical learning in America was co-extensive with the Revolutionary generation, from about 1760 to 1790. It was at this time that the American cult of antiquity was at its height, in the crepuscular afterglow of the Renaissance in this new Hesperia. The Founding Fathers, with a common core of knowledge from the obligatory traditional classical curriculum and from omnivorous adult reading, venerated the ancient commonwealths, statesmen, and the classical virtues as models of republicanism. In Revolutionary America love of liberty and political expertise were associated with classical learning. And so the Founding Fathers ransacked the Roman and Greek classics for usable lessons from the past, "the lamp of experience," in Patrick Henry's words, extracting therefrom analogies, parallels, and precedents as guidelines for public policy and partisan politics, as well as exemplars of civic and private virtue. There is perhaps no better epitome of the Revolutionary generation's commitment to classical learning than John Adams's exhortation to his son John Quincy in 1781: "In Company with Sallust, Cicero, Tacitus and Livy you will learn Wisdom and Virtue. . . . You will ever remember that all the End of study is to make you a good Man and a useful Citizen."[1]

The flood of applications of lessons and examples from the ancient world to the new republic crested in 1787–88, in the debates and polemics concerning the Constitution. America was never again to witness such an outpouring of historical and political precedents from antiquity.[2] The Founding Fathers were, however, not classical scholars but humanist statesmen, and the uses to which they put the classical heritage were a function of their quest for political freedom, not of a search for the truth. Insecure and inexperienced, they looked back for guidance to the "perfect Models of Antiquity," and plundered the classics for instant history—uncritically, selectively, opportunistically—constructing timeless models, political abstractions, stereotypes, ideals. These served timely needs indeed during the ardors and uncertainties of the Revolutionary Age, but for this flight into the past the Founding Fathers had to pay a price in the early national period when history propelled them turbulently into the future. The classical models and the traditional classical education were immediately challenged as obsolete in the dynamism of a unique, revolutionary, pluralistic, changing, progressive nation.[3]

Reconstruction of education along pre-Revolutionary lines was unacceptable to many American national leaders. The long-dominant classics, which had served useful functions in America for a century and a half, culminating in conceptual contributions to the Revolution and the Constitution, were now deemed by many to have exhausted their utility, to be, indeed, elitist, ornamental, impractical, even detrimental to republicanism. In their efforts to establish national institutions and a distinctive American culture, they feverishly sought to redirect education away from the classical curriculum to national forms and purposes. While plans for a national system of education and a national university came to naught, early national educational thought, generally nationalistic, utilitarian, and democratic, was by and large not supportive of the traditional classical curriculum.[4]

No sooner was the national life inaugurated under the Constitution in 1789 than classical learning began precipitously and conspicuously to decline in usefulness, acceptance, and vitality. Previous sporadic and meager opposition to the dead languages in America, largely on religious and utilitarian grounds,[5] now erupted into a massive campaign to dethrone the age-old sovereignty of Latin and Greek in the grammar schools and colleges, and to banish classical learning entirely from American intellectual life. In 1804 Josiah Quincy, later one of the great presidents of Harvard, deplored that a "whole mass of sages . . . in the United States . . . have been for these twenty years past, engaged in the great work of bringing into discredit the study of the languages and sciences of

Greece and Rome . . . [and of] preventing the further growth of
Greek and Latin learning among us, by discouragng its culture in
our schools and colleges, and so, by degrees, rooting it out of the
country."[6] Although the aged and venerable Franklin, autodidact
and apostle of utility, was not one of the leaders among these anti-
classical "sages," in 1789, near the end of his life, he entered the
battle over the classics in America with a formulation that clearly
defined the issues. Because the English School at the Academy of
Philadelphia which he had established decades before had closed its
doors, through faculty neglect and parental and student disinterest,
he issued an angry condemnation, fulminating that "learning the
ancient languages for the purpose of acquiring Knowledge is become absolutely unnecessary." "But," he continued, "there is in
Mankind an unaccountable Prejudice in favor of ancient Customs
and Habitudes, which inclines to a Continuance of them after the
Circumstances, which formerly made them useful, ceased to exist. . . . Thus the time spent in that Study might, it seems, be much
better employed in the Education for such a Country as ours."[7]

Franklin did not live to witness the barrage of arguments and the
vituperative language marshalled by the opponents and champions
of the classical languages in America, except perhaps those of his
friend and fellow Philadelphian Benjamin Rush, who was the most
vociferous and inflexible enemy of the classics, from 1788 to his
death in 1813. The battle over the role of the dead languages in
America continued unabated in the first four decades of the national period. The number of participants on both sides among the
first national generation was formidable, and the debate was carried
on in magazines, newspapers, books, essays, pamphlets, public addresses, and private correspondence.

A sense of urgency consumed the aggressive and clamorous enemies of classical learning. "Irony and ridicule have been levelled
against them," wrote a defender of the classics in 1790. "Declama-
tion and sophistry have opened their trenches. The powerful artillery of respectable names has thundered forth. The attack . . . is a
formidable one."[8] The bill of particulars against the dead languages
in America presents an impressive array of charges: Few obtain
more than a smattering of the dead languages, after seven to ten
years of study, and quickly forget them; therefore the time expended is too costly. Study of the classical languages as they are
taught, through formal grammar, does not develop taste. Formal
grammar has become an end in itself; students are not trained to
think. It is necessary to turn away from the study of words to the

study of things. Translations of all the ancient authors are available. Study of the classical languages does not develop polished gentlemen but "mere scholars." Knowledge of English and modern foreign languages is more useful. Knowledge of Latin and Greek is not necessary for learning English grammar or the etymology of English words. Doctors and lawyers no longer need a knowledge of Latin. Classical learning is elitist, unresponsive to the needs of the common people. The classical languages are not useful knowledge to most Americans, especially those designed for nonprofessional careers. Study of the dead languages acts as a fetter on the diffusion of other forms of knowledge, especially of science and practical knowledge needed for a new country. Study and veneration of classical models in literature act as a brake on national literary creativity. The classics do not inculcate patriotism and republicanism; the *Iliad* and the *Aeneid* especially are not compatible with republican ideology. The classics are deleterious to morality and religion. Classical mythology is filled with absurdities and immorality. As a consequence of the classical curriculum, women have been excluded from access to higher education.[9]

One may judge the virulence of the anticlassical assault by the acrimonious and vituperative language used, e.g.: "these obsolete languages"; "the clamour of pedantry in favour of Greek and Latin . . . the rigid friends of antiquity"; "absurdity and folly . . . this dry and unfruitful study"; "unaccountable prejudice" for the classical curriculum; "the quackery of literature"; "this formidable enemy of human reason"; "the idolatry of Greece and Rome"; "the present indiscriminate and preposterious mode of teaching the dead languages"; "monkish learning"; "offal learning"; "folly and madness"; "useless subjects"; "the murder of time"; "the tyranny of Greek and Latin"; "the long and gloomy portico of Latin and Greek"; "those who go out as knights-errant against Latin and Greek"; "those who are governed by an indiscriminating and impotent hatred of classical learning."[10] Benjamin Rush in 1789 was sanguine that the anticlassicists would triumph: "I expect to prevail in my attempt to bring the dead languages into disrepute."[11] And it was Samuel Miller's pessimistic judgment in 1803 that "the popular prejudice against [classical literature] is strong and growing; and there is too much reason to fear that this prejudice will, at no great distance of time, completely triumph."[12]

Throughout the entire early national period the continuing attacks on the classics elicited repeated methodical briefs for the traditional curriculum and classical learning, which were, on the whole, defensive parrying of the charges of the opponents of the classics. Study of the classics, it was argued, was useful and essential for many reasons: It disciplines the mind and trains thinking and judgment. It develops habits of precision in use of language. Develops the ability to write and speak well. Develops mastery of the English language. It cultivates taste and standards of criticism. Develops the imagination, and trains the memory. Inculcates principles of universal grammar. The classics are exquisite models of literature in every genre. The etymology of English words is clarified. Translations of the classics cannot do justice to the originals. Knowledge of the classical languages is necessary for the professions. It is indispensable for knowledge of modern languages. It helps to understand technical terms in the arts and sciences. The classics are a storehouse of useful knowledge in many fields. The classics teach fine sentiments and maxims. Enlightened morality is inculcated through the study of classical models. Heroes of Greece and Rome serve as models of patriotism. Training in republican ideology and statesmanship is provided through the lessons of ancient history. Classical mythology is necessary for reading modern literature.[13]

"For classical learning I have ever been a zealous advocate," wrote Jefferson on "this litigated question," for "the classical languages are a solid basis for most, and an ornament to all the sciences," and "the basis of good education. . . . indispensable to fill up the character of a 'well-educated man.'"[14] For John Adams, too, the classics were "indispensable."[15] George Tucker, ardent supporter of classical studies, could descend to the recommendation that "a good classical scholar is rarely seen to be an habitual gamester or sot";[16] and the Reverend John Mason concluded that "it is now too late . . . to dispute what has been ratified by the seal of ages."[17]

And yet the dispute did not subside. One of its manifestations was a recrudescence of the Battle of the Books, which had run its course in France and England at the end of the seventeenth and early eighteenth centuries. From about 1785 on, as an American national culture began to be molded, there arose a clamor for the immediate production of an indigenous literature. In their yearning for freedom from cultural dependence, American intellectual patriots in the early national period hurled challenges against the long venerated "exquisite models" of antiquity. "We are called to sing a New Song," wrote Nathaniel Appleton, "a Song that neither We nor our Fathers were able to sing before."[18]

It is not possible here to document and analyze the vigorous efforts made in the first few decades of the national period to depreciate the classical authors and to demonstrate that the American "moderns" were superior to the "ancients." The quest for American superiority in literature, pursued by militant nationalists among the Anti-Federalists, democrats, Connecticut Wits, was accompanied by attacks on the reverence for the classics as a deterrent to creative originality in America.[19]

In 1829 Caleb Cushing declared in the *North American Review* that "time has been, when all that was most perfect in matters of taste . . . was claimed as the exclusive birthright of the ancients. . . . In many things the ancients were unquestionably inferior to us, if they were not in all. . . . Any alleged superiority of ancient writings, if it existed, would not prove that we cannot surpass the ancients."[20] However, despite the demand for a native literature, from 1776 to 1830 American literature remained derivative and imitative, dependent on British and classical models. In the mid-1830s Emerson pointed out that fifty years of exhortations for a great American literature produced none at all.[21] Yet, while the campaign for a national literature did not then produce positive results, the attendant devaluation of the classical models contributed to the decline in acceptance of classical learning in America.

Contributing also to the vulnerability of classical learning in America at this time was a graver problem—the superficiality of classical scholarship and the prevailing methods of teaching. Throughout the early national period there resounds an almost unrelieved litany of censure of both teachers of the classical languages and their methods of instruction. This criticism came not only from enemies but also supporters of the classics. Over and over again we hear of the inadequacy of the schoolmasters in the grammar schools, who were poorly equipped in knowledge and stayed on for a short time en route to preparation for other professions. Most teachers were merely drillmasters, concentrating on grammar, parsing, and inculcating forms and rules through rote memory. Even the conservative *Port Folio*, warm supporter of classical learning, severely criticized "the gross imperfections of our system of education."[22] The frequency of the use of the phrase, "a smattering of the dead languages," and the widespread acknowledgement of the superficialty of classical learning in America are evidence of deterioration of the quality of knowledge of the classics.[23]

The versatile and learned Philadelphian Francis Hopkinson called American schoolmasters "Haberdashers of Moods & Tenses," and he had nothing but contempt for their lack of aesthetic taste for the languages and the authors, and for their ignorance of the contents of the works they taught. "The time may come," he wrote, "when teachers will be convinced that languages are not to be squared by rule and compass."[24] Benjamin Rush had compassion for schoolboys in the Latin school: "There is no play common among children that strikes me with an idea of half the folly that I am struck with every time I look into a Latin school and see thirty or forty little boys pinioned down to benches and declining nouns, conjugating verbs, or writing Latin versions."[25] Even advocates of the utility of the classical languages warned that attention to grammatical construction alone was but "trifling knowledge."[26]

This poor teaching and the poverty of the results obtained therefrom were much deplored, but not effectively combatted and reformed. As one cause of the low standards and the superficiality of classical learning, there was adduced the permissive widespread use of translations of classical texts, a practice deemed prejudicial to the knowledge of the languages as well as to the inculcation of habits of hard work;[27] also cited were the unsettled conditions of the country after the Revolution, local circumstances, and the ongoing debate over the relative importance of classical learning and the sciences.[28]

In the colleges, low standards of admission and the low pay of professors were acknowledged as contributing to the superficial knowledge of Latin (and less Greek).[29] Even John Adams conceded to Benjamin Rush, in 1811, in their long dispute over the utility of the classical languages for America, that "we need not fear that Latin and Greek will ever be too much studied. Not one in ten thousand of those who study them in schools and colleges ever make any great proficiency in them."[30] In New England it was reported that "the metropolis of Massachusetts does not contain more than two or three ripe Latin Scholars. . . . As to Greek I shall say nothing at present. . . . This reflects no credit on the general system of prevalent education. . . . A smattering of Latin is common enough among us."[31] The standards at Harvard in 1808 were pitiful, lamented the *Monthly Anthology:* "Though knowledge, at the present day, may be more widely diffused, yet it is, at the same time, more superficial than at former periods; and, notwithstanding the late improvements in our University, it is questionable, whether it can at the present boast of any scholars, equal to those who flourished half a century since."[32]

At Yale, as Julian M. Sturtevant (class of 1826), later president of Illinois College, recalled, tutors were just "good drill masters," who "did not bring their students as they might have done into sympathy with classic authors as models of literary excellence." He quoted James L. Kingsley, professor of Latin and Greek (one of the authors of the Yale Report in 1828) as once saying, after reading Tacitus' *Agricola* with a group of students, "Young gentlemen, you have been reading one of the noblest productions of the human mind without knowing it."[33] Harsh words were uttered by Americans concerned with the development of a high culture in the country. The Reverend Joseph Stevens Buckminster (Harvard, class of 1800), in a famous Phi Beta Kappa address at Harvard on Aug. 31, 1809, declared: "It is our lot to have been born in an age of tremendous revolution. . . . When we look back to the records of our learning before the American revolution, we find or think we find (at least in New England) more accomplished scholars than we have since produced . . . , men . . . who had not learned to be ashamed of being often found drinking at the wells of antiquity."[34] In 1813 the *Analectic Magazine* was full of pessimism: "Classical literature [in America] . . . is now at the lowest ebb. . . . Though learned men are few, yet seminaries of learning of the highest pretensions abound; the consequence of which is, that many of them, invested with all the powers and dignities of colleges, will not bear a comparison with the grammar-schools of England, or the second grade of French schools."[35]

Joseph Green Cogswell, writing from Europe in 1819, when he was a student abroad, condemned American classical education on all levels as a waste of eight to nine years. He criticized the "mere task work" which was soon forgotten, blaming the situation on poor teachers, bad methods of teaching, low standards of admission to college, and the use of translations. "But in all that relates to classic learning, [the academies] are totally deficient; there is not one, from Maine to Georgia, which has yet sent forth a single first rate scholar; no, not one since the settlement of the country, equal even to the most ordinary of the thirty or forty, which come out every year from Schule Pforta, and Meissen. . . . It is impossible for a man to teach what he does not understand himself, or to excite in others a taste, which he has never acquired. The remark may be applied to most of the instructors of the classic schools in America; they are mere language masters, not scholars. . . . It cannot be expected that the masters should be good, as long as the system of education, which they are required to follow, is wholly defective. The object of learning is misunderstood in America, or rather, it is valued only as far as it is practically useful."[36] A decade later, about 1829, Hugh Swinton Legaré, distinguished Charlestonian, anguished over the wretched methods of teaching classical languages and the incompetent teachers: "One such example of a practice, scandalously at variance with profession, does more harm in such a country as this, than the speculative opinions of a hundred men like Dr. Rush and his school. . . . The system of education, we repeat it, which obtained universally in this country a few years ago, and is far from being reformed now, was the most profligate and insane waste of time and money, that was ever tolerated by an intelligent people."[37]

The sterility of American education, critical scholarship, and letters in the early national period led to a movement to elevate standards through adoption of European scholarship and critical methods. A small wave of American students flowed to Europe for study at this time, especially to Göttingen. The most famous of these came from Harvard: George Ticknor, Edward Everett, Joseph Green Cogswell, George Bancroft.[38] In 1815 for example, when Edward Everett was appointed the first professor of Greek at Harvard—at the age of twenty-one!—he was immediately given a leave of absence to go abroad to study at the universities;[39] he did not return until 1820. In 1816 Ticknor wrote Jefferson of his design to have German scholarly pursuits "transplanted into the U. States, in whose free and liberal soil I think it would, at once, find congenial nourishment."[40] Cogswell, too, was optimistic; in 1819 he wrote of the inspiration of German classical scholarship: "It is applying the remedy exactly where it is most wanted, a taste once created for classical learning at the College, and the means furnished for cultivating it, and the long desired reform in education in my opinion is virtually made. . . . We are not wanting in good lawyers and good physicians, and if we could but form a body of men of taste and letters our literary reputation would not long remain at the low stand, which it now is."[41]

There was, however, a fundamental difficulty involved in the effort to transplant German classical learning to America at this time. The country had never before had specialized classical scholars. Liberal scholarship had been integrated with life, both public and private, and this tradition—particularly during the Revolutionary Age—had given an acceptable public image to classical studies in

America. George Bancroft identified the alien character of German scholarship: "A German man of letters," he wrote, "is very different from the ideas formed of a scholar in America. . . . It is attended to as a trade, is cultivated merely because one can get a living by it."[42] Despite the efforts of Ticknor and Everett at Harvard, and similar endeavors at Yale, proposals to institute reforms for elevating the level of scholarship failed.[43] The American college remained virtually unchanged, continuing to be little above a German gymnasium. In addition to the dead hand of tradition, contributing factors were the mushrooming of college foundations in the early national period, the paucity of resources, and the increasing deterioration in the quality of teachers.

On the secondary level private academies in great numbers (by 1830 there were about 1,000 incorporated academies in the United States)[44] displaced the Latin grammar schools, an institution demolished in the Revolutionary Age. The most advanced experiment for transplanting German standards to America was the establishment of the Round Hill School at Northampton, Massachusetts, by Cogswell and Bancroft. Modeled on the German gymnasium, it was founded in 1823, and by 1825 had a faculty of twelve, "the ablest body of instructors in the country," Ticknor said. The core of the curriculum was the classical languages, primarily Latin; standards were high; and students flocked to it from all parts of the country. But by 1834 it closed its doors, an institution alien and unassimilable in American education of the time.[45]

Equally fugitive was a movement launched in 1820 by admirers of Greek literature to give Greek priority over Latin in the schools, indeed to elevate Greek to the role of first and principal study in the classics. During the early national period, when the validity of the traditional curriculum had been under attack, the study of Greek was more vulnerable than Latin. It had received but marginal attention in the grammar schools—to satisfy minimal college entrance requirements—and was relegated to a minor place in the college curriculum. Unlike Latin, its usefulnes, except to those preparing for the ministry, had long before been doubted; to some it was a "matter of meer Curiosity."[46] In 1788 there appeared in the *New-Haven Gazette* the following dismissal of Greek: "Can you conceive why we should vent so much of our spleen on Greek. It is surely a harmless amusement enough.—To pretend that it is useful would be quite too much."[47] By 1803 Samuel Miller noted that in American colleges the study of Greek was a mere "smattering which scarcely deserves the name of knowledge," and that popular

hostility to Greek was so pronounced that "in some colleges it requires the exertion of all the authority vested in the immediate instructors, and the governors, to prevent popular ignorance and
prejudice from expelling the study of Greek from their plans of education."[48] The anticlassical rebellion at Yale, and elsewhere, in the
first decade of the nineteenth century was directed principally at
the study of Greek.[49] George Ticknor said that early in the century
"a copy of Euripides in the original could not be bought at any
bookseller's shop in New England."[50] In South Carolina many students avoided the study of Greek entirely, or received only the
most superficial instruction in the language.[51] Accompanying this
anti-Greek trend was a growing crescendo of attacks on the study of
Homer's *Iliad* (as well as Vergil's *Aeneid*) on political, moral, and
utilitarian grounds. Most dramatic was the rejection of Homer by
Joel Barlow in the preface to his epic *The Columbiad* (first published 1807). While venerating Homer's genius as a poet, Barlow
condemns him as a writer whose "existence has really proved one
of the signal misfortunes of mankind."[52]

Yet advocates of the study of Greek were not lacking at this time.
The *Port Folio* of Philadelphia extolled Greek as the finest language
there has ever been, and ranked it above Latin.[53] In Boston it was
argued that "Greek [as] an engaging and important part of American education" was justified by its usefulness in fostering republicanism.[54] In 1811 John Adams, noting a revival of interest in Greek
language and culture, ventured to explain this development as a
consequence of the American Revolution, which motivated, he believed, the first formal histories of Greece, by Gillies and Mitford in
England.[55] In 1813 Adams wrote Jefferson: "Lord! Lord! what can I
do with so much Greek?"[56] Jefferson himself, after the sale of his
great second library to Congress, accelerated his purchase of Greek
books abroad, with the help of George Ticknor.[57]

Even before the influence on American students of the new humanism of Germany, with its emphasis on Greek studies, the
American "discovery" of Greece itself began in the first decade of
the nineteenth century.[58] While in Greece in 1806 Nicholas Biddle
of Philadelphia wrote in his diary: "I had long felt an ardent desire
to visit Greece. . . . The soil of Greece is sacred to genius and to
letters."[59] The most famous voyager to the "sacred soil of Greece"
at this time was Edward Everett, who made the pilgrimage just before his return to Cambridge in 1820, to become "the foremost
American Hellenist," giving lectures at the university on Greek language and literature, and public lectures in Boston on the antiqui-

ties of Athens, "the first such lectures delivered to public audiences in America."[60] Emerson was later to hail the year 1820 as the dividing line between a sterile generation that preceded and the impulse to critical scholarship given by Edward Everett when he returned after five years of study abroad.[61] It was a premature judgment on Emerson's part, at least as far as classical studies were concerned.

Yet for the first time concern for the accuracy of Greek texts published in this country emerged. As early as 1809 Wells of Boston reprinted Griesbach's edition of the New Testament, "the first Greek book to be printed in the United States with great accuracy."[62] Publications supportive of Greek learning began to come off American presses. In 1818 appeared John Pickering's book *On the Pronunciation of the Greek Language*, and in 1826 his *Comprehensive Lexicon of the Greek Language*, "the best Greek-English dictionary before Liddell-Scott."[63] Edward Everett, as Eliot Professor of Greek Literature at Harvard, published in 1822 his translation of Philip Buttmann's *Greek Grammar*, and in 1823 of Frederick Jacob's *Greek Reader*.[64] A reprinting in 1826 of the Tauchnitz edition of *Demosthenis Opera* was hailed because of the encouragement it might give to the study of Demosthenes in the original.[65]

In 1820 this campaign to give Greek priority over Latin in American education was supported by the belief that the change would reinvigorate classical learning in America. H. M. Fisher in the *North American Review* was "convinced that on this depends the advancement of our classical and polite learning."[66] Though the proposal was not adopted anywhere in American schools and colleges, the *Port Folio* continued to assert that knowledge of Greek was more desirable than Latin.[67] The learned Charlestonian Hugh Swinton Legaré, editor of the *Southern Review,* as late as 1828 was an advocate of the Greek language and literature as superior to Latin, indeed "by far the most extraordinary and brilliant phenomenon in the history of the human mind. . . . If Americans are to study any foreign literature at all, it ought undoubtedly to be the Classical, and especially the Greek."[68]

The proponents of Greek were, however, out of touch with the prevailing American reality. Conservative tradition prevailed. In Kentucky, for example, both teachers and parents advised against learning Greek.[69] When Cogswell and Bancroft planned their German-model academy at Round Hill in 1823, they put Latin at the core of the curriculum, conceding that, though Greek surpasses Latin, "none need learn it."[70] Finally, in 1827 George Bancroft himself, acknowledging the great opposition to the classics in general in America, asked "whether it is worth our while to study Greek in this country."[71]

Greater progress in improving the quality of classical education in the early national period was made in another sphere: the classical texts and textbooks used in schools and colleges. Those interested in classical studies in America were troubled by two realities: almost all texts continued as before to be imported from Europe, especially England; and those books reprinted in this country were of inferior quality, both as to typography and accuracy. As late as 1823 it could be lamented that all grammars used in the schools were "disgraced by errors or defects."[72] The lack of resources that James Otis referred to when he explained that his study of Greek prosody, written in 1760, could not be printed here because "there were no Greek types in the country, or, if there were, there was no printer who knew how to use them"[73] was remedied beginning with independence from Britain. In 1776 school texts began to be printed on this side of the Atlantic, both in Greek and Latin; they were, however, reprints of books of foreign origin.[74]

In the 1790s there began a more substantial effort on the part of American printers to supply school texts in Greek and Latin.[75] The year 1795 was memorable for the publication of "the *first* of the kind, that has been written and published in the *United States*," Caleb Alexander's *A New Introduction to the Latin Language*.[76] It was written, Alexander declared, "to prevent the necessity of sending to Europe for books that are wanted and used in American schools. . . . To the *Republican Sons of America* this reason will appear not only plausible but conclusive." Even if the book had no originality, the author said, and might be inferior to European productions, it was native American.[77]

Concerted efforts to improve the quality of texts for classical studies printed by American publishers were launched at the start of the nineteenth century. In 1802 William Poyntell & Co. of Philadelphia established the Classic Press for reprinting valuable European books cheaper and of at least equal quality, with priority to be given to "the *invaluable* writings of antiquity."[78] By 1806, under the imprint of the Classic Press, Poyntell had published American editions of Caesar, Horace, Sallust, Vergil, Ovid, Lucian, and Xenophon.[79] The editor of the *Port Folio* expressed pleasure at this evidence of the advancement of learning in America, "because, from the genius of our government, from the gross imperfections of our systems of education, and from the manners and principles of the people, we consider the circumstance as a sort of miracle."[80]

Now, he enthused when Poyntell's *Virgil* appeared, "for the honor of our country, for the benefit of studious youth, and for the promotion of current taste in literature, we hope that the works of Virgil, one of the most splendid specimens of ancient wit, will be perused at every Grammar School, and College in America."[81]

Poyntell's venture was probably motivated by the establishment of the New York Association of Booksellers in 1801–02, a consortium whose first publication was *Cicero's Select Orations*, printed in 1802.[82] By 1804 American publishers had already produced a total of about thirty books related to the field of classical learning.[83]

In 1805, when a new, natively prepared edition of Sallust was published at Salem, a reviewer was ecstatic: "*Ecce monstrum!* . . . We record it as a memorable fact in the annals of our literature, that in the year of our Lord 1805 appeared the first edition of an ancient classick ever published in the United States, which was not a professed reimpression of some former or foreign edition."[84] Shortly after, the University Press at Harvard published an edition of Horace's *Carmina* for students, which the *Monthly Anthology* excoriated for many reasons, including the fact that it was an expurgated text. "With pain and regret have we proceeded at every step in this examination of a book, printed under the auspices of the first university in America. . . . Let it be forgotten in the history of American typography. Its clumsy shape . . . , its vicious text, its infantine notes, the incalculable absurdities of its punctuation. . . ."[85] But when a new American edition of Sallust, edited by Professor P. Wilson of Columbia, was published by the New York firm of Swords in 1809, the same magazine was pleased, but maintained reserve about American scholarship: "To the honour of giving a truly critical edition of an ancient classick, we can hardly aspire in this Western World. Our means are so few, our literary labour so little subdivided and parcelled out, our pursuits are so loose and general, and the distance between men of similar studies is so great in this extensive country, that we can hardly think of doing a greater service to ancient literature, than to add to the convenience of our school books."[86]

In 1807 the *Monthly Anthology* began a retrospective of works relating to classical scholarship in America, singling out for praise as a masterly treatise James Otis's book on Latin prosody, published in 1760, as well as James Logan's translation of Cicero's *Cato Major*, printed by Benjamin Franklin in 1744, "the first translation of a classick, and the best which has appeared in this country."[87] Skeptical voices were heard questioning the productivity of American publishers in the field of classical books and also the interest of the public in such books. William Bentley, for example, in 1806, seeing a shipment of German classical works opened in Wells's Bookstore in Boston, considered the event the first of its kind in America, and declared, "Indeed, I date from this arrival the Commencement of a Classical Collection of Books for general sale in the country."[88]

But in fact plans were in the making for more American publications of the classics. Remarkable for the time was the proposal to publish a text edition of Tibullus.[89] In New York plans were broached in 1807 to publish editions of the classics, beginning with Vergil, as well as classical dictionaries;[90] and a new edition of the still popular Rollin's *Ancient History* (in eight volumes) was projected in Boston.[91] In Philadelphia, in 1806, when announcement was made of the forthcoming publication, by subscription, of Lemprière's *Classical Dictionary*, the *Port Folio* was ecstatic: "We cannot omit to express our exultation that so many of our countrymen begin to regard, with more than complacency, whatever relates to ancient literature."[92] In 1808 a proposal was announced in Philadelphia to establish the American Classic Association—for the printing and publishing of works of ancient literature. The prospectus contained the following rationale: "Whereas the ancient works of literature, written in the Grecian, Roman, Hebrew and other Oriental langauges, exhibit the most excellent models of composition, and contain a fund of information highly useful to the general scholar, and to men in the literary professions. . . . And whereas the rapid improvement in the arts, science and literature, with which Divine Providence has favoured the United States of America, has created a demand for books which cannot be readily supplied from foreign countries. . . . And whereas the printing of such books in this country would . . . promote the diffusion of useful and ornamental knowledge."[93] Nothing came of this venture.

In 1810 the Boston firm of Wells & Wait proposed to publish, by subscription, the complete Latin classics (from the best European editions), under the title *Scriptores Romani*, beginning with Cicero. Thereupon the *Monthly Anthology* commented with enthusiasm: "The utility, and even the necessity, of an undertaking like the present, in the United States, will . . . little be disputed. It is a fact, notorious to all who have any acquaintance with our seminaries for academick education, that the progress of Classical literature is materially obstructed by the almost total want of good editions of the ancient writers."[94] Nothing came of the proposal at this time. It was renewed in 1815 by Wells & Lilly of Boston, who planned to issue a complete Cicero in twenty volumes. It soon became apparent, however, that there was little support for this project. The *North American Review* was dispirited, for only Harvard as an institution supported the project to publish all classical texts. "Is there not something of lukewarmness towards classick literature, in thus neglecting an exertion in the cause of which they are all instituted to support."[95] The *Analectic Magazine*, hailing the project of Wells & Lilly, animadverted that "there is a portion of the European literary world with whom a valuable critical edition of all the Latin Classics will add more to our national reputation than the invention of the steamboat, the defence of New Orleans, or the victories of the lakes."[96]

The quality of American books for classical studies was a continuing concern. About 1816 Robert Finley, later president of the University of Georgia, proposed national uniformity in textbooks, in order to restore accuracy, and to remove obscene passages repugnant to religion and morals. "The Latin and Greek authors printed in this country," he declared, "abound so exceedingly with typographical errors that very great injury is sustained from the use of them in school. . . . [It is] a fact disgraceful and humiliating to American scholars" to have to keep a European edition of the authors ready for reference as the standard.[97] In 1818 John Bristed was distressed that "the United States have produced scarcely a single *learned* writer, in the strict acceptation of that term; indeed, I do not know one American work on classical literature, or that betrays any intimate acquaintance with the classics. And, excepting Cicero's works, printed accurately and well by Wells and Lilley, at Boston, the only classical productions of the American press are the republication of a few common schoolbooks."[98]

It was not until the return of Edward Everett in 1820 from his studies abroad that a new level of scholarly classical works began to appear in this country.[99] Besides Everett's own texts, in 1824 Harvard published the fourth American edition of Dalzel's *Collectanea Graeca Majora*, edited by Professor John S. Popkin. George Bancroft hailed it as "this very correct edition," in which "ten thousand" errors had been removed, and he concluded, "it augurs well of the state of learning."[100] In 1826 Sidney Willard welcomed with high enthusiasm P. A. Gould's edition of Vergil, published also by Harvard, because of its accuracy, elegant typography, and omission of translations and other crutches. "It is not long since," Willard declared, "we were dependent mainly on our parent country for books in the learned languages, to be used in our schools and colleges; and the few that were reprinted here were generally so inaccurate, as to be wholly undeserving of confidence. But the time has come when we must rely on our own presses to supply the demand for such books."[101]

But one or two swallows do not make a spring. The appearance in 1830 of the edition of Horace by Professor Charles Anthon of Columbia was hailed with rapture by a reviewer in the *American Quarterly Review*: "A critical edition of a classical author, elaborated in America, by an American, and for American consumption, is a new thing under the sun. . . . But mere school-books are not the subject of our story. Here is a work which has, no doubt, been many years in preparation, and which lays claim to a higher character than any former cis-Atlantic publication in the department."[102] Yet the dependency of the country on Britain, and Germany, for classical texts did not end, and still exists. In the mid-1830s Alexis de Tocqueville noted that "Almost all important English books are republished in the United States. The literary genius of Great Britain still darts its rays into the recesses of the forests of the New World."[103]

All the indicators reveal that pervading the first four decades of the national period there was an awareness of marked deterioration of classical studies in America, of a sharp decline in standards and popular esteem. At the end of the eighteenth century an English visitor to the United States observed with regard to the falling off of interest in the classics that "the habits and manners of America were so different from those of Europe, that they did not want to breed up men of deep speculation and abstract knowledge, for a man amongst them, was no more valuable there as he was useful in improving the state of the country."[104] Especially in the first decade of the nineteenth century there was a flood of expressions of alarmed concern about the neglect, decay, status, and vulnerability of classical studies in America. President Samuel Stanhope Smith of Princeton warned that "they are beginning to be greatly neglected."[105] The *Port Folio* in 1802–03 lamented "the almost universal neglect of classical literature in this country."[106] Samuel Miller in 1803 declared his verdict that "in America the decline of classic literature is especially remarkable and prevalent . . . [and that] the diminished . . . public respect for classic literature . . . still continues to operate with undiminished force. . . . The popular prejudice against it is strong and growing; and there is too much reason to fear that this prejudice will, at no great distance of time, completely triumph." Miller also deplored "the prevailing and increasing disposition to neglect this department of study . . . as among the fashionable follies of the age," and he regretted that the classics were "regarded by a large portion of the literary world, as among the most useless objects of pursuit."[107]

When Charles Nisbet, first president of Dickinson College, staunch supporter of classical learning, died in January 1804, Benjamin Rush recommended Samuel Miller as his successor. Rush wrote Miller: "You will have the honor of introducing a system of education into our country accommodated to the forms of our government, and to our state of society and manners. You will be able to abolish customs, and studies in the College of monkish origin, and which have nothing but antiquity to recommend them."[108] Miller declined. In the same year Josiah Quincy, then a state senator in Massachusetts, wrote of the "unremitting . . . labours to bring Greek and Roman science into universal neglect and disrepute" in the United States, and that if the issue of the advantages of classical learning "were to be decided by *'hand vote,'* in the United States, it would be carried against me by a very great majority. . . . I know that the great mass of my contemporaries, when such evidence is produced, think that all questions concerning the advantage of that learning are at an end."[109] The *Monthly Anthology* was pessimistic in 1807: "Since the revolution . . . the coin, which passes in all other parts of the civilized world . . . is neither current by authority of our government, nor stamped with the approval of our people. . . . By this specious word *reform*, democracy has undermined the most venerable fabricks of antiquity, and has, in a moment, levelled with the dust the labours of ages."[110]

The *Monthly Anthology* might declare with exasperation that "the world has long been sick of formal disquisitions on the merits of the classical and established authors,"[111] but the recognition of deterioration was profound. The Reverend Joseph Buckminster in his Harvard Phi Beta Kappa address in August 1809, exhorting the students to rededication to scholarship, spoke with sadness: "The foul spirit of innovation and sophistry has been seen wandering in the very groves of the Lyceum, and is not yet completely exorcised, though the speed is broken. . . . But so gravely have our habits of thinking been distorted by the revolutions of the last thirty years, the progress of our education, and the course of the character of our learning have not a little suffered."[112]

In the next decade the gloom continues. For example, the Reverend James Wilson, president of the newly established Bedford

Academy, warned in 1812 that "some pretenders to literary reform are labouring to banish at once all classical literature from our seminaries, or are attempting to confine it to limits so narrow as to render it both contemptible and useless."[113] The *Analectic Magazine* in 1813 deplored "the unsatisfactory state of classical education in our colleges."[114] De Witt Clinton noticed the avoidance of classical allusions by lawyers, a tendency which is "now professional with the bar."[115] The *Port Folio* in 1816 lamented that "the general spirit of the United States is to decry the merits of the ancients. Even our physicians and lawyers have united with the merchants in preaching the inutility of classical knowledge."[116] "I sincerely wish," said Timothy Dwight ca. 1818, "that the knowledge of the ancient languages was now holden in . . . estimation."[117] In 1819 Joseph Green Cogswell, criticizing American education, condemned "the common opinion about the value of classical learning [which is] . . . generally under-valued, and of course neglected."[118]

In the 1820s there was no respite in awareness of decline and neglect of the classics. Characteristic are the reactions of the *Western Review* in 1820 that "we cannot suffer ourselves for a moment to believe that classical learning is destined to fall into general disrepute"; of De Witt Clinton in a Phi Beta Kappa address at Union College, who was apprehensive of the deterioration in the quality of classical learning in the country; and of George Watterston, Librarian of Congress, who regretted the neglect of the learned languages in the United States.[119] In 1828 Hugh Swinton Legaré spoke a valedictory to the classical learning of America as it had once existed, in the Revolutionary Age: "There is something melancholy in the reflection, that the race of such men is passing away, and that our youth are now taught to form themselves on other models."[120]

In comparison with such doomsday utterances, expressions of optimism about a revival and reinvigoration of classical studies in America are exceedingly rare. In every decade from 1790 to 1830 predictions of a resurgence are heard. For example, Samuel Miller in 1803, despite his gloomy analysis of the status of classical learning in America, saw the "promising appearance of a revival of classic literature," in some parts of the country.[121] In 1808 the *Port Folio* announced that, despite the opposition, "the study of the ancient authors is unquestionably more and more fashionable in America"; yet in 1809 the editor bewailed the fact that classical learning had been "ignominiously neglected," and comforted himself with its elitist character, saying, "yet in spite of the sneers of some, and the theories of others, there is a favourite few, who have successfully studied the fine authors of Greece and Rome."[122] John Adams, in his continuing debate with Benjamin Rush on the role of the classics in America, predicted that "the admiration of Greek and Roman science and literature will increase. Both are increasing very fast," and he made the claim that "the second resurrection of learning" in Europe at the time, under the impulse of Napoleon, was due to the American Revolution, which had turned men's interests to the study of Greek and Greek civilization.[123] In 1817 Augustus B. Woodward, presiding judge of the Supreme Court of Michigan, in presenting a plan for the establishment of a university in Michigan, indulged his classical enthusiasm riotously. He proposed to name the university *Catholepistemiad* and suggested grandiloquent Greek titles for the professors of the various disciplines, e.g., *anthropoglossica* (for literature), *iatrica* (medicine), *polemitactica* (military science).[124] In 1824 George Bancroft saw symptoms of an "increasing fondness for classical learning" in the country.[125] Yet in 1827 the faculty of Amherst sadly reported that "the rage of the present day is to leave the great high way of knowledge, which had been trodden for ages."[126]

The climax and resolution of the debate over the role of classical studies in America for forty years came with the famous Yale Report of 1828. Mounting pressure by advocates of vocational and practical subjects led to a momentous resolution placed before the Yale Corporation to change the entrance requirements so as to omit the dead languages. After much debate and investigation the definitive report, written by President Jeremiah Day and Professor James L. Kingsley, professor of Greek and Latin was adopted. It reaffirmed the traditional classical curriculum as the best possible one for liberal education in America. In the report the conventional arguments in defense of the classical languages were marshalled anew by Professor Kingsley. President Day acknowledged that American colleges were closer in their character to the German gymnasium than to the German university, and that "ancient literature is too deeply inwrought into the whole system of the modern literature of Europe to be so easily laid aside." "The learned world long ago settled this matter, and subsequent events and experience have confirmed their decision," said the report. "We are the people, the genius of whose government and institutions more especially and imperiously than any other, demands that the field of classical learning be industriously and thoroughly explored and cultivated. . . . The models of ancient literature, which are put into the hands of the young student, can hardly fail to imbue his mind with the principles of liberty; to inspire the liveliest patriotism, and to excite to noble and generous action, and are therefore peculiarly adapted to the American youth." The Yale Report—the most influential document in American higher education in the first half of the nineteenth century—assured the entrenchment of the classics, not only at Yale but throughout the country, until after the Civil War.[127] "For the next two generations the American college would remain, at its best, a 'well-disciplined high school.' "[128]

Thus by the end of the administration of John Quincy Adams (1825–28) and the beginning of Andrew Jackson's presidency, classical learning ceased to be a "dynamic force in American public life."[129] It had ceased to be useful knowledge for the larger society, and no longer offered guidelines for the nation. Henceforth advocates of the classics championed their cause as preservers of a tradition, guardians of a heritage. This transformation of classical studies in America from its Golden Age, when the classics nourished the "living patriotism" of students and molded their professional lives, to a Silver Age, during which it gradually became the exclusive preserve of the schoolmasters, was noticed by Daniel Webster in 1826. In his joint eulogy of Thomas Jefferson and John Adams, both of whom died on July 4 of that year, the jubilee of the Declaration of Independence, he observed: "Men have seen that [classical learning] might exist . . . without good taste, and without utility. . . . Those whose memories we honor were learned men; but their learning was kept in its proper place and made subservient to the uses and objects of life."[130]

The guardians of the heritage might hurl academic thunderbolts at the enemies of the classics, as, for example, the *Western Review:* "We cannot suffer ourselves for a moment to believe that classical learning is destined to fall into general disrepute. We trust there will always be found zeal and talent enough to oppose the innovating spirit of those who would exclude the study of the ancient languages from our systems of education, and we shall ever be ready to lend our feeble aid to the efforts of those, who appear as champions of the venerated classics. Should the time ever come, when Latin and Greek should be banished from our Universities . . . we should regard mankind as fast sinking into absolute barbarism, and the gloom of mental darkness as likely to increase, till it should become universal."[131] But Thomas Smith Grimké, that vociferous anticlassicist, could in 1835 call the traditional education in America, with classics and mathematics at the core, "decidedly *un*-American"; and an anonymous New Yorker in the same year declared that "there is not a country on earth, where there is less reverence for antiquity, than in the United States," a judgment confirmed at this very time by Alexis de Tocqueville.[132]

But the classics were successfully protected by its guardians in the colleges and academies, and the curriculum and methods remained unchanged for decades. Before American classical studies could attain to its Heroic Age a generation later, it needed the courage and learning of a Basil Gildersleeve, who could say, even if retrospectively, of the state of classical learning in his student days in the mid-nineteenth century "my American teachers did not understand their business."[133]

Notes

1. *Adams Family Correspondence*, ed. L. H. Butterfield (Cambridge, Mass., 1963–73), vol. IV, p. 117.
2. The bibliography of the classical tradition in Early America has been collected in Meyer Reinhold, *The Classick Pages: Classical Reading of Eighteenth-Century Americans* (University Park, Pa., 1975), and in Chapter XII, below.
3. Cp. Merle Curti, *American Paradox: The Conflict of Thought and Action* (New Brunswick, 1956; rpt. 1973), pp. 8–18; Henry Steele Commager, "The American Enlightenment and the Ancient World," *Proc. Mass. Hist. Soc.* 83 (1971), pp. 3–15; idem, *Jefferson, Nationalism and the Enlightenment* (New York, 1975), pp. 123–139.
4. Allen O. Hansen, *Liberalism and American Education in the Eighteenth Century* (New York, 1926; rpt. 1965); Frederick Rudolph, ed., *Essays on Education in the Early Republic* (Cambridge, Mass., 1965); David Tyack, "Forming the National Character: Paradox in the Educational Thought of the Revolutionary Generation," *Harvard Educational Review* 36 (1966), pp. 29–41.
5. "Opponents of Classical Learning in America during the Revolutionary Period," Chapter IV, above; "The Quest for Useful Knowledge in Eighteenth-Century America," Chapter II, above.
6. *Port Folio* 4 (1804), p. 89. Quincy at this time wrote under the pseudonym Climenole. He deplored the rancor and the great prejudice that had been aroused against the classics.
7. *Observations Relative to the Intentions of the Original Founders of the Academy*, in Thomas Woody, *The Educational Views of Benjamin Franklin* (New York, 1931), pp. 220–227; John H. Best, *Benjamin Franklin on Education* (New York, 1962), pp. 173–174.
8. T. Q. C., in *New-York Magazine* 1 (1790), p. 277.
9. See, e.g., Francis Hopkinson, *Miscellaneous Essays and Occasional Writings* (Philadelphia, 1792), vol. II, pp. 41–57 ("On the Learned Languages"); idem, letter to Franklin, May 24, 1784, in *The Life and Works of Francis Hopkinson*, ed. George E. Hastings (Chicago, 1926), p. 420; "Thoughts on Education," *United States Chronicle*, Feb. 8, 1787; Noah Webster, "On the Education of Youth in America," *American Magazine*, Dec., 1787, pp. 232–236 (rpt. in *A Collection of Essays and Fugitiv Writings on Moral, Historical, Political and Literary Subjects* [Boston, 1790], pp. 1–35). A Countryman [Roger Sherman?], *New-Haven Gazette and Connecticut Magazine*, June 12, 1788; *Massachusetts Magazine* 1 (1789), pp. 736–737; Hugh Williamson, "Extract of a Letter to the Honorable William Samuel Johnson, L.L.D., President of Columbia College,"

Massachusetts Magazine 1 (1789), pp. 746–749 (also in *American Museum* 7 [1790], pp. 33–35, 103–105); Benjamin Rush, "An enquiry into the Utility of a knowledge of the Latin and Greek langauges, as a branch of liberal studies, with hints of a plan of liberal education without them, accommodated to the present state of society, manners, and government of the United States," *American Museum* 5 (1789), pp. 525–535 (also in *Essays, Literary, Moral & Philosophical* [Philadelphia, 1798], pp. 21–56); idem, letter to the Reverend James Muir, principal of the Alexandria Academy, Va., in 1791, in *Letters of Benjamin Rush*, ed. L. H. Butterfield, *Memoirs of the American Philosophical Society*, no. 30 (Philadelphia, 1951), vol. I, pp. 604–607; Thomas Paine, "Age of Reason," in *Life and Major Writings of Thomas Paine*, ed. Philip S. Foner (New York, 1945), pp. 491–492; "On Education," *Massachusetts Magazine* 7 (1795), pp. 202–206; Philip S. Freneau, "Epistle to a Student of Dead Languages," *Poems of Philip Freneau, Poet of the American Revolution*, ed. Fred L. Pattee (Princeton, 1902–07), pp. 121–122; Benjamin Henry Latrobe, *The Journal of Latrobe* (New York, 1905), pp. 65–82 (letter to Ferdinand Fairfax, 1798); Climenole [Josiah Quincy], *Port Folio* 4 (1804), pp. 81–83, 89–91; Samuel Miller, *A Brief Retrospect of the Eighteenth Century* (New York, 1803), vol. II, pp. 36–38; Joel Barlow, *The Columbiad* (Philadelphia, 1807), vol. I, pp. vi–vii, vol. II, pp. 194–195; *North American Review* 28 (1829), pp. 313–314; *Port Folio*, 6th ser., 1 (1826), pp. 343–344. Cp. Howard Mumford Jones, *The Theory of American Literature*, rev. ed. (Ithaca, 1965), pp. 27–33; A. Owen Aldridge, "Thomas Paine and the Classics," *Eighteenth Century Studies* 1 (1968), pp. 370–380; "The Quest for Useful Knowledge in Eighteenth Century America," Chapter II, above; "Opponents of Classical Learning in America during the Revolutionary Period," Chapter IV, above; Edwin L. Miles, "The Young American Nation and the Classical World," *Journal of the History of Ideas* 35 (1974), pp. 259–274.

10. Hopkinson, *Miscellaneous Essays*, p. 46; Noah Webster, *A Grammatical Institute of the English Language*, pt. 1 (first published 1783), cited in Ervin C. Shoemaker, *Noah Webster: Pioneer of Learning* (New York, 1936), pp. 44–47, 54–55; *Massachusetts Magazine* 1 (1789), pp. 736–737; Franklin, *Observations*, pp. 225–226; idem, *Pa. Mag. Hist. & Biog.* 29 (1905), p. 27 (both in 1789); Rush, "An enquiry," pp. 525–535; idem, *Letters*, vol. I, pp. 604–607, vol. II, pp. 1066–1068, 1080–1081; *The Spur of Fame: Dialogues of John Adams and Benjamin Rush, 1805–1813*, ed. John A. Schutz and Douglass Adair (San Marino, 1966), pp. 168–170, 178 (from letters to Adams in 1810–11); Hugh Williamson, "Extract of a Letter," pp. 747–749; *North American Review* 24 (1827), pp. 155–156.

11. Letter to John Adams, July 21, 1789, in Rush, *Letters*, vol. I, pp. 524–525.

12. Ibid., vol. II, pp. 36–37.

13. See, e.g., Philanthropos, "On the Study of the Latin and Greek Languages," *United States Chronicle*, Oct. 12, 1786; Hopkinson, *Miscellaneous Essays*, vol. II, pp. 41–48; William Duke, *Remarks Upon Education, with Respect to the Learned Languages* (Philadelphia, 1795); Onkelos, "The Dead Languages," *Massachusetts Magazine* 8 (1796), pp. 420–422, 473–475, 550–553, 661–664; Samuel Knox, *An Essay on the Best System of Liberal Education, Adapted to the Genius of the Government of the United States* (Philadelphia, 1799) (=Rudolph, *Essays on Education*, pp. 271–372); John C. Kunze, "Letter to Dr. Stuber of Philadelphia, Concerning the Learned Languages," *New-York Magazine* 1 (1790), pp. 276–277, 347–349, 396–398, 467–469, 510–512, 585–588, 643–646; John Clarke, *Letters to a Student in the University at Cambridge, Massachusetts* (Boston, 1795), pp. 42–52; R. D. W. Connor, Louis R. Wilson, and Hugh T. Lefler, eds., *A Documentary History of the University of North Carolina, 1776–1799* (Chapel Hill, 1953), pp. 168–170 (document of

1792); Jefferson, letter to Joseph Priestley, 1800, in *Writings of Thomas Jefferson*, Memorial Edition (Washington, D.C., 1905), vol. X, pp. 146–148; Miller, *Brief Retrospect*, vol. II, p. 43; *Monthly Anthology and Boston Review* 1 (1804), pp. 225–227; Climenole [Josiah Quincy], *Port Folio* 4 (1804), pp. 89–91; "Falkland," "An examination of the causes that have retarded the progress of literature in the United States," *Port Folio*, n.s., 4 (1807), pp. 356–357; Jacob Van Vechten, *Memoirs of John M. Mason* (New York, 1856), pp. 239–240 (describing Mason's views in 1805); Charles Nisbet, "On the Ancient Languages and Classical Education," *Port Folio*, n.s., 4 (1807), pp. 385–386, 403–404, and vol. 5 (1808), pp. 5–8, 19–21, 56–58; "Classical Learning," *Harvard Lyceum* 1 (1810), pp. 4–6 (efforts to degrade the classics called by Harvard seniors a "literary heresy"); "Remarks on the Utility of Classical Learning," *Monthly Anthology and Boston Review* 8 (1810), pp. 227–236, 367–376; vol. 9 (1810), pp. 7–17; T. C., "Classical Education," *Port Folio*, 4th ser., 1 (1813), pp. 567–582; T. C., "On University Education," *Port Folio*, 4th ser., 5 (1815), pp. 349–359; Hugh Henry Brackenridge, *Law Miscellanies* (Philadelphia, 1814), pp. xii–xiii; "Carré and Sanderson's Seminary, or Remarks on Classical and Moral Education," *Port Folio*, 4th ser., 6 (1815), pp. 413–420; John Bristed, *America and Her Resources* (London, 1818), pp. 345–347; *North American Review* 6 (1819), pp. 324–331; Jefferson, letter to John Brazier, Aug. 14, 1819, in *Writings*, vol. XV, pp. 207–211; *Western Review* 1 (1819), pp. 413–423; George Tucker, "On Classical Education," in *Essays on Various Subjects of Taste, Morals, and National Policy, By a Citizen of Virginia* (Georgetown, D.C., 1822), pp. 89–108, 296–298; "On the Study of the Classics," *Port Folio*, 5th ser., 16 (1823), pp. 308–313; George Bancroft, "The Value of Classical Learning," *North American Review* 19 (1824), pp. 125–137; idem, *North American Review* 23 (1826), pp. 142–150; Hugh Swinton Legaré, "Classical Learning," *Southern Review* 1 (1828), pp. 1–49.

14. Letter to Thomas Cooper, Oct. 7, 1814, in Jefferson, *Writings*, vol. XIV, p. 200; letter to John Brazier, Aug. 24, 1819, *Writings*, vol. XV, pp. 209–211; minutes of the Board of Trustees of the University of Virginia, Oct. 4, 1824, in *Thomas Jefferson and Education in a Republic*, ed. Charles F. Arrowood (New York, 1930), pp. 169–170.

15. *The Works of John Adams* (Boston, 1850–56), vol. X, p. 105.

16. "On Classical Education," Tucker, *Essays*, p. 107.

17. *Memoirs of John M. Mason*, p. 238 (the date of Mason's disquisition on classical education is 1805).

18. Cited by Russel B. Nye, *The Cultural Life of the New Republic, 1776–1830* (New York, 1960), p. 238.

19. Attention to the Battle of the Books in America was first directed by A. Owen Aldridge, in his paper "The Concept of Ancients and Moderns in American Poetry of the Federal Period," published in *The Classical Traditions in Early America*, ed. John W. Eadie (Ann Arbor, 1976), pp. 99–118. On the quest for a national literature in the early Federal Period see Nye, *Cultural Life*, pp. 235–267; Benjamin T. Spencer, *The Quest for Nationality, an American Literary Campaign* (Syracuse, 1957); M. F. Heiser, "The Decline of Neo-classicism, 1810–1848," in *Transitions in American Literary History*, ed. Harry Hayden Clark (New York, 1954; rpt. 1975), pp. 93–159.

20. 28 (1829), pp. 313–314, 338.

21. Nye, *Cultural Life*, pp. 251, 261.

22. 5 (1805), p. 253.

23. For detailed criticism of teachers, methods, and the general thinness of classical learning, see Philenos, "On the Living Languages," *Massachusetts Magazine* 8 (1796), pp. 657–660; *Port Folio* 2 (1802), p. 374; Miller, *Brief Retrospect*, p. 400 ("The *Classic Literature* of the United States . . . is almost every where

superficial"); David Ramsay, *The History of South-Carolina* (Charleston, 1809), pp. 372–376; *Port Folio*, 4th ser., 6 (1815), p. 414; Bristed, *America and Her Resources*, p. 327 (rote memory, "senseless jargon . . . superficial smattering . . . [teachers who are] unlettered foreign adventurers" or young Americans who do not stay in the profession); John C. Gray, *North American Review* 11 (1820), p. 414; Francis Glass, writing in 1824, in *A Life of George Washington, in Latin Prose* (New York, 1835), pp. 218–220. In 1816 a machine for teaching grammar was advertised: *Analectic Magazine* 8 (1816), p. 99. Yet in 1823 a writer "On the Art of Teaching" approved the traditional curriculum and methods (*Port Folio*, 5th ser., 16 (1823), pp. 313–321).

24. Letter to Benjamin Franklin, 1784, in George E. Hastings, *The Life and Works of Francis Hopkinson* (Chicago, 1926), p. 420; Hopkinson, *Miscellaneous Essays*, vol. II, pp. 41–48 (whimsical lecture "On the Learned Languages" at the commencement of 1786 at the College of Philadelphia).

25. Letter to the Reverend James Muir, Aug. 24, 1791, in Rush, *Letters*, vol. I., pp. 604–607.

26. T. Q. C., "Observations *on* the Utility *of the* Latin and Greek Languages," *New-York Magazine* 1 (1790), p. 510.

27. Miller, *Brief Retrospect*, vol. II, pp. 273, note y, 434–435; *The Diary of William Bentley* (Salem, 1905–14), vol. II, p. 12 (entry of 1793); *Port Folio*, 5th ser., 16 (1823), pp. 455–461. In this period booksellers' catalogues, under the caption "School Classics," carried numerous texts with parallel translations.

28. *North American Review* 9 (1819), pp. 188–199, esp. 188.

29. Miller, *Brief Retrospect*, vol. II, pp. 37–38; Noah Webster, "Education" *American Magazine*, Dec., 1787, pp. 232–236; *Port Folio* 1 (1801), p. 378; *Port Folio*, n.s., 4 (1807), pp. 356–357; *Analectic Magazine*, 2 (1813), pp. 309–310; *Port Folio*, 4th ser., 5 (1815), pp. 349–350.

30. Adams and Rush, *Spur of Fame*, p. 177.

31. "Boston Latin Literature," *Monthly Anthology* 2 (1805), pp. 304–305.

32. Ibid., 5 (1808), p. 222.

33. Richard Hofstadter and Wilson Smith, *American Higher Education: A Documentary History* (Chicago, 1961), vol. I, pp. 274–275; Brooks M. Kelley, *Yale: A History* (New Haven, 1974), p. 161.

34. J. S. Buckminster, "On the Dangers and Duties of Men of Letters," *Monthly Anthology* 7 (1809), p. 146.

35. *Analectic Magazine* 2 (1813), pp. 309–311.

36. [Joseph G. Cogswell], "On the Means of Education, and the State of Learning, in the United States of America," *Blackwood's Edinburgh Magazine* 4 (1819), pp. 546–553, 639–647 (esp. 547–548). Cp. James McLachlan, *American Boarding Schools: A Historical Study* (New York, 1970), pp. 30–32. The *North American Review* 9 (1819), pp. 242–252, carried a weak reply in defense of American teachers as good scholars.

37. "Classical Learning," *Southern Review* 1 (1828), pp. 1–49, esp. 9–11; *Writings of Hugh Swinton Legaré* (Charleston, 1845–46), vol. II, pp. 5–51, 217–218. The new Jesuit college in the Midwest, St. Louis College, founded in 1829 (Latin and Greek were first taught there in 1830–32), was woefully inadequate in instruction in the classics. Father Peter Kenney, visitor of Missouri, reported in 1832 that "the young men go forth superficially educated in every way. They speak proudly of eloquence, rhetoric, and of its figures, but of the Greek and Latin authors there is ignorance profound." See Gilbert J. Garraghan, *The Jesuits of the Middle United States* (New York, 1938), vol. I, pp. 324–325.

38. Orie William Long, *Literary Pioneers: Early American Explorers of European Culture* (Cambridge, Mass., 1935; rpt. 1967), pp. 3–158; Cynthia S. Brown, "The American Discovery of the German University: Four Students at Göttin-

gen 1815-1822" (Ph.D. diss., Johns Hopkins, 1964); John Edwin Sandys, *A History of Classical Scholarship* (Cambridge, 1908; rpt. 1967), vol. III, pp. 453-455; McLachlan, *American Boarding Schools*, pp. 50-70; Hofstadter and Smith, *American Higher Education*, pp. 257-263. Between 1781 and 1825 there were nineteen American students at Göttingen (Brown, pp. 309ff.). On classical studies in the early nineteenth century see the very general statement of Ernst Sihler, "Klassische Studien und klassischer Unterricht in den Vereinigten Staaten," *Neue Jahrbücher für Pädagogik* 10 (1902), pp. 503-507; Elizabeth A. Atwater, "A History of Classical Scholarship in America" (Ph.D. diss., Pittsburgh, 1938), pp. 27-29, 109-110.

39. *North American Review* 1 (1815), pp. 127-130.
40. Long, *Literary Pioneers*, p. 24.
41. Ibid., p. 116.
42. Ibid., p. 120.
43. Hofstadter and Smith, *American Higher Education*, vol. I, pp. 251-252.
44. McLachlan, *American Boarding Schools*, pp. 34-35.
45. Ibid., pp. 71-101.
46. E.g., Hopkinson, "On the Learned Languages" (1786), *Miscellaneous Essays*, pp. 41-48; *Diary and Autobiography of John Adams*, ed. L. H. Butterfield (Cambridge, Mass., 1962), vol. I, p. 55.
47. *New-Haven Gazette and Connecticut Magazine*, June 12, 1788, written by "A Countryman" (thought to be Roger Sherman). See Roger S. Boardman, *Roger Sherman, Signer and Statesman* (Philadelphia, 1938), pp. 267-268.
48. Miller, *Brief Retrospect*, vol. II, p. 36-37.
49. "Greek Literature," *Monthly Anthology* 4 (1807), p. 656. This was perhaps written by John Sylvester John Gardner. Cp. Lewis P. Simpson, ed., *The Federalist Literary Mind* (Baton Rouge, 1962), pp. 188-192.
50. John Edwin Sandys, *A History of Classical Scholarship* (Cambridge, 1908; rpt. 1967), vol. III, p. 453.
51. David Ramsay, *The History of South-Carolina* (Charleston, 1809), vol. II, p. 376.
52. [Richard Beresford], *A Plea for Literature: More Especially the Literature of Free States* (Charleston, 1793), pp. 29-30; Latrobe, *The Journal of Latrobe*, p. 74 (letter of 1798); Joel Barlow, *The Columbiad* (Philadelphia, 1807; 2nd ed. 1809), vol. I, pp. v-vii; vol. II, pp. 194-195; Adelphian, "Critical Comments on Homer," *Portico* 3 (1817), pp. 313-316.
53. N.s., 3 (1807), p. 119.
54. *Monthly Anthology* 7 (1809), p. 16.
55. Rush, *Letters*, vol. II, pp. 1076-1078 (also in Adams and Rush, *Spur of Fame*, p. 177), letter of Jan. 10, 1811.
56. Adams, *Works*, vol. X, p. 49.
57. Long, *Literary Pioneers*, pp. 10, 21. The leading cultural magazines saw a marked increase in interest in Greek and Greek literature in the second decade of the nineteenth century. See, e.g., *Port Folio*, 3rd ser., 7 (1812), pp. 181-182, 289, 394-396; 4th ser., 3 (1814), pp. 409-422; *Monthly Anthology* 7 (1809), pp. 11-16; *Portico* 3 (1817), pp. 409-410.
58. Stephen A. Larrabee, *Hellas Observed: The American Experience of Greece, 1775-1865* (New York, 1957), pp. 11-19.
59. Ibid., p. 12. In 1816 James Eastburn of New York wrote a poem, "The Temple of Theseus," the earliest poem by an American on a Greek architectural masterpiece. See *Port Folio*, 5th ser., 4 (1817), pp. 87-88. It is interesting to note the effect of the vogue of Greek in student life at Princeton. In the Revolutionary Age the secret names used by students in the Cliosophic Society were mostly from the Roman tradition. In 1819 Greek names were in a majority. This information is supplied from a paper on "Classical Names, American

Identities," by James McLachlan, in Eadie, *The Classical Traditions in Early America*, pp. 81–98.
60. Larrabee, *Hellas Observed*, pp. 32–35, 40–41. Emerson thought that his lectures on Greek antiquities contained much material that "is easily acquired from common books." See *The Letters of Ralph Waldo Emerson*, ed. Ralph L. Rusk (New York, 1939), vol. I, p. 128.
61. Ralph Waldo Emerson, "Historic Notes on Life and Letters in New England," in *Lectures and Biographical Sketches*, vol. X of *Complete Works* (Boston, 1904), pp. 325–330.
62. Brown, "American Discovery," p. 25.
63. See *North American Review* 9 (1819), pp. 92–113; 10 (1820), pp. 272–290; Jefferson's reaction to Pickering's views in Jefferson, *Writings*, vol. XV, pp. 181–185, 216–218; *Dictionary of American Biography*, vol. XIV, p. 565.
64. George Bancroft, *North American Review* 18 (1824), pp. 99–106, welcomed the books, taking it as a good omen "that the pursuits of classical literature are making advances among us"; *North American Review* 18 (1824), pp. 280–284. Notice is taken here also of an improved edition of an elementary Greek book published in Kentucky.
65. J. C. Gray, *North American Review* 22 (1826), pp. 34–52.
66. "On the Priority of Greek Studies," *North American Review* 11 (1820), pp. 209–218.
67. *Port Folio*, 5th ser., 13 (1822), p. 155; 16 (1823), p. 316.
68. *Southern Review* 1 (1828), pp. 40, 48.
69. *Western Review* 1 (1819), p. 58.
70. *Prospectus of a School to Be Established, at Round Hill, Northampton, Massachusetts, by Joseph G. Cogswell and George Bancroft* (Cambridge, Mass., 1823), pp. 10–12.
71. *North American Review* 24 (1827), p. 155. Yet at the same time there appeared in this country a brilliant, sophisticated review of Friedrich August Wolf's *Prolegomena ad Homerum*, in the *American Quarterly Review* 2 (1827), pp. 307–337.
72. "On Grammars," *Port Folio*, 5th ser., 16 (1823), pp. 223–227.
73. Adams, *Works*, vol. X, p. 275.
74. E.g., for Greek, E. Wetenhall's *Graecae Grammaticae Institutio Compendiaria in Usum Scholarum* (Philadelphia, 1776); for Latin, *A Short Introduction to Grammar. For the Use of the College and Academy in Philadelphia, Being a New Edition of Wetenhall's Latin Grammar*, was published as early as 1762 by Steuart in Philadelphia. The latter was full of errors: see Reinhold, *The Classick Pages*, p. 23.
75. Esp. Greek texts of Epictetus's *Enchiridion* (from Upton's edition, with Latin translation) in 1792 and 1793, by Matthew Carey in Philadelphia (the Greek is difficult to read). I owe these references to the kindness of Edwin Wolf 2nd, librarian of the Library Company of Philadelphia. See also Caleb Alexander, *A Grammatical Institute of the Latin Language: Intended to the Use of Latin Schools in the United States* (Worcester, 1794).
76. Worcester, 1795.
77. Preface, pp. ix–x. Cp. George E. Littlefield, *Early Schools and School-Books of New England* (Boston, 1904), pp. 266–267. Caleb Alexander also compiled *A Grammatical System of the Grecian Language* (Worcester, 1796), based on eight English grammars. The author asks "the candid, benevolent *reader, without being requested, [to] forgive inaccuracies and cherish* even feeble *attempts to promote any kind of useful knowledge, in this rising Empire*" (Preface).
78. *Port Folio* 3 (1803), pp. 390–391. Texts were to include Vergil, Horace, Ovid, Caesar, Sallust, the Greek Testament, the Latin Testament, and a Latin dictionary. Cp. Adolph Growoll, *Book Trade Bibliography in the United States in the Nineteenth Century* (New York, 1898; rpt. 1939), pp. vi–vii.

79. *Port Folio* 4 (1804), pp. 252–253, 286; 5 (1804), p. 253; *Monthly Anthology* 2 (1805), pp. 436–437; 3 (1806), p. 54.
80. *Port Folio* 5 (1805), p. 253.
81. *Port Folio* 4 (1804), p. 286.
82. Growoll, *Book Trade Bibliography*, pp. iv–vi. It was based on William Duncan's Aberdeen edition; this first American edition was revised by Malcolm Campbell.
83. Ibid., Appendix: "Catalogue of All the Books Printed in the United States" (Boston, 1804); Katherine H. Packer, *Early American School Books: A Bibliography Based on the Boston Booksellers Catalogue of 1804* (Ann Arbor, 1954).
84. *Monthly Anthology* 2 (1805), p. 549.
85. *Monthly Anthology* 4 (1807), pp. 380–387.
86. *Monthly Anthology* 7 (1809), p. 55.
87. "Retrospective Notice of American Literature, II," a review of James Otis's *Rudiments of Latin Prosody* (Boston, 1760), in *Monthly Anthology* 5 (1808), pp. 222–224; "Retrospective . . . , III," review of James Logan's *M. T. Cicero's Cato Major* (Philadelphia, 1744), ibid., pp. 281–282, 340–342, 391–396. American translations of the classics were rare in the eighteenth century. An increased tempo of translations and imitations took place in the early national period. The most memorable are: Robert Munford's of the first book of Ovid's *Metamorphoses*, in *A Collection of Plays and Poems* (Petersburg, 1798), pp. 113–163; John Quincy Adams's of the 13th and 7th satires of Juvenal, in *Port Folio* 1 (1801), pp. 6–8; 5 (1805), pp. 150–152, both in rhymed couplets, together with Latin text; William Munford's *Homer's Iliad* (Boston, 1846), composed 1802–25. On Adams's translations see Irving N. Rothman, "Two Juvenalian Satires by John Quincy Adams," *Early American Literature* 6 (1971–72), pp. 234–251; Linda K. Kerber and Walter John Morris, "Politics and Literature: The Adams Family and the *Port Folio*," *Wm. & Mary Quart.*, 3rd ser., 23 (1966), pp. 450–476. On Munford's *Iliad* see Richard Beale Davis, *Literature and Society in Early Virginia, 1608–1840* (Baton Rouge, 1973), pp. 278–286. Munford's was the most distinguished translation of a classical work by an American in the early national period. An anonymous translation of Juvenal's 3rd satire in 1806, was severely criticized in the *Monthly Anthology* 3 (1806), pp. 592–595: "His apology for publishing is one, which we have heard before, but wish *never* to hear again. It is, that the production is American."
88. Bentley, *Diary*, vol. III, p. 247 (entry of Sept. 16, 1806).
89. *Port Folio*, n.s., 4 (1807), pp. 366–367; *Monthly Anthology* 4 (1807), pp. 284, 381.
90. *Monthly Anthology* 4 (1807), p. 683.
91. By Etheridge and Bliss: *Port Folio*, n.s., 4 (1807), p. 331.
92. *Port Folio*, n.s., 1 (1806), Frontispiece and pp. 280, 358.
93. *Articles for the Establishment of a Society for the Printing and Publishing of the Ancient Works of Grecian, Roman, Hebrew and Other Oriental Literature: To Be Denominated the "American Classic Association"* (Philadelphia, 1808). Shares were to be issued, and a board of directors established consisting of eight "men skilled in Classical Literature," and five business men.
94. *Monthly Anthology* 8 (1810), pp. 69–72.
95. *North American Review* 2 (1816), pp. 129–139; 4 (1817), pp. 269–270. In 1817 Wells & Lilly also published the first American edition of Tacitus (republication of the Oberlin text): *North American Review* 7 (1818), pp. 324–331.
96. *Analectic Magazine* 6 (1815), pp. 337–338.
97. Hofstadter and Smith, *American Higher Education*, vol. I, pp. 220–221.
98. Bristed, *America and Her Resources*, p. 355. In connection with the purchase of Jefferson's library by Congress three years before, in the debate on the floor

of the House it was argued by some that "it abounded with productions of an atheistical, irreligious and immoral character—a fourth of such books were in foreign languages and many in the dead languages." See William Dawson Johnson, *History of the Library of Congress* (Washington, D.C., 1904), vol. I, p. 87.

99. See pp. 181–182, above.
100. *North American Review* 23 (1826), pp. 142–150.
101. *North American Review* 23 (1826), pp. 220–224.
102. *Q. Horatii Flacci Poemata*, ed. Charles Anthon (New York, 1830), reviewed in *American Quarterly Review* 8 (1830), pp. 72–93.
103. Alexis de Tocqueville, *Democracy in America* (New York, 1945), vol. II, p. 58. Tocqueville's work was first published in 1835–40.
104. *Henry Wansey and His American Journal, 1794*, ed. David John Jeremy (Philadelphia, 1970), p. 130.
105. Louis E. Snow, *The College Curriculum in the United States*, Teachers College, Columbia University, Contributions to Education, no. 10 (New York, 1907), pp. 113–114.
106. *Port Folio* 2 (1802), p. 374; 3 (1803), p. 198.
107. Miller, *Brief Retrospect*, vol. II, pp. 36–43, 54.
108. Nathan S. Goodman, *Benjamin Rush, Physician and Citizen, 1746–1813* (Philadelphia, 1934), pp. 339–340.
109. Climenole [Josiah Quincy], *Port Folio* 4 (1804), pp. 81–83, 89–91; cp. 4 (1804), p. 366; n.s., 4 (1807), p. 357. See also Linda K. Kerber, *Federalists in Dissent: Imagery and Ideology in Jeffersonian America* (Ithaca, 1970), pp. 95–134 ("Salvaging the Classics").
110. "Scaliger," in 4 (1807), pp. 65–71, 184. Cp. *Port Folio* 5 (1805), p. 325; *Monthly Anthology* 5 (1808), pp. 222–224.
111. 5 (1808), p. 197.
112. Buckminster, "On the Dangers and Duties of Men of Letters," p. 146.
113. *Port Folio*, 3rd ser., 7 (1812), p. 450.
114. 2 (1813), p. 309.
115. *Port Folio*, 4th ser., 6 (1815), p. 148.
116. *Port Folio*, 5th ser., 2 (1816), p. 122.
117. Timothy Dwight, *Travels in New England and New-York* (New Haven, 1821–22), vol. I, p. 482.
118. [Joseph Cogswell], "On the Means of Education, and the State of Learning, in the United States of America," *Blackwood's Edinburgh Magazine* 4 (1819), pp. 550, 559. See also Tucker, *Essays*, p. 90; Jefferson, *Writings*, vol. XIV, pp. 200–201 (letter of 1814); *Port Folio*, 4th ser., 6 (1815), p. 148; 5th ser., 1 (1816), pp. 414–415 ("[The classics] are . . . pretty generally proscribed in the United States. . . . The most strenuous opposition to the study of the dead languages exists in the commercial classes of society"); *Port Folio*, 5th ser., 2 (1816), pp. 116–122.
119. *Western Review* 3 (1820), p. 145; William W. Campbell, *The Life and Writings of De Witt Clinton* (New York, 1849), pp. 355–356; *North American Review* 19 (1824), pp. 128, 133.
120. *Southern Review* 1 (1828), pp. 1–49, esp. p. 3, note; *Writings of Hugh Swinton Legaré* (Charleston, 1845–46), vol. II, pp. 5–51, 217.
121. Vol. I, p. 470.
122. N.s., 5 (1808), p. 158; 3rd ser., 1 (1809), p. 93. For editor Joseph Dennie's uncompromising advocacy of classical models as the ultimate authority in American letters, see Randolph C. Randall, "Joseph Dennie's Literary Attitudes in the *Port Folio*, 1801–1812," in *Essays Mostly on Periodical Publishing in America*, ed. James Woodress (Durham, 1973), pp. 66, 88.

123. Adams and Rush, *The Spur of Fame*, pp. 170–171, 177. On other optimistic views on the classics, see Cantabrigiensis, *Massachusetts Magazine* 1 (1789), pp. 117–118; *Port Folio* 5 (1805), p. 325; n.s., 1 (1806), p. 358; *Monthly Anthology* 4 (1807), p. 656.
124. Hofstadter and Smith, *American Higher Education*, vol. I, pp. 189–191; Howard H. Peckham, *The Making of the University of Michigan 1817–1967* (Ann Arbor, 1967), pp. 5–7.
125. *North American Review* 18 (1824), pp. 99, 280.
126. Review of *Substance of Two Reports of the Faculty of Amherst College* (Amherst, 1827), in *North American Review* 28 (1829), p. 303.
127. "Original Papers in Relation to a Course of Liberal Education," *American Journal of Science and Arts* 15 (1829), pp. 297–351; Snow, *College Curriculum*, pp. 143–154; Hofstadter and Smith, *American Higher Education*, vol. I, pp. 275–291; R. Freeman Butts, *The College Charts Its Course* (New York, 1939), pp. 118–125; Richard Hofstadter and C. DeWitt Hardy, *The Development and Scope of Higher Education in the United States* (New York, 1952), pp. 15–17; Brooks M. Kelley, *Yale: A History* (New Haven, 1974), pp. 161–165; Sol Cohen, *Education in the United States: A Documentary History* (New York, 1974), vol. III, pp. 1441–1451.
128. McLachlan, *American Boarding Schools*, p. 96.
129. Howard Mumford Jones, *O Strange New World. American Culture: The Formative Years* (New York, 1952), pp. 265–266.
130. *The Works of Daniel Webster* (Boston, 1853), vol. I, p. 143; Louis B. Wright, "Thomas Jefferson and the Classics," *Proc. Amer. Philos. Soc.* 87 (1943–44), p. 233; Emily E. F. Ford and Emily E. F. Skeel, eds., *Notes on the Life of Noah Webster* (New York, 1912), vol. I, p. 31.
131. *Western Review* 3 (1820), p. 145; cp. Samuel Miller, *Letters from a Father to His Sons in College* (Philadelphia, 1852), pp. 131–139. Miller's letters were written in 1843.
132. Thomas Smith Grimké, *Oration on American Education* (Cincinnati, 1835), p. 10; "Our Own Country," *The Knickerbocker, New-York Monthly Magazine* 5 (1835), pp. 416–417; Tocqueville, *American Democracy*, vol. I, p. 327; vol. II, pp. 65–67, 70, 85 ("Democratic Communities . . . care but little for what occurred at Rome and Athens").
133. *American Journal of Philology* 37 (1916), p. 495. Henry E. Dwight wrote in 1830 (Hofstadter and Smith, *American Higher Education*, vol. I, p. 305): "The want of competent teachers is one of the principal reasons, why the Classics have been studied with little enthusiasm in our country." On the classical curriculum of the mid-nineteenth century see Edwin C. Broome, *A Historical and Critical Discussion of College Admission Requirements* (New York, 1903), p. 40.

VII. "A New Morning": Edward Everett's Contributions to Classical Learning

$$\mathbf{I}$$n the early national period the very survival of classical learning in America was in the balance, not only because of concerted efforts by militant nationalists to restructure education along utilitarian lines for national purposes, and to create an indigenous literature free from cultural dependence but also because of the superficiality of classical scholarship, the sterility of traditional methods of teaching, the inadequacy of schoolmasters as scholars and teachers, and the poverty of the results.[1]

In the second decade of the nineteenth century there was a sharp awareness of the sterility of classical scholarship, and of the need to elevate standards by adopting European critical methods and scholarship. Prominent among the first wave of American students who went to Europe, especially to the University of Göttingen, was Edward Everett, who, it was hoped, would invigorate and set standards for classical scholarship, and reform the teaching of the classics in America.

In the fall of 1819 there was an air of buoyant expectancy at Harvard and in Boston intellectual circles. "Waiting for Everett" was at an end: he was returning after four and a half years of study and travel abroad to assume his new post as professor of Greek literature and, as America's first systematically trained classical scholar, to lay the foundations of critical scholarship as a whole in this country.

Emerson heralded Everett's return as the turning point in America to both scholarship and high culture. "Germany," he wrote, "had created criticism in vain for us until 1820, when Edward Everett returned . . . and brought to Cambridge his rich results. . . . The rudest undergraduate found a new morning opened to him in the lecture room of Harvard Hall. . . . It was not original thought, but the manner of presentation [brought] a new perception of Grecian beauty, to which he had opened our eyes."[2] "There was an influence on the young people from Everett's genius which was almost comparable to that of Pericles of Athens."[3] He was acknowledged as the "greatest Hellenist in America," its "foremost classical scholar." He was, in fact, the only one in his day.

The distinguished scholar in Cambridge, as he was called, taught a new course in the history of Greek literature (to the Middle Ages), required of seniors, and also occasionally an optional course in antiquities. In his teaching Everett discarded the traditional American recitation method of drill and testing of assignments. He decided to use the German lecture method. This was a revolutionary innovation which met with resistance from students, unaccustomed to German-style teaching, note taking, and learning. The administration, too, was soon troubled by the procedure. For Emerson, in his senior year at Harvard, and for some other students, the novel experience was a thrilling one, particularly the unique content and Everett's manner of presentation.

Everett's aspirations and energies were not confined to Harvard Yard. He was for years editor of the influential *North American Review*, and for intellectual circles in Boston he delivered two series of popular lectures in the winter of 1822–23, on antiquities and on ancient art. Emerson acclaimed his idol at this time thus: "He has this winter delivered a noble course of Lectures on Antiquities . . . , all of which I heard—only desire to hear more," though, Emerson demurred, "much of his matter is easily acquired from common books."[4] In his *Journal* Emerson recorded that "though the lectures contain nothing original, and no very remarkable views, yet it was an account of antiquities betraying everywhere that fine Roman hand, and presented in the inimitable style of *our Cicero*."[5] There is, however, something Emerson did not know: in the still unpublished Everett Papers[6] at the Massachusetts Historical Society there is preserved a massive set of very precise and detailed notes (361 manuscript pages!) taken down at Professor Welcker's lectures at Göttingen in 1817 on "Archaeology, Or of Ancient Art."

To live the role of scholar—German style—Everett began to publish learned articles, the first of their kind in America in the field of classical studies. They appeared in the fourth volume (1821) of the *Memoirs of the American Academy of Arts and Sciences.* One contained the *editio princeps* of a Latin "Inscription from the Columbarium of the Freedmen and Slaves of Livia Augusta." This was the first ancient inscription published in America, a small one procured by him in Rome in the winter of 1818–19. His edition of the inscription is, in part, erroneous; and it has remained buried in the *Memoirs*, never finding its way into the *Corpus Inscriptionum Latinarum.* The second article was simply a descriptive catalogue of eight manuscripts procured by Everett abroad for Harvard: seven Greek (mostly biblical), procured by him in Constantinople in 1819; and one Latin, a translation of three of Aristotle's works, obtained in Florence. Everett's effort to date the manuscripts is faulty; and he was, moreover, poorly informed in his belief that they were the only Greek manuscripts in the country.

Like many German scholars, Everett also produced school texts. Books for Greek and Roman studies—manuals, grammars, dictionaries—were nearly all imported from Europe. Now in 1822 there appeared Everett's eagerly awaited translations from the German of Philip Buttmann's *Greek Grammar*, and the next year the companion translation of Jacob's *Greek Reader.* Everett was himself not sanguine about these efforts. In the preface of the *Greek Grammar* he wrote, "The translator is not without fear that, at least at first, it may be found somewhat in advance of the state of philological studies in this country." And he was right! It did not find acceptance in American schools.

Yet it was, in Emerson's words, a "new morning" for classical studies in America. Here for the first time was an all-round classical scholar: innovative teacher, contributor to the increase in classical knowledge, textbook author, dazzling lecturer to the general public. But let us look at the cultural context in which Everett sought to create the beginnings of classical learning in America in the 1820s. At this very time classical learning in America was at its lowest ebb. After a Golden Age of classical learning during the Revolutionary period (from 1760–90), classical studies underwent a precipitous and disastrous decline in the early national period.[7] This resulted, in part, from the frenetic quest for national American values for the new republic. So the classical models and the traditional classical education were vigorously challenged as obsolete, elitist, ornamental, and unsuitable in the dynamism of unique, revolutionary, pluralistic, turbulent, future-oriented society.

With regard to the study of Greek, which Everett sought to foster, it had always been in America far to the rear of Latin, dismissed as "a smattering which scarcely deserves the name of knowledge."[8] It was in this grim atmosphere that, to stem the anti-Greek tide, an anonymous donor (who later was revealed to be Samuel Eliot) established the professorship of Greek literature at Harvard in 1814. The statutes of the professorship specified that the professor be a master of arts (the Ph.D. degree was unknown in the United States), and his duties were specified as "Professor of the Greek Language and of Greek Literature." Young Everett, one of Harvard's most brilliant graduates (class of 1811), and protégé of President Kirkland, was appointed the first professor of Greek literature, and ceremoniously inaugurated on April 12, 1815, the day after his twenty-first birthday! Four days later he sailed, with George Ticknor, for Europe, for there were no facilities in America for the training of a classical scholar. In an unprecedented and generous move, the Corporation and Board of Overseers of Harvard granted Everett leave to study abroad, with generous financial support, to fit himself as a Greek scholar for the prestigious chair. Adams, as Washington before him, was opposed to sending American youth to Europe for education. Jefferson, predictably, advised Ticknor in 1815 to go abroad to study, because it was impossible to become a scholar in this country.

But how ignorant responsible Americans were about what it would require to perfect a classical scholar! The Harvard Corporation originally granted Everett one year for study abroad; but this was quickly extended to two years, and eventually to four and a half. Everett's principal goal was intensive study at the University of Göttingen, then the best university in Europe for classical studies. Although Everett's obligation was to perfect himself as the first American classical scholar, he spent only two years at Göttingen, where he was tireless in his studies. The remainder of his long leave he traveled purposefully, in England, France, Holland, Germany, and finally in Italy and Greece.

As for the American students who descended on Göttingen at this time, their dreams and ambitions were naive, flamboyant, visionary—and precarious. Everett, Ticknor, Joseph Cogswell, and George Bancroft were starry-eyed innocents abroad in the advanced scholarly world of Germany. Ticknor wrote home in November of 1813, "What a mortifying distance there is between a European and an American scholar. We do not yet know what a Greek scholar is; we do not even know the process by which a man is to be made one."[9] Cogswell complained in May of 1817, "What can men think when they say two years are sufficient to make a Greek scholar. . . . It is true very few of what Germans call scholars are needed in America; if there were only one to begin with. . . ."[10] In 1818, Cogswell was still sceptical: "[A scholar] could never be formed in America. . . . Is there any one willing to make such a sacrifice? I answer that it is the sacrifice made by almost every man of classical learning in Germany."[11] Everett wrote in 1815, "A German scholar sits and smokes and drinks coffee, and studies his eighteen hours a day, partly because it feels good."[12]

The Americans at Göttingen soon became painfully aware that they were not prepared to absorb and bring back the systematic scholarship of Germany. Where could they begin in America to teach and promote the values and emphases of German Neo-humanism, with its Graecomania, its emphasis on Greek language, culture, and creativity in such varied fields, its critical historical study of all *Altertumswissenschaft* (so different from the American uncritical veneration of the "Sacred Classics"), its dedication to un-tiring research and publication of such research, its emphasis on philology as the capstone of humanistic education, on classical phil-ology as a specialized field, on a life of commitment to study, re-search, publication, and teaching? Our American innocents abroad could not assimilate this complex experience in so short a time, or find a congenial atmosphere for such learning in America. Not one of them came back a finished classical scholar.

The resources of the library at Göttingen were awesome to the Americans. Although Göttingen was founded in 1737, a century after Harvard's beginnings, in eighty years the library had over 200,000 volumes, while Harvard's, the largest in the country, pos-sessed about 24,000 at the time, a mere "closetful of books" Tick-nor called it. He wrote back to Jefferson from Göttingen, "In America we look on the library at Cambridge as a wonder. . . . [But] it is much less remarkable that our stock of learning is so small than that it is so great, considering the means from which it is drawn are so inadequate." "We are mortified and exasperated be-cause we have no learned men, and yet make it *physically* impossi-ble for our scholars to become such. . . . [We give] them a library from which hardly one, and *not one* of them, can qualify to execute the duties of his office."[13]

Everett himself was fully aware of the difficulties of absorbing German scholarship and living as a classical scholar in America. Still, he applied himself feverishly for two years, and was granted the Ph.D. degree on September 17, 1817, the first American to be awarded the degree, but without writing the dissertation and without oral defense of a thesis.

Edward Everett left Germany in the fall of 1817 for England and France. On a previous visit to England, on his way to Göttingen, he had gone to see the Elgin marbles in London, and he wrote in his journal in June, 1815, that he was disappointed in his expectations. But when he returned to see them again in the spring of 1818, he was more confident and perceptive: "These mutilated remains speak a Truth & Nature, which all the freshness of modern art cannot reach—I felt proud of being a Greek professor, as I surveyed them." By contrast, when he was in Leipzig in 1816, where he met a teacher-librarian, a Herr Spohn, a very learned man indeed, he recorded in his journal, "I felt ashamed of my title when I heard him called plain Master."[14]

Everett's classical pilgrimage in Italy took him as far south as Pompeii and Paestum; in Rome he diligently visited the museum, and read in the Vatican Library. Then on to the "sacred soil of Greece." At Göttingen he had become aware of the importance of studying every facet of antiquity: architecture, sculpture, coins, gems, manuscripts, inscriptions, as well as the texts. When he visited August Boeckh and Philip Buttmann in Berlin in the fall of 1816, there was much talk of the forthcoming publication by Boeckh of Greek inscriptions (the *Corpus Inscriptionum Graecarum*). Like Nicholas Biddle of Philadelphia in 1806, Everett copied a number of Greek inscriptions, and one in Latin, while he traveled in Greece. But, curiously, he did not send a single one of the texts to Boeckh, or publish them himself. They lie buried in his unpublished journal. He seems to have felt obliged to pay some attention to visible remains of antiquity in his travels, but so overwhelming was the experience in so short a time that he simply resorted to tokenism.

After four and a half years Everett returned to Harvard and his post as professor of Greek literature in the fall of 1819. From the very start of his professorship, his efforts to fulfill his duties as a classical scholar and to introduce German-style scholarship to America were not appreciated. Indeed, though he threw himself into his duties conscientiously and methodically, he was a solitary voice crying in the wilderness. In time some of the overseers were critical of the "useless erudition" and display of learning that were of no benefit to the students. Everett's own inner conflicts are revealed in a letter he wrote to one of the Harvard overseers, Judge

Joseph Story, on April 12, 1821 (Everett was then twenty-seven years old): "I find I am a poor professor. From the very first week of my return hither, I saw that our University . . . would furnish me little scope for the communication of the higher parts of ancient literature, and that a good grammatical driller, which I cannot consent to be, is wanted. . . . In short, I die daily of a cramped spirit, fluttering and beating from side to side of a cage."[15] He wanted, he insisted, to be a professor of Greek literature. They, he said, wanted a "drill master."

Among his aspirations was to create an atmosphere of receptivity in America to the Greek language and to Hellenism. In the period 1820–30, he mounted a concerted campaign in America to tilt classical studies to Greek and Hellenism. Emanating from Everett and his friends, articles appeared in the *North American Review*, the *Port Folio* in Philadelphia, the *Southern Review*, and the *Western Review* to promote the study of Greek to higher priority than Latin, indeed even to supplant it in the curriculum. But ten years of effort came to naught. The proposal was out of touch with the mainstream of American education and society. Conservative tradition prevailed.[16]

Everett met other failures in his efforts to promote Hellenism in America. A famous painting, *Panorama of Athens*, by Henry Barker and John Burford, was the rage in London. Theodore Lyman, Jr., a friend of Everett, purchased a copy in London and presented it to Harvard. The *Panorama* was exhibited with much fanfare in Boston to raise funds for a permanent building to house the large painting. Everett lectured on it to a fashionable and brilliant audience in Boston, but he managed to raise less than four hundred dollars. The plan for the building was shelved; the painting was destroyed by fire in 1845.

Another blow to his self-esteem came in 1824, when, during the Greek War of Independence, he aspired to be appointed agent of the United States government to promote American interests in Greece. John Quincy Adams, then secretary of state, rejected him as "too partisan," and an editorial in the *National Advocate* of New York declared "the Professor" unsuitable because what was needed was a shrewd politician, not a Greek scholar and periodical writer, in short, a "mere scholar." It was indeed a blow to be thought a mere scholar, a derogatory term in America.

In August of 1824, Everett was invited to give the annual Phi Beta Kappa oration at Harvard. By coincidence the aged Lafayette, who was visiting the United States, was in the audience. Everett, whose topic was the development of a national American literature, concluded with a dazzling peroration eulogizing patriotism—and Lafayette. The speech created an unprecedented sensation. Shortly after, he was nominated for Congress, and elected by a landslide vote in November, 1824. "He orated himself into Congress," Samuel Eliot Morison said of him. Everett fully expected to hold on to his professorship while he was a member of Congress in Washington. But the law of nonresidence was invoked against him by the overseers, and his professorship was declared vacated at the end of the academic year. Everett wrote later in an autobiographical sketch that he had not contemplated retirement from academic life.

Emerson, however, was distressed by Everett's withdrawal from the world of scholarship. "This man," he wrote, "had neither intellectual nor moral principles to teach. He had no thought. . . . Only in new perspectives of Grecian beauty had he opened our eyes." Emerson lamented finally, "This bright new morning had a short continuance. Mr. Everett was soon attracted to the vulgar prize of politics, and quit coldly the splendid career opening before him."[17] Emerson was himself keenly aware, as he stated, that it was easier to demand a native American literature than to produce one. It was equally premature for him to expect a native classical scholarship at this time.

A further egregious misjudgment of the national temper by Everett in his fervor for Hellenism was the advice he gave to the distinguished American sculptor Horatio Greenough in 1832. Then a member of the House of Representatives in Washington, representing Massachusetts, he counseled Greenough to take as his model the colossal Olympian Zeus of Phidias for the monumental statue of Washington commissioned by Congress to serve as a national symbol. The statue, now a curiosity housed in the Museum of Natural History and Technology of the Smithsonian Institution, was rejected with a mixture of national indifference, hostility, and ridicule.[18]

Everett had given ten years of his life to classical learning. Alternative careers opened up before him: he became successively governor of Massachusetts, president of Harvard, secretary of state under Lincoln. The failure of his aspirations in academic life should not be attributed to his inability to stay at one activity very long, as has been charged, but to a host of factors not in his control. Classical learning was not yet a professional field in the United States, and thus his efforts to act the role of German-type scholar were doomed to failure. He sensed the importance of reaching out to general audiences with his popular lectures, and of writing suitable textbooks for students, and he sought to publish learned articles in the field (even if his contributions to classical scholarship remained minimal). Neither the scholarly apparatus nor the institutional structure for specialization of this kind was yet at hand. Libraries were inadequate for scholarly research, and there were no specialized media for disseminating learned publications in the field, nor scholarly colleagues in the country with whom to communicate. The traditional emphasis in American collegiate education on veneration of the Greek and Roman classics and on drill and testing discouraged critical scholarship. For many reasons, indeed, the American college remained virtually unchanged long after Everett's time, continuing to be little above the level of the German gymnasium.

In sum, Edward Everett was ahead of his time in scholarly aspirations, methods, and comprehensive scope of the field he envisaged. Though he did not reach the promised land, he saw what needed to be done. He deserves to be remembered as the earliest pioneer in the promotion of classical scholarship in America.

Notes

1. See "The Silver Age of Classical Studies in America, 1790–1830," Chapter VI, above. Cp. the self-knowledge of James Priestley, one of the South's famed classical scholars, teacher especially of Greek (in Virginia, Maryland, and Kentucky), president of Cumberland College (from 1809–16), in a letter to Bishop John Carroll of Baltimore, Sept. 10, 1807: "[I have more demands on my time] than ten professors in a European University, & less qualification than perhaps any one of them. . . . It is impossible to study, & without study it is impossible to be rightly prepared to teach, especially when the teacher has himself been so ill-instructed as all in this country have been—I have been for thirty years, almost, laboring to mend the defects of my own education, and I have not yet got it done." See John H. Thiveat, "James Priestley: Classical Scholar of the Old South," *Tennessee Historical Quarterly* 39 (1980), pp. 421–439.
2. Ralph Waldo Emerson, "Historic Notes of Life and Letters in New England," in *Lectures and Biographical Sketches*, vol. X of *Emerson's Complete Works* (Boston, 1884), pp. 312–316.
3. *Journals of Ralph Waldo Emerson*, ed. Edward Waldo Emerson and Waldo Emerson Forbes, vol. VI (Boston, 1911), pp. 255–256.
4. *The Letters of Ralph Waldo Emerson*, ed. Ralph L. Rusk (New York, 1939), vol. I, pp. 131–132.
5. Emerson, *Journals*, vol. VI, p. 207.
6. Everett Papers, vol. 218, microfilm reels XXXIV–XXXV, Massachusetts Historical Society, Boston.
7. See "The Silver Age of Classical Studies in America, 1790–1830," Chapter VI, above, pp. 175–178.
8. Samuel Miller, *A Brief Retrospect of the Eighteenth Century* (New York, 1803), vol. II, pp. 36–37.
9. George Ticknor, *Life, Letters, and Journal* (Boston, 1909), p. 53.

10. Richard Hofstadter and Wilson Smith, eds., *American Higher Education: A Documentary History* (Chicago, 1961), vol. I, p. 262.
11. Ibid.
12. Everett Papers, reel XXXIV.
13. Orie William Long, *Literary Pioneers: Early American Explorers of European Culture* (Cambridge, Mass., 1935), pp. 12–13.
14. Everett Papers, reels XXXIV–XXXV.
15. Long, *Literary Pioneers*, pp. 74–75.
16. See "Philhellenism in America in the Early National Period," Chapter VIII, below.
17. Emerson, *Journals*, vol. VI, p. 256.
18. Nathalia Wright, *Horatio Greenough: The First American Sculptor* (Philadelphia, 1963), p. 191; W. Craven, "Horatio Greenough's Statue of Washington and Phidias's Olympian Zeus," *Art Quarterly* 26 (1963), pp. 429–440.

VIII. Philhellenism in America in the Early National Period

When John Adams was a young man he asked the leading Boston lawyer Jeremiah Gridley whether he should study Greek. Gridley replied drily, "It is a matter of meer Curiosity."[1] Greek, in fact, had only a token role in the traditional humanistic curriculum of the colonial period. And when classical learning was politicized in the Revolutionary Age, Greek and Hellenism receded into the shadows. Latin was for centuries the elite subject, and for American libertarians the Roman republic became the archetypal model, "the lamp of experience," the pure fountain of lessons for the building of the first modern republic.

In their search for analogs in antiquity, the Founding Fathers discounted the Greek experience, especially Athens, largely because of the turbulent and fugitive character of many Greek commonwealths. True, there were occasional rhetorical flourishes to Sparta as the "land of the free and home of the brave," to Athens as the "nursery of liberty and the arts," to the valor of the coalition of small Greek states that defeated the Persian monarch. James Wilson wrote in 1790: "At the mention of Athens, a thousand refined and endearing associations rush immediately into the memory." And Jefferson's special love of Homer, "this rich source of delight," is well known.[2]

But these were tangential judgments. For example, in 1787 Jefferson gave his verdict that in the study of foreign languages "I think

Greek the least useful"—the general view. In the massive efforts to restructure American education after the Revolution, the study of Greek was widely assailed as dispensable. By 1803 Samuel Miller, in his famous *Brief Retrospect of the Eighteenth Century*,[3] noted that the study of Greek in American colleges was endangered, that it was a mere "smattering of knowledge," and that popular hostility to Greek was so marked in some colleges that the college authorities had to exert great effort "to prevent popular ignorance and prejudice from expelling the study of Greek." At Yale and elsewhere the anticlassical student rebellion in the first decade of the nineteenth century was directed primarily against the study of Greek.

At the same time there was taking place in the early national period a steady disenchantment with and emancipation from the previously revered classical political models: they were now deemed unsuitable for the American national character and experience. Charles Pinckney of South Carolina had said at the Constitutional Convention in 1789: "Can we copy from Greece and Rome? . . . We surely differ from the whole. Our situation is unexampled."[4] In reality, the Roman pattern known to the Founding Fathers was but a stereotype, a timeless abstract model, a canonical standard for a free, virtuous republic; but it soon became apparent that dynamic, pluralistic, disorderly America could not be forced into the classical mold. This retreat from the Roman model—dare I say "Paradigms Lost"?—was in full swing in the early national period.[5]

And what did the future have in store for classical learning in America? No sooner was the national life inaugurated in 1789 than classical learning declined precipitously from its Golden Age in the Revolutionary period into a Silver Age—and worse—in the following decades. There ensued a sharp deterioration in classical studies, superficiality of scholarship and teaching, low standards, decline in popular esteem, and virtual stagnation. In 1793 Hugh Henry Brackenridge in his satirical novel-miscellany *Modern Chivalry* could portray an illiterate Irishman passing himself off as a professor of Greek in an American college on the strength of his heavy Irish brogue.

But in the midst of this disarray there emerged, like the phoenix from the ashes, the first intimation of a rebirth: a burst of philhellenism in America. In 1811 John Adams discerned this new trend in classical learning in America: a new interest in the Greek language and Hellenic culture. He ventured to explain this development—simplistically, it must be noted—as a consequence of the

American Revolution, which, he averred, motivated the first formal histories of Greece, and thus opened up this new interest in antiquity. It was indeed in the 1780s that Greek history was for the first time since antiquity taken seriously on both sides of the Atlantic.

This nascent American philhellenism was, as a matter of fact, not influenced by the sentimental idealization by the English poets of the eighteenth century of ancient Greece as an idyllic Arcadia and symbol of beauty, repose, and liberty, or even initially by the New Humanism in Germany, with its Hellenic renaissance in classical studies and its Greek aestheticism, associated with Winckelmann, Herder, Lessing, Schiller, Goethe, Hölderlin.

No, Americans began to discover Greece by themselves—by travel. In 1806 one of the first Americans to set foot in Greece was the Philadelphian Nicholas Biddle, whose reverence for Greece took him there, and who wrote back, that "the soil of Greece is sacred to genius and to letters." Others in increasing numbers brought back descriptions of Greek lands and romantic enthusiasm for Hellenism.[6]

Thus, in the first three decades of the nineteenth century William Munford of Virginia composed a new verse translation of the *Iliad*, the most distinguished translation of a classical work by an American in the early national period. In his preface Munford eulogized Homer and "the almost unparalleled sublimity and beauty of the original. . . . Surely, the venerated bard . . . must be admitted to be one of the most moral and religious of all ancient heathen authors." Compare this with the full-scale assault on Homer by the Jeffersonian Federalist Joel Barlow in 1807 in the preface of his flawed American epic *The Columbiad*, and his conclusion that "the Iliad has done more harm than good. Its existence has really proved one of the most signal misfortunes of mankind."[7]

It was exactly at this time (the year is 1808) that in Tennessee young Sam Houston at the age of sixteen fell in love with the *Iliad* —in Pope's translation. Though he was an undistinguished student at the local academy, he related later in his *Autobiography* that "I had got possession of two or three books, among them Pope's translation of the *Iliad*, which I read so constantly that I could repeat it almost entirely from beginning to end." His modern biographer Wisehart attributes to Houston's addiction to the *Iliad* his personal flamboyance and heroic self-image, and concludes that it colored his oratorical and literary style, and inspired him to give an heroic posture to all his actions.[8]

Much more diffusive was the influence of a wave of American students who descended upon Europe in the first two decades of the nineteenth century, especially in Göttingen, then steeped in the new German Hellenic studies. The most famous of these young Americans were George Ticknor, Edward Everett, Joseph Cogswell, and George Bancroft. In 1815 Edward Everett was appointed the first Eliot Professor of Greek at Harvard—at the age of twenty-one—and was at once given leave to study abroad. At Göttingen he was molded into an outstanding Greek scholar. In 1816 he wrote home from Göttingen with excitement: "I have seen a genuine Greek, a fellow-countryman of Homer." Everett also traveled extensively in Greece before returning to Harvard in 1819, to become "the foremost American Hellenist," and the only one, giving lectures at the university in Greek language and literature and public lectures in Boston on the antiquities of Greece, the first such delivered to a public audience in America. They created a sensation.

On the wave of this nascent American Hellenism, a campaign was launched in 1820 by admirers of Greek literature to give priority to Greek over Latin in the schools and colleges, in short, to elevate Greek to the role of the principal study in the traditional curriculum which for centuries was dominated by Latin. Professor H. M. Fisher of Harvard wrote in 1820 in the influential *North American Review* that he was "convinced that on this depends the advancement of our classical and polite learning." Hugh Swinton Legaré of Charleston wrote in the first issue of his new *Southern Review* in 1828 that Greek is "by far the most extraordinary and brilliant phenomenon in the history of the human mind. If Americans are to study any foreign literature at all, it ought undoubtedly to be the Classical, and especially the Greek."[9] Needless to say, the Greek War of Independence also stirred fervent sympathies in America.

For this Greek revival there was a basic desideratum: Greek texts. Those previously printed in this country were notoriously inaccurate. Such new texts and tools for the study of Greek were now forthcoming: especially John Pickering's *On the Pronunciation of the Greek Language* and his *Comprehensive Lexicon of the Greek Language*—the best Greek-English dictionary before Lidell-Scott; a Greek grammar and Greek reader, both by Everett—but both translations from German texts.

But this movement to upgrade Greek, orchestrated at Harvard, with ardent followers in various parts of the country was stillborn. It was out of touch with the mainstream of American education and American society. In 1827 George Bancroft sadly asked "whether it is worth our while to study Greek at all in this country."[10]

By 1830 efforts to tilt classical studies away from Latin and Romanism to Greek and Hellenism had evaporated. But, remarkably, at this very time Hellenism indeed triumphed and won national acceptance in one of the arts—architecture. Jefferson's neoclassical Roman Revival architecture (dominant in America from 1780–1820), intended for public buildings and derived mostly from books, was an import from the European Palladian style. Jefferson's architectural credo was that buildings "should be more than things of beauty and convenience, above all, they should state a creed." His creed in this domain was to link the newness and rawness of the American experience with universal patterns of acknowledged beauty; particularly, he aimed at evoking the idealized Roman republic on American soil through "architectural quotations," as it were, from Roman grandeur.[11]

But in this he was myopic. For the Roman Palladian style was soon attacked as lavish, ornamental, and ponderous in its stately magnificence. Manifestoes were promulgated aimed at substituting the Parthenon for the Pantheon, Greek architecture for Roman. Simplicity, chaste style, and economy were to be the guiding principles, as more consonant with the American national character. Benjamin Latrobe, a naturalized Englishman, was the pioneer in launching the Hellenic Revival in America. In 1811 in an oration to American artists in Philadelphia he eulogized Greece as the fountainhead of the arts, proving in its stupendous creativity that the arts are compatible with freedom, and he prayed that "the days of Greece may be revived in the woods of America, and Philadelphia become the Athens of the Western world."[12]

Thus the Greek temple style was born, and it rapidly won central importance in American life; it became our first national style in architecture, gradually spreading all over the country, as the dominant form from 1820 to 1860. Besides being relatively simple to construct, the Greek temple form embodied a polyvalent symbolism: it cloaked the newness, changeability, and materialism of American culture with an aura of sanctity, linked it with the "land of liberty" and aesthetic creativity, and evoked an intimation of something eternal.

Robert Mills, our first native-born professional architect, wrote about the Greek Revival in America as follows: "It was fortunate that this style was so early introduced into our country, both on the ground of economy and of correct taste, and it exactly suited the character of our political institutions, and pecuniary means. Mr. Jefferson was a Roman in his views of architecture. . . . It required all the talents and good taste of such a man as Mr. Latrobe to correct it by introducing a better. The national good taste and the unprejudiced eye of our citizens required only a few examples of the Greek style for public structures, and its simplicity recommended its introduction into our private dwellings."[13] It is interesting to listen to a character in one of James Fenimore Cooper's lesser novels, *Home as Found* (1838): "Public sentiment just now runs almost exclusively and popularly into the Grecian school. We build little besides temples for our churches, our banks, our taverns, our court houses, and our dwellings,"—even breweries.[14]

It is thus one of the paradoxes of the people of paradox that, in the middle decades of the nineteenth century, while the Roman models lost their age-old authority for Americans, and the Greek language, too, failed to win pride of place over Latin in elitist academic circles, and indeed remained a "meer Curiosity," the Greek temple style, with its visual symbolism of simplicity, sanctity, and eternity, swept the nation and won popular acceptance. This was in essence a creedal statement in America's ceaseless groping for a sense of community. But it was the last time that the classical world was to furnish us with a collective value-laden theme, one that linked us visually, if not spiritually, with "purer fountains" of Western civilization.

Notes

1. *Diary and Autobiography of John Adams*, ed. L. H. Butterfield (Cambridge, Mass., 1962), vol. I, p. 55.
2. *The Works of James Wilson*, ed. Robert G. McCloskey (Cambridge, Mass., 1967), vol. I, p. 400; Meyer Reinhold, *The Classick Pages: Classical Reading of Eighteenth-Century Americans* (University Park, Pa., 1975), p. 130.
3. Samuel Miller, *A Brief Retrospect of the Eighteenth Century* (New York, 1803), vol. II, pp. 36–37.
4. *Secret Proceedings and Debates of the Convention* (Richmond, 1839), p. 175.
5. See "Classical Influences and Eighteenth-Century American Political Thought," Chapter III, above, pp. 105–109.
6. See "The Silver Age of Classical Studies in America, 1790–1830," Chapter VI, above.
7. William Munford, *Homer's Iliad* (Boston, 1846), vol. I, pp. vii–xii; Joel Barlow, *The Columbiad*, 2nd ed. (Philadelphia, 1809), vol. I, pp. v–vii; vol. II, pp. 194–195.
8. Susan Ford Wiltshire, "Sam Houston and the Iliad," *Tennessee Historical Quarterly* 32 (1973), pp. 241–254; M. K. Wisehart, *Sam Houston, American Giant* (Washington, D.C., 1962), pp. 4–5.

9. See "The Silver Age of Classical Studies in America, 1790–1830," Chapter VI, above, pp. 183–185.
10. *North American Review* 24 (1827), p. 155.
11. Martin O. Snyder, "The Icon of Antiquity," in *The Usefulness of Classical Learning in the Eighteenth Century*, ed. Susan Ford Wiltshire (University Park, Pa., 1977), pp. 32–34.
12. Benjamin Latrobe, *Anniversary Oration Pronounced before the Society of Artists of the United States* (New York, 1811), pp. 16–17.
13. H. M. Pierce Gallagher, *Robert Mills* (New York, 1935), p. 142.
14. Snyder, "The Icon of Antiquity," p. 42.

IX. Vergil in the American Experience from Colonial Times to 1882

$\mathbf{I}$n 1881, in commemoration of the nineteenth centenary of Vergil's death, Tennyson composed his stately eulogy "To Virgil." Across the Atlantic there was no American accolade, not even a ceremonial compliment in remembrance of Rome's greatest poet.

We need to understand this silence, since for about 250 years Vergil's works were in unbroken continuity read and studied by all Americans who experienced the academic curriculum, transported from the British educational model, in the colonial and early national grammar schools, the academies, high schools, and colleges. From the beginning knowledge of Vergil's *Aeneid* was, indeed, required of college-bound students. By 1655 ¹ Harvard College (founded in 1636, a year after the establishment of the Boston Latin School), specified an entrance examination on ability to "read and understand Tully, Virgill, or any such ordinary Classical Authors." This statute set the pattern: it was uniformly followed by American colleges. Ability to "Read, Construe and Parce Tully, Virgil, and the Greek Testament" was written into the admission requirements of Yale in 1745, and by King's College (later Columbia) in 1754. Similar admission standards were adopted by the other six colonial colleges, and then by the numerous colleges that sprang up like mushrooms in the first century of the national period.¹ In the South, the Midwest, the western territories and western states, like-

221

wise, knowledge of Vergil's *Aeneid* was mandated in entrance requirements of colleges, with some variations in expectations and scope.[2]

Accordingly, preparatory studies for college students included the *Aeneid*, sometimes also the *Eclogues* and the *Georgics*. At the exemplary Boston Latin School, under the famed master Ezekiel Cheever, Vergil was standard fare, as Cotton Mather recalled in his memorial tribute to Cheever.[3] In 1712 the seven-year curriculum at the Boston Latin School specified Vergil in the sixth and seventh years. When the curriculum was telescoped into four years in 1789, study of Vergil was required in the third and fourth years; after 1826, in the fourth and fifth years; after 1870 in the third, fourth, fifth, and sixth years.[4]

Consider the experience of typical American students with Vergil. Silas Bigelow (Harvard, 1765) recorded in his diary under September 4, 1759, about his preparatory work: "What I have learned is almost the 1st A Knieed in Virgil, viz: Studied it over to myself the second time (for I learned to the 8th A:d before I left off . . . , looking over the grammar again."[5] In preparing for Harvard, Nathanial Pynchon in 1759 "had gone through the Ecologues, three Eneid and had got forty or sixty lines at the beginning of every Eneid to the eleventh. Some parts of it four times."[6] Elihu Hubbard Smith, one of the lesser Connecticut Wits, began his study of Latin at age nine at Judah Campion's school at Litchfield, Massachusetts, in May, 1780, and by the age of ten had studied, among other authors, Vergil's *Eclogues* and seven books of the *Aeneid*.[7] In the South, where tutors for a long time were common on the plantations, at Nomini Hall in the Tidewater region of Virginia, Philip Vickers Fithian, tutor to the Carter family, prepared the master's sons in Vergil.[8] In 1797 Daniel Webster, as he recalled, studied in grammar school "Virgil & Tully" and "conceived a pleasure in the study of them, especially the latter."[9]

In the college curriculum of the seventeenth, eighteenth, and nineteenth centuries in America, Vergil continued to be studied: college students were likely to read the *Eclogues* and *Georgics*.[10]

From this exposure to Vergil American teenagers and youths found memories of the *Aeneid* highly distasteful. American students were introduced to Vergil at a very young age, and the experience was uninspiring, indeed repugnant to most. The text of the *Aeneid* as studied in the grammar schools, academies, and later the high schools served simply as a *corpus vile* for drilling grammar, for construing and parsing Latin, and for scanning verses. Francis

Bowen, who edited an edition of Vergil for schools and colleges in 1842, commmented candidly on the folly of this method of instruction. "Virgil," he wrote, "is more generally read and less appreciated than any other classic. . . . These elegant and delightful poems call up, in the minds of most persons, no more pleasant images than those of the spelling-book, the recitation room, and perhaps, the rod." As a result, he concluded, Vergil is generally neglected, read not as a poet but "as a crabbed and difficult exercise in Latin."[11] John Trumbull (Yale, 1769), one of the Connecticut Wits, in his comic satire *The Progress of Dulness* (1772–73) mocked the neglect of belles lettres in America:

> our youth with grammar teazing,
> Untaught in meaning, sense or reason;
> ⋯⋯⋯⋯⋯⋯⋯⋯⋯⋯⋯⋯⋯⋯
> From thence to murd'ring *Virgil's* verse,
> And construing *Tully*, into farce,
> ⋯⋯⋯⋯⋯⋯⋯⋯⋯⋯⋯⋯⋯⋯
> Read antient authors o'er in vain,
> Nor taste one beauty they contain.[12]

Benjamin Rush, vociferous opponent of classical learning in America, in 1791 ridiculed the study of the *Aeneid* (or the *Iliad*) by mere boys, who, he says, carry away from school "but a smattering of the classics."[13] Francis Hopkinson of Philadelphia deplored that, though study of modern history was needed in America in the late eighteenth century, instead the time of the youth "is consumed in reading the delectable and lamentable story of *Aeneas* and queen *Dido*." Learning languages by means of grammar alone is sheer folly, he asserted, and schoolmasters were mere "Haberdashers of Moods & Tenses," with no feeling or taste for the authors they teach. "What would Virgil think could he hear his beautiful poems frittered into its grammatical component parts in one of our schools."[14] In 1806 study of the *Georgics* even on the college level was questioned: "all our industry could not select more unprofitable, because more unintelligible, reading for a school-boy than this celebrated poem," because, said the writer, it is a treatise on agriculture which requires technical expertise in that field, even at times in astronomy.[15] In 1811 a graduate of Phillips Academy Andover lamented the aims and methods of the early formal education as "excessive memorizing . . . of entire Greek and Latin grammars." "The whole business," he continued, "and it was the same all over the land, was a melancholy misunderstanding of the function of education."[16]

Moreover, the textbooks employed in teaching Vergil's works were not conducive to the development of understanding and appreciation. While the *Port Folio*, prestigious magazine published in Philadelphia, might applaud the announcement of an American edition of Vergil's works declaring, "for the promotion of correct taste in literature, we hope that the works of Virgil, one of the most splendid specimens of ancient wit, will be perused at every Grammar School and College in America,"[17] decade after decade school texts of Vergil were either far beyond the competence of young boys and young men or were so simplified and provided with so many crutches that initiative and challenge were destroyed. For many decades the Delphin text, by Carolus Ruaeus (Charles de la Rue, SJ) held the field: the first American edition was published in Philadelphia in 1804, and it was frequently reprinted for decades thereafter. The commentary was in Latin, even the preface. At the other extreme was the popular English Vergil by Davidson, first published in Britain in the middle of the eighteenth century:[18] it provided the Latin text, the Latin in order of sense on the same page, and also an English translation and brief notes. Vergil texts authored by Americans for use in schools and colleges began to appear early in the nineteenth century. The best known were those edited by Malcolm Campbell,[19] by J. G. Cooper (to bridge the extremes of the editions of Ruaeus and Davidson),[20] Edward Moore,[21] G. A. Gould,[22] and by Charles Anthon, whose editions were often reprinted and often criticized for hasty, careless workmanship, errors, and plagiarisms from German editions.[23]

Outside the schools and colleges, interest in Vergil's works, from colonial times through the nineteenth century, is evidenced by the frequency with which texts and translations of Vergil are found in private libraries.[24] Most Americans read Vergil in Dryden's translation, often reprinted in America well into the nineteenth century.[25] In 1796 Caleb Alexander published a prose translation of Vergil's works, for school use. He hailed it proudly, but cautiously, in his preface as "the first AMERICAN translation." "Elegant it cannot be," he wrote, but "why should Americans be dependent on European translations and printers for the Latin or Grecian Classics?"[26] It is, however, noteworthy that, while in the first decades of the nineteenth century, a new verse translation of the *Iliad* was composed by a Virginian, William Munford, a work that is the most distinguished translation of a classical work by an American in the early national period,[27] no American translation of the entire *Aeneid* in verse was undertaken.

It is true that translations of limited parts of Vergil's works began to appear. In 1806 the *Port Folio* enthusiastically reprinted from the *Kentucky Gazette* "A New Translation of Virgil's First Pastoral."[28] It was an inelegant effort, in the form of a dialogue between Tityrus and Meliboeus, yet the editor of the *Port Folio* with patriotic zeal hailed it as a "very great curiosity," and commented that "a classical imitation, by a woodsman of the west is . . . stupendous. . . . This forester's translation, though occasionally meritorious, does not always emulate the sense of the original. But we think the very attempt is wonderful in a savage region." In 1807 Lucius Manlius Sargent, Boston lawyer and litterateur, published a verse translation of the *Culex*. The influential *Monthly Anthology and Boston Review*, while doubting the authenticity of the *Culex*, and deploring the trivial nature of the theme, complimented Sargent on the accuracy of the translation, and saluted the publication of it as "this small accession to the specimens of American literature."[29] In 1814 the *Port Folio* printed a verse translation of *Aeneid* 2.268–280, by a youth of fourteen, which the editors praised as a creditable effort.[30] As a result, the editors solicited more verse translations of the *Aeneid*, proposing as texts two "beautiful and celebrated passages," 4.173–188 (beginning *Extemplo Libyae magnas it Fama per urbes*) and 4.693–705 (beginning *Tum Iuno omnipotens longum miserata dolorem*). The editor was sanguine that he could expect such an effort from "some of the literary youth of our country, to whom we cannot too often repeat the advice which we have already given, *never to neglect their classical learning.*"[31] Shortly after they published translations of these passages—routine, uninspired ones.[32] Not long after, there appeared a verse translation of the fourth *Eclogue*.[33] In 1820 William Ellery (Harvard, 1747), signer of the Declaration of Independence, in his old age was engaged in translating part of the *Aeneid*.[34] Despite these tentative efforts to create an American Vergil, no creditable translations appeared until the twentieth century. For Americans in the eighteenth and nineteenth centuries, in reading the *Iliad* and the *Aeneid* "in English, it is not so much Homer and Virgil that we admire as Pope and Dryden."[35]

It is therefore curious to find Americans expending creative energies not on efforts to interpret and appreciate Vergil's works but on travesties. In Maryland the Reverend Thomas Cradock (1718–70) wrote travesties (still unpublished) of all ten *Bucolics*. In these he incorporated major concerns of Chesapeake rural life and society, such as corrupt and incompetent clergymen, the loves of black slaves, the antics of wicked indentured servants, drunkenness among the provincials, the spread of marital and religious infidelity (Deism) in the colony, a lovesick woman soliciting charms to win back her lover, the greed of whites against the Indians and their lands, and, finally, consolation to a friend whose beloved married another while he went to England. Cradock's *Eclogue* 1 begins:

> Beneath the shade of these wide-spreading Trees,
> Dear Split-Text. You can smoke your chunk at Ease;
> I hapless wretch! must bid such joys Adieu,
> Stript of my Credit, & my Income [too?].

Eclogue 10 contains the lines

> Begin his gen'rous Passion let us sing,
> While warbling Mock-Birds usher in the Spring,

and ends with the forsaken lover lamenting that he had ever fallen in love, and deciding to leave for the frontier.[36]

In 1774 Rowland Rugeley published a travesty of book 4 of the *Aeneid*.[37] It was written, he says in the preface (xiv–xv) "for fun," and he acknowledged inspiration from Charles Cotton's well-known British burlesque of the *Aeneid*, *Scarronides*, though Rugeley does not descend to the grossness and coarse, scatalogical verses of Cotton. Rugeley begins his travesty of book 4:

> Aeneas finish'd here his ditty
> Of old King Priam and his city;
> The Tyrians at a tale so deep,
> And wondrous moving, fell—asleep.
> Not so the Queen. . . .

Dido's soul at the end of book 4 at the hands of Rugeley suffers this indignity:

> "And thus I set at liberty
> Your restless headstrong spirit—die."
> This said—she gave a lusty pluck at
> The lock, and Dido kick'd the bucket.[38]

While there were travesties of the *Aeneid* in England also, there were many distinguished translations of Vergil's poems, and the scholarship on and appreciation of his works from the sixteenth century on remained on the whole of a high order.[39] In Latin America, too, by contrast with the English colonies and the early American national period, the influence of Vergil was substantial, beginning as early as the second half of the sixteenth century and continuing through the nineteenth. For example, the *Aeneid* was the model for Alonso de Ercilla y Zuñiga (1569–90) in the composition of the national Chilean epic *La Araucana*. In the war between the Spaniards and the Araucanian Indians the fall of Troy is echoed in the capture of Concepción, and there are elaborate games and a romance of the Dido-Aeneas model.[40] Translations, centos, imitations, echoes of the *Aeneid*, *Eclogues*, and *Georgics* abound, composed in Mexico, Guatemala, Cuba, Venezuela (noteworthy is the influence of Vergil on Andrés Bello, 1781–1865), Chile, Argentina.[41]

It is also striking that the *Aeneid* was not as popular in America in the seventeenth, eighteenth, and nineteenth centuries as the *Iliad* (known mostly from Pope's version). Such potentially transportable themes as the birth of a new nation in a new land, the wandering of a divinely guided people, the struggle between the settlers and the native people, the transplantation of culture—these did not, in general, leave their mark on American thought and literature.[42]

Far more in tune with American life and thought than the epic themes and grandeur of the *Aeneid* were the agrarian-pastoral models of the *Eclogues* and *Georgics*. From the seventeenth century well into the middle of the nineteenth, many aspects of American life attracted Americans to the idyllic landscape and fantasy of the *Eclogues* and the rural values and moral exaltation of agriculture in the *Georgics*: traditional American primitivism, the politico-ethical content of American agrarianism, the Sabine Farm ideal, and the paradigms of Cincinnatus and the virtuous yeoman-citizen-soldier.[43] Particularly welcome and pertinent was the moral didacticism of the *Georgics*, the message of the work ethic and the rewards of labor, the anxieties in the *Eclogues* about the intrusion of history and the real world that threatens to shatter the sheltered pastoral world with its idealized *otium* and stability. The ideal of a rural retreat with intellectual pursuits as refuge from the city and the political world was widespread among Americans, both in the North and the plantations of the South.[44] "Vergil's *Eclogues* are the true fountainhead of the pastoral stream in our literature."[45]

Thus, while the *Aeneid* remained virtually untried, translations
and imitations of the *Eclogues* and *Georgics* were composed (none,
it is true, memorable). For example, a Pennsylvanian calling himself Agricola produced a mediocre imitation of a Vergilian pastoral,
"The Squabble, A Pastoral Eclogue," in the form of a dialogue between Thyrsis and Corin.[46] In 1772 the poet Nathaniel Evans published "Daphnis and Menalcas. A Pastoral Eclogue."[47] At the end of
the eighteenth century John Miller Russell composed a verse translation of *Eclogues* 1–6.[48] Moreover, the *Georgics* (in translation)
was a favorite of many Americans, for instance, Eliza Lucas Pinckney of South Carolina, one of America's distinguished women of
the eighteenth century. In 1742 she wrote: "I have got no farther
than the first volume of Virgil but was most agreeable disapointed
to find my self instructed in agriculture as well as entertained by
his charming poem; for I am persuaded that tho he wrote in and for
Italy it will in many instances suit Carolina."[49] In 1759 there appeared a paraphrase of *Georgics* 2.148ff. (beginning *O fortunatos
nimium*).[50] The *Georgics* and *Eclogues* were read and appreciated
not only in the South but on the landed estates of New York in
the 1780s.[51]

Royall Tyler's autobiographical novel of 1797, entitled *The Algerine Captive*, the first novel about life in New England, contains
numerous references to Vergil's works. The hero Updike Underhill,
son of a struggling farmer, was sent to school, where for years he
studied only Greek and Latin. Because of family financial difficulties Updike was called back to the farm, where he proceeded to give
Greek names to all the farming tools, and to recite hexameter
verses to the cattle. The only book he took with him into the fields
was a copy of Vergil (the Delphin edition). One day he tried to apply some practical knowledge he learned from the last book of the
Georgics: he killed a cow, and tried to raise a swarm of bees "after
the manner of Virgil; which process, notwithstanding I followed the
directions in the georgics, some how or other failed." Accordingly,
he was sent away from the farm back to school.[52]

In the nineteenth century the *Eclogues* in particular, transmitted
"a delicate blend of myth and reality that was to be particularly relevant to American experience."[53] In particular *Eclogue* 1, with its
theme of the dispossessed, the intrusion of history unhinging the
rural myth, had significant influences, e.g., on Hawthorne, Thoreau, Emerson.[54] In the middle of the nineteenth century, however,
when industrialization burgeoned, the assault on the Vergilian pastoral mode in America mounted. In 1850, for example, Thomas

Eubank, commissioner of patents, declared, "A steamer is a mightier epic than the Illiad, and Whitney, Jacquard, and Blanchard might laugh even Virgil, Milton and Tasso into scorn."[55] On the day the Northern Railroad was inaugurated in New Hampshire Daniel Webster, lauding railroads, progress, profits, dismissed Vergilian pastoralism out of hand: "New Hampshire is no classic ground. She has no Virgil and no Eclogues."[56]

But the positive influences of Vergil on Americans were not inconsiderable. The first native-born American poet, Benjamin Tompson (1642–1714; Harvard, 1662), was a grammar school teacher of extensive experience (Boston Latin School, Braintree School, Roxborough Latin School). Despite his knowledge of classical authors, he wrote bad verse in English. But he knew his Vergil. In his poem "New England's Crisis" (1676), about incidents in King Philip's War, he recalls Aeneas at the fall of Troy in describing a massacre by Indian warriors; and in praising the efforts of the women of Boston to help fortify the city, he quotes *Dux Foemina Facti*.[57] In "The Grammarian's Fame," in commemoration of Robert Woodmancy, he begins:

> Eight Parts of *Speech* this Day wear *Mourning Gowns*,
> Declined Verbs, Pronouns, Participles, Nouns,

and he identifies in the funeral procession a group of classical authors including Vergil.[58] It was Benjamin Tompson, too, who in 1702 wrote the Latin hexameters that serve as preface to Cotton Mather's *Magnalia Christi Americana*. These lines of Tompson echo Vergilian phrases, notably from *Eclogue* 4.7:

> Haec nova Progenies, veterum sub Imagine, coelo
> Arte Tua Terram visitans, demissa salutat,

and from *Aeneid* 1.600, 609:

> Grates persolvimus omnes.
> Semper Honos, Nomenque tuum, Mathere, manebunt.

In his *Magnalia* Cotton Mather sought to signal in the very opening words the epic grandeur of the exploits of the Puritan Founding Fathers in New England by an analogy to the *Aeneid*: "I write the wonders of the Christian religion, flying from the Depravations of *Europe*, to the *American Strand*." While the analogy is not carried

out systematically by Mather, among his numerous direct quotations and adaptations from Latin authors in the *Magnalia* there are
over thirty from Vergil, mostly from the *Aeneid*.[59] In his tribute to
his teacher at the Boston Latin School, Ezekiel Cheever, Mather
wrote in 1708:

> Our stately *Virgil* made us but Contrive
> As our *Anchises* to keep him Alive
> . . . .
> Young *Austin*[60] wept, when he saw Dido dead,
> Tho' not a Tear for a *Lost Soul* he had:
> Our Master would not let us be so vain,
> But us from *Virgil* did to *David* train.[61]

Despite Puritan wariness about the corrupting influences of pagan
literature, and traditional Puritan injunctions against aesthetic
pleasure and belles lettres, Mather could write his son: "I cannot
wish you a Soul that shall be wholly *unpoetical*. . . . I wish you may
so understand an *Epic* poem, that the Beauties of an *Homer* and a
Virgil may be discerned with you."[62]

If there was no profound influence of Vergil's poems on American thought and literature, familiarity with his works is evidenced
by the facility with which Vergilian tags flowed from the pens and
tongues of Americans—phrases, lines, passages. For example, at
Harvard the Latin orations of John Leverett (in 1686, 1709, 1711)
and of Urian Oakes (in 1672, 1678) were dotted with direct quotations and adaptations from Vergil.[63]

Moreover, conventional general tributes to Vergil as poet and
moral writer are scattered liberally in essays, poems, and letters. A
poem by the Bostonian Benjamin Church (Harvard, 1754; physician, classmate of John Hancock), entitled *The Choice*, contains the
lines,

> *Homer*, great Parent of Heroick Strains,
> *Virgil*, whose genius was improv'd with Pains.[64]

Francis Hopkinson, first graduate of the College of Philadelphia,
wrote in 1762 in a commencement poem,

> But now glad *Science* to this riper Age
> Unlocks the Treasures of the Classic Page
> . . . .

> *Virgil* for him awakens the tuneful Lyre
> ·································
> Pious *Aeneas*! who attends thy woe
> But deeply feels the sympathetic Glow?
> Thro' ev'ry Page engaging Virtues shine
> And frequent Precepts grace each moral Line.[65]

The preface to a collection of poems by John Beveridge, published in 1765, complimented Beveridge by associating him with Homer and Vergil:

> His tow'ring thought and soft enchanting lays
> Long since have crown'd him with immortal Bays:
> But ne'er did Maro such high glory seek
> As to excel Maeonides in Greek.[66]

In the rousing poem "The Rising Glory of America," authored by Philip Freneau and Hugh Henry Brackenridge, and recited at the commencement at Princeton in 1771, the influence of Vergil (and Milton) is apparent in the epic tone and phrases.[67]

But from all these comments and references, both laudatory and negative, critical analyses and understanding of Vergil as poet and thinker rarely emerge. In his elaborate statement of the intellectual experience at Harvard at the end of the eighteenth century, the Reverend John Clarke lauded "the Sacred Classicks" in general, and expatiated on the virtues of Vergil. The limits of his appreciation are found in his praise of "his truly correct poem," "the beauties of his composition," "the smoothness of his numbers."[68] It is noteworthy, too, that the perceptive and brilliant Fisher Ames, early America's greatest Congressional orator, extolled Homer as epic poet but was silent about Vergil: "Shall we match," he wrote, "Joel Barlow against Homer or Hesiod?"[69]

In the first decade of the nineteenth century, in the midst of the great debate of the time on the suitability of the classical curriculum for America, there appeared a flurry of essays in praise of Vergil. The *Literary Magazine and American Register*, published in Philadelphia, printed a review of a new British translation of the *Georgics* (by Sotheby, for whom see below). The reviewer mused: "I have taken down from its shelf my old academic Virgil, over which I have kindled into rapture, and passed many a happy hour."[70] Later, the same magazine, in an ongoing debate on whether classical literature inculcated immoral and anti-Christian sentiments, extolled Vergil as preeminent in elegance and tenderness, despite his descriptions of war and battles and the fact that his vision of the afterlife conflicted with Christian views.[71] The *Port Folio*, too, carried biographies and comments on the works of Vergil (very superficial), bestowing high praise on "the prince of Latin poets."[72] In New England, the *Monthly Anthology and Boston Review*, assessing the extent of Vergil's imitation of his predecessors, concluded that in the *Bucolics*, except for *Eclogues* 1, 4, 5, and 6, Vergil's pastorals were but "elegant translations" of Theocritus. "This is not said, however, to detract from his merit as a poet."[73]

Jefferson's love of Vergil's poems was summarized by him in the oft-quoted "But as we advance in life . . . things fall off one by one, and I suspect that we are left with Homer and Vergil, perhaps with Homer alone."[74] His second library, eventually sold by him to Congress, contained one of the largest assortments of Vergilian books in early America: a variety of texts, even Maffei Veggio's *Thirteenth Book* (with English translation), the Dryden translation, an Italian verse version (by Annibale Caro), and a French translation (by Didot).[75] In his youthful commonplace books (composed mostly from 1764–72), Jefferson copied a great range of quotations from classical authors. Yet there were only six passages from Vergil, four from the *Aeneid*, two from the *Eclogues*.[76] Jefferson was interested in theories about Vergil's tomb, and cited lines from Vergil's poems in his comments on metrics.[77] But in his voluminous letters, essays, speeches there is hardly any evidence of his great love of Vergil. Indeed, as he grew older, under pressure of public affairs he confessed that his relish for poetry had deserted him, so that "at present I cannot read even Virgil with pleasure."[78]

John Adams's interest in Vergil extended through his entire life and was more varied and vocal. In 1756, the year after his graduation from Harvard, he set himself the task of reading with care thirty to forty lines of Vergil every day.[79] In 1756 he set down his thoughts on poetic genius and ranked among the writers of antiquity Homer, Vergil, and Ovid as "most perfect in their several kinds." In imagination even Milton's *Paradise Lost*, Adams judged, "falls short of the Aeneid or Iliad." The "Aeneid is like a well ordered Garden, where it is impossible to find any Part unadorned, or to cast our Eyes upon a single Spot that does not produce some beautiful Plant or Flower." In these musings, when he wrote on the beauties of country life he quoted *Georgics* 4.467–470, substituting *hic* three times for Vergil's *at* in these lines. And he commented that "in his Georgicks he has given us a Collection of the most delightful Landskips that can be made out of Fields and Woods, Herds of Cattle, and Swarms of Bees."[80] In an entry in his diary in 1758 he quoted *Aeneid* 4.2, *vulnus alit venis, et caeco carpitur igni*, which he translated thus: "He nurses a Wound in his Veins, and is consumed by a blind hidden fire." Then he named five young men among his acquaintances consumed by secret fires of love.[81] In the same year he was interested in poetic genius and wrote to a correspondent on "sublime Passages in [various authors] including Virgill." Poetic genius, he wrote, has been exhibited "in a surprising degree by Milton, and Shakespeare, Homer, Virgil, &c."[82] On his voyage to France in 1778, when he experienced a fierce storm at sea, he noted in his diary that "every School Boy can turn to more than one description of a storm in Virgil."[83] Adams's great library contained, like Jefferson's, various texts and translations of Vergil.[84] In retirement he was pleased to learn in 1823 that his grandson Thomas Boylston Adams had "made such progress in Virgil."[85] Yet during the Revolutionary War it was not poetry that Adams deemed essential for the times. In 1781 he exhorted his son John Quincy, then a student abroad: "In Company with Sallust, Cicero, Tacitus and Livy you will learn Wisdom and Virtue. . . . You will ever remember that all the end of study is to make you a good Man and a useful Citizen."[86]

Political science was at a premium for the Revolutionary generation, and the cult of antiquity was at its height in America, as the Founding Fathers ransacked the Roman and Greek classics for republican models and classical virtues. It was at this time that the Great seal of the United States was created, adopting its mottoes from Vergil. In 1782, the year of the eighteenth centenary of Vergil's death, Congress approved the design of the official seal. One of the consultants to the committee that drew up the seal was Charles Thomson, Secretary of Congress, who had been a teacher of Latin in Philadelphia. The seal (now on the obverse of the dollar bill), contains three Vergilian tags: ANNUIT COEPTIS (adapted from *Aen.* 9.625 and *Georg.* 1.40 (*audacibus adnue coeptis*); NOVUS ORDO SECLORUM (adapted from *Ecl.* 4.5 (*magnus ab integro saeclorum nascitur ordo*), and E PLURIBUS UNUM (adapted from *Moretum* 103: *color est e pluribus unus*). However, the motto *e pluribus unum* appears to have been taken over, not from the *Moretum* directly, but from the legend on the title page of the British *Gentleman's Magazine*, popular on this side of the Atlantic.[87] These mottoes embodied a statement of the classical heritage and humanistic origins of the first modern republic, even if the heraldic emblems and the devices would have been understood only by educated Americans.

One such American was Peter van Schaack of Kinderhook, New York, whose love affair with Vergil continued throughout his life. A graduate of King's College, 1766, lawyer and accomplished Latin scholar, he opted for the Loyalist cause, and so lived for seven years in exile until his citizenship was restored in 1784. His letters from abroad, to John Jay, his son, and his brother, display throughout Vergilian tags, appreciations, and encouragement to continued study of his favorite author. His motto in exile was *superanda fortuna ferendo* (adapted from *Aen.* 5.710); his despair was expressed by *fuimus Troes, fuit Ilium* (*Aen.* 2.135); his admonition to his son *labor improbus omnia vicit* (*Georg.* 1.145–146). In his exile Vergil was to van Schaack "my favorite," "the modest and amiable Virgil," "that sweet poet, about whom one may say *decies repetita placebit.*"[88]

One of the principal literary influences on the poems of Philip Freneau (1752–1832), America's first important poet, was Vergil. His poems are full of classical allusions, including echoes, epigraphs, and references from the *Aeneid, Eclogues, Georgics.*[89]

John Trumbull, another early American poet, possessed a more perceptive aesthetic appreciation of Vergil. In 1770 he composed as a "collegiate exercise," a verse translation of the Orpheus and Eurydice story in the *Georgics*, entitled "The Speech of Proteus to Aristaeus." Trumbull set down first the Latin text of the 75 lines, *Georgics* 4.453–527 (from *non te nullius exercent numinis irae* to *Eurydicen toto referebant flumine ripae*), then his translation in 104 lines of rhymed couplets.[90] Later, his influential poem *M'Fingal* (1782) contained imitations and adaptations from the *Aeneid*, e.g., the speech of Hector's ghost to Aeneas in book 2, and an adaptation of Aeneas' experience in Hades.[91] In the 1820s, in his old age, he judged that Vergil lacked Homer's descriptive skill, but noted that Vergil had a penchant for the letter *m* (which Trumbull approved), and possessed "meritorious judgement," "force of expression," and "elegant correctness."[92] Though Trumbull was one of the small number of Americans who were not completely turned away from Vergil as the result of students' experience in the grammar schools, in his youth he had satirized the methods of teaching classical authors in his poem *The Progress of Dulness* thus:

> Read antient authors o'er in vain,
> Nor taste one beauty they contain;
> . . . .
> And plodding on in one dull tone,
> Gain antient tongues, and lose their own.[93]

It is curious that Plutarch, whose works were not part of the required curriculum of schools and colleges but read by adults, was never adversely criticized by Americans. Indeed, he was greatly admired by them. The reasons for the hostility to and rejection of Vergil are complex: familiarity from school days and the emphasis on grammar and parsing, and wariness on religious, moral, and political grounds. For example, in the late seventeenth century Robert Calef, fulminating on the dangers of exposing children to "Heathen writers," condemned "the pernicious works of pagan learning in Virgil, Ovid, and Homer" and defended his own views with "If I err, I may be shewed it from Scripture or sound reasoning, and not by quotations out of Virgil."[94] In 1769 John Wilson, teacher in the Friends Latin School in Philadelphia, motivated by Quaker utilitarian educational views and by moral and religious objections, resigned from his position and wrote in a letter to the overseers of the school that instruction in classical authors "is the grossest absurdity that ever was practiced. It has contributed more to promote Ignorance, Lewdness & Profanity in our Youth than anything I know besides. . . . Will the Lasciviousness of Ovid teach them Chastity? the Epicurean Horace Sobriety? the impudent Juvenal Modesty? or the atheistick Lucretius Devotion? & tho Virgil commonly is excepted from this guilty List yet with the impious Notion Of both the 2d and 8th Eclogues & his representing the Ungrateful Lustful Perfidious Aeneas as the particular Friend & Favorite of Heaven are shocking to every System of Morality."[95]

Similarly, the Quaker teacher and humanitarian Anthony Benezet of Philadelphia deplored the religious and moral influence of Vergil: "the prodigious hurt done by these romantic & mad notions of heroism &c. which are early implanted in the tender minds from the use of these Heathen Authors Ovid, Virgil, Homer &c. which they are generally taught in, which nourishes the spirit of war in the Youth & in other respects is so diametrically opposed to our Christian Testimony."[96]

American pragmatism and the quest for useful knowledge motivated many in their rejection of study of the classics. In New York William Livingston (later governor of New Jersey) wrote in 1768: "We want hands . . . more than heads. The most intimate acquaintance with the classics will not move our oaks, nor a taste of the *Georgics* cultivate our lands."[97]

But the most sustained challenge to the reputation of Vergil in America occurred in the early national period, when rising American nationalism created an American version of the Battle of the

Books, or "La Querelle des Anciens et Modernes," a vigorous debate which had exercised the French and English in the late seventeenth and early eighteenth centuries, coming to an end across the Atlantic about 1720. In the nascent United States the clamor for an immediate native literature was accompanied by manifestoes of freedom from cultural dependence that depreciated the great literary models of antiquity and denounced slavish imitation of them as absolute standards as deterrents to creative originality in America.[98] "We are called to sing a New Song," wrote Nathaniel Appleton, "a Song that neither We nor our Fathers were able to sing before."[99] In the very first issue of the new national periodical the *Massachusetts Magazine* there was published a poem entitled "Anticipation of the Literary Fame of America" which predicted the rise of an American Livy, Cicero, Euripides, Ovid, Aristotle, Plato, and

> Some future *Virgil* shall our wars rehearse
> In all the dignity of epic verse.[100]

Foreshadowing the American aspirations for native epics, as early as 1772 Timothy Dwight (later president of Yale) at the age of twenty delivered in New Haven a disquisition in which he argued that the Bible as literature is superior to all the ancient literary genres. "Shall we," he wrote, "be blind . . . to Poetry more correct and more tender than *Virgil?*" Further, he repudiated the conventional view that "*Homer* and *Virgil* . . . were sent into the world to give Laws to all other authors."[101] In 1791 a declaration was made that America had already produced a Homer, a Vergil, and a Horace.[102] The writer was alluding to Timothy Dwight himself, whose huge biblical epic, *The Conquest of Canaan*, had appeared in 1785; to Joel Barlow as the American Vergil—his epic *The Vision of Columbus* was first published in 1787; and to Philip Freneau as the American Horace.

In the *Conquest of Canaan*, in ten thousand lines, Dwight took as his subject the victory of the biblical hero Joshua over the Canaanites. He was the first American to write in the epic genre, and he sought to replace in this way the appeal of Homer's *Iliad* among Americans. Similarly, Barlow's American epic was composed to supersede the *Aeneid* as well. In 1807, to promote a new original national literature with native didactic-moral-poltical content, he produced a revised version of his epic entitled *The Columbiad*. In the preface to this version he unleashed a vigorous assault on Homer for inculcating glorification of war, as supporter of the divine right of kings, promoter of military plunder, violence, and false notions of honor. "The moral tendency of the Eneid of Virgil," he added, "is nearly as pernicious," though Vergil's artistry elicited his praise. "But Virgil wrote and felt like a subject, not like a citizen. The real design of his poem was to increase the veneration of the people for a master, whoever he might be, and to encourage, like Homer, the great system of military depradation."[103] Nevertheless, *The Columbiad* opens with Vergilian echo:

> I sing the Mariner who first unfurl'd
> An eastern banner o'er the western world.

Dwight's epic is virtually unknown today, and Joel Barlow's, despite the national theme and his promotion of the doctrine of progress, remains one of the most dismal failures in the history of American poetry.

The efforts of Dwight and Barlow to create American epics replicated the striving in sixteenth- and seventeenth-century Europe to supersede Homer and Vergil with vernacular epics on biblical and national themes as statements of national literary achievement. The best known of these are Camoens's *Lusiads* (1572), Ronsard's *La Franciad* (1572), and Milton's *Paradise Lost* (1667). In France alone from 1653–70 some dozen such biblical and national epic poems were composed. Though all these turned from the contents of the great classical models, repudiating the themes and intellectual standards and values associated with antiquity, they all clung to classical form and style, as did Dwight and Barlow. And, like the American epics, none of the French epics has enjoyed any lasting reputation.[104]

In 1793 Richard Beresford of South Carolina attacked the moral content of the Homeric and Vergilian epics. In particular, he faulted "the pious Aeneas [who] took occasion to involve a homeless race of men in all the horror of desolation and slaughter," and he condemned Vergil's *parcere subjectis et debellare superbos* (*Aen.* 6.853) for its emphasis on the use of raw power to subdue others by force and to keep them in obedience. "No longer are the *Iliad* and *Aeneid* perused as exemplars in moral, but in poetic excellence."[105] In the face of such depreciation, Fisher Ames, a fervent advocate of classical learning, declared that modern poets cannot find such inspiring themes as those of the *Iliad* and *Aeneid*, "for no such subject worthy of poetry exists [in the United States]. Commerce . . . is the passion of the multitude."[106] In 1814 the *Port Folio* published an accolade to the poetry of Vergil who, it proclaimed, "wrote for *immortal renown*," while British poets wrote to please the multitude. "After a lapse of two thousand years, the writings of Vergil are still in the prime—the zenith of their fame. Two thousand years hence, what will have become of the writings of Lord Byron!"[107]

In the 1830s, in the face of waning influence of neoclassical symbols and thought in America (except for Hellenic Revival architecture), the militant South Carolinian anticlassicist Thomas Smith Grimké, moved by religious and patriotic fervor, dismissed Vergil (and Homer, too) as not providing useful knowledge or edification for America. "As for their morals, who would be willing to have a son, or brother, like . . . the mean and treacherous Aeneas, the hero of the Aeneid, if indeed it has a hero." Grimké condemned Aeneas not only for meanness but for ingratitude and perfidy toward Dido, and also for killing Turnus. "The beauties of Shakespeare are worth all the beauties of Homer and Virgil." Instead of these, Americans should read *Paradise Lost* and *Paradise Regained*. "I do not doubt, that the Paradise Lost is worth the Iliad, Odyssey, and the Aeneid all together; there is more sublime, rich and beautiful descriptive poetry in Childe Harold than half a dozen Georgics."[108] Indeed, in his Phi Beta Kappa address at Yale in 1830 he proclaimed, "I would rather read that great impeccable and glorious poem 'Gertrude of Wyoming' than the Fourth Book of the Aeneid."[109] Now this poem was not an American work at all but by Thomas Campbell, a Scot who had never set foot in America, though he sympathized with the American Revolution. The poem was a romanticized narrative, in Spenserian stanzas, of the Wyoming Valley massacre in 1778 in eastern Pennsylvania in the Susquehanna River country, based on events involving American patriots and the Continental forces battling Loyalists and Indians, with resultant brutality on both sides. The poem created a sensation in America—it was even edited by Washington Irving. It opens with the line "On Susquehanna's side, fair Wyoming." Campbell's admiring biographer later judged "Gertrude of Wyoming" to be a "third-rate poem, containing a few first-rate lines."[110]

Grimké and others might campaign against the classics and Vergil, but in the Adams family John Adams's admiration for Vergil was, as it were, a legacy. When John Quincy Adams was a young student abroad, his father urged him (the time is 1780–81) to "study in Latin, above all, Virgil and Cicero."[111] At this time, when John Quincy translated the *Eclogues* in his notebooks he commented, "What a difference between this study and that of a dry, barren Greek Grammar."[112] In July 1783 he copied down the Latin text of all ten *Eclogues*, and for each wrote down a translation in rhymed couplets; in a collection of early translations made by John Quincy we find a copy of Dryden's version of "Virgil's Fourth Pastoral, or Pollio," following which he wrote his own prose translation of the first five *Eclogues*.[113] Next he copied the text of *Georgics* 1.12–73, and wrote a prose translation of all four books (from November 1783 to February 1784).[114] Later, when he wrote for the *Port Folio*, he reviewed a new English translation of the *Georgics* by William Sotheby (published in an American edition in 1808), giving it high praise and comparing it favorably with Dryden's translation. Adams here called the *Georgics* "the most perfect composition, that ever issued from the mind of man," lauding its "transcendent excellence." Some passages in the *Georgics*, he added, "have been the special delight of twenty centuries," and "will enchant the ear of harmony and transport the soul of fancy as long as taste and sentiment shall last among mankind." With characteristic American concern for practicality, he added that the didactic parts "will not be of much . . . use to our practical farmers."[115] John Quincy Adams kept six bronze busts in his study at Quincy which he called his "Household Gods." One of these was Vergil.[116]

The most extensive appreciation of Vergil that we have in America during the nineteenth century is to be found in the diary of John Adams's grandson, Charles Francis Adams. As a student in 1820 he was committed to daily study of Vergil.[117] In 1831 he decided to assess the genius of Vergil, who, he judged, would have risen to higher rank as a poet if he had exhibited greater originality.[118] Then in 1832 he began to read systematically through all of Vergil's works in Latin. About the *Eclogues* he commented that "they are fine specimens of the highest polish of which verse is susceptible. Vigorous but smooth."[119] Then he read through the *Georgics* in less than a week, dismissing the details of "rural Economy," and lauding the *Georgics* as a whole as "models for that specimen of composition, a sign of which is that all subsequent times have only imitated them."[120] In the next five weeks (March–April 1832) he read through the entire *Aeneid*.[121] "It is a very great mistake committed," he wrote, "to make boys or men read Virgil first and Homer afterwards."[122] The morality of book 4 he considered dubious: "The pious Aeneas is little better than a rascal for the desertion of Dido after seducing her," though he felt inclined to mitigate this criticism on the ground that it was "poetic," and, in any case, "agreeable to nature."[123] Book 6 he thought the masterpiece. "The imagination, the description, the versification combine wonderfully."[124] Taken as a whole the *Aeneid* is "an honour to the human intellect for imagination, for pathos, for perfect harmony, for beauty, and there is moral in it, so far as the Ancients allowed themselves to have moral."[125]

The greatness of the *Aeneid*, he concluded, is unfortunately not appreciated by boys, who are too young for the experience, and are poorly taught. "It is a great mistake I think to submit such things to be hammered over in such a way until return to them at a future moment is disgusting from the Association it brings up."[126] Then from August 1833 to January 1834 he reread Vergil entire once more.[127] On the *Georgics* he wrote: "I find the Poetry of the Georgics more exquisite than ever. The high polish, the ease and familiarity with which the versification is conducted, and the beauty of it throughout are now and must remain unequalled monuments of ancient mental exertion."[128] Again he recorded his condemnation of Aeneas for his behavior toward Dido. "I do not greatly admire his hero in this business. His cold heartedness is a vice past defence." But, taking the *Aeneid* as a whole, "I have read it with pleasure." "I find repetition of a Classic only shows me how much I let escape before."[129]

In the next two decades Vergil was a leading inspiration for Henry Thoreau, for descriptions of nature, for man's closeness to the soil, the idyllic pastoral life, and even the concept of a golden age.[130] From 1837–57 quotations from Vergil recur in his writings —from the *Aeneid*, the *Eclogues*, the *Georgics*. For example, in 1859 he recorded in his *Journal* that Vergil's account of a winter in *Georgics* 1.291 "applies well-nigh to New England."[131] In 1837 he found in the *Eclogues* confirmation of the eternal sameness of human beings. "I would read Virgil if only that I might be reminded of the identity of human nature in all ages. . . . It was the same world, and the same men inhabited it."[132]

For a long time it was difficult for poetry to find a home and proper appreciation in the United States: practical concerns, politics, materialism dominated American life. Moreover, the pastoral image had faded by the middle of the nineteenth century. In 1847 Daniel Webster had dismissed Vergil and his *Eclogues* (see above). In 1866, in an address before the prestigious Academy of Arts and Sciences in Boston, entitled "Remarks on Classical and Utilitarian Studies," Jacob Bigelow, M.D., dismissed the works of Homer and

Vergil because of the "absence of all moral or poetical justice" in them.[133] The transformation of education in America in the first hundred years of the nation is patent in the views of John Adams's great-grandson, Charles Francis Adams, Jr. In a Phi Beta Kappa address at Harvard in June, 1883, he delivered a major assault on the traditional classical curriculum in the universities and colleges, declaring it irrelevant and useless.[134]

By the last decades of the nineteenth century classical learning had ceased to provide moral, political, aesthetic models for educated Americans; it became the province of classical scholars. It is, however, mere coincidence that the first scholarly studies on Vergil's poetry were published at this time—just about the nineteenth centenary of Vergil's death. In July, 1880, at the annual meeting of the American Philological Association in Philadelphia Ernest G. Sihler presented a paper on "Virgil and Plato," which was that year published by the association.[135] In the following years several articles on Vergil appeared in the *American Journal of Philology*.[136] But in the *Proceedings* of the Association for 1881, 1882, and 1883, Vergil is not mentioned at all. No American classical scholar at the time, no teacher of the classics, no American poet was moved to salute, with Tennyson, "Roman Virgil," *Wielder of the stateliest measure ever moulded by the lips of man.*

Notes

1. See, e.g., Edwin C. Broome, *A Historical and Critical Discussion of College Admission Requirements*, Columbia University Contributions to Philosophy, Psychology, and Education, vol. XI, nos. 3–4 (New York, 1903), pp. 17–39, 41; Richard Hofstadter and Wilson Smith, *American Higher Education: A Documentary History* (Chicago, 1961), vol. I, pp. 54, 109; Meyer Reinhold, *The Classick Pages: Classical Reading of Eighteenth-Century Americans* (University Park, Pa., 1975), pp. 3–6.
2. Broome, *Admission Requirements*, pp. 40–69; Edgar W. Knight, *A Documentary History of Education in the South Before 1860* (Chapel Hill, 1949–53), vol. IV, pp. 53, 297, 308–309.
3. See n. 61, below.
4. Kenneth H. Murdock, "The Teaching of Latin and Greek at the Boston Latin School in 1712," *Publ. Colon. Soc. Mass.*, vol. XXVII (1931), *Transactions*, 1927–30, pp. 21–29; Pauline Holmes, *A Tercentenary History of the Boston Public Latin School 1635–1935* (Cambridge, Mass., 1935), pp. 256–260, 264, 287, 330–331; Reinhold, *The Classick Pages*, p. 4; John E. Rexine, "The Boston Latin School's Curriculum in the Seventeenth and Eighteenth Centuries," *Classical Journal* 72 (1977), pp. 261–266.
5. "Diary of Rev. Silas Bigelow, The First Minister of Paxton, Mass.," *Proceedings Worcester Society of Antiquarians* 17 (1900), p. 263.

6. From diary of the Reverend John Ballantine, his teacher, quoted in Sibley's *Harvard Graduates* (John L. Sibley and Clifford K. Shipton, *Biographical Sketches of Harvard University Graduates* [Cambridge, Mass., 1873-], vol. XV, p. 478).

7. *Diary of Elihu Hubbard Smith (1771-1798)*, ed. James E. Cronin (Philadelphia, 1973), pp. 28-29, 31, 33.

8. *Journal and Letters of Philip Vickers Fithian, 1773-1774*, ed. Hunter D. Farish, new ed. (Williamsburg, 1957), pp. 99, 182, 250.

9. *Papers of Daniel Webster: Correspondence*, vol. I, ed. Charles M. Wiltse (Hanover, 1974), p. 10.

10. Broome, *Admission Requirements*, pp. 40-69; Colyer Meriwether, *Our Colonial Curriculum 1607-1776* (Washington, D.C., 1907; rpt. 1976), pp. 94-96; Francis L. Broderick, "Pulpits, Physics, and Politics: The Curriculum of the College of New Jersey, 1746-1794," *Wm. & Mary Quart.*, 3rd ser., 6 (1949), pp. 42-50; Knight, *Documentary History*, vol. III, pp. 22-25, 39-41, 46-49, 53, 101-102, 207.

11. *P. Virgilii Maronis Bucolica, Georgica, et Aeneis*, ed. Francis Bowen (Boston, 1842), Preface.

12. *The Progress of Dulness*, pt. 1, lines 43-44, 49-50, 131-132, in *The Satiric Poems of John Trumbull: The Progress of Dulness and M'Fingal*, ed. Edwin T. Bowden (Austin, 1962).

13. Edwin L. Wolf, "The Classical Languages in Colonial Philadelphia," in *Classical Traditions in Early America*, ed. John W. Eadie (Ann Arbor, 1976), pp. 79-80; Reinhold, *The Classick Pages*, pp. 14-15; idem, "Opponents of Classical Learning in America during the Revolutionary Period," Chapter IV, above, pp. 128-133.

14. *Miscellaneous Essays, and Occasional Writings* (Philadelphia, 1792), vol. II, pp. 7, 57; *The Life and Works of Francis Hopkinson*, ed. George E. Hastings (Chicago, 1926), p. 420. On the content and quality of the teaching of classical authors at Yale in the 1820s Julian M. Sturtevant (later president of Illinois College) criticized the professors as mere drillmasters. James L. Kingsley, professor of Latin and Greek (he was one of the authors of the influential Yale Report in 1828 that mandated the classical curriculum throughout the country for a half century) is recorded to have said, after reading Tacitus' *Agricola* with a class: "Young gentlemen, you have been reading one of the noblest productions of the human mind without knowing it." See Julian M. Sturtevant, *An Autobiography* (New York, 1896), pp. 84-85, 90-91.

15. "Classical Obscurities," *The Literary Magazine and American Register* 6 (1806), pp. 394-396.

16. Claude M. Fuess, *An Old New England School: History of Phillips Academy Andover* (Boston, 1917), pp. 170-171.

17. *Port Folio* 4 (1803), p. 286.

18. There were numerous editions of Davidson's Vergil published in America, e.g., *The Works of Virgil, Translated into English Prose* (New York, 1811).

19. *The Works of Virgil*, ed. Malcolm Campbell (New York, 1803). This was in substance a revised version of Davidson's Vergil.

20. E.g., *P. Vergilii Maronis Opera*, ed. J. G. Cooper (New York, 1829).

21. *The Bucolics, Georgics, and Aeneid of Virgil*, ed. Edward Moore (Boston, 1849).

22. *Publius Virgilius Maro, Bucolica, Georgica, et Aeneis*, ed. B. A. Gould (Boston, 1826). The text was based on editions of Heyne, Hensius, Burmann, and Wakefield. "One of the principal objects of studying the language," he wrote in his preface, is "that mental discipline which is acquired by the practice of critical and exact analysis." The *North American Review* 23 (1826), pp. 220-224, published a very favorable review of Gould's Vergil by Sidney Willard, who

praised it for accuracy of text, good typography, and avoidance of too much aid for the student.

23. *The Aeneid of Virgil*, ed. Charles Anthon (New York, 1843); *The Eclogues and Georgics of Virgil*, ed. Charles Anthon (New York, 1847). Anthon's editions were attacked by the *North American Review* in 1849 and 1850 as impeding real progress in classical education in America because of their basic faults. Cp. Stephen Newmyer, "Charles Anthon, Knickerbocker Scholar," *Classical Outlook* 59 (1981–82), pp. 40–41.

24. See, e.g., *The Charter, Laws and Catalogue of Books of the Library Company of Burlington* [N.J.] (Philadelphia, 1758); *A Catalogue of Books Sold by Noel and Hazard* (New York, 1771); *William Young's Catalogue for 1787* (Philadelphia, 1786); *William Pritchard, Catalogue of Books for 1788* (Philadelphia, 1788); *Matthew Carey's Catalogue of Books* (Philadelphia, 1794); *The Writings of Colonel William Byrd*, ed. John S. Bassett (New York, 1901), pp. 431–435 ("Catalogue of the Books in the Library of Westover Belonging to William Byrd, Esq."); Louis B. Wright, *The First Gentlemen of Virginia: Intellectual Qualities of the Colonial Ruling Class* (San Marino, 1940), pp. 136, 153; Farish, *Journal and Letters of Philip Vickers Fithian*, pp. 285–294 (catalogue of the library of Robert Carter); Walter B. Edgar, "Some Popular Books in Colonial South Carolina," *South Carolina Historical Magazine* 72 (1971), p. 177; Edwin Wolf 2nd, *The Library of James Logan of Philadelphia 1674–1751* (Philadelphia, 1974), pp. 500–502; Reinhold, *The Classick Pages*, pp. 133–136; Richard Beale Davis, *Intellectual Life in the Colonial South 1585–1763* (Knoxville, 1978), vol. II, pp. 506, 539–540.

25. E.g., *The Works of Virgil, Translated by John Dryden* (Baltimore, 1818; New York, 1825).

26. Caleb Alexander, *The Works of Virgil, Translated into Literal English Prose* (Worcester, 1796). The volume contained also the Latin text and brief notes. John F. Latimer, in "American Scholarship and Caleb Alexander," *Trans. Amer. Philolog. Assn.* 80 (1949), pp. 403–412, is charitable to Alexander's efforts at "scholarship." For translations of Vergil's works across the Atlantic in English, French, German, Dutch, Danish, Swedish, Polish, see, e.g., Joseph W. Moss, *A Manual of Classical Bibliography*, 2nd ed. (London, 1837), pp. 722–726.

27. William Munford, *Homer's Iliad* (Boston, 1846); cp. "Philhellenism in America in the Early National Period," Chapter VIII, above, p. 216.

28. *Port Folio*, n.s., 1 (1806), pp. 207–208.

29. 4 (1807), pp. 211–213. On Sargent (1786–1867) see *Dictionary of American Biography*, vol. XVI, pp. 367–368.

30. *Port Folio*, 3rd ser., 3 (1814), pp. 593-594. The editor exhorted the young man "to perseverance in his classical studies, assuring him that nothing else is necessary to rank him, at no very distant period, among the elegant scholars in his country."

31. *Port Folio*, 3rd ser., 4 (1814), pp. 103–105.

32. By Vivian, *Port Folio*, 3rd ser., 4 (1814), pp. 224–225.

33. By C, *Port Folio*, 3rd ser., 5 (1815), pp. 294–298.

34. William M. Fowler, Jr., *William Ellery: Rhode Island Politico and Lord of Admiralty* (Metuchen, 1973), pp. 180–181.

35. John C. Gray, "Study of the Classics," *North American Review* 11 (1820), p. 415.

36. "Maryland Eclogues in Imitation of Virgil's By Jonathan Spritly, Esqr., Formerly a Worthy Member of the Assembly, Revis'd & Corrected by his Friend Sly Boots," manuscript at Maryland Historical Society. See the detailed analysis in Davis, *Intellectual Life*, vol. III, pp. 1393–1395; Richard Beale Davis et al., *Southern Writing, 1585–1920* (New York, 1970), pp. 136–140.

37. *The Story of Aeneas and Dido Burlesqued* (Charleston, 1774); Oscar Wegelin, *Early American Poetry*, 2nd ed. (New York, 1930), vol. I, p. 67.
38. On Charles Cotton (1630–87), poet and friend of Izaak Walton, and his burlesque of Vergil's *Aeneid*, see *Dictionary of National Biography*, vol. IV, p. 1224. Many editions of his *Scarronides* appeared in his lifetime. On the frivolous travesties of the *Aeneid* in Italy, France, and England in the seventeenth century see Fritz Görschen, *Die Virgiltravestien in Frankreich* (Dresden, 1937), including versions by Paul Scarron (1649), and by the brothers Perrault (1649); Lewis W. Brüggemann, *A View of the English Editions, Translations, and Illustrations of the Ancient Greek and Latin Authors* (London, 1797; rpt. New York, n.d.), pp. 552–553; H. H. Huxley, "Virgilian Parodies and Imitations," *Proceedings of the Virgil Society* 2 (1962–63), pp. 9–16.
39. Martin L. Clarke, *Classical Education in Britain, 1500–1900* (Cambridge, 1959), pp. 76, 169, 171; idem, "Virgil in English Education Since the Sixteenth Century," *Virgil Society Lectures*, no. 39 (1957).
40. Marcelino Menéndez y Pelayo, *Historia de la Poesía Hispano-Americana* (Santander, 1948), vol. II, p. 226; idem, *Historia de la Poesía Chilena (1569–1892)* (Santiago, 1957), pp. 9–34.
41. Menéndez y Pelayo, *Poesía Hispano-Americana*, vol. I, pp. 81–82, 92–93, 178–180, 222–223, 226; vol. II, pp. 333, 336, 345–347; Tom B. Jones, "Classics in Colonial Hispanic America," *Trans. Amer. Philolog. Assn.* 70 (1939), pp. 37–45; Irving A. Leonard, *Books of the Brave* (Cambridge, Mass., 1949), pp. 164, 208–209, 219; L. Correa, "Andrés Bello y Virgilio," *Cultura Venezuelana* 14 (1931), pp. 145–153; A. G. Rostrepo, "Virgilio en la America Latina," *Colombo* 22 (1930), pp. 1–5.
42. The suggestion that Captain John Smith served as an Aeneas figure for early Virginians lacks documentation. The proposal was made by Howard Mumford Jones, *The Literature of Virginia in the Seventeenth Century*, 2nd ed. (Charlottesville, 1968), pp. 25–29; cp. E. Bradford, "That Other Republic: *Romanitas* in Southern Literature," in *The Classical Tradition in the South*, special issue of *Southern Humanities Review*, 1977, pp. 7, 10.
43. Douglass G. Adair, "The Intellectual Origins of Jeffersonian Democracy: Republicanism, the Class Struggle, and the Virtuous Farmer" (Ph.D. diss., Yale, 1943), pp. i–ii, 27–30, 65–95, 272–295; Alfred W. Griswold, *Farming and Democracy* (New York, 1948), pp. 18–46; Ernest Cassara, *The Enlightenment in America* (New York, 1975), pp. 29–30; Marilyn B. Silver, "The Farmer in Early American Literature," *Gypsy Scholar* 4 (1977), pp. 17–26; Leo Marx, *The Machine in the Garden: Technology and the Pastoral Ideal in America* (New York, 1964), p. 3; "Classical Influences and Eighteenth-Century American Political Thought," Chapter III, above, p. 99.
44. Louis P. Simpson, *The Dispossessed Garden: Pastoral and History in Southern Literature* (Athens, Ga., 1975), pp. 1–3. An anonymous poem, "Old Virginia Georgics" (by a member of the patrician landed gentry of the South, who knew both the Roman authorities on agriculture and the *Eclogues* and *Georgics*) appeared in *Farmers Register* 1 (1834), pp. 551–552. A satire on the lackadaisical farming of the time, it contains tags from the *Aeneid*, *Eclogues*, and *Georgics*, and begins with the lines:

I sing the tillage old Virginia knows,
Which cheats with hope the husbandman who sows;
Not such as Maro sung in deathless strains,
To piping shepherds and Italian swains.

See Clarence Gohdes, "Old Virginia Georgics," *Southern Literary Journal* 11 (1978), pp. 44–53.

45. Marx, *Machine in the Garden*, p. 19.
46. 2nd ed. (Philadelphia, 1764). The anonymous author claimed in the preface that "the following Piece was really written by a Country Farmer . . . from my Farm on the Banks of the River————." The frontispiece contains two illustrations, captioned "Thyrsis with a Presbyterian Nose; Corin with a Quakerian Nose."
47. In *Poems on Several Occasions* (Philadelphia, 1772; rpt. 1970), pp. 1–6.
48. *The Pastoral Songs of P. Virgil* [sic] *Maro* (Boston, 1799).
49. *Letterbook of Eliza Lucas Pinckney 1739–1762*, ed. Elise Pinckney (Chapel Hill, 1972), pp. 35–36. She was the mother of two eminent South Carolinians, Charles Cotesworth Pinckney and Thomas Pinckney. She was an avid reader who admired not only the *Georgics* but Plutarch's *Lives*.
50. *New American Magazine* 1 (1759), pp. 436–437, 468–469.
51. Henry C. van Schaack, *The Life of Peter van Schaack* (New York, 1842), pp. 221, 230. In a letter to his son, written from London, van Schaack advised him to inform his farmers how husbandry was carried on in Vergil's time, "but do not quote the *Georgics* to them." "By the way," he wrote to him, "do you not often read the first Eclogue with peculiar sensibility when you think of public troubles? Who will be the happy man of whom it shall be said *Deus nobis haec otia fecit!* (a god brought about this peace for us)." *Eclogue* 1, he wrote, is "so suitable to the times. When you read the fourth turn to Pope's Messiah."
52. *The Algerine Captive*, ed. Jack B. Moore (rpt. Gainesville, 1967), vol. I, pp. 41–42; cp. George T. Tanselle, *Royall Tyler* (Cambridge, Mass., 1967), p. 57; Ada L. Carson and Herbert L. Carson, *Royall Tyler* (New York, 1979), pp. 60, 66. Updike's father concluded that "if Updike went to college, I should think he should learn, not *hard words*, but *useful things*" (vol. I, p. 39).
53. Marx, *Machine in the Garden*, p. 19.
54. Ibid., pp. 20–21, 243–244.
55. Ibid., p. 203.
56. Ibid.
57. *Benjamin Tompson, 1642–1714: First Native Born Poet of America: His Poems*, ed. Howard J. Hull (Boston, 1924), pp. 29–30, 64, 70, 79. Cp. Richard M. Gummere, *The American Colonial Mind and the Classical Tradition: Essays in Comparative Culture* (Cambridge, Mass., 1963), pp. 145–146.
58. Tompson, *Poems*, p. 117.
59. Cotton Mather, *Magnalia Christi Americana Books I & II*, ed. Kenneth B. Murdock (Cambridge, Mass., 1977), pp. 45, 89–90, 107, 200; Leo M. Kaiser, "On the Latin Verse Passages in Cotton Mather's *Maganalia Christi Americana*," *Early American Literature* 10 (1976–77), pp. 301–306; idem, "Six Notes," *Early American Literature* 13 (1978–79), p. 298. The Vergilian quotations and adaptations are from all books of the *Aeneid* except 5, 8, 9, 10.
60. I.e., St. Augustine.
61. Cotton Mather, *Corderius Americanus* (Boston, 1708), p. 31.
62. Cotton Mather, *Manductio ad Ministerium. Dissertation for a Candidate of the Ministry* (Boston, 1726), p. 38.
63. Leo M. Kaiser, "The Oratio Quinta of Urian Oakes, Harvard 1678," *Humanistica Lovaniensia* 19 (1970), pp. 485–508; "Tercentenary of an Oration: The 1672 Commencement Address of Urian Oakes," *Harvard Library Bulletin* 21 (1973), pp. 75–87; "John Leverett and the Quebec Expedition of 1711: An Unpublished Latin Oration," *Harvard Library Bulletin* 22 (1974), pp. 309–316; "Seventeenth Century Latin Prose: John Leverett's Welcome to Governor Sir Edmund Andros," *Manuscripta* 18 (1974), pp. 30–37; "Prae Gaudio, Prae

Luctu: The First Commencement Address of President John Leverett," *Harvard Library Bulletin* 24 (1976), pp. 381–394.

64. Benjamin Church, *The Choice* (Boston, 1757), lines 75–76.

65. Francis Hopkinson, *Science. A Poem* (Philadelphia, 1762), lines 59–60, 63, 65–68. On Hopkinson see *The Life and Works of Francis Hopkinson*, ed. George E. Hastings (Chicago, 1926).

66. John Beveridge, *Epistolae Familiares et Alia Quaedam Miscellanea* (Philadelphia, 1765), Preface.

67. *A Hugh Henry Brackenridge Reader, 1770–1815*, ed. Daniel Marder (Pittsburgh, 1970), p. 56.

68. John Clarke, *Letters to a Student in the University of Cambridge, Massachusetts* (Boston, 1796), pp. 45, 50–51. Cp. the superficial bantering mutual criticism in "A Dialogue between Homer and Virgil," in *Christian's, Scholar's & Farmer's Magazine*, Oct.–Nov., 1789, pp. 465–466. At Princeton about this time the Whig Society's device (engraved by Charles F. Mercer in 1799–1800), depicted a youth being guided to a Temple of Virtue on a mountain. En route he faced a tablet on which were inscribed the names of Demosthenes, Xenophon, Homer, Cicero, Tacitus, and Vergil. See James McLachlan, "The *Choice of Hercules:* American Student Societies in the Early 19th Century," in *The University in Society*, ed. Lawrence Stone (Princeton, 1974), vol. II, pp. 491–492.

69. "American Literature," in *Works of Fisher Ames*, ed. Seth Ames (Boston, 1854), vol. II, p. 430.

70. 2 (1804), pp. 112–117.

71. "Classical Literature," *Literary Magazine and American Register* 7 (1807), p. 392.

72. *Port Folio*, n.s., 3 (1807), pp. 164–169, 227–228; 5 (1808), pp. 103–106 ("Classical Learning"); 3rd ser., 4 (1814), pp. 105–106.

73. 6 (1809), pp. 376–379 ("Theocritus and Virgil").

74. *Writings of Thomas Jefferson*, Memorial Edition (Washington, D.C., 1905), vol. XVIII, p. 448. The time is after 1789, probably during the years he served as secretary of state.

75. *Catalogue of the Library of Thomas Jefferson*, ed. Millicent Sowerby (Washington, D.C., 1952–59), vol. III, pp. 419–423; Charles B. Sanford, *Thomas Jefferson and His Library* (New Haven, 1977), p. 85.

76. *The Literary Bible of Thomas Jefferson: His Commonplace Book of Philosophers and Poets*, ed. Gilbert Chinard (Baltimore, 1928), p. 12; Marie Kimball, *Jefferson: The Road to Glory 1743–1776* (New York, 1943), p. 113. There are far more excerpts from Euripides (70), Homer (21), Cicero (20), Horace (14).

77. In a letter to William Short, Sept. 20, 1788, in *Writings of Thomas Jefferson*, ed. Paul Leicester Ford (New York, 1892–99), vol. V, p. 51. On his technical knowledge of the classics see Thomas Fitzhugh, "Letters of Thomas Jefferson Concerning Phillogy and the Classics," *University of Virginia Alumni Bulletin*, 3rd ser., II (1918), pp. 168–187, 337–395; 12 (1919), pp. 66–78, 155–177.

78. *Writings*, ed. Ford, vol. VIII, p. 65.

79. *Diary and Autobiography of John Adams*, ed. L. H. Butterfield (Cambridge, Mass., 1962), vol. I, pp. 37–38, 41.

80. Adams Family Papers, microfilm reel 187, Massachusetts Historical Society, Boston ("Miscellany, Literary Commonplace Book"), pp. 31–38.

81. *The Earliest Diary of John Adams*, ed. L. H. Butterfield (Cambridge, Mass., 1966), p. 68.

82. Ibid., pp. 72–73, 76.

83. *Diary and Autobiography of John Adams*, vol. IV, p. 13.

84. "Catalogue of His Library," Adams Family Papers, microfilm reel 193, pp. 35–37; *Catalogue of the John Adams Library in the Public Library of the City of Boston* (Boston, 1917), pp. 256–257.

85. Adams Family Papers, microfilm reel 124 (the date is March 29, 1823).
86. *Adams Family Correspondence*, ed. L. H. Butterfield (Cambridge, Mass., 1963–75), vol. IV, p. 117.
87. For the phrase "one out of many" cp. Aristotle *Politics* 1.5.3; Horace *Epistles* 2.2.212 (*de pluribus una*); Cicero *De Officiis* 1.17.56 (*Pythagoras vult in amicitia ut unus fiat ex pluribus*); St. Augustine *Confessions* 4.8 (*ex pluribus unum*). Benjamin Franklin's nephew Benjamin Mecom published for a few months in 1758 the *New England Magazine of Knowledge and Pleasure*, which carried on its title page the motto *E Pluribus Unum*. See Monroe E. Deutsch, "E Pluribus Unum," *Classical Journal* 18 (1922–23), pp. 387–407; B. J. Cigrand, *History of the Great Seal of the United States* (Cambridge, Mass., 1903); Gaillard Hunt, *History of the Great Seal of the United States* (Washington, D.C., 1909); Frank H. Sommer, "Emblem and Device: The Origins of the Great Seal of the United States," *Art Quarterly* 24 (1961), pp. 57–76.
88. *Dictionary of American Biography*, vol. XIX, pp. 213–214; H. van Schaack, *The Life of Peter van Schaack*, especially the letters from London 1778–83, pp. 129, 206, 212, 220, 284, 338.
89. Ruth Wentworth Brown, "Classical Echoes in the Poetry of Philip Freneau," *Classical Journal* 45 (1949), pp. 32–33; Harry Hayden Clark, "The Literary Influences of Philip Freneau," *Studies in Philology* 22 (1925), pp. 7, 20; Philip M. Marsh, *The Works of Philip Freneau: A Critical Study* (Metuchen, 1968), pp. 20, 181.
90. *The Poetical Works of John Trumbull* (Hartford, 1820), vol. II, pp. 131–138. The translation appeared first in *The American Museum* 2 (1787), pp. 95–97.
91. Canto 4, lines 81–89, 104–110, 610–612.
92. Victor E. Gimmestad, *John Trumbull* (New York, 1974), pp. 131, 138; Katherine A. Conley, "A Letter of John Trumbull," *New Engl. Quart.* 11 (1938), 372–374.
93. *The Progress of Dulness*, pt. 1, lines 131–132, 137–138, in Bowden, *The Satiric Poems of John Trumbull*.
94. Richard M. Gummere, *Seven Wise Men of Colonial America* (Cambridge, Mass., 1967), p. 23.
95. James Mulhern, *A History of Secondary Education in Pennsylvania* (Philadelphia, 1933), pp. 43–44, 122; Wolf, "The Classical Languages in Philadelphia," p. 71.
96. George S. Brookes, *Friend Anthony Benezet* (Philadelphia, 1937), p. 389, letter of John Pemberton, May 29, 1783; cp. letter to Robert Pleasants, Oct. 2, 1780, pp. 351–352, on the deleterious effect on religion from the reading of Ovid, Vergil, and Horace.
97. *A Letter to the Right Reverend Father in God, John, Bishop of Landaff* (New York, 1768), pp. 23–24. Cp. Rutherford E. Delmage, "The American Idea of Progress, 1750–1800," *Proc. Amer. Philos. Soc.* 91 (1947), p. 307.
98. Benjamin T. Spencer, *The Quest for Nationality, an American Literary Campaign* (Syracuse, 1957); M. F. Heiser, "The Decline of Neoclassicism 1810–1848," in *Transitions in American Literary History*, ed. Harry Hayden Clark (New York, 1954; rpt. 1975), pp. 93–169; A. Owen Aldridge, "The Concept of the Ancients and Moderns in American Poetry of the Federal Period," in Eadie, *Classical Traditions in Early America*, pp. 99–108; "The Silver Age of Classical Studies in America, 1790–1830," Chapter VI, above.
99. Cited by Russel B. Nye, *The Cultural Life of the New Republic, 1776–1830* (New York, 1960), p. 238. It is noteworthy that Philip Freneau at his commencement in 1771 at Princeton participated in a forensic debate on the topic "Does Ancient Poetry Excel the Modern," taking the affirmative.
100. By Cantabrigiensis, in *Massachusetts Magazine* 1 (1789), pp. 117–118.

101. *A Dissertation on the History, Eloquence and Poetry of the Bible* (New Haven, 1772).
102. By The Meddler, *New Haven Gazette* 1, no. 4, June 26, 1791.
103. Joel Barlow, *The Columbiad* (Philadelphia, 1809), vol. I, pp. v–vii; vol. II, pp. 194–195. Cp. Arthur L. Ford, *Joel Barlow* (New York, 1971), pp. 74–84; James Woodress, *A Yankee's Odyssey: The Life of Joel Barlow* (Philadelphia, 1958), pp. 245–250. On Vergil as subservient to Augustus, currying favor with a monarch, flattering him and his countrymen, cp. "Literature of the Ancients," by "R" in *Monthly Anthology and Boston Review* 4 (1807), pp. 57–59. George Bancroft, "Value of Classical Learning," *North American Review* 19 (1824), p. 130, also criticized Vergil for "servile adulation," and failure to sustain in his later work the "republicanism of his earlier days."
104. Hans Kortum, *Charles Perrault und Nicolas Boileau: Der Antike-Streit im Zeitalter der klassischen französischen Literatur* (Berlin, 1966), pp. 136–145.
105. [Richard Beresford], *A Plea for Literature, More Especially of the Literature of Free States* (Charleston, 1793), pp. 29–30, 35.
106. *The Works of Fisher Ames*, ed. Seth Ames (New York, 1854; rpt. 1971), p. 468.
107. *Port Folio*, 3rd ser., 4 (1814), pp. 105–106 ("Ancient and Modern Poets"). On the other hand, Crito in the *Literary Magazine and American Register* 3 (1805), pp. 165–167 ("Virgil's Mornings") judged that English poets were superior to Vergil in descriptions of mornings.
108. Thomas Smith Grimké, *Oration on American Education* (Cincinnati, 1835), pp. 16–17, 39.
109. *Oration . . . before the Connecticut Alpha of the Phi Beta Kappa Society, Sept. 7, 1830* (New Haven, 1831).
110. Mary Ruth Miller, *Thomas Campbell* (New York, 1978), pp. 58–68; J. Cuthbert Hadden, *Thomas Campbell* (Edinburgh, 1899), p. 97; Charles Duffy, "Thomas Campbell and America," *American Literature* 13 (1941–42), pp. 346–355.
111. *Adams Family Correspondence*, vol. III, pp. 308–309; vol. IV, p. 144.
112. Adams Family Papers, microfilm reel 13, Oct. 4, 1781.
113. Ibid., reel 238.
114. Ibid.
115. *Port Folio* 3 (1803), pp. 43–44, 50–51, 58–59, 66–68. Cp. Linda K. Kerber and Walter J. Morris, "Politics and Literature: The Adams Family and the *Port Folio*," *Wm. & Mary Quart.*, 3rd ser., 23 (1966), pp. 455–456. The library of John Quincy Adams contained two texts of Vergil, including an edition published in London in 1824, which he annotated thoroughly, as well as a French translation.
116. *Diary of Charles Francis Adams*, ed. Aida di Pace Donald and David Donald (Cambridge, Mass., 1964–68), vol. III, p. vii. The others were of Homer, Socrates, Plato, Demosthenes, and Cicero.
117. Ibid., vol. I, pp. 4–7.
118. Ibid., vol. IV, p. 114.
119. Ibid., p. 247.
120. Ibid., pp. 249–253. The text he used and annotated (see above, n. 116) had the following notation at the end in his hand: "These books have never been equalled."
121. Ibid., pp. 254–279.
122. Ibid., p. 255.
123. Ibid., p. 256.
124. Ibid., p. 267.
125. Ibid., p. 279.
126. Ibid., p. 276.
127. Ibid., vol. V, pp. 147–250.

128. Ibid., p. 174.
129. Ibid., pp. 213, 250.
130. Ethel Seybold, *Thoreau: The Quest and the Classics* (New Haven, 1951), pp. 16, 37, 121–123. Cp. Kenneth W. Cameron, *Companion to Thoreau's Correspondence* (Hartford, 1964), pp. 17, 35.
131. *Journal*, vol. XIII of *The Writings of Henry David Thoreau*, ed. Bradford Torrey (Boston, 1906; rpt. 1968), entry under Dec. 13, 1859.
132. Ibid., entry under Nov. 20, 1837. Cp. Seybold, *Thoreau*, pp. 29, 55.
133. *Remarks on Classical and Utilitarian Studies* (Boston, 1867).
134. "College Fetich," in Charles Francis Adams, *Three Phi Beta Kappa Addresses* (Boston, 1907), pp. 3–47. Cp. "Survey of the Scholarship on Classical Traditions in Early America," Chapter XII, below, pp. 282–283.
135. *Trans. Amer. Philolog. Assn.* 11 (1880), pp. 72–82.
136. Clement L. Smith, "Virgil's Instructions for Ploughing, Fallowing, and the Rotation of Crops, Georgics II, 43–83," *American Journal of Philology* 2 (1881), pp. 425–445; R. Ellis, "On the Culex and Other Poems of the Appendix Vergiliana," *American Journal of Philology* 3 (1882), pp. 271–284; Thomas R. Price, "The Color System of Vergil," *American Journal of Philology* 4 (1883), pp. 1–20.

X. Plutarch's Influence in America from Colonial Times to 1890

The most popular work of ancient literature (always excepting the Bible) in America for about 250 years was Plutarch's *Lives*.[1] Though Plutarch was not a subject in the curriculum of American grammar schools, academies, high schools, or colleges, there was hardly a library—private, public, or college—or bookseller's catalogue that did not possess a copy, whether in the elegant Tudor prose of Sir Thomas North's translation (1579) from Amyot's great French version, or the so-called Dryden translation, by several hands (1683), or that of the brothers John and William Langhorne (1770), or, in the nineteenth century, the improved Dryden version revised by Arthur Hugh Clough.[2] While Homer, the Greek tragedians, Aristophanes, Plato, Aristotle, Vergil, Cicero, Horace, Ovid, Seneca were criticized, frowned upon, or denounced in greater or lesser measure, Plutarch always stood unequivocally in high favor in America.[3] For centuries, a recent biographer of Plutarch reminds us, "Plutarch's *Lives* and *Morals* [were] among the formative books of western civilisation."[4] In his universality and expansive scope Plutarch caught the essence of the cosmopolitan culture of the classical world, celebrating many of the highest ideals, achievements, and great men of Greco-Roman civilization. From the renaissance to the mid-nineteenth century, both in Europe and America, Plutarch was cherished and imitated as one of the foremost mediators of the norms of life associated with the *humanitas*

250

ideal of classical antiquity. In America, from Cotton Mather's plaudits to Emerson's homage to him as "the elixir of Greece and Rome,"[5] he gave pleasure, instruction, and inspiration to numerous Americans, to whom he endeared himself by his memorable portrayals of the virtues and vices of the great figures of antiquity, his high moral ideals, geniality, charming style, anecdotal talent, and vivid narrative craftsmanship. And, as Emerson pointed out, "One proof of Plutarch's skill as a writer is that he bears translation so well."[6]

In Puritan New England Plutarch's *Lives* were in tune with the late Renaissance reverence for and moralistic interpretation of history.[7] In the Massachusetts Bay Colony, as early as the 1660s America's first woman poet, Anne Bradstreet (1612–72), in the revised second edition (published posthumously in Boston in 1678) of her long poem "The Four Monarchies" (which was based for the most part on Sir Walter Raleigh's *History of the World*), incorporated some details she had culled from her reading of North's Plutarch's *Lives*.[8] Regarding Artaxerxes Memnon of Persia she interpolated:

> Such as would know at large his warrs and reign,
> What troubles in his house he did sustain,
> His match incestuous, cruelties of th' Queen,
> His life may read in *Plutarch* to be seen.
> Forty three years he rul'd, then turn'd to dust,
> A King nor good, nor valiant, wise nor just.

And regarding Eumenes, she wrote:

> He that at large would satisfie his mind,
> In *Plutarchs Lives* his history may find.[9]

To Cotton Mather, Plutarch was "the incomparable Plutarch,"[10] guide to historical writing and the genre biography as model for moral instruction. And though it was the work of a pagan moralist, for Mather his precepts and pragmatic philosophy did not clash with Christian moral doctrine.[11] Mather freely proclaimed his great debt to Plutarch: "I must, in a way of Writing, like that of *Plutarch*, prepare my Reader for the intended Relation, by first searching the *Archives* of Antiquity for a *Parallel*." And he expressed his admiration for him as model of integrity thus: "[I am] entirely of Plutarch's mind, that it is better it should never be said there was such a man as Plutarch at all, than to have it said, that he was not an *honest* and *worthy* man."[12]

The eighteenth century was a veritable *aetas Plutarchana*. Like Rousseau on the other side of the Atlantic, many an American was introduced early in life to the *Parallel Lives* and "knew them off by heart." Benjamin Franklin is a memorable case in point. He tells us in his *Autobiography* that Plutarch was his first love for general reading: "My Father's little library consisted chiefly of Books in polemic Divinity most of which I read, and have since often regretted, that at a time when I had such a Thirst for Knowledge, more proper books had not fallen in my way. . . . Plutarch's Lives there was, in which I read abundantly, and I still think that time I spent to great Advantage."[13] Among the first books ordered by Franklin in 1737 for what was to become the Library Company of Philadelphia was a copy of Plutarch's *Lives*.[14] One of Franklin's cronies in Philadelphia, John Breitnall, had Plutarch "at his finger tips." In 1729, in a contribution to the *American Mercury*, he treated at length the incident in Plutarch's life of Timoleon leading up to the famous saying: "I rejoice to see the time when every man in Syracuse may speak freely what he thinks."[15] Similarly, Plutarch was a favorite with that remarkable South Carolinian Eliza Lucas Pinckney, mother of the American patriots and statesmen Charles Cotesworth Pinckney and Thomas Pinckney. In 1742, when she was a young woman, her beloved *Plutarch* was almost thrown into the fire by an older woman friend who feared that so much classical reading would addle her mind and injure her chances of making a proper match.[16]

From the middle of the century Americans read Plutarch's *Lives* with an eye not only to moral instruction but to political enlightenment and historical models as well.[17] As men turned more and more from theological concerns to political instruction, history became a central interest. Americans studied the past voraciously and intensively, ransacking especially ancient history for parallels, analogies, lessons, role models. In 1753 William Smith (later provost of the College of Philadelphia) defined the prevailing interest thus: "History is a Lesson of *Ethics* and *Politics*—an useful Rule of Conduct and Manners thro' Life. . . . The Youth are thus sent into the World well acquainted with the History of those Nations they are likely to be most concerned with in Life, and also the History of *Greece* and *Rome*, which may be justly called the History of *Heroism, Virtue,* and *Patriotism.* . . . It is History that, by presenting those bright Patterns to the eyes of Youth, awakens Emulation and Calls them forth steady Patriots to fill the Offices of State." And in his exposition of specifics on how to study ancient history he cites numerous examples from Plutarch's *Lives*.[18]

One of Smith's protégés was the youthful Benjamin West, later to achieve international fame abroad as a painter and president of the Royal Academy in England. Under Smith's tutelage West became enamored of the picturesque stories in Plutarch's *Lives*. In 1756, at age eighteen, he painted in Lancaster, Pennsylvania, *The Death of Socrates*, which was to remain the only classical subject he treated while in America. According to West's earliest biographer, the work was commissioned by a certain William Henry of Lancaster, who suggested the subject to him and read West the story from a translation of Plutarch. Of course, the death of Socrates is not recounted anywhere in Plutarch. It is more likely that the model of the work, particularly the central group, was the engraving on the frontispiece of the fourth volume of the famous best-seller of the eighteenth century, Charles Rollin's *Ancient History*.[19] Indeed, several generations of Americans in the eighteenth and early nineteenth centuries were nurtured by the eminently readable histories of antiquity by the distinguished French educator Charles Rollin. His *Ancient History* and *Roman History*, both quickly translated into English, were standard shortcuts to the classics, providing instruction in morals and politics. Much of Rollin's material was culled from Plutarch.[20]

At bottom it was Plutarch's *Lycurgus* that engendered the widespread admiration of Sparta prevailing in the eighteenth century, both in Europe and America. It was not Athens but Sparta that appealed to Americans for generations: admired were her stability, maintenance of freedom as a commonwealth for about five hundred years, emphasis on civic virtue, simplicity of life, agricultural base, checks and balances in a mixed constitution, her citizen militia, inner harmony, equilibrium between the extremes of absolute monarchy and extreme democracy, and the dedication of her magistrates and citizens to the republic. Thus it was "as brave and free a people as ever existed," declared John Dickinson in 1768, citing with approval the disciplined behavior of the Spartans described in Plutarch's *Lycurgus*.[21] Samuel Adams, indeed, looked forward to a "Christian Sparta" in Boston.[22]

Attracted especially to the ancient lawgivers and champions of liberty in Plutarch, Americans drew from him role models of republican heroes as their classical "saints and martyrs," together with numerous historical *exempla* of virtues and vices, republicanism in action, and dedication to liberty, as well as exemplary anecdotes and quotable moral apothegms.[23] George Bernard Shaw could call Plutarch's *Lives* a "revolutionists' handbook."[24] In 1774, for example, Josiah Quincy peppered his arguments against the Boston

Port Bill with quotations and incidents from several of the *Lives:*
Caesar, Solon, Tiberius Gracchus, Lysander, Pompey, Brutus, and
Galba. Typical are the following illustrations by Quincy: "Private
soldiers (said Tiberius Gracchus from the Roman Rostrum) fought
and died to advance the wealth and luxury of the great"; "Will you
never have done (exclaimed Pompey) with citing laws and privi-
ledges to men who wear swords"; "It had been easy (said the great
lawgiver Solon to the Athenians) to repress *the advance* of tyranny
and prevent it's establishment, *but now it is established* and grown
to some height it would be MORE GLORIOUS *to demolish* it"; "Resolved as we are (replied the hero [Cassius] to his friend [Brutus])
. . . let us march against the enemy, for *tho' we should not conquer,
we have nothing to fear.*"[25]

What did Americans see in these Plutarchan heroic models?
Among their favorites were the *Cicero,* portraying the life of a self-
made man, brilliant orator, and dedicated patriot fighting to the
death for republicanism against tyranny; *Solon,* depicting politics
joined with morality, patriotism, military exploits on behalf of
one's country, integrity, the lawgiver promoting balance and moderation, the primacy of the public good, and exemplifying the mod-
erate life-style of a leader; the *Phocion,* for patriotism, principled
integrity, and unmerited attacks on an honorable statesman; the
Timoleon,[26] portraying hostility to tyrants, disinterested public service, withdrawal from the seats of power after serving, and support
for due process and freedom of speech; the *Demosthenes,* exalting
love of liberty, hostility to tyranny, the role of the orator-statesman,
and the call to sacrifice for freedom.[27]

The most immensely popular of Plutarch's *Lives* in eighteenth-
century America was the *Cato Uticensis.* For Cato was idealized (in
England as well) as the impeccable model of patriotism, private and
public virtue, republicanism, unrelenting opposition to tyranny, in-
corruptibility, and dedication to public service. Americans knew
the Catonic model mediated through a contemporary play based in
large part on Plutarch's life, Joseph Addison's *Cato,* the first great
neoclassical English tragedy. First performed in 1712, it was received in London with thunderous applause, and the acclaim rever-
berated throughout the century, in Britain, on the continent, and in
America, serving as a clarion call to dedication to virtue, civic duty,
and freedom. The play was very popular in the colonies also, especially in the 1760s and 1770s: there were numerous performances
from South Carolina to New Hampshire, and it was played in
Washington's presence in the winter of 1777–78. In Addison's *Cato*

Americans frequently heard the sententious lines: "It is not now a Time to talk of aught / But Chains, or Conquest; Liberty, or Death"; "What Pity is it / That we can die but once to serve our Country!"[28]

The Revolutionary generation, however, had no Charlotte Corday, who before she assassinated Marat spent the day reading Plutarch. But, like Madame Roland, learned French Girondist leader in the French Revolution, many an American might have proclaimed with her, "Plutarch disposed me to become a republican." Indeed, General Charles Lee of the Revolutionary army, writing to Robert Morris in 1782, said much the same: "I have ever from the first time I read Plutarch been an Enthusiastick for liberty . . . and for liberty in a republican garb."[29] There is more than rhetoric in Charles Mullett's oft-quoted conclusion that "Classical authors are to be counted among the 'founding fathers.' . . . The heroes of Plutarch became the heroes of the revolutionary American leaders. Not less than the Washingtons and the Lees, the ancient heroes helped to found the independent American commonwealth."[30]

It is curious, however, that among the Founding Fathers the two most devoted to classical learning, Jefferson and Adams, had so little to say about Plutarch. Jefferson's one single reference to him is to the *Pericles*, regarding the establishment of colonies (cleruchies) by Pericles.[31] Adams, too, referred to Plutarch only once, instancing Aratus' views that small autonomous cities of Achaea could not survive unless united by bonds of common interest, communication and connectedness.[32]

Plutarch was, however, a high favorite of Alexander Hamilton, whose classical education was limited. When Hamilton was a captain in the Artillery Company of New York in 1777, he spent leisure time excerpting on blank pages of his pay account extensive passages with commentator's notes (fifty-one pages of quotations) from the Dryden translation of the first four lives: Theseus, Romulus, Lycurgus (largest number of quotations), and Numa Pompilius.[33] Hamilton was about twenty years of age at the time. The excerpts reveal two major interests of Hamilton at that time: political institutions and sex.[34] In the mounting tempo of polemics over the political institutions of the new country, Hamilton's knowledge of Plutarch's *Lives* emerged. In 1782 he repudiated the common image of a virtuous Sparta as model for America, derogating as visionary the notion of establishing a republic based on a virtuous people led by virtuous leaders. "We might as soon," he wrote, "reconcile ourselves to the Spartan community of goods and wives, to their iron coins, their long beards, or their black broth. There is a total dissimulation in the circumstances, as well as the manners of society among us; and it is as ridiculous to seek for models in the simple ages of Greece and Rome, as it would be to go in quest of them among the Hottentots and Laplanders."[35]

Both Hamilton and Madison in the debates over the formulation of the new constitution put their knowledge of Plutarch to practical use. In the list of books to be bought for the reference library of Congress in 1783 Madison included the Langhorne translation of the *Lives*.[36] *The Federalist* papers demonstrate that both had been doing their homework in Plutarch.[37] In "Federalist," no. 6 Hamilton discusses the causes of hostility among nations, and warns that private motives of leaders are sometimes transformed into public policies, citing as precedent Pericles' destruction of Samos at the instigation of Aspasia, "a prostitute," and his unleashing the Peloponnesian War through the Megarian decrees to avoid persecution on a charge of being an accomplice of Phidias in illegalities and peculation, or to avoid accusations of misuse of public moneys for private purposes.[38] In "Federalist," no. 18 Madison and Hamilton jointly discuss at length the inadequacies of Greek federal leagues, warning that "it happened but too often, according to Plutarch, that the deputies of the strongest cities, awed and corrupted those of the weaker, and that judgment went in favor of the most powerful party."[39] In "Federalist," no. 38 Madison, in discoursing on the constitutions of ancient states, cites the Plutarchan figures of Solon, Lycurgus, Romulus, and Numa.[40] Later, in 1792, Hamilton, in a letter to Gouverneur Morris, agreed to the use of a cypher for confidential correspondence, listing code names for members of the executive, for specific senators and representatives. Of twenty-six Americans, classical names were to be used for all but three, and about half of the code names were taken from Plutarch's *Lives*.[41]

Hamilton himself always wrote his pamphlets under pen names, following the standard custom of the late eighteenth century. The pseudonym Publius, shared by Hamilton, Madison, and Jay, derived from Plutarch's Publius Valerius, who consolidated the Roman Republic after the overthrow of Tarquinius Superbus. At various stages of his career it was Hamilton's practice to use pseudonyms derived from Plutarchan heroes: Phocion in 1784; Tully in 1790; Camillus, 1795; Pericles, 1803. The nom de plume Phocion he signed to a plea for generosity and justice to ex-enemies, following the example of the fourth-century conservative Athenian leader. Here Hamilton was pleading with New Yorkers to end the persecution of Tories and restore them to full civic rights. The pseudonym Tully he used in an attack on the Whiskey Rebels, reminiscent of Cicero's denunciation of Catiline; Camillus for a defense of the Jay Treaty; and Pericles for justification of the proposition that the United States must become an imperial power, like democratic Athens under Pericles. These four pseudonyms out of Plutarch, the import of which was readily understood by educated Americans, demonstrate, taken together, as Douglass Adair has shown, Hamilton's own estimate of his destiny at each time. All of Plutarch's heroes had this in common, that they were men of heroic virtue and had contempt for the people whom they nevertheless served devotedly, and that all four were misjudged and persecuted by the populace. But, as Plutarch concludes in each biography, the people in each case later came to regret their repudiation of these leaders and honored them posthumously.[42] In 1791, at a Cabinet meeting, Hamilton, basing his view on Plutarch's life of Caesar, declared that "the greatest man . . . that ever lived was Julius Caesar." Adair concluded that we must take into consideration in judging Hamilton how his use of Plutarch and his vision of antiquity "affected his view of his own destiny and the policies appropriate to achieve it."[43]

Among the Loyalists, too, Plutarchan models existed. It was especially Peter Oliver, last royal chief justice of Massachusetts who was influenced by Plutarch. Writing in exile for an English audience, he narrated the history of the Revolution as he viewed it with Plutarchan biographical methodology, adorning his own heroes with classical Stoic virtues.[44]

The popularity of Plutarch in America reached its height at the end of the eighteenth century. A case in point is the action taken by a board of three commissioners who met in New York City on July 3, 1790, to give names to twenty-five new townships in lands to be distributed to veterans around Lake Cayuga, New York. Of the names decided upon twenty were taken from classical antiquity, and of these twelve were lifted directly out of Plutarch's *Lives*: Lysander, Hannibal, Cato, Camillus, Cicero, Tully, Marcellus, Romulus, Scipio, Fabius, Cincinnatus, and Solon. The choice of Dryden as one of the names reveals that the translation of Plutarch being used by the commissioners was the Dryden version.[45]

It is also interesting to observe that during the period of national mourning for Washington, from December 14, 1799, to February 22, 1800, numerous analogies to classical heroes were made in the approximately 350 funeral eulogies pronounced over Washington, from Maine to Georgia. Washington was most frequently compared to Plutarchan heroes, especially to Fabius Maximus, Cincinnatus, Solon, Lycurgus, Cimon, Scipio, Philopoemen, Pompey, Timoleon, Epaminondas, and Aristides. Typical of the Plutarchan reminiscences were the remarks of Fisher Ames of Massachusetts, Congress's greatest orator of the time and a devotee of ancient history, who eulogized Washington thus: "Some future Plutarch will search for a parallel to his character. Epaminondas is perhaps the highest name of all antiquity. Our Washington resembled him in the purity and ardor of his patriotism; and like him, he first exalted the glory of his country." But Ames hastened to add, "There it is to be hoped the parallel ends; for Thebes fell with Epaminondas."[46] John Davis declared, "If we were to select the character, among the great men of antiquity exhibiting the nearest resemblance to Washington, it would be Timoleon."[47] Francis Adrian van der Kemp, speaking at Oldenborneveld, Oneida County, New York, eulogized Washington as greater than the Plutarchan heroes Aristides, Phocion, Camillus, and Manlius because he did not suffer the eventual violent persecution of his fellow countrymen.[48]

As American nationalism and pragmatism became dominant, and internal partisan strife escalated, the usefulness of classical knowledge in the public arena waned. It is at this time that, in the vigorous debate over the place of the classical curriculum in American schools and colleges, men like Hugh Henry Brackenridge rose to the defense of classical learning. In 1804 he wrote: "Political studies ought to be the great object with the generous youth of a republic, not for the sake of place or profit, but for the sake of judging right and preserving the constitution inviolate. Plutarch's Lives is an admirable book for this purpose. I should like to see an edition of 10,000 volumes bought up in every state. Plutarch was a lover of virtue, and his reflections are favorable to all that is great and good among men."[49] The prestigious literary magazine *Port Folio*, published in Philadelphia, wrote that Plutarch's *Lives* are "far more interesting than the histories of national events and revolutions, because they come nearer to our own business and bosoms, and possess a much stronger claim to our attention."[50] Even Benjamin Rush, vociferous anticlassicist that he was, could nevertheless quote with approval from Plutarch. He was especially fond of the statement attributed to Brutus near the end of his life, "I early devoted myself to my country, and I have ever since lived a life of liberty and glory."[51] In 1817 Francis Walker Gilmer wrote to his son Thomas (later secretary of the navy, 1844): "You & William must read Plutarch's *Lives*, frequently. I had rather you should read no history for 5 or 6 years—if you can obtain Biographies of great men; great in my sense of the word. You cannot read Plutarch too often."[52]

John Quincy Adams had a copy of Plutarch's *Lives* in 1809 as he voyaged to his diplomatic post in Russia. En route he reread the lives of Lycurgus and Solon.[53] In 1811 he received from the Sardinian minister Count De Maistre the manuscript of his French translation of Plutarch's essay "The Delay of Divine Justice." Adams commented in his diary: "The translation is too much dilated. There are two points in the character of Plutarch's style which the French denominate *bonhommie* and *naiveté*; they are well represented in the old translation of Amyot, but I do not find them in that of Maistre. . . . Plutarch reasons well, but leaves too much of the mysterious veil over his subject."[54] The Adams family's reverence for Plutarch continued into the third generation with Charles Francis Adams.[55]

In the middle of the nineteenth century the enormous influence of Plutarch of the preceding century as "guide for princes and ordinary men" began to fade in both Europe and America.[56] The reasons for this are complex: contemporary German positivistic scholarship had demolished Plutarch as a reliable source for Greek and Roman history and thought; history itself as the biographies of great men was giving way to the annals of peoples; romanticism was creating new concepts of the heroic.[57] Indeed, as antiquity in general was losing its bloom as absolute standard for political institutions and for civic virtue, Plutarch's usefulness and appeal waned steadily. Moreover, American heroes, especially Washington, were now treasured as role models.

It is therefore a veritable anomoly that Ralph Waldo Emerson (1803–82), living in the twilight of the *aetas Plutarchana*, should have so admired, utilized, and exploited Plutarch in the highest throughout his entire career. From Plutarch the biographer, the essayist, the moralist Emerson took his views on the ethical nature of history, expressed in the lives of great men, his adoption of the essay genre and manner of teaching by use of moral anecdotes and epigrams.[58] Before he was twenty he began his lifelong love affair with Plutarch (the earliest *Journal* reference to Plutarch's *Lives* is in 1822). Indeed, throughout his life his favorite author remained Plutarch, and the *Moralia* (little appreciated before Emerson) was his favorite work (he began to read it in 1825).[59] It must be stressed that Emerson's knowledge of classical literature was not based on reading of the originals but on translations. For Plutarch he relied on the Dryden and Langhorne versions for the *Lives*, and on the translation "by several hands" for the *Moralia*.[60]

"We cannot read Plutarch," wrote Emerson, "without a tingling of the blood."[61] Plutarch remained for Emerson "the elixir of Greece and Rome, that is the book which nations went to compose. If the world's library were burning, I should as soon fly to rescue that, as Shakespeare and Plato, or next afterwards." "I must think we are more deeply indebted to him than to all the ancient writers."[62] It was to Plutarch that Emerson owed the revival of the cult of the moral essay, his neo-Hellenic predilection for the Greeks over the Romans as model of simple natural nobility and heroism, his Spartomania, his conception of the hero as moral exemplar, his debt to Stoicism (a sort of loose practical idealism, a "Stoicism of the blood," as he called it), and not least his anecdotal and apotheg-matic style and his assimilation of American and Plutarchan he-roes.[63] In his essay on Abraham Lincoln, delivered in Concord as eulogy in 1865, Emerson used as caption the lines from President Lowell's "Commencement Ode" at Harvard: "Here was a type of the true elder race, / And one of Plutarch's men talked with us face to face."[64]

The last appreciation of Plutarch written in America by a well-known writer, before the publication of scholarly articles on Plu-tarch began to appear, was Emerson's impressionistic essay written in 1870. In his essay, entitled "Plutarch," composed as introduction to a new version of the *Moralia* by William W. Goodwin (actually a revision of the older translation by several hands), he assigns to him "a unique place in literature as an encyclopedia of Greek and Roman antiquity." His popularity, he wrote at a time when few were still reading Plutarch, is due to his humanity, his delight in magnaminity and self-sacrifice, which have made his works "a bible for heroes." And he concluded that "Plutarch will be perpetu-ally rediscovered from time to time as long as books last."[65]

Plutarch, like Vergil, gradually became the preserve of classical scholars, and by the end of the century the learned journals in America began to publish articles addressed to specialists.[66] Still, the older influence of Plutarch in America as literary model occa-sionally manifested iself. For example, in Herman Melville's poem "Timoleon" (ca. 1886–88), he used Plutarch's life of Timoleon to probe his own concerns about his family (especially his relationship to his brother, on the model of Timoleon's to his brother Timo-phanes) and about his own views and dilemmas (Melville appears to have used the Langhorne translation).[67] And even in the twentieth century the usefulness of Plutarch's *Lives* for political models and moral instruction has not completely drawn to a close.[68]

Notes

1. Rudolf Hirzel, in *Plutarch, Das Erbe der Alten*, vol. IV (Leipzig, 1912), pp. 194–195, deals very briefly with Plutarch in America, citing only Franklin and Emerson; Gilbert Highet, in *The Classical Tradition: Greek and Roman Influences on Western Literature* (London, 1949), is silent about the American experience with Plutarch.
2. The *Moralia* was rarely read before Emerson's consuming interest in Plutarch's essays, beginning 1825. Cp. Edmund G. Berry, *Emerson's Plutarch* (Cambridge, Mass., 1961), p. 38. The *Moralia* was read in Philemon Holland's version of 1603 or in *Plutarch's Morals*, translated by several hands (London, 1684–94).
3. In Europe Plutarch did not escape adverse criticism in the eighteenth century. Cp. Martha W. Howard, *The Influence of Plutarch in the Major European Literatures of the Eighteenth Century* (Chapel Hill, 1970), passim.
4. Donald A. Russell, *Plutarch* (London, 1978), Preface.
5. Berry, *Emerson's Plutarch*, p. 35 (quotation from the *Journals*).
6. Ralph Waldo Emerson, "Plutarch," in *Lectures and Biographical Sketches*, vol. X of *Emerson's Complete Works* (Cambridge, Mass., 1883), p. 302. Emerson himself probably did not read Plutarch in the original (Berry, *Emerson's Plutarch*, pp. 297–298, n. 6).
7. E.g., Kenneth B. Murdock, *Literature and Theology in Colonial New England* (Cambridge, Mass., 1949), pp. 67–69. John Harvard's library, given to Harvard in 1638, contained North's *Plutarch*. See Thomas Goddard Wright, *Literary Culture in Early New England, 1620–1730* (New Haven, 1920), p. 31, and for other early New England libraries possessing Plutarchs, pp. 36, 60, 129, 135. Cp. *Early English Books at the University of Virginia*, ed. William Miller (Charlottesville, 1941), pp. 7, 10 (North's *Plutarch* and Philemon Holland's *Moralia*).
8. There is no evidence that Anne Bradstreet could read Greek or Latin: Josephine K. Piercy, *Anne Bradstreet* (New York, 1968), p. 58.
9. *The Works of Anne Bradstreet*, ed. John H. Ellis (New York, 1932), pp. xi, xlii–xliv, xlix, 246, 297; Piercy, *Anne Bradstreet*, pp. 50–66.
10. *Magnalia Christi Americana* (Hartford, 1830), vol. I, p. 27 (the first American edition from the London edition of 1702).
11. Gustaaf van Cromphout, "Cotton Mather as Plutarchan Biographer," *American Literature* 46 (1974–75), pp. 465–481.
12. *Magnalia Christi Americana Books I & II*, ed. Kenneth B. Murdock (Cambridge, Mass., 1977), p. 277; van Cromphout, "Cotton Mather," p. 475; Murdock, *Literature & Theology*, pp. 68–69; idem, "Clio in the Wildnerness: History and Biography in Puritan New England," *Church History* 24 (1955), pp. 222–223; E. G. Berry, "Plutarque dans l'Amérique du XIXe Siècle," *Actes du VIII. Congrès, Association Guillaume Budé, 1968* (Paris, 1969), pp. 578–582; C. J. Gianakaris, *Plutarch* (New York, 1970), pp. 132–133. The second quotation from Mather is a parody of Plutarch's remark: "I would rather have people say there is no such person as Plutarch than that Plutarch is an unstable, changeable person" ("Superstition," *Moralia* 170A).
13. *The Autobiography of Benjamin Franklin*, ed. Leonard W. Labaree et al. (New Haven, 1964), p. 58. Curiously there is almost no reference to Plutarch in all of Franklin's voluminous papers. Cp. Richard M. Gummere, "Socrates at the Printing Press: Benjamin Franklin and the Classics," *Classical Weekly* 26 (1932), pp. 57–59.

14. Austin K. Gray, *Benjamin Franklin's Library* (New York, 1937), p. 9.
15. Elizabeth C. Cook, *Literary Influences in Colonial Newspapers, 1704–1750* (New York, 1912; rpt. 1966), pp. 81–83.
16. *The Letterbook of Eliza Lucas Pinckney 1739–1762*, ed. Elise Pinckney (Chapel Hill, 1972), p. 33.
17. See Thomas E. Keys, "Popular Books in the Colonial Library," *Wilson Library Bulletin* 14 (1940), pp. 726–727; Wilson Ober Clough, *Intellectual Origins of American National Thought: Pages from the Books Our Founding Fathers Read*, 2nd ed. (New York, 1961), pp. 80–89; H. Trevor Colbourn, *The Lamp of Experience: Whig History and the Intellectual Origins of the American Revolution* (Chapel Hill, 1965), p. 78, and appendix II ("History in Eighteenth-Century American Libraries"), pp. 204–206, 217, 222; Walter B. Edgar, "Some Popular Books in Colonial South Carolina," *South Carolina Historical Magazine* 72 (1971), p. 177; Meyer Reinhold, *The Classick Pages: Classical Reading of Eighteenth-Century Americans* (University Park, Pa., 1975), pp. 39–47; Richard Beale Davis, *A Colonial Southern Bookshelf: Reading in the Eighteenth Century* (Athens, Ga., 1979), pp. 35, 92.
18. *A General Idea of the College of Mirania* (New York, 1753), pp. 28–30, 51–55. Cp. Carl L. Becker, *Everyman His Own Historian* (New York, 1935), p. 49: The typical college student of the time knew "the Parallel Lives of Plutarch . . . almost by heart, and was never weary of descanting on the austere morality and virtuous republicanism of those heroic times."
19. Joseph T. A. Burke, *A Biographical and Critical Study of Benjamin West, 1738–1792* (Master's essay, Yale, 1937), p. 19; William Sawitzky, "The American Work of Benjamin West," *Pa. Mag. Hist. & Biog.* 62 (1938), p. 461; James Thomas Flexner, "Benjamin West's American Neo-Classicism," *New York Historical Society Quarterly* 36 (1952) pp. 6–7, 19–34.
20. On Rollin see Reinhold, *The Classick Pages*, pp. 157–158; William Gribbin, "Rollin's Histories and American Republicanism," *Wm. & Mary Quart.*, 3rd ser., 29 (1972), pp. 611–622; Peter Gay and Victor G. Wexler, *Historians at Work* (New York, 1972), vol. II, pp. 220–226. There was an English translation of Rollin's *Ancient History* (London, 1738).
21. *Letters from a Farmer in Pennsylvania to the Inhabitants of the British Colonies* (Philadelphia, 1768), letter III.
22. Richard M. Gummere, *The American Colonial Mind and the Classical Tradition* (Cambridge, Mass., 1963), p. 116.
23. Charles F. Mullett, "Classical Influences on the American Revolution," *Classical Journal* 35 (1939–40), pp. 92, 96.
24. Cited by Howard Mumford Jones, *Revolution & Romanticism* (Cambridge, Mass., 1974), p. 136.
25. Josiah Quincy, *Observations on the Act of Parliament Commonly Called the Boston Port-Bill* (Boston, 1774), pp. 31, 34, 52, 63, 81–82.
26. On the Timoleon cult of the late eighteenth and early nineteenth centuries see Berry, *Emerson's Plutarch*, pp. 25–26.
27. The exemplary models of historical villains were especially Sulla, Alexander, Caesar, Antony.
28. Paul Leicester Ford, *Washington and the Theatre* (New York, 1899; rpt. 1967), pp. 1–2, 25–26; Frederic W. Litto, "Addison's *Cato* in the Colonies," *Wm. & Mary Quart.*, 3rd ser., 23 (1966), pp. 431–449; Reinhold, *The Classick Pages*, pp. 147–151.
29. *The Lee Papers*, vol. IV, Collections of the New-York Historical Society for the Year 1874 (New York, 1875), p. 26.
30. Mullett, "Classical Influences," p. 104.
31. *The Commonplace Book of Thomas Jefferson*, ed. Gilbert Chinard, Johns Hopkins Studies in Romance Literatures and Languages, extra vol. II (Baltimore, 1926), p. 184. The quotations were compiled by Jefferson ca. 1774–76.

32. From *Life of Aratus* 24.4–5. In Adams's *Defence of the Constitutions of Government of the United States of America*, in *The Works of John Adams*, ed. Charles Francis Adams (Boston, 1850–56), vol. IV, pp. 504–505.

33. E. P. Panagopoulos, "Hamilton's Notes in his Pay Book at the New York State Artillery Company," *American Historical Review* 62 (1956–57), pp. 316–319; *Alexander Hamilton's Pay Book*, ed. E. P. Panagopoulos (Detroit, 1961), pp. 7–12, 45–68; *The Papers of Alexander Hamilton*, ed. Harold C. Syrett, vol. I (New York, 1961), pp. 391–407.

34. Hamilton, however, wrote: "These notes are selected more for their singularity than use—though some important facts are comprehended" (*Papers*, vol. 1, p. 39).

35. "The Continentalist, no. 6," July, 1782, in Hamilton, *Papers*, vol. III (New York, 1962), p. 103 and n. 6 (Hamilton's source in Plutarch).

36. "Report on Books for Congress, Jan. 23, 1782," in *Papers of James Madison*, ed. William T. Hutchinson and William M. E. Rachal, vol. VI (Chicago, 1969), p. 77. Of 307 titles, 16 concerned Greek history and antiquities, Roman history and antiquities, Plato's *Republic*, Aristotle's *Politics*, Roman law. There was a Latin (but not a Greek) dictionary.

37. For Plutarch at the Constitutional Convention see Epaminondas P. Panagopoulos, "Classics and the Framers of the Constitution" (Ph.D. diss., Chicago, 1952), p. 90.

38. Hamilton, *Papers*, vol. IV (New York, 1962), pp. 310–311. Hamilton's notes include his source: Plutarch's *Pericles*.

39. Ibid., p. 379 (quoting from Plutarch's *Demosthenes*); Benjamin Fletcher, ed., *The Federalist* (Cambridge, Mass., 1961), pp. 35, 172; Jacob E. Cooke, ed., *The Federalist* (Middletown, Conn., 1961), p. 618.

40. Wright, *The Federalist*, pp. 272–273; Cooke, *The Federalist*, pp. 240–241.

41. Hamilton, *Papers*, vol. XI (New York, 1969), pp. 545–546.

42. [Douglass Adair], "A Note on Certain of Hamilton's Pseudonyms," *Wm. & Mary Quart.*, 3rd ser., 12 (1955), pp. 282–297; also in *Fame and the Founding Fathers, Essays by Douglass Adair*, ed. H. Trevor Colbourn (Williamsburg, 1974), pp. 272–285.

43. Adair, "Hamilton's Pseudonyms," pp. 290, 296.

44. Thomas H. Howards, "Peter Oliver: Plutarch of the American Revolution," *North Dakota Quarterly* 42 (Summer, 1974), pp. 77–101.

45. George E. Stewart, *Names on the Land: A Historical Account of Place-Naming in the United States*, rev. ed. (Boston, 1958), p. 184. The migration of Plutarch to the west of the United States is evidenced in the library of John Breckenridge, Virginia lawyer and farmer, who, before moving to Kentucky, ordered 150 volumes from London which included Plutarch's *Lives*. See Lowell H. Harrison, "A Virginian Moves to Kentucky, 1793," *Wm. & Mary Quart.*, 3rd ser., 15 (1958), pp. 208–209.

46. "An Oration on the Sublime Virtues of General George Washington" (Boston, June 8, 1800), in *Eulogies and Orations on the Life and Death of General George Washington* (Boston, 1800), p. 128.

47. "A Eulogy on General George Washington" (Boston, Feb. 19, 1800), *Eulogies and Orations*, pp. 153–155.

48. "Eulogy of George Washington," by Francis Adrian van der Kemp, in *Washington Eulogies: A Checklist of Eulogies and Funeral Orations on the Death of George Washington* (New York, 1916), p. 10.

49. Claude M. Newlin, ed., *Modern Chivalry* (New York, 1962), p. 433. Cp. *Port Folio* 1 (1801), p. 375, announcing a new edition of the Langhorne translation of Plutarch's *Lives*: "To the fame of Plutarch, little can be added, except the testimony of a good scholar, who assured us, that the Lives of Plutarch he read at school, during those hours in which he might have slept, and to the perusal of

this ancient biography, he was indebted for some of the finest and most liberal dispositions of his mind."

50. *Port Folio* 5 (1805), p. 19.
51. *The Autobiography of Benjamin Rush*, ed. George W. Corner (Princeton, 1948), p. 108 (cp. p. 199, mention of Plutarch's *Alexander*); *Letters of Benjamin Rush*, ed. L. H. Butterfield (Princeton, 1951), vol. II, p. 1123 (to John Adams, Feb. 12, 1812).
52. *Tyler's Quarterly Historical & Genealogical Magazine* 6 (1925), p. 241.
53. *Memoirs of John Quincy Adams*, ed. Charles Francis Adams (Philadelphia, 1874), vol. II, pp. 5–6. A letter of John Quincy Adams to George Washington Adams (March 7, 1813) contains citations from Plutarch's *Lycurgus* and *Solon*, taken from the Langhorne translation. See *Letters of Mrs. Adams*, ed. Charles Francis Adams, 4th ed. (Boston, 1848), p. 453.
54. John Quincy Adams, *Memoirs*, vol. II, pp. 296–297; vol. X, p. 123.
55. *Diary of Charles Francis Adams*, ed. Marc Friedlaender and L. H. Butterfield, vol. VI (Cambridge, Mass., 1974), pp. 349–350 (on March 11, 1836, he read the *Camillus*, to compare with Livy's account).
56. "The Silver Age of Classical Studies in America, 1790–1830," Chapter VI, above.
57. Russell, *Plutarch*, p. 161; Berry, *Emerson's Plutarch*, pp. 3, 25–26.
58. Berry, *Emerson's Plutarch*, pp. 15–20.
59. Berry, ibid., pp. 38–43, 261; C. J. Gianakaris, *Plutarch* (New York, 1970), pp. 137–139.
60. Berry, *Emerson's Plutarch*, pp. 35–36, 297–298; Kenneth W. Cameron, *Ralph Waldo Emerson's Reading* (Raleigh, 1941); idem, *A Commentary on Emerson's Early Lectures (1833–1836)* (Hartford, 1961), p. 126. Berry, p. 5, cites a book in Emerson's library entitled *The Beauties of Plutarch*.
61. "Uses of Great Men," in *Emerson's Representative Men and Other Essays*, ed. Ezra K. Maxfield (Boston, 1929), p. 8.
62. Cited by Berry, *Emerson's Plutarch*, p. 35; *The Early Lectures of Emerson*, ed. Stephen E. Whicher et al. (Cambridge, Mass., 1966–72), vol. II, pp. 329–330.
63. Berry, *Emerson's Plutarch*, pp. 29–33, 54, 63–65, 81–85, 115–116, 249–285; Whicher, *The Early Lectures*, vol. I, pp. 94–95.
64. Cited by Berry, *Emerson's Plutarch*, p. 262.
65. "Plutarch," in *Lectures and Biographical Sketches*, pp. 217–230; cp. Berry, *Emerson's Plutarch*, p. 33.
66. A. Gudeman, "A New Source in Plutarch's Life of Cicero," *Trans. Amer. Philolog. Assn.* 20 (1889), pp. 139–158; idem, "The Codex Matritensis of Plutarch and Plut. *Cic.* 29," *American Journal of Philology* 11 (1890), pp. 312–318; Arthur Fairbanks, "On Plutarch's Quotations from the Early Greek Philosophers," *Trans. Amer. Philolog. Assn.* 28 (1897), pp. 75–87.
67. Robert Shulman, "Melville's 'Timoleon': From Plutarch to the Early Stages of *Billy Budd*," *Comparative Literature* 19 (1967), pp. 351–361; Berry, *Emerson's Plutarch*, pp. 33–34.
68. President Harry S. Truman once said of Plutarch's *Lives*: "My father used to read me out loud from that. And I've read Plutarch through many times since. I have never figured out how he knew so much, I tell you. They just don't come any better than old Plutarch. He knew more about politics than all the other writers I've read put together. When I was in politics, there would be times when I tried to figure somebody out, and I could always turn to Plutarch, and nine times out of ten I'd be able to find a parallel in there." See Merle Miller, *Plain Speaking: An Oral Biography of Harry S. Truman* (New York, 1973), pp. 69–70; cp. p. 111. President Truman's use of Plutarch's *Lives* is indeed the manner in which Plutarch intended them to be read.

XI. American Visitors to Pompeii, Herculaneum, and Paestum in the Nineteenth Century

Hail! glorious vestiges of ancient art,
Ye proud memorials of an age unknown.

—*Henry Pickering,*
The Ruins of Paestum *(1822)*

The vogue of making the Grand Tour for eighteenth-century English gentlemen remained almost a ceremonial *rite de passage* well into the nineteenth century. The pilgrimage to the classic ground usually culminated in Naples and its environs. A constant cavalcade of English travelers (and some French, German, and Russian visitors) made their way to the bustling metropolis of southern Italy, sampling, as time allowed, Posilipo, Baiae, "Vergil"'s tomb, Capri, Vesuvius, Herculaneum, Pompeii, and— for the more intrepid—Paestum.[1] The rediscovery and excavation of Herculaneum and Pompeii in the first half of the eighteenth century and the disclosure of Paestum to the world in 1755 placed these classical sites high on the itineraries of European visitors and evoked enthusiasm in writers and artists.[2]

On the other side of the Atlantic, however, neither European Etruscomania nor the romance of the classical sites near Naples created much of a ripple of excitement. Few Americans indeed braved the rigors of ocean travel to make the Grand Tour or undertake extensive travel in Europe until the second third of the nineteenth century, when regular transatlantic steamship navigation began.[3] It is true that the second half of the eighteenth century was the Golden Age of classical learning in America, but the predominant interest was in the classics of Roman and Greek literature, not in classical sites, archaeological discoveries, or antiquities, for there were no visible relics of the Greek and Roman presence, as there were in Europe, to memorialize the continuity with classical antiquity.[4] Characteristic was the disclaimer of Hector St. John Crèvecoeur (written ca. 1774): "many persons are continually going to visit Italy.—That country is the daily resort of modern travelers. . . . I fancy their object is to trace the vestiges of a once flourishing people now extinct. There they amuse themselves in viewing the ruins of temples and other buildings which have very little affinity with those of the present age, and must therefore impart a knowledge which appears useless and trifling."[5]

Most of the Founding Fathers were trained under the traditional classical curriculum, and reached back to antiquity for models and analogies in their political thought, but it is striking that few of them and of other American patriots who went to Europe in the late eighteenth century visited Italy or were indeed receptive to the fine arts. In January, 1775, Josiah Quincy (father of Josiah Quincy, who was later president of Harvard), on a political mission in England, visited a certain Colonel Barré, an eminent Whig, who showed him engravings of the ruins of Herculaneum but cautioned him about books of art: "let them get abroad, and you are ruined. They will infuse a taste for buildings and sculpture, and when people get a taste for the fine arts, they are ruined."[6]

Nevertheless, it was in that very year, 1775, that some Americans did visit the classical sites near Naples, the first apparently to do so: the painter John Singleton Copley, the remarkable Gulian Verplanck, and Ralph Izard (later diplomat and senator) of Charleston, with his wife and a Mr. Archer. In January of that year Copley and Verplanck visited Pompeii and Herculaneum. Copley, commenting on the private houses of Pompeii, and the mosaics, streets, and temples, was deeply impressed by "a people of great luxury," by the "wonderful scenes," the sculptures found at Herculaneum. Together with the Izards and Archer, Copley visited Paestum in February. Though they stayed there only three hours, Copley was deeply moved by the experience and wrote: "This place I am glad to have seen, though I should not have extended my Tour so far, had not Mr. Izard invited me to accompany him their from Naples." He noticed the walls of Paestum, the remains of three or four temples, and an amphitheater. "This is all that remains to be seen at this Day. the Ground for Ages has been plowed and so little has this place been known that it is not menshoned by any Author, tho a place of such curiossity as any I have seen, except Pompei and

Herculaneam. from its antiquiety and singular Stile of Architecture it derives its curiosity, it being older than Rome and it[s] Architecture that of the first dawning of that Science among the Greeks."[7] This brief experience was apparently the beginning of Copley's abiding interest in classical antiquity.

Neither John Adams, nor Benjamin Franklin, nor John Quincy Adams when they were abroad for years made the slightest effort to visit Italy. But Jefferson, during his stay in France, in April of 1787 toured southern France (where he fell in love with the Maison Carrée at Nîmes) and northern Italy (where he visited especially Turin, Milan, Genoa, Pavia). Because time did not allow, he "scarcely got into classical ground," as he said. His friend and active correspondent William Short, chargé d'affaires of the American legation in Paris, got far more than Jefferson's "peep into Elysium." In February of 1789 he wrote Jefferson, very briefly, about his visit to "Herculanum," where only the theater was to be seen, and "Pompeia" and the climb up Mt. Vesuvius. "I shall not tire you," he wrote, "of a country which I still hope you will one day or other see. I hope it first for your own sake and secondly for that of your friends."[8]

William Short's account of a visit to Herculaneum and Pompeii, brief as it is, together with his participation in the fashionable ascent of Vesuvius and his failure to venture south to Paestum, was typical of the experience of early American visitors there. Books containing detailed descriptions of Pompeii and Herculaneum were available to an informed person like Jefferson; and Paestum was in a desolate, malaria-ridden area. Thus in 1805 Washington Irving was at Naples, and from there on March 14 and 15 visited Pompeii, climbed Vesuvius, and stopped at Herculaneum. Irving recorded in his journal some details of various sights in Pompeii, but, he added, "It is needless to give a very particular account of this place as it has so frequently been described." He expressed chagrin that the King of the Two Sicilies, living in luxury in Naples, had not provided funds to continue the excavations of Pompeii. At Herculaneum there was, of course, little to be seen: the theater, some private houses, and the superb little museum at Portici. For Washington Irving, as for many other European and American visitors, the climb to the crater of Vesuvius was a must, but Paestum was out of the way.[9]

Similar conventional itineraries were followed by other Americans who visited the area in the early national period, from 1801 to 1818, and wrote undistinguished accounts of visits to Mt. Vesuvius, Herculaneum, Pompeii. For example, William Berrian followed the standard pattern, and recorded that all this "causes emotion."[10] Joseph Sansom regretted that the papyri found at Herculaneum turned out to contain "nothing but uninteresting Treatises upon Music, Rhetoric, and Theology," instead of lost books of Tacitus, Livy, or Polybius. "We have not seen," he acknowledged, "the three Dorick Temples of Paestum, the ancient Possidonia of the Greeks, which have lately risen from the midst of the Calabrian Thicket."[11] An anonymous American traveler in 1805 wrote of his visit to "Pompeia" that a new room with frescoes had just been uncovered and, with characteristic American practicality, noted that the ancients knew the art of glassmaking but did not have wooden casks.[12]

Beginning with the classical pilgrimage of four young Americans from Harvard who went to Göttingen between 1815 and 1820 to absorb and bring back to Cambridge German scholarship, the desolate country at Paestum began to be more frequently visited. Edward Everett, George Ticknor, Joseph Green Cogswell, and George Bancroft were among the early intrepid travelers to Paestum. Everett, professor of Greek at Harvard, en route to Greece after his years of study at Göttingen, passed a month in the Naples area, visiting also Baiae, Misenum, Vesuvius, Paestum, Herculaneum, and Pompeii. It is indeed regrettable that the reactions of this perceptive young American scholar, particularly of the ruins of Paestum, are not known because, unfortunately, the portion of his enormous journal containing elaborate details of places seen there has not been located.[13] Fired with German neo-Hellenism, all four ventured to Paestum. In 1818 Cogswell traveled south of Naples and Salerno to explore the Greek temples at Paestum, which he called "the sublimest monument anywhere to be found of the destruction of time. . . . Nothing has left such an impression upon me as Paestum."[14] The most extensive account of a visit to Paestum at this time is that of George Bancroft, later the famed historian and diplomat. He spent several weeks in the environs of Naples, from which he visited Pompeii, Herculaneum, and finally Paestum, where he spent several days. About Pompeii he wrote, from Naples, to friends in Cambridge: "when you see it, you will declare it interesting enough to employ the thoughts for days together." "The ruins around Rome are more grand and sublime, but those near Naples are more singular." On March 7, while at Paestum, he wrote a lengthy account of his visit and impressions of the ruins. He had been writing "Pestum," but now records that "this should be spelled Paestum." "We entered and felt the power which a scene like this exercises on the soul." "The three public buildings of Paestum which yet stand in glorious ruin, form the most admirable monument of the high minds of its ancient inhabitants." Concerning the temple of Neptune, which he analyzed in very sophisticated technical detail, he wrote that it was "the model of ruins. It is the most perfect, most picturesque, most beautiful wreck of a temple in the world." "The temple has an air of imposing grandeur, which inspires awe into the mind. . . . I repeat this is the ne plus ultra of beautiful ruins."[15] Ticknor, however, did not visit Herculaneum, Pompeii, and Paestum until May, 1857, when he sojourned at Naples.[16]

Another venturesome American traveler who made it to Paestum was Matthias Bruen, who visited the area about 1820 (seeing also Pompeii and Herculaneum). He has left us an extensive effort at a description of Paestum, but his account of the walls and the three temples is quite trivial. He comments on "the rare union of beauty and majesty in these remains." But he viewed Paestum from a moral and religious perspective, and at Pompeii ("We have all read so much of Pompeii before we see it") and Herculaneum, all was steeped in pagan superstition. The state of morals then was so "loathsome" that "the Paestum and Pompeii of the world still stand in ruin to warn us."[17] This moralizing theme of the destruction of the ancient cities because of their moral depravity reechoes in the accounts of more than a few American travelers to the "dead cities."

But the romantic appeal of remains of antiquity was also spreading. By the third decade of the eighteenth century Paestum was sufficiently well known in America for a native poet, Henry Pickering, to compose a long poem, *The Ruins of Paestum*, in 1822. It is not known whether Pickering (son of the distinguished political figure Timothy Pickering of Massachusetts) visited Paestum or merely read accounts of it (he does describe the three temples in a long note). The poem begins thus:

> Hail! glorious vestiges of ancient art,
> Ye proud memorials of an age unknown,
> That here, sav'd from the wreck of envious Time,
> In solitary grandeur awful stand—
> Say whence your origin?

And in the concluding section he salutes

O PAESTUM! Here each votary too of art
Shall glad resort, and gazing on thy proud
Remains. . . .
Confess the hands which made them were divine.
And when the setting sun, with lingering beams,
No more these mouldering columns shall illume,
But all their glories prostrate shall be laid—
E'en then the pious wanderer on those shores
Shall point exulting to the desert spot,
And to the skies proclaim, that here, the source
Of all that is in art sublime, was found.

My Country! thou whose destiny august
Some few revolving years must clear unveil,
Shall monuments like these, (except in their
Decay) thy happier shores in time adorn?[18]

For many other Americans Paestum, with its lonely ruins and wild, desolate scenery, was far more affecting than a mere romantic travelers' interlude. It was revered as representative of the arts of Greece itself, and it seemed to visitors as if they had stepped onto the sacred soil of Greece.[19] The voyage to Greece itself was too hazardous yet: of the four Harvard scholars only Everett made his way to Greek sites, after his visit to Paestum.

For a long time after Copley's early visit in 1775, American artists did not come to the Naples area. But in the third decade of the century they began to descend on Italy in earnest, and some ventured as far south as Paestum. Robert Walter Weir, later one of the Hudson River school of landscape painters, visited Paestum with an English architect, measured the temples, and made extensive notes on the buildings.[20] The painter Rembrandt Peale was at Pompeii in 1830, climbed Vesuvius, but did not go to Paestum.[21] In 1832 Thomas Cole (1801–48), founder of the Hudson River school, after two weeks at Naples set off with a small group for the solitudes of the malarial Paestum. An Englishman who had just returned from the ruins, asked him: "Why do you go to Paestum? You will see nothing but a few old buildings." While there Cole painted a view of the scene for an American woman. Later William Cullen Bryant, in his funeral eulogy for Cole, said that he saw there "the grandest and most perfect remains of the architecture of Greece" in a pestilential place where "the air is sweet with violets running wild."[22]

The classic scenes in the Naples region soon began to influence literary compositions. As early as 1831 Sumner Lincoln Fairfield of Massachusetts (1803–44), poet and editor of the *North American Review* from 1832–38, who had been abroad in 1826, completed a long poem entitled "The Last Night of Pompeii." This was a fictionalized treatment of the famed event, in which he emphasized the corrupt morals of the Pompeians. In his preface he noted that "the excavations of the last forty years have furnished the tourist, the antiquarian, the novelist, and the poet, with many a subject of picturesque and glowing description." Fairfield later charged Bulwer-Lytton with plagiarism, claiming that he had sent him a copy of his poem two years before the publication of Bulwer-Lytton's famous novel *The Last Days of Pompeii.*[23]

In 1848 another New England minor poet, William Giles Dix, wrote a longish poem "Pompeii," which is in part fictionalized but also appears to be based on personal observation of the site. The poem includes sections entitled "The Roman Song of Life," "The Roman Patriot's Song," "Cicero's Meditation," and "The Martyr's Hymn" (about a Christian in the amphitheater of Pompeii). The poem includes the lines,

> Thou seest not all Pompeii's size,
> Yonder, a part yet covered lies.[24]

Famous American authors who traveled abroad and visited Italy often made their way south to see Pompeii, Herculaneum, and Paestum. James Fenimore Cooper, who visited the classical sites in 1828–30, has left an extensive account filled with many details of things seen, though he was aware, as he said, that they had been described "for the thousandth time." About Pompeii (which he visited twice) he expressed a little disappointment: "Perhaps our expectations were wrought up too high, for, certainly, I have apprehended no place in Europe with the same feverish excitement." Cooper commented on the very slow pace of the excavations but was among the first to acknowledge the need for prudent care "in the interest of knowledge." He suggested, however, the desirability of restoring at least one house, with roof and with objects from the museum. About Herculaneum, there was only the theater to be seen, but he thought Herculaneum of greater importance than Pompeii. There is, he wrote, "a sublimity in the catastrophe of Herculaneum, a grandeur in desolation, that has no parallel." He was aware of the generality of his observations and indicated that "I have only given you my first impressions on visiting these two remarkable places, as volumes exist filled with their details, arranged with care, and collected with accuracy." He made the popular ascent of Vesuvius and also ventured to Paestum. The temple of Neptune he considered "the most impressive, and I had almost said the most imposing, edifice I know." Like many others of the time Cooper dated the ruins of Paestum to the time of the pyramids of Egypt and ventured to place them in the new civilization that emerged after the biblical flood. "What a speck does the history of America become in this long vista of events."[25]

Ralph Waldo Emerson in March, 1833, climbed Vesuvius and saw Pompeii and Herculaneum. "I have seen all the best of the wonders, but have not visited Paestum as I would."[26] In June, 1835, William Cullen Bryant, too, climbed Vesuvius and made excursions to Pompeii and Herculaneum.[27] The novelist Catharine Maria Sedgwick (1789–1867), when she was abroad in 1839–40, went to Pompeii, which she described in considerable detail. There she met two Englishmen who repeatedly said it was "all a d——d bore, those old rattle-trap places." Paestum stirred intense romantic emotions in her. "There they stand, between the mountains and the sea, . . . scarcely ruins, but monuments of the art, wealth and faith of a nation long effaced from the earth—temples erected to an unknown God by an unknown people. . . . You must see them in this affecting solitude with God's temples, the mountains behind them, the sea sweeping before them, and the long grass waving from the crevices, to *feel* them—class the sensations they produce with those excited by the most magnificent works of nature, Niagara and the Alps." We also learn from her comments that one of her correspondents had cork models of the temples at Paestum.[28]

A few years later, in 1844, that dour Puritan, the distinguished New England historian Francis Parkman (1823–93), climbed Vesuvius, visited Pompeii, which he found but little edifying, and dismissed Herculaneum as "scarce worth seeing." Parkman, like many other American tourists, had little historical perspective about antiquity, preferring the oddities of Naples and its social life.[29] On the other hand, Herman Melville, who in 1857 visited the region, climbing Vesuvius and visiting Pompeii briefly, preferred Pompeii to Paris, though he found it "like any other town, same old humanity."[30] William Dean Howells in 1864–65 spent a day in Pompeii and a half-hour at Herculaneum to visit the theater. He found Pompeii "full of marvel and surprise," "the revelation of another life, and the utterance of the past . . . here more perfect than anywhere else in the world." Howells admired especially the murals of Pompeii and the sculptures from Herculaneum in the museum.[31]

No account of a visit to Pompeii by an American has been so widely read as that of Mark Twain (Samuel Langhorne Clemens) in *The Innocents Abroad.* On a journalistic tour as correspondent for the *Daily Alta California* and the *New York Tribune*, he reported on his ascent of Vesuvius and visit to "the Buried City of Pompeii" in August, 1867. The version in *Innocents Abroad*, written in 1868, is only slightly altered from the original dispatches. Twain commented on the houses, mosaics, frescoes, streets, shops, temples, halls of justice, shelters, baths, theaters, lupanars, tombs, the skeletons of the dead, and the warning sign "Beware the Dog." The luxurious tastes and habits of the Pompeians, their exquisite bronzes, cameos, and engravings he found noteworthy. The murals he deemed "often much more pleasing than the celebrated rubbish of the old masters of three centuries ago." He also highlighted, with rhetorical inflation, the story of the Roman soldier in full armor who died at his sentry post at the city gate ("We never read of Pompeii but we think of that soldier"). He reminded his American readers that "the sun shines as brightly down on old Pompeii to-day as it did when Christ was born in Bethlehem" and "when the Disciples were preaching the new religion," and he moralizes on "the unsubstantial unlasting character of fame."[32] Somehow he got the date of the eruption of Vesuvius wrong; he gives it as November 9, A.D. 79; the actual date of the eruption, vividly described by Pliny, was August 24.[33] Twain obviously found the ascent of Vesuvius more newsworthy, for he devoted far more space to it than to Pompeii. It is unfortunate that Mark Twain's facetious comments on Pompeii have been interpreted as typical of American tourists' lack of veneration for the historic past and the monuments of antiquity. If he laughed at some of the relics of the Old World, and boasted of the superiority of the New World, it goes too far to call him "defiantly American."[34]

A generation before Mark Twain's journalistic visit to the Naples region, thousands of Americans got their impressions of the ascent of Vesuvius and the ruins of Pompeii, Herculaneum, and Paestum from the travel essays prepared for the *New York Mirror* in 1833 by Nathaniel Parker Willis (1806–67). His letters from abroad were much admired, e.g., by Daniel Webster and Bayard Taylor, and they may well have been known to Mark Twain, and influenced his comments. Willis had little to say about Herculaneum, and his account of Pompeii, though very detailed, was quite ordinary. "It would be tedious," he wrote, "to enumerate all the curious places to which the guide led us in this extraordinary city." Mark Twain's dutiful soldier dying at his sentry post is recounted here, and embellished with reference to sixty other soldiers who died at their posts. But, "I have neither time nor room to enumerate the curiosities found here and in other parts of the city." The elegant "Villa of Diomed" was "occupied by its last family *while our Savior was walking the world.*" Willis was especially thrilled to visit the "*house of Sallust, the historian*" at Pompeii. "I have seen nothing in my life as remarkable as this disentombed city." He admired a statue of Balbus, who, Willis wrote, was "proconsul of Herculaneum." The ruins of Paestum he called "temples of inimitable beauty." At the site of Paestum there "seemed to be a general feeling in the party that silence and solitude were the spirits of the place." "We walked among the ruins for hours." "To think that these very temples were visited as venerable antiquities in the time of Christ!" "What an extraordinary succession of objects were embraced in the fifty miles between Paestum, Pompeii, Vesuvius, Herculaneum [and Naples]."[35]

Ten years later, in March, 1843, Joel Tyler Headley (1813–97), an editor of the *New York Tribune*, whom Edgar Allen Poe called "The Autocrat of all the Quacks," sent back pedestrian accounts of his visits of Herculaneum, Pompeii, and Paestum. "I cannot go into details," he wrote, "they have been written over a hundred times." When he left Pompeii, he wrote, oddly, "a feeling of indescribable sadness stole over me, and I rode away without the wish ever to see it again."[36]

Like the comments of Headley, the accounts of many American tourists who traveled abroad in the first half of the nineteenth century read as if they were following a guidebook. By far the most popular guidebook for the Naples area at the time was that of Mariana Starke.[37] It contains the story of the soldier who died at his post in Pompeii, and highlights the house of "Sallust the historian." The book contains a superb description of the temple of Neptune at Paestum. Most tourists who went to Naples and its vicinity climbed Vesuvius, many went to Pompeii, fewer ventured to Paestum. Among the travelers who then published typical conventional accounts were: Nathaniel Hazelton Carter, who visited all four places in May, 1826; Henry Theodore Tuckerman, who went only to Pompeii, in 1833–34; Wilbur Fisk, president of Wesleyan College, Connecticut, who visited Paestum, Pompeii, and Herculaneum in 1837; Fanny W. Hall, who stopped only at Herculaneum in 1835; Rev. Charles Rockwell, who saw Paestum, Pompeii, and Herculaneum in 1842; George Stillman Hillard, who visited Pompeii and Herculaneum and climbed Vesuvius in 1847–48; Horace Binney Wallace, who climbed Vesuvius in 1849 or 1852; Mrs. A. T. J. Bullard, who saw Herculaneum, Pompeii, and Vesuvius in 1850; Rev. George Foxcroft Haskins, who went to Pompeii and Herculaneum in 1855; Howard Payson Arnold, who climbed Vesuvius and visited Herculaneum and Pompeii in the early 1860s.[38]

Some noteworthy comments made by these tourists are: the temple of Neptune at Paestum is the oldest building in existence (Carter); human nature has always been the same (Tuckerman; Haskins); the ruins of Paestum are the most perfect in existence, affective in "their lonely grandeur" (Fisk); the moral degradation and depravity of Pompeii and Herculaneum have their biblical analogies in the fate of Sodom and Gommorah (Rockwell; Arnold); the obscenity of the sculpture and frescoes is repulsive, "representations, which cannot be described, hardly alluded to . . . , subjects delineated which no man should look on a second time" (Hillard).

One of the best such accounts was that of Christopher Pearse Cranch, critic, poet, painter, who visited all four places in 1848. About Pompeii, he wrote, "It is a place for a poet to dream in days and days. . . . Here are the dreams of the architect, the poet, the painter, the sculptor, vivid as of old." At Paestum he made sketches, and was rapturous: "Never have I seen anything more perfect, such exquitiste proportion. . . . Mysterious, beautiful temples! . . . standing there for over two thousand years. It is almost like going to Greece."[39] At about the same time James Jackson Jarves, newspaper editor, critic, art collector, visited Pompeii and wrote an extensive, widely read account. With practical eye for modern conveniences at Pompeii, he complimented their municipal administration for its good water supply, baths, sewers— cultural conveniences superior to those of Naples at the time, and even Paris but a short time before. "The spirit of Yankeedom moved within me. Would it not be a 'good operation' to buy up Pompeii, reserve the corner lots, sell the intervening, and appropriate the temples to public schools?" It was, he wrote, "my pleasantest day of travel in Europe." But he deplored that the Pompeians were licentious and lacked "American delicacy"; their art was prurient, very obscene, depravities which fortunately Christianity banished. "The number and magnitude of public buildings in so small a town astonishes, in particular, the American traveler, who seldom finds anything worth visiting for architectural beauty at home in cities much greater than Pompeii."[40]

By far the most perceptive and precise treatment of the ruins of Pompeii and Herculaneum written by early American tourists was the account of Benjamin Silliman, professor of chemistry and natural history at Yale 1802–53, the leading scientific mind in America during the first half of the nineteenth century. After retirement he visited Pompeii and Herculaneum in May, 1851. He observed everything with the eye of a scientist and with sensitive artistic appreciation: numerous details about types of stone, methods of construction, manufacture of glass, city planning, etc. He did not, like many others, moralize about the frescoes. "We saw nothing in Pompeii or Herculaneum, worthy of so much criticism in point of taste." "No scenes of my life have ever interested me so much" as what he saw at Pompeii and Herculaneum. Silliman's conclusion is worth quoting at length because of his interest in a fuller understanding of antiquity and his appreciation of the importance of archeological finds for such understanding.

> The classical studies of our youth make us more or less acquainted with the learning of the Romans, with their eloquent orators and historians, with their beautiful poetry, their rhetorical lore, their moral disquisitions and sentiments, and in no small degree with their domestic and social manners. But the resurrection of these cities from their forgotten tombs, has brought Roman life vividly before us in their family scenes, and at the period of their greatest power, and luxury, and glory. There is indeed much in them to approve and admire, and much that is worthy of imitation.[41]

It was not, however, until after the Civil War, as American classical scholarship began to advance rapidly and the dawn of modern archeological methods arrived, that books on Pompeii, Herculaneum, and Paestum appeared in America that were less dilettantish, more accurate and professional.[42]

Notes

1. William E. Mead, *The Grand Tour in the Eighteenth Century* (Boston, 1914), pp. 328–329; Paul F. Kirby, *The Grand Tour in Italy (1700–1800)* (New York, 1952), pp. 113–122.
2. See, e.g., Jean Seznec, "Herculaneum and Pompeii in French Literature of the Eighteenth Century," *Archaeology* 2 (1949), pp. 150–158; Fiske Kimball, "The Reception of the Art of Herculaneum in France," in *Studies Presented to David Moore Robinson* (St. Louis, 1953), vol. II, pp. 1254–1256; Charles F. Mullett, "Englishmen Discover Herculaneum and Pompeii," *Archaeology* 10 (1957), pp. 31–38; Pierre Grimal, *In Search of Ancient Italy* (New York, 1964), pp. 135–161; G. W. Bowersock, "The Rediscovery of Herculaneum and Pompeii," *American Scholar* 47 (1978), pp. 461–470. Dora Wiebenson has cata-

logued the works published on the ruins of Paestum from 1766 to 1798, by Morghen, Berkenhout, Major, Dumont, Comte de Caylus, Delagordette, and Francesco Piranesi (*Sources of Greek Revival Architecture* (London, 1969), pp. 72, 120–124).

3. See, e.g., Giuseppe Prezzolini, *Come gli Americani Scoprirono l'Italia (1750–1850)* (Milan, 1933); Paul R. Baker, *The Fortunate Pilgrims: Americans in Italy 1800–1860* (Cambridge, Mass., 1964), pp. 69–73; Geoffrey Trease, *The Grand Tour* (London, 1967), pp. 4, 206–217; Erik Amfitheatrof, *The Enchanted Ground: Americans in Italy 1760–1980* (Boston, 1980), p. 3.

4. On early American aloofness from ancient art and archaeology see William B. Dinsmoor, "Early American Studies in Mediterranean Archaeology," *Proc. Amer. Philos. Soc.* 87 (1943–44), pp. 74–104.

5. *Letters from an American Farmer* (1782; Garden City, n.d.), letter I (written ca. 1774), p. 16.

6. Josiah Quincy, *Memoir of the Life of Josiah Quincy, Junior, of Massachusetts* (Boston, 1825), pp. 289–290; "Journal of Josiah Quincy, Jun.," *Proc. Mass. Hist. Soc.* 50 (1916–17), p. 452.

7. *Correspondence of Mr. Ralph Izard, of South Carolina from the Year 1774 to 1804* (New York, 1844), p. 43; Martha Babcock Amory, *The Domestic and Artistic Life of John Singleton Copley* (Boston, 1882), pp. 144–148; *Letters and Papers of John Singleton Copley and Henry Pelham 1739–1776*, Massachusetts Historical Society Collections, vol. LXXI (Boston, 1914), pp. 329–330; Dinsmoor, "Early American Studies," p. 75; Jules David Prown, *John Singleton Copley in England* (Cambridge, Mass., 1966), p. 251.

8. *Papers of Thomas Jefferson*, ed. Julian P. Boyd (Princeton, 1950–), vol. XII, p. 127; vol. XIV, p. 574; Edward Dumbauld, *Thomas Jefferson, American Tourist* (Norman, 1946), p. 102.

9. Washington Irving, *Notes and Journal of Travel in Europe 1804–1805* (New York, 1921), vol. II, pp. 164–168; vol. III, pp. 1–3; idem, *Journals and Notebooks* (Madison, 1969), vol. II, pp. 223–254.

10. Rev. William Berrian, *Travels in France and Italy in 1817 and 1818* (New York, 1921), pp. 170–179, 197–200.

11. A Native of Pennsylvania [Joseph Sansom], *Letters from Europe, During a Tour Through Switzerland and Italy, in the Years 1801 and 1802* (Philadelphia, 1805), vol. II, pp. 196–227. Similarly, when Jefferson in retirement at Monticello heard a rumor that 2,000 papyrus rolls had been discovered in Athens, he commented: "If true, we may recover what has been lost of Diodorus Siculus, Polybius, and Dion Cassius. I would rather, however, it should have been of Livy, Tacitus, and Cicero." See Meyer Reinhold, *The Classick Pages: Classical Reading of Eighteenth-Century Americans* (University Park, Pa., 1975), p. 82.

12. *Monthly Anthology and Boston Review* 4 (1807), pp. 483–485.

13. Edward Everett, "Auto-Biographical Sketch of Hon. Edward Everett" (written in 1833), in Everett Papers, microfilm reel XXV, Massachusetts Historical Society, Boston; Paul Revere Frothingham, *Edward Everett, Orator and Statesman* (Boston, 1925), p. 59; "A 'New Morning': Edward Everett's Contributions to Classical Learning," Chapter VII, above. Everett's brother, Alexander Hill Everett, may be the author of *Journal of a Tour in Italy, in the Year 1821 . . . , by an American* (New York, 1824), which contains the usual details of the ascent of Vesuvius and visits to Pompeii and Herculaneum (but not to Paestum), and conventional remonstrances about human mortality, even of monarchs. "No man ever visited this place for the first time, without considering that day an era in his life" (p. 113).

14. Letter to William Hickling Prescott, March 28, 1818, Prescott Collection, Massachusetts Historical Society, Boston. Cp. Baker, *Fortunate Pilgrims*, pp. 72–73.

15. Letters of Feb. 23 and Mar. 2 to Samuel A. Eliot; Mar. 5 to Andrews Norton; Mar. 7, written at Paestum itself, Bancroft Papers, Massachusetts Historical Society, Boston. Cp. M. A. De Wolfe Howe, *The Life and Letters of George Bancroft* (New York, 1908), vol. I, pp. 143–145; Russel B. Nye, *George Bancroft, Brahmin Rebel* (New York, 1944), p. 55.

16. *Life, Letters, and Journals of George Ticknor* (Boston, 1909), vol. II, p. 350 (letter to William H. Prescott).

17. An American [Matthias Bruen], *Essays, Descriptive and Moral; on Scenes in Italy, Switzerland and France* (Edinburgh, 1823), pp. 3–22.

18. [Henry Pickering], *The Ruins of Paestum; and Other Compositions in Verse* (Salem, 1822), pp. 5–20, 109–113. Pickering also wrote *Athens; and Other Poems* (Salem, 1824). William Cullen Bryant, in a review of Pickering's *Ruins of Paestum*, has faint praise for the poem but reflects on the allure of those "wonderful and venerable ruins . . . which still offer models of architecture to the world" (*North American Review* 19 (1824), pp. 42–46).

19. Cp. Grimal, *In Search of Italy*, pp. 205–207.

20. Dinsmoor, "Early American Studies," p. 81.

21. Rembrandt Peale, *Notes on Italy Written During a Tour in the Years 1829 and 1830* (Philadelphia, 1831), pp. 73–84; *Dictionary of American Biography*, vol. XIV, pp. 348–350.

22. William Cullen Bryant, "Thomas Cole. A Funeral Oration Delivered Before the National Academy of Design, May 4, 1848," in *Orations and Addresses* (New York, 1873), pp. 19–20; Louis Legrand Noble, *The Life and Works of Thomas Cole*, ed. Elliot Vesell (Cambridge, Mass., 1964), pp. 119–120.

23. Sumner Lincoln Fairfield, "The Last Night of Pompeii: A Poem in Three Cantos," in *The Poems and Prose Writings* (New York, 1832), vol. I, pp. 43–166; *Dictionary of American Biography*, vol. VI, pp. 258–259; M. R. Peterson, "Sumner Lincoln Fairfield: His Life and Charge of Plagiarism Against Bulwer-Lytton" (Ph.D. diss., Brown University, 1930).

24. William Giles Dix, *Pompeii and Other Poems* (Boston, 1848), pp. 3–48.

25. J[ames] Fenimore Cooper, *Excursions in Italy* (Paris, 1838), pp. 103–115, 164–168, 177–182; idem, *Gleanings in Europe: Italy* (Albany, 1981), pp. 90–105, 150–153, 161–165.

26. *The Letters of Ralph Waldo Emerson*, ed. Ralph L. Rusk (New York, 1939), vol. I, pp. 367–369, 371; *Journals of Ralph Waldo Emerson*, ed. Edward Waldo Emerson and Waldo Emerson Forbes, vol. III (Boston, 1910), p. 74.

27. William Cullen Bryant, *Prose Writings*, ed. Parke Godwin (New York, 1884; rpt. 1964), vol. II, p. 96.

28. Catharine Maria Sedgwick, *Letters from Abroad to Kindred at Home* (New York, 1881), vol. I, pp. 246–250, 269–271; *Dictionary of American Biography*, vol. XVI, pp. 547–548.

29. *The Journals of Francis Parkman*, ed. Mason Wade (New York, 1947), vol. I, pp. 101, 172; Mason Wade, *Francis Parkman, Heroic Historian* (New York, 1942), p. 123; *Dictionary of American Biography*, vol. XIV, pp. 247–250.

30. Herman Melville, *Journal of a Visit to Europe and the Levant, Oct. 11, 1856–May 6, 1857* (Princeton, 1955), pp. 176–177.

31. William Dean Howells, *Italian Journeys* (Boston, 1867), pp. 89–115.

32. Mark Twain [Samuel L. Clemens], *The Innocents Abroad, or The New Pilgrims' Progress* (New York, n.d.), pp. 213–233; *Traveling with the Innocents Abroad: Mark Twain's Original Reports from Europe and the Holy Land*, ed. Daniel M. McKeithan (Norman, 1958), pp. vii, 76–97; Leon T. Dickinson, "Mark Twain's Revisions in Writing *The Innocents Abroad*," *American Literature* 19 (1947), p. 152, note; Van Wyck Brooks, *The Dream of Arcadia: American Writers and Artists in Italy 1760–1915* (New York, 1958), pp. 155–156.

33. Pliny the Younger *Epistles* 6.10.

34. Wolfgang Leppermann, *Pompeii in Fact and Fiction* (London, 1968), pp. 82–83, 157–159. Leppermann deplores the fact that, though Longfellow, Hawthorne, and Henry James repeatedly visited Naples, they did not pay much attention to classical sites.

35. N[athaniel] P[arker] Willis, *Pencillings By the Way* (New York, 1844), pp. 90–109; *Dictionary of American Biography*, vol. XX, pp. 306–308; Henry A. Beers, *Nathaniel Parker Willis* (Boston, 1885), pp. 117–119; Cortland P. Auser, *Nathaniel Parker Willis* (New York, 1969), pp. 31, 33, 38; Kenneth L. Daughrity, "The Life and World of Nathaniel P. Willis, 1806–1836" (Ph.D. diss., University of Virginia, 1935).

36. J. T. Headley, *Letters from Italy*, new ed. (New York, 1848), pp. 70–102; *Dictionary of American Biography*, vol. VIII, pp. 479–480.

37. *Travels in Europe* (London, 1828).

38. N[athaniel] H[azelton] Carter, *Letters from Europe Comprising the Journal of a Tour . . . in the Years 1825, 1826, 1827* (New York, 1827), vol. II, pp. 262–288; Henry T. Tuckerman, *The Italian Sketch Book*, 3rd ed. (New York, 1848), pp. 138–139 (the first edition was published anonymously in Philadelphia, 1835); Wilbur Fisk, *Travels in Europe*, 4th ed. (New York, 1838), pp. 205–211; Fanny W. Hall, *Rambles in Europe* (New York, 1839), pp. 138–148; Rev. Charles Rockwell, *Sketches of Foreign Travel and Life at Sea* (Boston, 1842), pp. 114–123; George Stillman Hillard, *Six Months in Italy* (Boston, 1853), vol. II, pp. 110–153; Horace Binney Wallace, *Art, Scenery and Philosophy in Europe* (Philadelphia, 1855), pp. 237–242; Mrs. A. T. J. Bullard, *Sights and Scenes in Europe: A Series of Letters from England, France, Germany, Switzerland and Italy in 1850* (St. Louis, 1852), pp. 155–164; Rev. Howard Payson Arnold, *European Mosaic* (Boston, 1864), pp. 276–302; Rev. George Foxcroft Haskins, *Travels in England, France, Italy, and Ireland* (Boston, 1856), pp. 183–186, 196–197.

39. Leonora Cranch Scott, *The Life and Letters of Christopher Pearse Cranch* (Boston, 1917), pp. 136–137; *Dictionary of American Biography*, vol. IV, pp. 501–502. Cranch later composed a creditable translation of Vergil's *Aeneid: The Aeneid. Translated into English Blank Verse* (Boston, 1872).

40. James Jackson Jarves, *Italian Sights and Papal Principles, Seen Through American Spectacles* (New York, 1856), pp. 158–223 ("A Day at Pompeii"); *Dictionary of American Biography*, vol. IX, pp. 618–620.

41. Silliman also adds: "Their defects and errors arose simply from a false religion." Prof. Benjamin Silliman, *A Visit to Europe in 1851* (New York, 1853), vol. I, pp. 355–379; *Dictionary of American Biography*, vol. XVIII, pp. 160–163.

42. E.g., E. P. Evans wrote a very learned and comprehensive review of six scholarly publications on Pompeii by European scholars in *North American Review* 106 (1868), pp. 397–446.

XII. Survey of the Scholarship on Classical Traditions in Early America

On January 1, 1801, David Ramsay, distinguished physician, political leader, historian, speaking before a glittering audience in Charleston, offered an invocation for our present labors. "Let those who follow us in the 20th [century]," he said, "have as much reason to respect our memories, as we have to venerate those who have gone before us." Lest I mislead you about Ramsay's fellow feeling for classical learning, I ask you to reserve judgment on what he intended until later.[1] But I will give you a hint that Ramsay was strongly under the influence of his beloved teacher Dr. Benjamin Rush of Philadelphia, who for a generation was an untiring and vociferous opponent of classical education in the new republic. Jefferson, however, in 1782 noted that "the learning of Greek and Latin, I am told, is going into disuse in Europe. I know not what their manners and occupations may call for; but it would be very ill-judged in us to follow their example." John Adams, too, remained loyal to the classics in the midst of the national debate in the early national period on the future of the classics in America. In 1814, after Rush died, unrepentant, Adams wrote Jefferson: "Classics, in spite of our friend Rush, I must think indispensable."

Nineteenth-Century Judgments

At the very beginning of the nineteenth century an attempt was made to appraise the state of classical learning by Samuel Miller in his extraordinary book *A Brief Retrospect of the Eighteenth Century*,[2] a work which was called by a contemporary a "funeral sermon of the 18th century,"[3] and recently by an American historian "the first systematic study of intellectual history by an American."[4] Surveying the evolution of education in the colonies and in the early national decades, Miller concluded that classical learning suffered a steady decline during the century. The reasons he assigned to this were complex: exclusiveness of the classical curriculum; emphasis on language and grammar to the neglect of the content of the classics; the pervasive utilitarian spirit of the country; competition by other branches of learning, including the living languages; the democratization and general diffusion of knowledge. At the end of the century these developments culminated in widespread loss of confidence in the usefulness of the classics, especially in America, where its study was pitifully superficial. Miller also concluded that the decline in the study of Latin and Greek was in part the result of ready availability of many translations of the classics in the eighteenth century, which he called the "Age of Translations." The national character, above all, was the determinative force, for it was disposed to favor more immediately practical and useful knowledge. "The spirit of our people," said Miller, "is *commercial*. It has been said, and perhaps with some justice, that the *love of gain* peculiarly characterises the inhabitants of the United States." Thus, by the end of the century the classics "came to be regarded by a large portion of the literary world as among the most useless objects of pursuit." As for himself, Miller deplored the strong popular prejudice against the classics and the decline in their study as "among the fashionable follies of the age."[5]

Despite his closeness to the times, we would be ill-advised to accept Miller's summary of the role of the classics in the eighteenth century. Not only were his conclusions not based on a methodical study of extensive evidence for developments throughout the century, but his pessimistic assessment reflects the vigorous contemporary debate on the suitability of the classics in American education in the early Federal period from 1783 to 1803. To single out a few lacunae at random, Miller has no understanding of the history and varied roles of the classics in the different colonies and sections of the country; and he is unaware of the massive upsurge in the cult of antiquity during the Revolutionary period.[6]

After Miller's superficial and flawed survey a curtain descends for almost a century on the study of the intellectual history of early America. Nineteenth-century American historians of the formative age of our country, men such as George Tucker, George Bancroft, Richard Hildreth, and Francis Parkman, were intensely nationalistic and patriotic "drum-and-trumpet school" writers. Convinced of the poverty of American cultural life during the eighteenth century, and of the self-generating uniqueness of the American experience, they lavished their enthusiasm on political and military events, the lives of glamorous heroes, dramatic narratives of colorful episodes.[7]

Thus there was an almost universal silence about the mission of the classics in early America during the nineteenth century, broken only, to my knowledge—both impressionistic judgments—by Moses Coit Tyler and Charles Francis Adams, Jr., the great-grandson of John Adams. In his enduring work, *A History of American Literature*,[8] originally published in 1878, Tyler, then professor of rhetoric and English literature at the University of Michigan, wrote with an unparalleled conviction of the cultural worth of early America. About early American colleges he wrote with enthusiasm: "But the vast influence that our early colleges exerted upon literary culture can hardly be overestimated. Among all the people, they nourished those spiritual conditions out of which, alone, every wholesome and genuine literary culture must grow; and in their special devotion to classical studies, they imparted to a considerable body of men the finest training for literary work that the world is yet possessed of. It was of incalculable service to American literature that, even in those wild regions of the earth, the accents of Homer, of Thucydides, of Cicero, were made familiar to us from the beginning; that a consciousness of the aesthetic principle in verbal expression was kept alive here, and developed, by constant and ardent study of the supreme masters of literary form; and that the great, immemorial traditions of literature were borne hither across the Atlantic from their ancient seats, and were housed in perpetual temples, for the rearing of which the people gladly went to great cost."[9] Magnificent rhetoric!

Shortly after, Charles Francis Adams, in a Phi Beta Kappa address at Harvard on June 28, 1883, labeled the study of the classics in his day "A College Fetich," and at the same time, to bolster his case, belittled the knowledge John Adams and John Quincy Adams had had of classical languages, especially Greek. He insisted that

John Adams scorned Greek and that John Quincy Adams never read the language ("I suspect . . . he never could read it"), and that "it would have been better for him if he had also dropped his Latin."[10] The reliability of Charles Francis Adams on these matters can now be tested by the evidence of the Adams Family Papers. In John Adams's *Literary Commonplace Book* and his *Literary Notes and Drafts*,[11] as well as in his letters and other writings,[12] there is abundant evidence of his knowledge of and reading in Greek, as well as, of course, Latin authors. In John Quincy Adams's memoranda and commonplace books[13] we find excerpts from Aeschines, *Iliad, Odyssey*, Plutarch, Anacreon, among Greek authors. When John Quincy Adams entered Harvard in 1785 he had read, in his extensive reading program in the classics, parts of Aristotle's *Poetics*, of Plutarch's *Lives*, of Lucian, the Choice of Hercules from Xenophon, as well as several books of the *Iliad*.[14]

Early Twentieth-Century Neglect

Nineteenth-century American historians, mostly amateurs, wrote our early history as a filiopietistic hobby. At the turn of the century a new breed of professional historians abandoned the politico-military-nationalistic perspectives of American history for the "New History," promulgated by Edward Eggleston, who in 1900 proclaimed that "no other superstition has held so long as the classic. . . . Let us brush aside once and for all the domination of the classic tradition."[15] Soon afterward Eggleston expanded this theme in his great work *The Transit of Civilization from England to America in the Seventeenth Century*, in which he proceeded to brush aside the importance of classical education in early America as irrelevant for a pioneering society with pressing practical needs.[16]

About this time, in 1901, there appeared a substantial work on *The Revolutionary Movement in Pennsylvania 1760-1776*, which dealt, in part,with the books then influential in America. The range is comprehensive—from Milton to Voltaire—but not a single classical author is mentioned.[17] Moreover, that "noble ruin" of scholarship, Vernon Parrington's *Main Currents in American Thought*,[18] could range through the colonial period (vol. I, 1927) without a single mention of the American colleges or their classical curriculum. As late as 1935 the *Journal of American History* published an article on "Political Philosophy of the American Revolution," which examined such influences on the American Revolution as the Bible, Puritan thinkers, and English and French writers but ignored the authors of antiquity.[19]

Forerunners of the Study of the Classical Tradition

About this time the first serious proposals for studying the nature and depth of the classical tradition in early America were made—not by classicists, but by American historians of the colonial and early national periods. The first to suggest the need for such research was Carl Becker, who wrote in 1925: "Will not someone write a book showing how the revolutionary state of mind of the eighteenth century was also nourished on an ideal conception of classical republicanism and Roman virtue? . . . To know the answers . . . would help much to understand both the French and American revolutions."[20] Shortly afterwards came Gilbert Chinard's discovery and publication of Jefferson's commonplace book in 1928.[21] This dramatic event was to spur interest in research in many aspects of the classical tradition in America. Chinard concluded from Jefferson's utilitarian reading of the classics that "in those remote days the study of the classics was more than a luxury and a painful task. It was an essential part in the moral foundation of many of the men who framed the American institutions."[22] "We can hardly realize," Chinard observed, "the power exerted by the classics at a time and in a land where only a few books were available."[23] Later Chinard was to remark critically of American scholarship: "I have often proposed that our ignorance and neglect of this classical background vitiates most of our studies in eighteenth-century thought."[24]

It was, I surmise, the enthusiasm generated by Chinard's work on Jefferson's knowledge of the classics that launched the classicist Richard M. Gummere on his lifelong interest in the classical tradition in America. It was natural for him to begin his long series of studies in this area with the Philadelphia experience—a brief study published in 1932 on Benjamin Franklin and the classics.[25] Despite Gummere's dedicated work, there was no one yet in America to do first what Henri Peyre did, in a limited way, with regard to the methodological problems involved in studying the influence of classical authors on modern French literature.[26] As late as 1955 Douglass Adair, who combined a working knowledge of the classics with his gifts as American historian, could say, "alas, there is not even a beginning on the classics in Revolutionary America."[27]

The Discipline of Intellectual History and the Classical Tradition

Meanwhile, American intellectual history had come of age in the 1940s and 1950s. New perspectives, new techniques, and the study of a mass of previously neglected sources and data began to produce a comprehensive picture of the intellectual life of early America. In particular, in the reinterpretation of the Revolution diverse views emerged that assigned little or no place to the classical tradition. Neither the consensus school, reflecting continuity with the American past and unity of intellectual traditions in American society, nor the conflict school, that sees the Revolution as the climax of pluralistic pressures resulting from social and economic conflicts within American life, directed attention to the classical curriculum of the schools and colleges. Moreover, many American intellectual historians, espousing an Atlantic Community concept, gave special attention to European influences on early American culture and the Revolution, particularly the English traditions.[28] In consequence, in this radical rethinking of the intellectual life of early America little or no attention was given by American historians to the classical tradition. Characteristic was Clinton Rossiter's judgment in 1953 that the classics taught the Founding Fathers nothing new; he curtly brushed aside the use of ancient authors by early Americans as mostly window dressing. "The Americans," he wrote, "would have believed just as vigorously in public morality had Cato and the Gracchi never lived."[29]

About this time there appeared an influential article by a historian of English intellectual history, Charles F. Mullett, whose "Classical Influences in the American Revolution"[30] was a skillful identification of the Greek and Roman antecedents that contributed to the ideology of freedom, to the Revolution, and to the framing of the Constitution. The Founding Fathers cited the classics as unimpeachable authorities for republicanism and natural law, and they venerated classical heroes as ideals, particularly the ancient lawgivers and martyrs for freedom. Though Mullett concluded that "no less than the Washingtons and the Lees [the] ancient heroes helped to found the independent American commonwealth," it was his phrase "the window-dressing value of classical writers and incidents"[31] in contemporary oratory that was singled out by many American historians to characterize the classical tradition in America.

Richard M. Gummere's Work

While most Americanists in their exploration of a great range of influences on early America ignored or severely limited the classical influences, classicists have tended to overestimate the classical tradition. This was the proclivity of the pioneer among classicists in this field, Richard Mott Gummere,[32] as he labored to demonstrate, and celebrate, the classical influences on early Americans. Beginning in 1932, with brief studies of the classics in Philadelphia, Gummere devoted the remainder of his long scholarly career to explicating various aspects of the role of the classics in early America. He began these studies when he was headmaster of the Penn Charter School in Philadelphia, continued them through his tenure as chairman of the Committee on Admissions at Harvard, and then in his retirement, until his death in 1969. When he moved to Cambridge, Gummere began to apply to other colonial and Revolutionary leaders the same method he had already developed: biographical sketches with a focus on identification of the classical allusions and quotations used by them. From a study of John Adams[33] he turned to a similar treatment of James Wilson of Pennsylvania.[34] It was already evident that Gummere's principal purpose was to elucidate what he called "this glorified game of hide-and-seek through the pages of classical antiquity."[35]

There followed a study of John Witherspoon, famous president of the College of New Jersey (Princeton).[36] More comprehensive were his succeeding essays, which sought to evolve some general trends: "The Heritage of the Classics in Colonial North America. An Essay in the Greco-Roman Tradition"[37] and "The Classics in a Brave New World."[38] Both of these studies, as is the case with almost every one of Gummere's numerous contributions to this field, are characterized by a Herodotean stream of details, often digressive and irrelevant, and by exaggeration and antiquarianism. Gummere had a passion for the sport of hunting down classical quotations and tags, and for explicating the etymologies of Latinate English words used in the "classics-laden language" of the eighteenth century. "Volumes could be written," he wrote, "with lists of quotations from the ancients."[39]

Nevertheless, Gummere made two important contributions to American intellectual history: by his unrelenting documentation of classical references he demonstrated that the Founding Fathers were familiar not only with English and French writers on government but also the classical sources; and he introduced the concept of refraction to characterize how early Americans selected and adapted classical theory and practice of politics and government to their own needs.[40]

Gummere's typical procedure—biographical, discursive, exaggerated claims of classical influences—are also to be found in subsequent essays on: William Bartram,[41] John Adams,[42] Thomas Hutchinson and Samuel Adams,[43] John Cotton and Roger Williams,[44] John Dickinson,[45] John Wise,[46] Michael Wigglesworth,[47] Jonathan Boucher,[48] and Thomas Paine.[49] An article on "Some Classical Sidelights in Colonial Education"[50] stressed that the classics were not mere ornament and dealt with the relevancy of the classics to "the cultural and civic needs of a new nation," and with the diversified content of the classics, that provided both Whigs and Tories with intellectual weapons. The best and most enduring of Gummere's specialized studies is his article "The Classical Ancestry of the United States Constitution."[51] Here he demonstrated how classical concepts and experience, especially as expressed by Aristotle, Cicero, and Polybius, were adapted by the Founding Fathers to the new national government: Greek leagues, Greek colonies, ancient senates, mixed constitutions, natural law. Gummere concluded here that "there is no doubt that the Greco-Roman tradition was one of the basic contributors to the Constitution." Yet he claimed too much, for he neglected to explore the indirect ways, the immediate sources by which classical theories reached Americans; he insisted, for example, that Adams and Jefferson simply did not rely on "second-hand material" but went to the originals in Greek and Latin.[52]

In 1963, when Gummere was an octogenarian, there appeared his widely acclaimed book *The American Colonial Mind and the Classical Tradition: Essays in Comparative Culture.*[53] As Gummere revealed, his method was "largely biographical, rather than an impersonal 'thesaurus' of parallels or quotations, stastically classified." He cautioned, properly, that early Americans were amateurs, not professional classicists; and he concluded that the classical tradition "penetrated deeply," especially from 1750 to 1775. In eleven chapters, containing much material culled from his published short studies, he elucidated the many-faceted utilitarian appropriations from the classics by early Americans, the relevance of classical education to their needs, and the success of this type of training in developing a galaxy of extraordinary men. He deprecated the rigors of interdisciplinary methods by cautioning that "the Classicist should not pose as an authority on American history."[54]

The reviews of Gummere's book, by both classicists and American historians, were almost uniformly laudatory. Among classicists William M. Calder III described it as a "rich, suggestive book, and the best statement in print for the relevance of classics to the U.S.A.";[55] Henry C. Montgomery declared the whole volume "of utmost value" for the "formative period of American culture";[56] Leon Golden commended Gummere for showing that the classics were "a major influence" in early America and for demonstrating that "this vital classical tradition was a constant, almost omnipresent factor."[57] Among Americanists John Schutz called the book a "valuable and noteworthy contribution to scholarship";[58] Samuel Eliot Morison admired its "thorough investigation of the classical background to the Anglo-American minds" and deplored that "during the last century American historians have largely ignored" the classical background, for classical education produced "giants of intellect" and "marvelous constructive political scientists."[59] Frederick B. Tolles, too, deplored that the debt to the ancients has been neglected by American intellectual historians, and concluded that now "it will be hard for anyone who reads this book ever again to disregard it."[60]

Only Jack P. Greene[61] and Howard Mumford Jones[62] published unfavorable reviews. Greene regretted the failure of Gummere to "explain how the colonials used the classics and what their use of the classics reveals about them." Jones dealt with Gummere's method, which he called "agglutinative," that is, an assemblage of references, allusions, citations from classical antiquity. "In the nature of the case he cannot determine when classical tags come from *florilegia*, commonplace books, and the like, and when they result from an acquaintance with the total work of a classical author. He has not attempted to assess indebtedness to the thought of the ancient world but to indicate that this indebtedness exists. . . . His is a map-making, not a mining operation." But, Jones concluded, "his studies underline the sound truth that the United States is a product of a long cultural tradition and not, as some recent interpretations of American history tend to assume, a self-originating culture."

Gummere's last work, *Seven Wise Men of Colonial America*,[63] contains biographical studies of Hugh Jones of Virginia, Robert Calef of Salem, Michael Wigglesworth of Harvard, Samuel Davies of Virginia, Henry Melchior Muhlenberg of Pennsylvania, Benjamin Rush of Philadelphia, and Thomas Paine. Some of these men had strong anticlassical views, particularly Rush and Paine, but

Gummere—wearing rose-colored classical glasses—sought to demonstrate that they were not really hostile to the classics, since they frequently used classical quotations, but merely wanted to reform the teaching of the classics.[64] This book of Gummere was brusquely dismissed by Leo M. Kaiser, in the only serious critical review of the work.[65] Kaiser criticized the many irrelevancies and trivia, the careless quotations and translations, the errors in fact, and Gummere's concern with classical tags, references, and examples. "One cannot escape the conviction," said Kaiser, "that Gummere, as he read in colonial literature, jotted down every classical reference, and from an assemblage of these attempted to construct meaningful studies. I have serious misgivings about such a procedure."[66]

The censure of Kaiser, Greene, and Jones of Gummere's method deserves serious attention. One suspects that the approval often given to Gummere's studies by American intellectual historians who consider the classical influences to have been negligible or largely ornamental comes from this very emphasis on the ability of early Americans to use classical tags and *exempla* from ancient history. Gummere never came to grips with the fundamental question of the depth of the classical influences on early Americans, and the extent to which this knowledge of the classics was determinative of thought and action.

It should be added that contributions by classicists other than Gummere, such as Gerald F. Else,[67] Walter R. Agard,[68] and William H. Calder III,[69] have been general statements of the vitality of the classical tradition in early America. The essay of Herbert P. Houghton[70] was poorly informed. Johannes Urzidil's book, *Amerika und die Antike*,[71] emphasized the reliance of the Founding Fathers upon antiquity but touched only lightly on the seventeenth and eighteenth centuries.

American Historians and the Classical Tradition

Gilbert Chinard

One of the first to study the nature of the classical traditions in early America was Gilbert Chinard, who deplored that the impact of the classics in early America was generally ignored by American historians, urged study of the classical knowledge of the men of the Revolutionary period, but warned against claiming too much for the classics.[72] On Chinard's contributions see further below, under "The Constitution" and "Thomas Jefferson."

Louis B. Wright

The venerable American historian Louis B. Wright has been one of the principal advocates of the view that classical learning was responsible for the intellectual and moral qualities of the Americans who played a decisive role in the Revolution and among the post-Revolutionary generation. His important study, "The Purposeful Reading of Our Colonial Ancestors,"[73] deals especially with the Virginia gentry. Wright here clarifies the continuity of the humanistic tradition and English cultural ideals on American soil, the utilitarian reading of early Americans, especially in the ancient historians and moralists, for political knowledge and moral improvement. This theme is extensively documented in his study "The Classical Tradition in Colonial Virginia,"[74] which defines the classical interests of the Tidewater Virginia ruling class, for whom the classics were both the hallmark of gentlemen's culture as well as a repository of practical wisdom for historical and moral instruction. Special attention is given by Wright to the libraries of leading Virginians and to Jefferson's commonplace book. Wright concludes: "The Classics provided a philosophic and intellectual mooring. Nothing in our modern world is so certain and so unquestioned as the belief held by the men of 1787 in the wisdom of the ancients."[75]

Wright's masterful book *The First Gentlemen of Virginia: Intellectual Qualities of the Early Colonial Ruling Class*[76] devotes considerable attention (chap. IV, pp. 95–116) to the transplanting of the English educational system to America, the Virginian conviction that polite learning necessitated a classical education, and the effect of this training in producing Ciceronian orators and Latin-quoting statesmen. Ample attention is also given (chap. V, pp. 117–154) to the importance of books and libraries in the lives of eminent Virginians of the plantation gentry, such as William Fitzhugh, Ralph Wormeley II, Richard Lee II, the Carters, and the Byrds. Wright properly underscores their utilitarian reading and the scant interest in belles lettres, but he exaggerates the proportion of books dealing with the classics in their libraries and in their usual reading. Wright's useful article "Thomas Jefferson and the Classics"[77] concludes that for Jefferson the classics served practical purposes and was of the highest utility—a living thing throughout his entire life. Yet he combined an interest in science with his love of the classics, was not a classical pedant, and frequently used translations of the classics. He was most at home with the Roman historians and moralists, and worked out his own ethical system by combining classical morality with Christian ethics.[78]

Douglass Adair

Douglass Adair, who moved comfortably and competently in the classics, was, from the beginning of his scholarly career, convinced of the great influence of the classics on the Founding Fathers. His first study, "The Intellectual Origins of Jeffersonian Democracy: Republicanism, the Class Struggle, and the Virtuous Farmer,"[79] rejected the "frontier" theory ofFrederick Jackson Turner to account for the concept of the virtuous farmer as the basis of stable republican government. Instead he traced the Virginia planters' political philosophy back to Aristotle, Xenophon, Polybius, Cicero, Plutarch, and the Roman writers of the Augustan Age. The concept of the free agricultural commonwealth, made up of self-sufficient, economically independent farmers, according to Adair, stems from the classical tradition.[80] To the Virginia Tidewater gentry, steeped in classical education, ancient history was also contemporary history: the analogies uncovered in their reading of ancient authors were of exemplary seriousness. Americans also rediscovered the theory of the mixed constitution through their knowledge of Thucydides, Aristotle, Polybius, Cicero. Adair concluded that the early American debt to antiquity was great, and that "the impact of such knowledge in their thought cannot be denied."[81]

In his masterly article "Experience Must Be Our Only Guide: History, Democratic Theory, and the United States Constitution,"[82] Adair stressed the vitality and influence of the classics in the thinking of the Founding Fathers. "Did lessons from the antique past," he asked, "applied to their present situation, concretely affect their actions at Philadelphia? The evidence is overwhelmingly that they did." The Founding Fathers, convinced of the uniformity of human nature as a constant, employed the historical-comparative method in ransacking ancient history for guidance. "They were *obliged* to study Greece and Rome, if they would gain 'experimental' wisdom on the dangers and potentialities of the republican form."[83]

Merle Curti

Merle Curti's reading of the evidence led him to conclude that classical learning, though elitist and the status badge of the gentleman, was the educational vehicle for the training of professionals and was regarded by many Americans as a repository of secular wisdom throughout adult life.[84]

Adrienne Koch

Striving to untangle the knotty problem of the evidence for the Enlightenment in America, Adrienne Koch was convinced that "classical learning was more important in the American republic than in France"[85] and that modern behavioral scientists "will have to consider how it was that men who were classical scholars, students of philosophy and science, and moralists were also men in the key positions, defining and molding institutions for the democratic republic."[86]

Edward M. Burns

In his excellent study, "The Philosophy of History of the Founding Fathers,"[87] Edward McNall Burns emphasized the influence of ancient history on the Founding Fathers, who learned from antiquity the universality of human problems, the cyclical view of history, the corrupting force of power and luxury, the need for political safeguards through a mixed constitution, and the strength and weaknesses of Greek federal leagues. "It may be doubted," he wrote, "that any group of statesmen anywhere in the world was more conscious of the lessons of antiquity and more determined to profit from them."[88]

Howard Mumford Jones

Howard Mumford Jones takes a middle stand between Americanists who ignore the classical tradition and classicists who overvalue its influence. In *O Strange New World. American Culture: The Formative Years*,[89] Jones cautions that because of the decline of knowledge of the classics, today the notion that "the classical past has exerted an important influence on the culture of the United States seems to many absurd."[90] It is true that the classics touched the lives of only an elite minority, and that for many it was somewhat pedantic and thin, a veneer of gentlemen's culture; and that early American libraries contained only a small percentage of books in the classics.[91] Yet the classics constituted a powerful force, from the agitation over the Stamp Act until the end of John Quincy Adams's presidency in 1828. They served as sources for propaganda, historical precedents, the theory and practice of a republic, provided ancient heroes as models for the emulation of Roman virtue,[92] and legitimized the ideal of a Sabine Farm retreat. In his recent work, *Revolution & Romanticism*,[93] Jones explores the strong interest in the ancient world in the eighteenth century, the classical curriculum of schools and colleges, and the widespread use of translations of the classics.[94]

Bernard Bailyn

Bernard Bailyn's contributions to an understanding of the nature of the educational process in early America and of the ideological framework of the Revolution have been universally acclaimed. Treating education as the entire process of the transmission of a culture, Bailyn in *Education in the Forming of American Society: Needs and Opportunities for Study*[95] characterized the role of formal education in early America as slight, compared with the involvement of family, church, and community. Yet such formal education was highly utilitarian in preparing for specific roles in society; its principal vehicle, classical literature, provided practical subjects of instruction, though it was gradually assailed in its monopoly by other concepts of utility.[96] In his *Ideological Origins of the American Revolution*[97] Bailyn masterfully analyzed the literature of the Revolution, noting that the sources and traditions used were in general characterized by "random eclecticism."[98]

According to Bailyn the heritage of classical antiquity was very conspicuous in the writings of the Revolutionary period, but the learning exhibited was amateurish and superficial. It was very selective and limited in range, mostly political history from ca. 200 B.C. to A.D. 200, culled mainly from Plutarch, Livy, Cicero, Sallust, and Tacitus. The application of classical analogies to the Revolutionary present was abundant, but the citations "are everywhere illustrative, not determinative of thought."[99] For Bailyn the determinative sources were the radical thinkers of the seventeenth and eighteenth centuries in England and the continent, English common law and legal history, and the works of the radical Whigs. Thus, in regard to the Revolution itself, it was European thought, not the classical heritage, that provided the moving force.[100] Bailyn's conclusions have been frequently cited as authority for the insignificance of the classical tradition in early American intellectual history. It must be remembered, however, that Bailyn was concerned only with the Revolutionary period, and that it was not his purpose to consider the influence of the classics on other aspects of early American life, such as literary style, oratorical methods, and moral thought, among others.

Henry Steele Commager

In his provocative article "Leadership in Eighteenth-Century America and Today,"[101] Henry Steele Commager analyzes the impact of the classics as highly utilitarian, with influences on thought and style, providing lessons in history and morality, and defining the law of nature. American leaders in the political arena drew lessons from the classics of Greek and Roman literature, which they regarded as timeless verities and as providing ideal types of men for their imitation and instruction. In his "The American Enlightenment and the Ancient World: A Study in Paradox,"[102] Commager analyzes the eighteenth-century concept of history as utilitarian knowledge, as "philosophy teaching by examples," with the result that the classics were plundered for timeless precedents and *exempla* for both historical an moral knowledge. But while they exploited the classics, the Founding Fathers were not unaware of a disturbing paradox. On the one hand, they relied on universal, timeless models that epitomized order, stability, reason (especially in the concept of a balanced, rationally ordered constitution); on the other hand, they were supporters of the uniqueness and dynamism of the American experiment, the "epitome of the particular," a society inclined to disorderly change, pluralistic, progressive, future-oriented.

H. Trevor Colbourn

Colbourn's influential book, *The Lamp of Experience: Whig History and the Origins of the American Revolution*,[103] describes the practical uses of history in eighteenth-century America, with the past as a storehouse of examples and authoritative precedents. Among these were the lessons extracted from the classics,[104] for which Americans in general preferred translations, modern surveys, particularly of Roman history, and other shortcuts to history. Colbourn's appendix II is especially valuable for its analysis of the works of history in numerous American libraries, from which we can determine what were the "best-sellers" in ancient history in eighteenth-century America.

Gordon S. Wood

In his stimulating work, *The Creation of the American Republic 1776-1787*,[105] Gordon Wood points out that in "the incredible jumble of references from every conceivable time and place, adduced by the Revolutionary generation in their search for a comprehensive knowledge of history, the appeal to ancient republics and republicanism was very strong,"[106] however selective and superficial such random extraction was. "The American's compulsive interest in the ancient republics was in fact crucial to their attempt to understand the moral and social bases of politics." But Americans did not study "an original and unglossed antiquity. They often saw a refracted image," handed down since the Renaissance.[107] Wood's conclusion regarding the classical heritage is that "for the Americans the mid-eighteenth century was truly a neo-classical age —the highpoint of their classical period. . . . Such classicism was not merely a scholarly ornament of educated Americans; it helped to shape their values and their ideals of behavior."[108]

Classical Education

General

Since 1945 the history of early American education, including the classical component, has been rewritten with profound insights into the cultural milieu and with access to an enormous mass of documents. The works, for example, of Butts and Cremin,[109] Cremin,[110] Sheldon Cohen,[111] Madsen,[112] Bailyn,[113] Wilson Smith,[114] and Sol Cohen[115] provide excellent general surveys of early American education, including theories, contents, results, and documentary collections.

Grammar Schools

The experience of the Latin grammar school, an institution transplanted from England, was a sine qua non for college-bound students preparatory to training in the professions of the ministry, law, and medicine. This secondary school offered a seven-year curriculum for about 150 years, until the Boston Latin School in 1789 reduced its program to 4 years.[116] The aims, curriculum, teaching methods, textbooks of the American grammar schools are thoroughly known.[117] A desideratum is a comprehensive study of the grammar school teachers of early America, both famous and fugitive, from the establishment of the Boston Latin School in 1635 to the end of the eighteenth century.[118] The survival of the Latin grammar school in relatively unchanged form because of pedagogical conservatism, despite widespread doubts as to its continued efficiency and despite new national needs and the persistent demand for more practical, vocational subjects, is well documented. In this connection a valuable contribution to early American secondary education was made by Robert Seybolt in his studies of the many private schools and evening schools, both vocationally oriented, and the many new academies that offered more varied and flexible curricula than the classically anchored traditional grammar schools.[119]

Colleges

We now have at our disposal adequate data and studies for an understanding of the aims, admission requirements, curricular evolution, and the careers of many Americans who attended college from 1636–1800.[120] There are numerous histories—some with extensive documentary sources—of the nine colonial colleges and the new institutions of higher learning that sprang up in the last quarter of the eighteenth century.[121] Sibley's *Harvard Graduates*,[122] with its extensive documentation, is an unparalleled work of reference. Dexter's sketches of Yale graduates[123] is also useful; and we look forward with great expectations to James McLachlan's project, a biographical dictionary of Princeton graduates and their contributions to American life from 1747 to 1776, which is now in progress.[124]

With regard to the classical component in American colleges in the colonial and early Federal periods, it would be very desirable to have a comprehensive synthesis dealing with aims, growth of secularization, changes in curriculum that competed with the fixed body of classical learning, methods, books used, libraries available, professors, students, the graduates of the colleges and their future careers. We also need a special study of the aims and program of the master's degree in American colleges. Even more necessary is a comprehensive study of student attitudes to the classics, a subject on which almost nothing has so far been written. Only recently Professor James McLachlan has begun to make contributions to this important subject, with special reference to student societies in American colleges in the late eighteenth and early nineteenth centuries.[125] These societies served an important para-educational function of supplementing the circumscribed college curriculum with more extensive and sophisticated reading and opportunities for debate and discussion, through the initiative of the students left to their own resources.[126] A great variety of still untapped material for such a study is to be found in unpublished commonplace books of students, their diaries, letters, comments written in books, their copy books, and their reminiscences in later life.

Clamor for Educational Reform

From the middle of the eighteenth century (Benjamin Franklin's efforts to break the monopoly of the dead languages and to introduce new subjects with utilitarian ends) to the first decades of the nineteenth century there were not infrequent proposals for basic educational reform. (See further below, under "Hostility to Classical Learning.") In the 1790s, in particular, numerous plans were offered for a national system of education. These sought to redirect American education, both on the secondary and collegiate levels, to pragmatic utilitarian goals, stressing the scientific method, a national ideology, a culture independent of past traditions, universal education for a distinctive American culture, and indoctrination for constructive citizenship and democratic ideology. A number of these programs were offered in response to a prize announced in 1797 by the American Philosophical Society for essays on a national system of education. These reform programs, ranging from proposals for complete elimination of the classical languages to schemes for higher priority to modern and utilitarian subjects, have been thoroughly studied, notably by Allen O. Hansen and Frederick Rudolph.[127] The evidence is clear that, despite all these reasoned and sometimes passionate proposals, the classical curriculum of the grammar schools and the colleges remained virtually unaltered.

American Libraries—Books and Reading Tastes

Studies in the reading interests of early Americans and the contents of numerous libraries in America in the seventeenth and eighteenth centuries have made it possible to determine fairly accurately the early American use of Greek and Latin texts, readers, grammars, dictionaries, translations of the classics, works on Roman and Greek antiquities, and contemporary books on Roman and Greek history. These books, almost all imported from Britain, are known to us from catalogues of college libraries, private libraries, wills, probate records of estates, parish libraries, lending collections, diaries, pamphlets, letters, commonplace books, speeches, bookdealers' catalogues and broadsides, and bills of sale and import vouchers, as well as estates of bookdealers themselves. While the humanistic tradition continued to influence reading tastes, it has been amply demonstrated that the percentage of books having anything to do with classical learning was relatively small, rarely exceeding 10–15 percent of holdings. A few characteristic examples will suffice: the library of James Logan of Philadelphia, the best classical library of the first half of the eighteenth century, contained about 13 percent in classical works; that of Edwin Lloyd IV of Maryland, a library of 2,250 volumes catalogued in 1796, contained about 5 percent in classics; that of William Munford of Virginia, translator of the *Iliad*, who catalogued his library in 1802, contained about 5 percent in this field; the library of the distinguished North Carolinian Archibald De Bow Murphey in 1822 contained 6.3 percent; George Washington's library, as catalogued in 1810, only 1 percent.[128]

It is now possible for us to determine with considerable accuracy the reading interests of early Americans by periods, sections, and classes of the population. Joe W. Kraus tells us that "it would be a staggering but not impossible task to compile a catalogue of all books known to have been owned by American colonists, and no doubt some day it will be done."[129] In my opinion, such a tabulation is not likely to reveal a component of books in classics in excess of 15 percent.

Sectional Differences

New England
The uninformed inclination to belittle Puritan thought as unsympathetic to liberal culture has been reversed by the magisterial studies of Samuel Eliot Morison and Perry Miller. In Morison's work on Harvard in its early days and in his *The Intellectual Life of Colonial New England*, he clarified the role of the classics in Puritan New England, demonstrating that, after initial hostility, the classics flourished there. Thus, the humanistic tradition on this continent was preserved, providing education for service to church and state, through the grammar schools, Harvard College, and the many libraries.[130] Perry Miller, in *The New England Mind: The Seventeenth Century*,[131] shows how the classics were assimilated in New England, even if used selectively and with reservations. The numerous grammar schools of New England and its colleges, particularly Harvard and Yale, with the classical curriculum at the center of their training, were the models for the other colonies.

Middle States
It is well known that the commercial and business interests of New York, and the Quakers, with their unfriendliness to ornamental knowledge, were long unresponsive to the learned languages. The utilitarian bent of the middle colonies delayed the establishment of traditional grammar schools and colleges until the middle of the eighteenth century. We do not have a thorough study of the classical tradition in New York. Pennsylvania, particularly Philadelphia, has been better served.[132] The contributions of William

Smith to the College of Philadelphia and of Charles Nisbet to Dickinson College have been adequately treated.[133]

Southern States

We are well informed about the classical interests of the plantation gentry, who naturalized English education in Maryland and the Tidewater regions. They stocked their libraries with works on the classics, read and quoted Latin and Greek authors both as gentleman's status badge and for utilitarian purposes. In the absence of cities as educational centers, they brought in tutors for their children, or sent their sons to be educated in England or on the continent.[134]

American Leaders and the Classics

Thomas Jefferson

Jefferson's lifelong love affair with classical learning is well known. His attachment to the classics was never ornamental but utilitarian in the highest degree, for public life and leisure. This is evidenced by his felicity as stylist, his development of a moral system based on the ancient moralists, his use of the Roman historians and ancient history as analogies to present problems, his revival of classical architecture in America. Despite the fact that no other of the Founding Fathers has had so many books written about him, there is as yet no satisfactory comprehensive study of all aspects of Jefferson as a student of classical antiquity.[135] Moreover, a new edition of his literary commonplace book, first edited by Gilbert Chinard, would be desirable.[136]

John Adams

Like Jefferson, John Adams was deeply committed from early years to classical learning as useful knowledge for America. His uses of classical heroes and politics as timeless models providing knowledge and examples for training in civic virtue, constitution making, and conduct of government have been collected and commented upon. We now need a comprehensive study of the classical learning in the life of John Adams.[137]

John Quincy Adams

Very little work has been done on the involvement of John Quincy Adams with the classics and classical learning.[138] The sources lie ready to hand, in his diaries, letters, poems, translations, and commonplace books.[139] A thorough study would be an important contribution to an understanding of his intellectual life and to the role of the classics at the end of the eighteenth century and the first quarter of the nineteenth.

Benjamin Franklin

Franklin's opposition to the monopoly of the classics in American education in the second half of the eighteenth century has been thoroughly studied. His efforts to supplant the priority of the classics with utilitarian subjects, especially English and science, failed because the conservative force of tradition was too strong.[140]

Benjamin Rush

In 1786 Benjamin Rush, distinguished physician, educator, patriot, wrote: "The Revolution is not over!" His conviction that a revolution in education was necessary for the new nation took the form of unrelenting hostility to the dead languages from 1787 to the end of his life in 1813. His educational plans to redirect the schools so as to create "republican machines," inculcate virtue, patriotism, republican ideology, and to disseminate knowledge universally (with new subjects for a new type of republic) have been adequately studied.[141]

James Logan

As a result of the work of Frederick B. Tolles and Edwin Wolf II we now have a comprehensive knowledge of "a belated Humanist," James Logan of Philadelphia, who possessed a scholar's working library in the classics, "beyond question the largest and finest collection of classical writings in colonial America" in the first half of the eighteenth century.[142]

Alexander Hamilton

Though some illuminating contributions have been made to an understanding of the knowledge and uses of the classics and ancient history by Alexander Hamilton, a comprehensive study of Alexander Hamilton and the classics is needed.[143]

Others

Specialized studies are needed on the classical background and the uses of classical learning by other leading Americans, e.g., Samuel Adams, Francis Hopkinson, Hugh Henry Brackenridge, and Fisher Ames.

The Uses of Ancient History

It has been adequately documented that the knowledge of history, especially of ancient history, was not an antiquarian interest in early America but highly utilitarian, "the lamp of experience." This dominant interest in antiquity was not, of course, uniquely American but a transplant from English neoclassical thought through the histories and commentaries Americans read. It is abundantly clear, too, that the utilitarian selectivity of American patriots in exploiting historical events and men of the ancient world was concerned mainly with the ancient republics as fountainheads of liberty, republican forms, civic virtues, and models of heroes. These classical analogies provided Americans with timeless ideals for a new type of society and a new type of man.[144] Lord Bolingbroke's dictum that "history is philosophy teaching by examples" provided the directive for the use of history for present politics, for moral and political education. The classics, especially the Roman historians, as a central organizing principle prefigured for Americans their problems and provided lessons for them in what they considered to be recurrent, typical phenomena.[145]

The tireless search for parallels and analogies from antiquity, based on the concept that human nature is uniform and that men will behave the same way under similar conditions, was, it is apparent from the sources, the almost universal practice.[146] Yet this zeal for analogies from antiquity began to be challenged early in the Federal period. The first systematic analysis of the dangers of the analogical-comparative method was made by William Vans Murray in 1787, in his *Political Sketches*,[147] a work not sufficiently appreciated today. Murray argued that analogies from antiquity were not valid, indeed dangerous, for he maintained the new nation was a unique society, and history had no lessons to teach America.[148]

The Constitution

Many strands of political theory and practice—English, continental, early American, classical—were woven into the complex fabric of the American Constitution in 1787. With regard to the classical influences, the ancestry of the Constitution in the thought of Plato, Aristotle, Polybius, and Cicero and in the constitutions and history of the Greek cities, Rome, and Carthage is too authentic to require repeated legitimization any longer.[149] Though the American appeal to natural law has its roots in antiquity (Aristotle,

Cicero [*De Leg.* 3.4.10], and Stoicism), Americans were indebted for this not so much through direct knowledge of the classical sources as from the English heritage of law and government, especially through Milton, Coke, Algernon Sidney, John Locke, and the continental jurists de Vattel, Pufendorf, and Burlamaqui.[150] Since the Founding Fathers analyzed and used the Greek leagues for guidance, it would be desirable to have a comparative study of the present state of our knowledge of these leagues and the ways in which the Founding Fathers exploited their knowledge.[151]

Miscellaneous Aspects of the Classical Tradition

Pseudonyms; Place Names

A comprehensive collection and study of classical pseudonyms used in early America has never been made.[152] Nor do we have a thorough collection and study of the history and use of classical place names in early America to 1800.[153]

The Classics as Belles Lettres

Aesthetic appreciation of Greek and Roman literature was shunted aside by the didactic, political, and moral interests of early Americans in the classical authors. It would be desirable to have a study of the extent to which belletristic interest in the classics existed. Cotton Mather's early warning against "a Conversation with the *Muses* that are no better than *Harlots*"[154] is characteristic of widespread objection to reading the classics for frivolous reasons, not only in Puritan New England but among the Quakers and even in Virginia. Few Americans knew the Greek lyric poets, and the ancient dramatists (except Terence) were in general ignored.[155]

Rhetoric and Oratory

The usefulness of Demosthenes, Cicero, and Quintilian for rhetorical studies and training in oratory in the early Federal period, for example, influenced early national poetry. A study of the influence of classical oratory on American public speaking would be desirable.[156]

There is also a need for a study of the classical component of the July Fourth orations from their inception to ca. 1825. They abound with classical references, and they were delivered before public audiences. It would also be desirable to have a study of the classical allusions in the funeral eulogies for Washington delivered from December 14, 1799, to February 22, 1800, the period of national mourning. About 350 of these are extant, and they contain numerous analogies to antiquity, particularly to Plutarchan heroes.

Classical Analogies to American Indians

The important work of Père Lafitau[157] on the customs of American Indians needs to be translated and equipped with a careful commentary. A study of his efforts to trace American Indians to peoples of antiquity would be rewarding.

Classical Art

John Singleton Copley's famous cri de coeur about the attitude of his fellow Americans to painting in the 1760s is a commentary on the conventional utilitarian-didactic-moralistic value put on art by Americans. "The people generally regard it no more than any other useful trade, as they sometimes term it, like that of a carpenter, tailor or shew maker, not as one of the most noble Arts in the World. . . . While the Arts are so disregarded I can hope for nothing."[158] However limited the classical influence on early American art may have been, it would be desirable to have a study of the impact of the classical tradition on American artists of the eighteenth century, especially classical themes in painting and sculpture, and American architecture.[159]

Classical Symbols and Iconography

There is need for a comprehensive study of the use of classical symbols, mottoes, and representations on seals, banners, diplomas, coins, certificates, monuments, etc. Ample evidence exists, for example, in the symbols of the Masonic Order in America (Paul Revere made engravings for diplomas and certificates of the order), the Great Seal of the United States, the symbols of the Society of the Cincinnati (established in 1783), coins, medals, and the emblems and diplomas of student societies.[160]

Neo-Latin in America

Leo Kaiser's careful studies of a number of examples of Latin speeches and poetry in early America[161] have only scratched the surface. A mass of still unexplored material is to be found in the documentary sources of American colleges, Lemay's catalogue of American poetry, and in American newspapers and magazines.[162] Kaiser's long-awaited book on neo-Latin in early America will, it is anticipated, add much to our knowledge.

Anthologies of Classical Readings

Wilson Ober Clough's[163] selected readings from "Our Long Heritage" were intended to illustrate some of the interests of eighteenth-century Americans. Clough, however, included some authors in whom early Americans had little or no interest and omitted more than a few that were commonly read by them, as well as the works on ancient history and Greek and Roman antiquities in wide circulation in America. In *The Classick Pages: Classical Reading of Eighteenth-Century Americans*[164] I have provided a general introduction to the cult of antiquity in America and have included extensive selections, with commentary, from translations of classical authors known to have been commonly read in early America, as well as excerpts from books on Roman life and government and the customs and manners of the Greeks and Romans.

Opponents of Classical Learning

From the founding of Harvard College to the end of the eighteenth century and into the early nineteenth, classical learning in America was never without its critics. At first this hostility came from the theologians, later from the advocates of utility, finally from supporters of a national education for a distinctive American culture. In their continuous quest for useful knowledge throughout the eighteenth century[165] Americans expressed discontent with the exclusive nature of the classical curriculum and the traditional veneration of classical literature. They also criticized the many years of a boy's youth devoted to Latin grammar school instruction, the quality of the instruction, and lack of time for study of English, science, and other modern subjects, including the living languages. We now have adequate treatments of many aspects of this hostility to the dead languages.[166]

Several aspects of the opposition to classical learning merit further attention. During the religious revival known as the Great Awakening, which erupted about 1740, there came to the surface a strong anti-intellectualism.[167] While the New Lights supported personal piety and assailed moralistic individualism as destructive of religion, the Old Lights continued to support high educational attainments of the traditional type. Some of the extreme New Lights were anticlassical, and tended to belittle formal education. We need a collection and study of all the evidence for the New Lights' hostility to the classics.[168]

At the end of the eighteenth century the victory of educational conservatism reaffirmed the continuing values of classical education, despite the assaults of the utilitarians, the nationalists, and the supporters of a new national literature without roots in the past. Further study, however, is needed of the political motivations behind the clash between opponents and supporters of classical learning at the end of the eighteenth and early nineteenth centuries. Many Federalists regarded the role of the classics as invaluable for developing good citizens, while the Democrats sought to dismantle the traditional forms of education at the same time as they sought to institute sweeping political reforms.[169]

In this connection a special analysis is needed of the mounting disenchantment with lessons of ancient history for the new society which began shortly after freedom from England and the promulgation of the Constitution. Even Jefferson and John Adams, lifelong devotees of the classics, began, late in life, to criticize aspects of ancient government and culture. Especially the dispute between John Adams and John Taylor over the usefulness of ancient history for America needs further study.[170]

As Howard Mumford Jones reminds us[171] all sides appealed to antiquity during the Revolutionary Age. But in the early Federal period widespread doubts began to be expressed about the usefulness of knowledge of the classical world for the new society. A fundamental paradox lurking in the uses of the ancient world by early Americans has been elucidated by Henry Steele Commager[172] and by other American historians who have analyzed the "people of paradox." The development of American society, based on an unstable, multidimensional pluralism and commitment to progress and change was incompatible with the absolute models of antiquity with their emphasis on the universal, on order, stability, reason, balance. The unique, dynamic American society, revolutionary, disorderly, future-oriented, could not long continue to venerate antiquity as before. Pride in achievement and self-confidence in national purpose produced conviction of American superiority over the ancient republics. Hence the jettisoning of the lessons of ancient history by most Americans. Even Jefferson could say: "I like the dreams of the future more than the history of the past." On this subject see my study of the decline of classical learning in America from its high point in the Revolutionary Age to a Silver Age, from 1790 to 1830, in Chapter VI, above.

New Directions for Research

In 1970 a working conference on the classical traditions in early America was held in Ann Arbor under the sponsorship of the Center for Coördination of Ancient and Modern Studies and the National Endowment for the Humanities.[173] The aim of this conference was to determine if the classical influences in early America were substantial and not merely ornamental, and, if so, to lay down a program of research for studying these influences.

The consensus of the participants was that the classical influences in early America were indeed substantial, but that thus far not much advance had been made through Gummere's work, which was criticized as antiquarian, biographical, belletristic and selective so as to overemphasize the role of the classics (Reinhold). It was pointed out (by Greene and Pocock) that we do not yet have a sense of function for the classics in America. Inadequate attention has been paid to the social function of the classics, which performed the role of an ideology expressing and solving needs of eighteenth-century society (Wood). We need greater clarity on any special uniqueness of the role of the classics in America, its special utilities for private and public purposes (Reinhold). Since the classics provided models, we need to study the sources and reading from which they constructed these classical models (Greene); of special value would be a study of the impact of Plutarch on the eighteenth century (Commager). Since selectivity, out of context, was characteristic of the use of the classics, we must study the principles of this selectivity, which were probably civic, republican, political (Pocock). More work in depth on the classical influences on political history and constitutional theory is needed, for Mullett "only begins to scratch the surface." With regard to classicism in American art, more study of such influence as a political and moral agent is needed (Wood). It would be productive also to investigate the concept of virtue in America, especially in its agrarian context (Eadie, Pocock). Attention should be paid to the uses of ancient history to validate stability and continuity in a culture based on pragmatism and rapid change (Commager). It would also be desirable to investigate how the classics influenced the way American leaders thought about themselves as leaders in classical terms (Wood). Finally, we know how Rome influenced early Americans, but not enough about the American valuation of Sparta and Athens (Pocock).[174]

How Deep Were the Classical Influences on Early Americans?

Many American historians are satisfied that Gummere's work has clarified the role of the classics in early America. If facility with classical quotations and allusions, as accumulated by Gummere from his extensive reading in early American sources, represents the depth of the classical influence, then we need not devote any further research to this field. Gummere has amply demonstrated how adept early Americans were with classical tags, quotations, references. But Howard Mumford Jones has pointed out[175] that Gummere's work is "a map-making, not a mining operation," and that "he has not attempted to assess indebtedness to the thought of the ancient world but to indicate that this indebtedness exists."

Our most urgent problem is to determine the extent to which classical learning in early America was not merely ornamental but deeply internalized. Here are some of the questions we must answer: To what extent did the classical education of the grammar schools and colleges really influence many Americans, especially considering the methods employed? How many Americans were really influenced in their thinking by the classical authors they studied and read? Since ownership of books does not assure that such books are read, can we assess influence merely by the books known to have been in a particular individual's library? Does reading a book really modify thought? And is there a causal nexus between ideas and political and social events? In short, can we prove that works read really influenced thought, and that thoughts were translated into deeds?[176]

It is well known that most of the signers of the Declaration and the delegates to the Constitutional Convention had a classical education.[177] Though they constituted an elite minority, their influence on the destinies of Americans was very great. For example, in the entire seventeenth century less than 600 went to college and only 465 were graduated.[178] In adult life most Americans, if they continued their interest in the classics, read translations. The quotations they were adept in using often came from books of proverbs and phrases, and they often made errors in the use of quotations. The themes of M.A. theses at Harvard reveal that out of several hundred very few were on classical topics.[179] The growth of student societies in colleges, which supplemented the classical education with modern subjects and topics in the late eighteenth and early nineteenth centuries,[180] represented a negative attitude on the part of college students to the traditional training. Henry Adams[181] condemned the educational system during the presidency of Jefferson as antiquated, "suited to children fourteen years of age." Harvard, he declared, "resembled a priesthood that had lost the secret of its mysteries." Joseph Green Cogswell in 1819 ridiculed the poor teaching methods, condemned the teachers as not being scholars, and declared, after coming to know the German secondary schools and universities, that American schools have not produced "a single first rate scholar, no, not one since the settlement of the country." The libraries he brushed aside as "pitiful," even that of Harvard, largest in the country.[182]

On the other hand, the traditional classical education was indeed an effective training ground for orators, through the discipline in disputation and logic; it trained many Americans in the niceties of style; equipped them with numerous exemplars from history for understanding contemporary events and behavior through comparative method; was a training tool for the memory; and endowed them with a storehouse of moral maxims plucked from the ancient moralists.[183]

In the 1640s Nathaniel Ward, educated in England, but writing in America, said: "I have been so *habituated* and *half-natured* into these Latins and Greeks, ere I was aware, that I neither can expel them, nor spell my own mother-tongue after my old fashion."[184] In 1825 Jefferson wrote to Henry Lee about the Declaration of Independence as follows: "It was intended to be an expression of the American mood. . . . All its authority rests then on the harmonizing sentiments of the day, whether expressed in conversation, in letters, in printed essays, or the elementary books of public right, as Aristotle, Cicero, Locke, Sidney."[185] Is Howard Mumford Jones right when he says, "It is of course difficult to estimate the effect of any educational pattern or the reading of any book or set of books upon those who study them. Only a few outstanding personalities in any generation show the direct influence of classical learning."[186]

Since the initial impulses given fifty years ago by Carl Becker and Gilbert Chinard to study of the role of the classical traditions in early America, there has been a steady appreciation of its significance. Are Clinton Rossiter and Bernard Bailyn closer to the truth in their valuation of the depth of the classical influence as superficial than Gilbert Chinard, Louis B. Wright, Douglass Adair, Gordon Wood? Daniel Boorstin wrote in 1948 about the effect of the classics on the Jeffersonians as follows: "It is hard to deny that they had been profoundly affected in thought and feeling."[187] Yet in 1789 David Ramsay, a contemporary, wrote about the Revolutionary period: "In these times of action, classical education was found of less service than good natural parts, guided by common sense and sound judgment."[188]

Notes

1. See below, nn. 28–31 for "The Discipline of Intellectual History and the Classical Tradition."
2. New York, 1803. *Brief Retrospect* was written before Miller was thirty-five. For the Reverend Samuel Miller's career (1769–1850) see *Dictionary of American Biography*, vol. XII, pp. 636–637; cp. n. 5 below. Worth reading is his later comprehensive and spirited case for the study of the classics, written in 1843 for his sons, in Samuel Miller, *Letters from a Father to His Sons in College* (Philadelphia, 1852), pp. 131–139.
3. Charles Nisbet, first president of Dickinson College. See James H. Smylie, "Charles Nisbet: Second Thoughts on a Revolutionary Generation," *Pa. Mag. Hist. & Biog.* 98 (1974), pp. 198–205.
4. John Higham, *Writing American History: Essays on Modern Scholarship* (Bloomington, 1970), p. 44.
5. *Brief Retrospect*, vol. II, pp. 35–54 ("Classical Literature"), 272–273, 400, 407, 409–410, 433. On Samuel Miller's work and its importance see Gilbert Chinard, "Progress and Perfectability in Samuel Miller's Intellectual History," in *Studies in Intellectual History* (Baltimore, 1953), pp. 94–122; idem, "A Landmark in American Intellectual History: Samuel Miller's *A Brief Retrospect of the Eighteenth Century*," *Princeton University Library Chronicle* 14 (1953), pp. 55–72; Jacob L. Susskind, "Samuel Miller's Intellectual History of the Eighteenth Century," *Journal of Presbyterian History* 49 (1941), pp. 15–37.
6. See in this chapter "Sectional Differences" and "The Constitution." However, some Harvard men of the first decade of the nineteenth century looked back nostalgically to the pre-Revolutionary period as the acme of classical learning in America: *Monthly Anthology and Boston Review* 5 (1808), p. 222; J. S. Buckminster, ibid., 7 (1809), p. 146.
7. See, e.g., *The Marcus W. Jernegan Essays in American Historiography*, ed. William T. Hutchinson (Chicago, 1937), pp. 1–59; Michael Kraus, *The Writing of American History* (Norman, 1953); Harvey Wish, *The American History: A Social-Intellectual History of the Writing of the American Past* (New York, 1960), pp. 58–179; George H. Callcott, *History in the United States 1800–1860* (Baltimore, 1970); John Higham, *Writing American History*, pp. 43–53; Richard C. Vitzthum, *The American Compromise: Theme and Method in the Histories of Bancroft, Parkman, and Adams* (Norman, 1974). On George Tucker see *Dictionary of American Biography*, vol. XIX, pp. 28–30; Robert C. McLean, *George Tucker, Moral Philosopher and Man of Letters* (Chapel Hill, 1961); and his defense of the classics in his *Essays on Various Subjects of Taste, Morals, and National Policy. By a Citizen of Virginia* (Georgetown, 1822), pp. 90–108 ("On Classical Education"—written 1813); on George Bancroft see *Dictionary of American Biogrpahy*, vol. I, pp. 654–657; Robert H. Canary, *George Bancroft* (New York, 1974); and Bancroft's defense of the classics in *North American Review* 19 (July 1824), pp. 125–137, and 23 (July 1826), pp. 142–150.
8. New York, 1878. His other great work, *The Literary History of the American Revolution 1763–1783* (New York, 1897), appeared when he was professor of

American history at Cornell. On Tyler see *Dictionary of American Biography*, vol. XIX, pp. 92–93; Howard Mumford Jones and Thomas E. Casady, *The Life of Moses Coit Tyler* (Ann Arbor, 1933); John Higham, "The Rise of American Intellectual History," *American Historical Review* 56 (1950–51), pp. 456–457.

9. I quote from the edition of 1879 (New York), vol. II, p. 309.
10. Charles Francis Adams, "A College Fetich," in *Three Phi Beta Kappa Addresses* (Boston, 1907), pp. 3–48.
11. Adams Family Papers, microfilm reels 187, 188, Massachusetts Historical Society, Boston.
12. See in this chapter under "John Adams."
13. Adams Family Papers, microfilm reels 199, 217, 220, 222, 223, 230, 239. On John Quincy Adams's training in both Latin and Greek, see, e.g., Marie B. Hecht, *John Quincy Adams* (New York, 1972), pp. 20–61; Samuel Flagg Bemis, *John Quincy Adams and the Foundations of American Foreign Policy* (New York, 1949), pp. 116–117.
14. Letter by John Adams in 1785 to Benjamin Waterhouse at Harvard, in *The Selected Writings of John and John Quincy Adams*, ed. Adrienne Koch and William Peden (New York, 1946), pp. 71–73.
15. "The New History," *Annual Report of the American Historical Association* 1 (1901), pp. 37–38.
16. New York, 1901. See esp. pp. 207–272, "The Tradition of Education," and his estimate of the grammar school training of early America (p. 219): "The vulgar utilities of English reading and writing and multiplying and dividing were much more suited to pioneers in America than Lilly's Latin grammar or even what was esteemed the 'rare and almost divine matter' of 'Tullies Offices.'"
17. Charles H. Lincoln, in *Publications of the University of Pennsylvania*, Series in History, no. 1 (Philadelphia, 1901), pp. 119–121.
18. 1927–30. Volume I (published in 1927) covers the *Colonial Mind (1620–1800)*. Cp. on Parrington, e.g., William T. Utter article in Hutchinson, *Jernegan Essays*, pp. 394–408; Wish, *The American History*, pp. 293–320.
19. William D. Houlette, "Political Philosophy of the American Revolution," *Journal of American History* 29 (1935), pp. 123–135.
20. *American Historical Review* 30 (1924–25), pp. 811–812. Under Becker's influence, Harold T. Parker produced the much-admired, but flawed, work, *The Cult of Antiquity and the French Revolutionaries: A Study of the Development of the Revolutionary Spirit* (Chicago, 1937; rpt. 1965). See now B. Récatas, "Quand l'Antiquité inspirait les hommes de la Révolution," *Annuaire de l'Institut de Philologie et d'Histoire Orientales et Slaves* [Mélanges Isidore Levy] 13 (1953), pp. 491–529; Fernando Diaz-Plaja, *Griegos y Romanos en la Revolución Francesa* (Madrid, 1960).
21. *The Literary Bible of Thomas Jefferson: His Commonplace Book of Philosophers and Poets*, ed. Gilbert Chinard (Baltimore, 1928).
22. Ibid., p. 4.
23. "Thomas Jefferson as a Classical Scholar," *American Scholar* 1 (1932), p. 135; "Thomas Jefferson as a Classical Scholar," *Johns Hopkins Alumni Magazine* 18 (1929–30), pp. 291–303, in which he cautions that "the influence of the older civilizations of the ancient world is too often disregarded" in the study of early America (p. 293).
24. "Jefferson Among the Philosophers," *Ethics* 53 (1942–43), p. 257.
25. "Socrates at the Printing Press: Benjamin Franklin and the Classics," *Classical Weekly* 26 (1932), pp. 57–59. Gummere exaggerated Franklin's knowledge of and use of the classics, to which, in fact, he harbored a lifelong antipathy. See also Gummere's article, "Apollo on Locust Street," *Pa. Mag. Hist. & Biog.* 56 (1932), pp. 68–92, which overestimates the impact of the classics on belles lettres in Philadelphia in the colonial period.

26. *L'Influence des littératures antiques sur la littérature française moderne: État des Travaux* (New Haven, 1941), esp. pp. 18–22, in which he suggests the need to determine, for example, which Greek and Latin authors were preferred in different periods, and which translations were read.
27. "A Note on Certain of Hamilton's Pseudonyms," *Wm. & Mary Quart.*, 3rd ser., 12 (1955), p. 289, n. 10.
28. Michael Kraus, "Literary Relations between Europe and America in the Eighteenth Century," *Wm. & Mary Quart.*, 3rd ser., 1 (1944), pp. 210–234; Franklin L. Baumer, "Intellectual History and Its Problems," *Journal of Modern History* 21 (1949), pp. 191–203; Higham, "The Rise of American Intellectual History," pp. 453–471; Kraus, *The Writing of American History*, pp. 345–376; Merle Curti, *American Paradox: The Conflict of Thought and Action* (New Brunswick, 1956; rpt. 1973), p. vii; John Higham, "American Intellectual History: A Critical Approach," *American Quarterly* 13 (1961), pp. 219–233; Arthur A. Ekirch, *American Intellectual History* (New York, 1963); Robert A. Skotheim, *American Intellectual Histories and Historians* (Princeton, 1966); William F. Streirer, Jr., "Conflict or Consensus? Recent Trends in the Historiography of the American Revolution," *Proceedings of the South Carolina Historical Association*, 1967, pp. 32–42; Higham, *Writing American History*, pp. 29–31; Felix Gilbert, "Intellectual History: Its Aims and Methods," *Daedalus* 100, no. 1 (1971), pp. 80–97; Arthur A. Ekirch, *American Intellectual History: The Development of the Discipline*, American Historical Association Pamphlets, no. 102 (Washington, D.C., 1973).
29. *Seedtime of the Republic* (New York, 1953), pp. 356–359.
30. *Classical Journal* 35 (1939–40), pp. 92–104.
31. Ibid., pp. 97,104.
32. For a biography and tribute to Gummere, see Frederick S. Allis, Jr., "Richard Gummere," *Proc. Mass. Hist. Soc.* 81 (1969), pp. 220–233. Gummere used to say that "the classicists dismissed him as a classicist *manqué*, while the historians dismissed him as an historian *manqué*" (p. 231).
33. "John Adams, Togatus," *Philological Quarterly* 13 (1934), pp. 203–210.
34. "Classical Precedents in the Writings of James Wilson," *Publ. Colon. Soc. Mass.* vol. XXXII (1938), *Transactions*, 1933–37, pp. 525–538.
35. Ibid., p. 535.
36. "A Scottish Classicist in Colonial America," *Publ. Colon. Soc. Mass.* vol. XXXV (1947), *Transactions*, 1942–46, pp. 146–161.
37. *Proc. Amer. Philos. Soc.* 99 (1955), pp. 68–78.
38. *Harvard Studies in Classical Philology* 62 (1957), pp. 119–139.
39. "The Heritage of the Classics" (see n. 37, above), p. 76.
40. Ibid., pp. 70, 72–75.
41. "William Bartram, a Classical Scientist," *Classical Journal* 50 (1955), pp. 167–170. Gummere claims for Bartram only a refraction of the classics in his "classically ornate" style and his use of Latinate words.
42. "The Classical Politics of John Adams," *Boston Public Library Quarterly* 9 (1957), pp. 167–182.
43. "Thomas Hutchinson and Samuel Adams, a Controversy in the Classical Tradition," *Boston Public Library Quarterly* 10 (1958), pp. 119–130, 203–210. Gummere's point is that both the defender of the crown in Massachusetts and the patriot firebrand used classical citations in support of opposing views on the status of colonies.
44. "Church, State, and the Classics: The Cotton-Williams Debate," *Classical Journal* 54 (1959), pp. 175–183. Most of the references used were patristic, but Gummere sees in their applications a broadening of the colonial mind through the classical heritage.

45. "John Dickinson: The Classical Penman of the Revolution," *Classical Journal* 52 (1956), pp. 81–88.
46. "John Wise, A Classical Controversialist," *Essex Institute, Historical Collections* 92 (1956), pp. 265–278.
47. "Michael Wigglesworth: From Kill-Joy to Comforter," *Classical Journal* 62 (1966), pp. 1–8.
48. "Jonathan Boucher, Toryissimus," *Maryland Historical Magazine* 55 (1960), pp. 138–145.
49. "Thomas Paine: Was He Really Anti-Classical?," *Proc. Amer. Antiq. Soc.* 75, pt. 2 (1965), pp. 253–259. Gummere cites Paine's use of classical tags and examples. But A. Owen Aldridge, in "Thomas Paine and the Classics," *Eighteenth-Century Studies* 1 (1967–68), pp. 370–380, demolished Gummere's claims for Paine as a classicist. Paine in fact had very little classical education, read very little of the classics even in translation, and, though he approved of some aspects of antiquity, considered the Enlightenment superior to ancient civilization. See also "Opponents of Classical Learning during the Revolutionary Period," Chapter IV, above, n. 86.
50. *Classical Journal* 55 (1959–60), pp. 223–232.
51. *American Quarterly* 14 (1962), pp. 3–18.
52. Ibid., p. 4.
53. Cambridge, Mass., 1963.
54. Ibid., pp. vii, ix, xi, 1.
55. *Gnomon* 38 (1966), pp. 637–638.
56. *Classical Journal* 60 (1964–65), pp. 134–135.
57. *Wm. & Mary Quart.*, 3rd ser., 21 (1964), pp. 469–471.
58. *American Historical Review* 69 (1964), pp. 1156–1157.
59. *New Engl. Quart.* 37 (1964), pp. 261–263.
60. *American Literature* 36 (1964–65), pp. 222–223.
61. *South Atlantic Quarterly* 63 (1964), pp. 594–595.
62. *Journal of American History* 51 (1964–65), pp. 490–491.
63. Cambridge, Mass., 1967.
64. See "Opponents of Classical Learning in America during the Revolutionary Period," Chapter IV, above.
65. *Wm. & Mary Quart.*, 3rd ser., 25 (1968), pp. 662–663.
66. Ibid., p. 663.
67. "The Classics in the New World," *Newsletter, American Council of Learned Societies* 16, no. 5 (1965), pp. 1–6.
68. "Our Classical Humanities—Refuge and Guide," *Virginia Quarterly Review* 38 (1962), pp. 232–235. Agard's comments are very superficial on the colonial and early Federal periods.
69. "Die Geschichte der klassischen Philologie in den Vereinigten Staaten," *Jahrbuch für Amerikastudien* 11 (1966), pp. 213–217.
70. "The Study of the Classics in the United States in the 17th, 18th, 19th, and 20th Centuries," *Humanitas* [Coimbra, Portugal], 2 (1948–49), pp. 345–350.
71. Zurich, 1964.
72. "Polybius and the American Constitution," *Journal of the History of Ideas* 1 (1940), pp. 38–58.
73. *ELH: Journal of English Literary History* 4 (1938), pp. 85–111.
74. *Papers of the Bibliographical Society of America* 33 (1939), pp. 85–97. Similarly, "Humanistic Education and the Democratic State," *South Atlantic Quarterly* 42 (1943), pp. 142–153; "The Prestige of Learning in Early America," *Proc. Amer. Antiq. Soc.* 83 (1973), pp. 15–27; "The Classics and the Eighteenth-Century Gentleman," in *Traditions and the Founding Fathers* (Charlottesville, 1975), pp. 106–116.
75. *Papers of the Bibliographical Society of America* 33 (1939), p. 97.

76. San Marino, Calif., 1940; rpt. 1964. Cp. *The Cultural Life of the American Colonies, 1607-1763* (New York, 1957), pp. 98-153 (on books, libraries, reading tastes, classical education).
77. *Proc. Amer. Philos. Soc.* 87 (1943-44), pp. 223-233.
78. See further on Wright in this chapter under "American Libraries—Books and Reading Tastes."
79. Ph.D. diss., Yale, 1943.
80. Ibid., pp. 122, 296-301.
81. Ibid., p. 122.
82. In *The Reinterpretation of Early American History: Essays in Honor of John Edwin Pomfret*, ed. Ray Allen Billington (San Marino, Calif., 1966), pp. 129-148; Jack P. Greene, ed., *The Reinterpretation of the American Revolution 1763-1789* (New York, 1968), pp. 396-416; *Fame and the Founding Fathers: Essays by Douglass Adair*, ed. Trevor Colbourn (New York, 1974), pp. 107-123.
83. Billington, *Reinterpretation of Early American History*, pp. 130, 136. For another significant contribution by Adair see under "Alexander Hamilton" in this chapter.
84. "The Transmission of Ancient Classics," in *The Growth of American Thought*, 3rd ed. (New York, 1960), pp. 76-81.
85. *The Philosophy of Thomas Jefferson* (New York, 1943), p. 2, n. 4.
86. "Pragmatic Wisdom and the American Enlightenment," *Wm. & Mary Quart.*, 3rd ser., 18 (1961), p. 326.
87. *The Historian* 16 (1954), pp. 142-168, esp. 142-147, 164-165.
88. Ibid., p. 142.
89. New York, 1952.
90. Ibid., p. 228.
91. Ibid., p. 240.
92. Ibid., pp. 227-272.
93. Cambridge, Mass., 1974.
94. Ibid., pp. 116-150.
95. Chapel Hill, 1960. For the importance of Bailyn's book see, e.g., J. Merton England, *American Historical Review* 68 (1962-63), pp. 235-236; Frederick D. Kershner, Jr., *Wm. & Mary Quart.*, 3rd ser., 18 (1961), pp. 579-581; Lawrence A. Cremin, *American Education: The Colonial Experience 1607-1783* (New York, 1970), pp. 577-578.
96. Bailyn, *Education* (see n. 95, above), pp. 18-19, 33-36.
97. Cambridge, Mass., 1967. This is a new edition of his introduction to volume I of *Pamphlets of the American Revolution 1750-1765* (Cambridge, Mass., 1965). See reviews by Jack P. Greene, *American Historical Review* 73 (1967), pp. 209-211; H. Trevor Colbourn, *Journal of American History* 52 (1965-66), pp. 609-611.
98. Bailyn, *Ideological Origins* (see n. 97, above), pp. 22-54.
99. Ibid., pp. 23-26.
100. See also Bernard Bailyn, *The Origins of American Politics* (New York, 1968), the thesis of which is the influence of British politics and constitution upon Americans.
101. *Daedalus* 90 (1961), pp. 652-673.
102. *Proc. Mass. Hist. Soc.* 83 (1971), pp. 3-15; also in *Jefferson, Nationalism, and the Enlightenment* (New York, 1975), pp. 123-139; first published in *Festschrift für Karl Lowenstein* (Tübingen, 1971).
103. Chapel Hill, 1965.
104. See especially on the classics pp. 21-25. Colbourn reminds us (pp. 191-192, n. 29) that "no one has done for the Founding Fathers what Harold T. Parker did for the French Revolutionaries in the 1780's and 1790's" (see above, n. 20).

105. Chapel Hill, 1969.
106. Ibid., pp. 48–53 ("The Appeal of Antiquity").
107. Ibid., p. 50.
108. Ibid., p. 49.
109. R. Freeman Butts and Lawrence A. Cremin, *A History of Education in American Culture* (New York, 1953), pp. 1–140.
110. Cremin, *American Education*, with excellent bibliographical essay, pp. 577–668.
111. Sheldon S. Cohen, *A History of Colonial Education: 1607–1776* (New York, 1974), a good general survey, with bibliographical essay, pp. 201–215.
112. David Madsen, *Early National Education: 1776–1819* (New York, 1974).
113. See above, n. 95.
114. Wilson Smith, *Theories of Education in Early America, 1655–1819* (Indianapolis, 1973), an excellent source book.
115. Sol Cohen, ed., *Education in the United States: A Documentary History* (New York, 1975), vol. I.
116. See Meyer Reinhold, *The Classick Pages: Classical Reading of Eighteenth-Century Americans* (University Park, Pa., 1975), pp. 3–4.
117. George E. Littlefield, *Early Schools and School-Books of New England* (Boston, 1904); Colyer Meriwether, *Our Colonial Curriculum 1607–1776* (Washington, D.C., 1907), pp. 63–109 (on "Ancient Languages" [antiquarian and inaccurate]); Walter H. Small, *Early New England Schools* (Boston, 1941), pp. 1–57; Emit D. Grizzel, *Origin and Development of the High School in New England Before 1865* (New York, 1923), pp. 1–27; Kenneth B. Murdock, "The Teaching of Latin and Greek at the Boston Latin School in 1712," *Publ. Colon. Soc. Mass.*, vol. XXVII (1931), *Transactions*, 1927–30, pp. 21–29; James Mulhern, *A History of Secondary Education in Pennsylvania* (Philadelphia, 1933), pp. 1–142; Robert F. Seybolt, *The Public Schools of Colonial Boston, 1635–1775* (Cambridge, Mass., 1935); Pauline Holmes, *A Tercentenary History of the Boston Latin School 1635–1935* (Cambridge, Mass., 1935), chaps. VIII–X (on curriculum, textbooks, methods of teaching; an act of homage to the oldest secondary school in the country, this volume teems with facts and reverent enthusiasm—and antiquarianism); Richard B. Ballou, "The Grammar Schools in 17th Century Colonial America" (Ph.D. diss., Harvard, 1940); Thomas Jefferson Wertenbaker, *The Puritan Oligarchy: The Founding of American Civilization* (New York, 1947), pp. 135–158; Homer H. Young, "Theory of Education During the Revolutionary Period 1743–1809" (Ph.D. diss., University of Texas, 1949), pp. 109–171 (on curriculum and utilitarian aims), pp. 284–289 (revolt against the classics); Rena L. Vassar, "Elementary and Latin Grammar School Education in the American Colonies 1607–1700" (Ph.D. diss., University of California, Berkeley, 1958) (best overview of the period; emphasizes growth of utilitarian perspectives); Robert Middlekauff, "A Persistent Tradition: The Classical Curriculum in Eighteenth-Century New England," *Wm. & Mary Quart.*, 3rd ser., 18 (1961), pp. 54–67; idem, *Ancients and Axioms: Secondary Education in Eighteenth-Century New England* (New Haven, 1963) (the best study of the curriculum; deals also with challenge to classical learning; based on much unpublished material in family papers, journals, commonplace books, letters, diaries).
118. See, e.g., Jean S. Straub, "Teaching in the Friends' Latin School of Philadelphia in the Eighteenth Century," *Pa. Mag. Hist. & Biog.* 91 (1967), pp. 434–456; Thomas C. Pears, "Francis Alison, Colonial Educator," *Delaware Notes* 17 (1944), pp. 9–22; Butts and Cremin, *A History of Education*, pp. 131–135; Willard S. Elsbree, *The American Teacher* (New York, 1939), pp. 1–24 ("The Colonial Schoolmaster"; a shabby piece of work). On the famous Latin teacher Ezekiel Cheever, see, e.g., his popular *"Accidence," A Short Introduction to the*

Latin Tongue: For the Use of the Lowest Forms in the Latin School (Boston, 1707) (it contains only rules of grammar, paradigms, principal parts of verbs in common use and of irregular verbs); Littlefield, *Early Schools and School-Books*, pp. 250–258; Elizabeth P. Gould, *Ezekiel Cheever: Schoolmaster* (Boston, 1904).

119. Butts and Cremin, *A History of Education*, pp. 115–131; Robert F. Seybolt, *The Evening School in Colonial America*, Bureau of Educational Research, College of Education, University of Illinois, Bulletin no. 24 (Urbana, 1925); idem, *Source Studies in American Colonial Education: The Private School*, ibid., Bulletin no. 28 (Urbana, 1925); idem, *The Private Schools of Colonial Boston*.

120. Edward J. Young, "Subjects of Master's Degree in Harvard College from 1655 to 1791," *Proc. Mass. Hist. Soc.* 18 (1880–81), pp. 119–151; Edwin C. Broome, *A Historical and Critical Discussion of College Admission Requirements*, Columbia University Contributions to Philosophy, Psychology, and Education, vol. XI, nos. 3–4 (New York, 1903), pp. 17–41; Lyon G. Tyler, "Early Courses and Professors at William and Mary College," *Wm. & Mary Quart.* 14 (1905–06), pp. 71–83; Louis F. Snow, *The College Curriculum in the United States*, Teachers College, Columbia University Contributions to Education, no. 10 (New York, 1907), pp. 20–55, 78–118, 132–134; Donald G. Tewksbury, *The Founding of American Colleges and Universities before the Civil War* (New York, 1932); Edward K. Rand, "Liberal Education in Seventeenth-Century Harvard," *New Engl. Quart.* 6 (1933), pp. 525–551; Allen G. Umbreit, "Education in the Southern Colonies, 1607–1776," *University of Iowa Studies in the Social Sciences*, vol. X, no. 3, *Abstracts in History* 2 (1934), pp. 17–31 (superficial); Agatho Zimmer, *Changing Concepts of Higher Education In America Since 1700* (Washington, D.C., 1938), pp. 1–22 (very general, unsatisfactory); Herbert W. and Carol Schneider, *Samuel Johnson, President of King's College* (New York, 1929); Edgar W. Knight, *A Documentary History of Education in the South Before 1860* (Chapel Hill, 1949–56), vol. I, and vol. II, pp. 1–40; Carl A. Hangartner, "Movements to Change American College Training, 1700–1830" (Ph.D. diss., Yale, 1955); Samuel E. Morison, *The Intellectual Life of Colonial New York*, 2nd ed. (New York, 1956), pp. 27–56; John S. Brubacher and Willis Rudy, *Higher Education in Transition. An American History: 1636–1956* (New York, 1958), pp. 3–21; Jerome S. Fink, "The Purposes of the American Colonial Colleges" (Ph.D. diss., Stanford, 1958) (valuable for charters, careers of graduates, curricula, conclusion that American colleges were originally liberal arts colleges, not theological seminaries); William D. Carrell, "American College Professors: 1750–1800," *History of Education Quarterly* 8 (1968), pp. 289–305; idem, "Biographical List of American College Professors to 1800," *History of Education Quarterly* 8 (1968), pp. 358–374; Cremin, *American Education*, pp. 611–615 (good bibliographical essay on the colleges); Margaret W. Masson, "The Premises and Purposes of Higher Education in American Society, 1745–1770" (Ph.D. diss., University of Washington, 1971).

Of special interest is James J. Walsh's *Education of the Founding Fathers: Scholasticism in the Colonial Colleges* (New York, 1935), and his article "Scholasticism in the Colonial Colleges," *New Engl. Quart.* 5 (1932), pp. 485–532. He argues for the primacy of scholasticism in colonial colleges, and the continuity of the medieval methods of Latin disputation in America. Clinton Rossiter, *Seedtime*, p. 486, calls this a "twisted argument"; Samuel Eliot Morison, *New Engl. Quart.* 8 (1935), pp. 455–457, a "strained argument."

121. For Harvard: Josiah Quincy, *The History of Harvard University* (Cambridge, Mass., 1840); Samuel Eliot Morison, *Harvard College in the Seventeenth Century* (Cambridge, Mass., 1936); idem, *Three Centuries of Harvard 1636–1936*

(Cambridge, Mass., 1937); for Yale: Franklin B. Dexter, *Documentary History of Yale University* (New Haven, 1916); Richard Warch, *School of the Prophets: Yale College, 1701–1740* (New Haven, 1973); Brooks M. Kelley, *Yale: A History* (New Haven, 1974), pp. 1–231; for Princeton: John Maclean, *History of the College of New Jersey From Its Origins in 1746 to the Commencement of 1854* (Philadelphia, 1877; rpt. 1969); George P. Schmidt, *Princeton and Rutgers: The Two Colonial Colleges of New Jersey* (Princeton, 1964); for King's College (Columbia): David C. Humphrey, "King's College in the City of New York, 1754–1776" (Ph.D. diss., Northwestern, 1968); for the College of Rhode Island (Brown): Reuben A. Guild, *Early History of Brown University* (Providence, 1897); Walter C. Bronson, *The History of Brown University 1764–1914* (Providence, 1914), pp. 1–154; for the College of Philadelphia (University of Pennsylvania): Edward Potts Cheney, *History of the University of Pennsylvania from its Foundation to A.D. 1770* (Philadelphia, 1900); for Dickinson College: Charles C. Sellers, *Dickinson College: A History* (Middletown, 1973), pp. 32–135; for Queen's College (Rutgers): William H. S. Demarest, *A History of Rutgers College, 1766–1924* (New Brunswick, 1924), pp. 1–215; Richard P. McCormick, *Rutgers: A Bicentennial History* (New Brunswick, 1966), pp. 1–35; Schmidt, *Princeton and Rutgers*; for North Carolina: Kemp P. Battle, *History of the University of North Carolina* (Raleigh, 1907–12), vol. I, pp. 1–229; Robert D. W. Connor, Louis E. Wilson, and Hugh T. Lefler, eds., *A Documentary History of the University of North Carolina 1766–1799* (Chapel Hill, 1953).

122. John L. Sibley and Clifford K. Shipton, *Biographical Sketches of Graduates of Harvard University* (Cambridge, Mass., 1873–), with 17 volumes to date, including class of 1771.

123. Franklin B. Dexter, *Biographical Sketches of Graduates of Yale College, with Annals of the College History* (New Haven, 1885–1912).

124. James McLachlan, *Princetonians 1748–1768* (Princeton, 1976); Richard A. Harrison, *Princetonians 1769–1775* (Princeton, 1980).

125. James McLachlan, "The *Choice of Hercules*: American Student Societies in the Early Nineteenth Century," in *The University in Society*, ed. Lawrence Stone (Princeton, 1974), vol. II, pp. 449–494. From 1750–1814 there were 38 such student library and debating societies in American colleges, such as the Whig Society and the Cliosophic Society in Princeton, the Dialectic Society and the Philanthropic Society in North Carolina.

126. Henry D. Sheldon, *Student Life and Customs* (New York, 1901), is a gold mine of information, with good bibliographies. See esp. pp. 89–94, 125–142, for the colonial and Revolutionary periods.

127. Allen Oscar Hansen, *Liberalism and American Education in the Eighteenth Century* (New York, 1926; rpt. 1965); Frederick Rudolph, ed., *Essays on Education in the Early Republic* (Cambridge, Mass., 1965); Jonathan Messerli, "Benjamin Franklin: Colonial and Cosmopolitan Educator," *British Journal of Educational Studies* 16 (1968), pp. 43–59; Merle M. Odgers, "Education and the American Philosophical Society," *Proc. Amer. Philos. Soc.* 87 (1943), pp. 12–24; Ervin C. Shoemaker, *Noah Webster: Pioneer of Learning* (New York, 1936); Harry R. Werfel, *Noah Webster, Schoolmaster to America* (New York, 1936).

128. Stephen Weeks, "Libraries and Literature in North Carolina in the Eighteenth Century," *Annual Reports of the American Historical Association 1895* (1896), pp. 169–267; Austin B. Keep, *The Library in Colonial New York* (New York, 1909); Julius H. Tuttle, "The Libraries of the Mathers," *Proc. Amer. Antiq. Soc.* 20 (1909–10), pp. 269–356; Philip A. Bruce, *Institutional History of Virginia in the Seventeenth Century* (New York, 1910), vol. I, pp. 402–441; George H. Abbott, *Short History of the Library Company of Philadelphia* (Phil-

adelphia, 1913); catalogue of the library of Archibald DeBow Murphey, 1822, in *The Papers of Archibald DeBow Murphey,* ed. William Henry Hoyt (Raleigh, 1914), vol. II, pp. 438–442; Worthington C. Ford, *The Boston Book Market 1679–1700* (Boston, 1917); *Catalogue of the John Adams Library in the Public Library of the City of Boston* (Boston, 1917); library of James Bowdoin, *Proc. Mass. Hist. Soc.* 51 (1918), pp. 362–368; E. V. Lamberton, "Colonial Libraries of Pennsylvania," *Pa. Mag. Hist. & Biog.* 42 (1918), pp. 193–234; Alfred C. Potter, "Catalogue of John Harvard's Library," *Publ. Colon. Soc. Mass.,* vol. XXI (1920), *Transactions,* 1919, pp. 190–203; Thomas G. Wright, *Literary Culture in Early New England 1620–1730* (New Haven, 1920); Eugene E. Prussing, *The Estate of George Washington, Deceased* (Boston, 1927), pp. 140, 418–433; Henry W. Boynton, *Annals of American Bookselling 1638–1850* (New York, 1932), pp. 17, 34–37, 124; William D. Houlette, "Plantation and Parish Libraries in the Old South," *University of Iowa Studies in the Social Sciences,* vol. X, no. 3, *Studies in History* 2 (1934), pp. 85–94; Austin K. Gray, *Benjamin Franklin's Library* (New York, 1937); Louis B. Wright, "The 'Gentleman's Library' in Early Virginia: The Literary Interests of the First Carters," *Huntington Library Quarterly* 1 (1937), pp. 3–61; George K. Smart, "Private Libraries in Colonial Virginia," *American Literature* 10 (1938–39), pp. 24–52 (based on about 100 private libraries; small proportion in classics); Donald G. Wing and Margaret L. Johnson, "The Books Given by Elihu Yale in 1718," *Yale University Library Gazette* 13 (1939), pp. 46–67 (only 14 on classics out of 417 titles); Wright, *The First Gentlemen of Virginia,* pp. 117–154, 197–210, 217–234, 239–248, 333–336; Joseph T. Wheeler, "Books Owned by Marylanders, 1700–1776," *Maryland Historical Magazine* 35 (1940), pp. 337–353; idem, "Reading Interests of the Professional Classes in Colonial Maryland 1700–1776," *Maryland Historical Magazine* 36 (1941), pp. 184–201, 281–301; idem, "Reading and Other Recreations of Marylanders, 1700–1776," *Maryland Historical Magazine* 38 (1943), pp. 37–55, 167–180; library of Robert Carter of Nomini Hall, Virginia, in *Journal & Letters of Philip Vickers Fithian, 1773–1774: A Plantation Tutor of the Old Dominion,* ed. Hunter D. Farish (Williamsburg, 1943), pp. 285–294; Carl L. Cannon, *American Book Collectors and Collecting from Colonial Times to the Present* (New York, 1941), pp. 13–49 (libraries of William Byrd, James Logan, Thomas Jefferson); Stuart C. Sherman, "Leman Thomas Rede's *Biblioteca Americana,*" *Wm. & Mary Quart.,* 3rd ser., 4 (1947), pp. 332–349; E. Millicent Sowerby, *Catalogue of the Library of Thomas Jefferson* (Washington, D.C., 1952–59); Joe Walker Kraus, "Book Collections of Five Colonial Colleges" (Ph.D. diss., University of Illinois, 1960) (Harvard, Yale, William and Mary, Princeton, Brown); Edwin Wolf 2nd, "The Reconstruction of Benjamin Franklin's Library: An Unorthodox Jigsaw Puzzle," *Papers of the Bibliographical Society of America* 56 (1962), pp. 1–16 (contained 4,276 volumes at time of Franklin's death; we need an analysis of titles of this library, called in 1787 "the largest and by far best private library in America"); Richard Beale Davis, *Intellectual Life of Jefferson's Virginia 1790–1830* (Chapel Hill, 1964), pp. 77–118; *The 1764 Catalogue of the Redwood Library Company at Newport, Rhode Island,* ed. Marcus A. McCorison (New Haven, 1965); John M. Jennings, *The Library of the College of William and Mary in Virginia, 1693–1793* (Charlottesville, 1968); Edwin Wolf 2nd, "The Library of Edward Lloyd IV of Wye House," *Winterthur Portfolio* 5 (1969), pp. 87–121; Walter B. Edgar, "Some Popular Books in Colonial South Carolina," *South Carolina Historical Magazine* 72 (1971), pp. 174–178; Edwin Wolf 2nd, "Great American Book Collections to 1800," *Grolier Club Gazette* 16 (1971), pp. 3–70; Norman S. Fiering, "Solomon Stoddard's Library at Harvard in 1664," *Harvard Library Bulletin* 20 (1972), pp. 255–269; Edwin Wolf 2nd, *The Library of James Logan* (Philadelphia, 1974); Joe W. Kraus, "Private

Libraries in Colonial America," *Journal of Library History* 9 (1974), pp. 31–53; William S. Simpson, Jr., "A Comparison of the Libraries of Seven Colonial Virginians, 1754–1789," *Journal of Library History* 9 (1974), pp. 54–65; Reinhold, *The Classick Pages*, pp. 6–8, 13.

129. J. W. Kraus, "Private Libraries," p. 49.

130. Pp. 17, 29, 133–151 (see n. 120, above).

131. Cambridge, Mass., 1954, p. 98.

132. See, e.g., Carl and Jessica Bridenbaugh, *Rebels and Gentlemen: Philadelphia in the Age of Franklin* (New York, 1942), pp. 26–69, 86–102 (excellent survey of evolution of education in Philadelphia; books and libraries with utilitarian interests); Gummere, "Apollo on Locust Street"; George S. Brookes, *Friend Anthony Benezet* (Philadelphia, 1937), pp. 360, 389–391, 492–495 (classics unsuitable for Quakers).

133. William Smith, *A General Idea of the College of Mirania* (New York, 1753); Albert F. Gegenheimer, *William Smith, Educator and Churchman, 1727–1803* (Philadelphia, 1943); Thomas F. Jones, *A Pair of Lawn Sleeves: A Biography of William Smith (1727–1803)* (Philadelphia, 1972). No adequate biography of Charles Nisbet exists. See, e.g., Smylie, "Charles Nisbet: Second Thoughts on a Revolutionary Generation," pp. 198–205; Sellers, *Dickinson College*, pp. 48–49, 54–153.

134. Martha W. Hiden, "Latin in Colonial Virginia," *Classical Weekly* 22 (1927–28), pp. 41–45 (antiquarian); Bruce, *Institutional History of Virginia in the Seventeenth Century*, pp. 316–330, 380–449 (education, William and Mary College, libraries, general culture); Wright, "The Classical Tradition in Colonial Virginia" (see n. 74, above); idem, *The First Gentlemen of Virginia* (see n. 76, above), pp. 95–116 (education, libraries); Mrs. P. W. Hiden, "Education and the Classics in the Life of Colonial Virginia," *Va. Mag. Hist. & Biog.* 49 (1941), pp. 20–28 (superficial); Thomas Jefferson Wertenbaker, *The Old South: The Founding of American Civilization* (New York, 1942), pp. 22–38 (education of Virginia and Maryland gentry); Herbert C. Lipscomb, "Humanistic Culture in Virginia," *Classical Journal* 43 (1947–48), pp. 203–208; Davis, *Intellectual Life*, pp. 34–118 (secondary schools, higher learning, reading interests, libraries).

135. Karl Lehmann's *Thomas Jefferson, American Humanist* (New York, 1947), is in many places impressionistic, speculative, uncritical. It is especially good on the neoclassical architecture of Jefferson (pp. 156–176).

136. The bibliography on Jefferson and the classics is voluminous: William D. Johnston, *History of the Library of Congress*, Vol. I, *1800–1864* (Washington, D.C., 1904), pp. 67–91; Thomas Fitzhugh, "Letters of Thomas Jefferson Concerning Philology and the Classics," *University of Virginia Alumni Bulletin*, 3rd ser., 11 (1918), pp. 168–187, 377–395; 12 (1919), pp. 66–78, 155–157; Fiske Kimball, *Thomas Jefferson, Architect* (Boston, 1916); Chinard, *The Literary Bible of Thomas Jefferson* (151 passages from Greek and Latin authors excerpted as practical rules of morality); Roy J. Honeywell, *The Educational Work of Thomas Jefferson* (Cambridge, Mass., 1931); Chinard, "Thomas Jefferson as a Classical Scholar," *American Scholar*, pp. 133–143; idem, "Thomas Jefferson as a Classical Scholar," *Johns Hopkins Alumni Magazine*; idem, *Thomas Jefferson, The Apostle of Americanism*, 2nd ed. (Boston, 1939, rpt. 1946), pp. 19–26, 33; idem, "Jefferson Among the Philosophers," pp. 255–268; Marie Kimball, *Jefferson: The Road to Glory, 1743 to 1776* (New York, 1943), pp. 84–87, 101–116; Fiske Kimball, "Jefferson and the Arts," *Proc. Amer. Philos. Soc.* 87 (1943–44), pp. 238–245; William Peden, "Thomas Jefferson: Book Collector" (Ph.D. diss., University of Virginia, 1942); Koch, *The Philosophy of Thomas Jefferson*, p. 1; Wright, "Thomas Jefferson and the Classics"; Edward Dumbault, *Thomas Jefferson, American Tourist* (Norman, 1946),

pp. 83–100; Eleanor D. Berman, *Jefferson Among the Arts* (New York, 1948); E. Millicent Sowerby, "Thomas Jefferson and His Library," *Papers of the Bibliographical Society of America* 50 (1956), pp. 203–228; idem, *Catalogue of the Library of Thomas Jefferson*; H. Trevor Colbourn, "Thomas Jefferson's Use of the Past," *Wm. & Mary Quart.*, 3rd ser., 15 (1958), pp. 56–70; *Crusade Against Ignorance: Thomas Jefferson on Education*, ed. Gordon C. Lee, Teachers College, Columbia University, Classics in Education, no. 6 (New York, 1961); Bruno Weil, *2000 Jahre Cicero* (Zurich, 1962), pp. 261–281 (on Jefferson; superficial); Susan Ford [Wiltshire], "Thomas Jefferson and John Adams on the Classics," *Arion* 6 (Spring, 1967), pp. 116–132 (excerpts from the correspondence); Henry C. Montgomery, "Epicurus at Monticello," in *Classical Studies Presented to Ben Edwin Perry*, Illinois Studies in Language and Literature, no. 58 (Urbana, 1969), pp. 80–87 (Jefferson's affinity to Epicurus's individualistic philosophy); Desmond Guinness and Julius T. Sadler, Jr., *Mr. Jefferson, Architect* (New York, 1973). See also in this chapter Douglass Adair, under "American Historians and the Classical Tradition."

137. On John Adams see especially: Gilbert Chinard, *Honest John Adams* (Boston, 1933), pp. 9–16 (on his early education); Gummere, "John Adams, Togatus"; Dorothy M. Robathan, "John Adams and the Classics," *New Engl. Quart.* 19 (1946), pp. 91–98 (descriptive of his knowledge, but little evaluation); Alfred Iacuzzi, *John Adams Scholar* (New York, 1952); Zoltán Haraszati, *John Adams and the Prophets of Progress* (Cambridge, Mass., 1952), pp. 14–25 ("John Adams Among His Books"); Gummere, "The Classical Politics of John Adams"; John R. Howe, Jr., *The Changing Political Thought of John Adams* (Princeton, 1966); John A. Schutz and Douglass Adair, eds., *The Spur of Fame: Dialogues of John Adams and Benjamin Rush, 1805–1813* (San Marino, 1966), esp. pp. 166–179 ("The Dead Languages").

138. Irving N. Rothman, "Two Juvenalian Satires by John Quincy Adams," *Early American Literature* 6 (1971–72), pp. 234–251; Bemis, *John Quincy Adams*, pp. 16, 132; Marie B. Hecht, *John Quincy Adams* (New York, 1972), pp. 20–61, on his education.

139. Still largely unexplored material in the Adams Family Papers, microfilm reels 6, 8, 13, 199, 217, 218, 220, 222, 223, 225, 230, 237, 238, 239, 240, 248.

140. See, e.g., Gummere, *American Colonial Mind*, pp. 125–131; M. Roberta W. Keiter, "Benjamin Franklin as an Educator" (Ph.D. diss., University of Maryland, 1957) (much that is naive and irrelevant); John Hardin Best, *Benjamin Franklin on Education*, Teachers College, Columbia University, Classics in Education, no. 14 (New York, 1962); Thomas Woody, *Educational Views of Benjamin Franklin* (New York, 1931), esp. pp. 58–68, 149–181; John J. O'Neill, "Analysis of Franklin's *Proposals* Relating to the Education of Youth in Pennsylvania as a Selection of Eighteenth Century Cultural Values" (Ph.D. diss., Harvard, 1960).

141. Harry G. Good, *Benjamin Rush and His Services to American Education* (Berne, Ind., 1918); Nathan G. Goodman, *Benjamin Rush, Physician and Citizen 1746–1813* (Philadelphia, 1934), esp. chap. XIV (education), chap. XV (Dickinson College); Lyman H. Butterfield, "Benjamin Rush as a Promoter of Useful Knowledge," *Proc. Amer. Philos. Soc.* 92 (1948), pp. 26–36; James A. Bonar, "Benjamin Rush and the Theory and Practice of Republican Education in Pennsylvania" (Ph.D. diss., Johns Hopkins, 1965); David F. Hawke, *Benjamin Rush, Revolutionary Gadfly* (Indianapolis, 1971), pp. 20, 284–285, 295–296; Donald J. D'Elia, *Benjamin Rush, Philosopher of the American Revolution, Trans. Amer. Philos. Soc.*, vol. LXIV, pt. 5 (Philadelphia, 1974); "The Quest for Useful Knowledge in Eighteenth-Century America," Chapter II, above. When Rush died, William Staughton, in *An Eulogium in Memory of the Late Dr. Benjamin Rush* (Philadelphia, 1813), sought to mitigate his unfriendliness to the classics (pp. 14–15).

142. Frederick B. Tolles, "Quaker Humanist: James Logan as a Classical Scholar," *Pa. Mag. Hist. & Biog.* 79 (1955), pp. 415–438; Edwin Wolf 2nd, "The Romance of James Logan's Books," *Wm. & Mary Quart.*, 3rd ser., 13 (1956), pp. 342–353; idem, "James Logan, Bookman Extraordinary," *Proc. Mass. Hist. Soc.* 79 (1967), pp. 33–46; idem, *The Library of James Logan.*

143. Gerald Stourzh, *Alexander Hamilton and the Idea of Republican Government* (Stanford, 1970), pp. 11–37, 63–70; [Douglass Adair], "A Note on Certain of Hamilton's Pseudonyms," *Wm. & Mary Quart.*, 3rd ser., 12 (1955), pp. 282–297 (four pseudonyms from Plutarch's *Lives* applied by him to different periods of his career); E. P. Panagopoulos, "Hamilton's Notes in His Pay Book of the New York Artillery Company," *American Historical Review* 62 (1956–57), pp. 316–319; *Alexander Hamilton's Pay Book*, ed. E. P. Panagopoulos (Detroit, 1961), pp. 9–21, 46–48.

144. Cp. Reinhold, *The Classick Pages*, pp. 16–18, with full bibliography.

145. Lord Bolingbroke, *Historical Writings*, ed. Isaac Kramnick (Chicago, 1972), particularly his "Letters on the Study and Use of History" (first edition 1752, preceded by a small private printing in 1738), and Kramnick's preface, pp. xvi–xvii; George H. Nadel, "New Light on Bolingbroke's Letters on History," *Journal of the History of Ideas* 23 (1962), pp. 550–557.

146. See, e.g., Colbourn, "Thomas Jefferson's Use of the Past"; Charles F. Mullett, "Ancient Historians and 'Enlightened Reviewers,'" *Review of Politics* 21 (1949), pp. 550–565; H. W. F. Stellwag, "The Psychological Significance of the Conceptions of Antiquity through the Ages," in *Studia Varia Carolo Guilielmo Vollgraff* (Amsterdam, 1938), pp. 139–154; William Gribbin, "Rollin's Histories and American Republicanism," *Wm. & Mary Quart.*, 3rd ser., 29 (1972), pp. 611–622 (Gribbin makes extravagant claims for the extent of Rollin's "influence" on American thought and actions); Peter Gay and V. G. Wexler, *Historians at Work* (New York, 1972), vol. II, pp. 200–224 (on Rollin); Colbourn, *The Lamp of Experience*; James W. Johnson, *The Formation of English Neo-Classical Thought* (Princeton, 1967), pp. 31–106 (role of historiography, importance of Greek and Roman models).

147. William Vans Murray, *Political Sketches* [written 1784–85] (London, 1787), also in *American Museum* 2 (Sept. 1787), pp. 222–235. Cp. Alexander de Conde, "William Vans Murray's *Political Sketches:* A Defence of the American Experiment," *Mississippi Valley Historical Review* 14 (1954–55), pp. 623–640.

148. See further "Opponents of Classical Learning in America during the Revolutionary Period," Chapter IV, above.

149. See, e.g., Gummere, *American Colonial Mind*, pp. 173–190; R. A. Ames and H. C. Montgomery, "The Influence of Rome on the American Constitution," *Classical Journal* 39 (1934), pp. 19–27; E. P. Panagopoulos, "Classicism and the Framers of the Constitution" (Ph.D. diss., Chicago, 1952); Winton U. Solberg, *The Federal Convention and the Formation of the Union of American States* (New York, 1958), pp. xix–xxiii; Henry Steele Commager, "Leadership in Eighteenth Century America and Today" (see n. 101, above); John P. Murphy, "Rome at the Constitutional Convention," *Classical Outlook* 51 (1974), pp. 112–114; Chinard, "Polybius and the American Constitution"; Gummere, "The Classical Ancestry of the United States Constitution" (see n. 51, above); Paul K. Conkin, *Self-Evident Truths* (Bloomington, 1974), pp. 145–149; Raoul S. Naroll, "Clio and the Constitution: The Influence of the Study of History on the Federal Convention of 1787" (Ph.D. diss., University of California, Los Angeles, 1953), pp. 11–12. For the use of analogies and references to ancient history and political experience at the Convention see especially Max Farrand, ed., *The Records of the Federal Convention of 1787*, rev. ed. (New Haven, 1931–37; rpt. 1966); *Notes of Debates in the Federal Convention of 1787*, Reported by James Madison (Athens, Ohio, 1966); Alexander Hamilton, James

Madison, and John Jay, *The Federalist*, ed. Benjamin F. Wright (Cambridge, Mass., 1961); *The Federalist*, ed. Jacob E. Cooke (Middletown, 1961).

150. See, e.g., Edward S. Corwin, *The "Higher Law" Background of American Constitutional Law* (Ithaca, 1955), pp. 149–185, 365–409; Benjamin Fletcher Wright, *American Interpretations of Natural Law* (Cambridge, Mass., 1931), pp. 4–7; Cornelia G. LeBoutillier, *American Democracy and Natural Law* (New York, 1950); Conkin, *Self-Evident Truths*, pp. 75–101.

151. See, Jakob A. O. Larsen's fundamental studies on Greek federal leagues: *Representative Government in Greek and Roman History*, Sather Classical Lectures, no. 28 (Berkeley, 1955); *Greek Federal States* (Oxford, 1968). The only critique of the limited knowledge and the manipulation of Greek leagues by the Founding Fathers appears in Edward A. Freeman, *History of Federal Government in Greece and Italy*, 2nd ed. (London, 1893; 1st ed. 1863), pp. 95–111, 243–245, 249 (the founders of the American Union were not scholars but practical politicians). Freeman deals incisively with some of their misconceptions and distortions regarding Greek leagues.

152. See, e.g., the brilliant study of Douglass Adair on Hamilton's pseudonyms, n. 143, above.

153. See, e.g., George R. Stewart, *Names on the Land: A Historical Account of Place-Naming in the United States*, rev. ed. (Boston, 1958), p. 184; Charles Maar, *New York State Historical Association Quarterly Journal* 7 (1926), pp. 155–167; Fictor S. Paltsits, "The Classic Nomenclature of Western New York," *Magazine of History* 13 (1911), pp. 246–249.

154. *Manductio ad Ministerium. Dissertation for a Candidate of the Ministry* (Boston, 1726), p. 42.

155. In preparation by Meyer Reinhold, "The Reception of Greek and Roman Drama in America from Colonial Times to 1880." On the classical influences on the American poet Philip Freneau (1752–1832)—Horace, Ovid, Lucretius, Vergil, Seneca, Juvenal, etc.—see Ruth Wentworth Brown, "Classical Echoes on the Poetry of Philip Freneau," *Classical Journal* 45 (1949–50), pp. 29–34; Harry Hayden Clark, "The Literary Influences of Philip Freneau," *Studies in Philology* 22 (1925), pp. 1–33.

156. See, e.g., Gordon E. Bigelow, *Rhetoric and American Poetry of the Early National Period*, University of Florida Monographs, Humanities, no. 4 (Gainesville, 1960); Porter G. Perrin, "The Teaching of Rhetoric in American Colleges Before 1750" (Ph.D. diss., Chicago, 1936).

157. [Joseph F.] Père Lafitau, *Moeurs des Sauvages Amériquains* (Paris, 1724); Father Joseph François Lafitau, *The Customs of the American Indians Compared with the Customs of Primitive Times*, ed. and trans. William N. Fenton and Elizabeth L. Moon (Toronto, 1974).

158. *Letters & Papers of John Singleton Copley and Henry Pelham, 1739–1776* (Boston, 1914; rpt. 1970), pp. 65–66.

159. See, e.g., James Thomas Flexner, "George Washington as an Art Collector," *American Art Journal* 4, no. 1 (1972), pp. 24–35; Walter M. Whitehill, *The Arts in Early American History: Needs and Opportunities for Study* (Chapel Hill, 1965); William B. Dinsmoor, "Early American Studies in Mediterranean Archaeology," *Proc. Amer. Philos. Soc.* 87 (1943–44), pp. 70–104; Wendell D. Garrett, "John Adams and the Limited Role of the Fine Arts," *Winterthur Portfolio* 1 (1964), pp. 243–255.

160. See, e.g., B. J. Cigrand, *Story of the Great Seal of the United States, or History of American Emblems* (Chicago, 1903); Gaillard Hunt, *The History of the Great Seal of the United States* (Washington, D. C., 1902); Frank H. Sommer, "Emblem and Device: The Origin of the Great Seal of the United States," *Art Quarterly* 24 (1961), pp. 57–76; Monroe E. Deutsch, "E Pluribus Unum," *Classical Journal* 18 (1922–23), pp. 387–407 (a masterly treatment); H. M. Jones,

Revolution & Romanticism, pp. 215–216; Cornelius Vermeuele, *Numismatic Art in America* (Cambridge, Mass., 1971), pp. 37–59; on the seal and membership certificate of the United States Military Philosophical Society, 1803–13, see Sidney Forman, "The United States Military Philosophical Society, 1802–1813: *Scientia in Bello Pax,*" *Wm. & Mary Quart.*, 3rd ser., 2 (1945), pp. 273–285; N. J. E. Budka, "Minerva versus Archimedes," *Smithsonian Journal of History* 1 (1966), pp. 61–64; James McLachlan, "The *Choice of Hercules*"; Edgar Erskine Hume, ed., *General Washington's Correspondence Concerning the Society of the Cincinnati* (Baltimore, 1941), pp. xii–xv, 2, 5–6; idem, "The Diplomas of the Society of the Cincinnati," *Americana* 29 (1935), pp. 7–47; Winslow Warren, *The Society of the Cincinnati: A History of the General Society of the Cincinnati, with the Institution of the Order* (Boston, 1929), pp. 25–26.

161. Leo M. Kaiser, "Seventeenth Century American Latin Prose: John Leverett's Welcome to Governor Sir Edmund Andros," *Manuscripta* 18 (1974), pp. 30–37; idem, "Oratio Comitialis by Samuel Johnson, King's College," *Classical Outlook* 46 (1969), pp. 113–115; idem, "The Oratio Quinta of Urian Oakes, Harvard 1676," *Humanistica Lovaniensia* 19 (1970), pp. 485–608; idem, "On the Latin in the Meserole Anthology," *Early American Literature* 6 (1971–72), pp. 165–166.

162. Joseph A. Leo Lemay, *A Calendar of American Poetry in the Colonial Newspapers and Magazines and in the Major English Magazines through 1765* (Worcester, 1972) (mostly anonymous and pseudonymous); Joshua Francis Fisher, "Some Account of the Early Poets and Poetry in Pennsylvania," *Memoirs of the Historical Society of Pennsylvania*, vol. II, pt. 2 (1830), pp. 53–103, including "Latin Poetry in America," pp. 78–81. On Thomas Makin's two Latin poems of 1728–29, dedicated to James Logan, *Encomium Philadelphiae*, and *In Laudes Pennsylvaniae Poema, seu Descriptio Pennsylvaniae*, in elegiac couplets, see Robert Proud, *The History of Pennsylvania in North America* (Philadelphia, 1797–98), vol. II, pp. 360–373, with English translation by Proud. The best Latin verse in Pennsylvania was written by John Beveridge. See his *Epistolae Familiares et Aliae Quaedam Miscellanea* (Philadelphia, 1765). He was professor of languages in the College and Academy of Philadelphia.

163. First published as *Our Long Heritage: Pages from the Books Our Founding Fathers Read* (Minneapolis, 1955). The second edition is entitled *Intellectual Origins of American National Thought: Pages from the Books Our Founding Fathers Read* (New York, 1961). Clough's brief treatment of "Why the Prestige of the Classics?" (pp. 284–285) does not correctly reflect the eighteenth-century appeal of the classics. He attributes early Americans' interest in classical authors as due to narrative interest, a remoteness from contemporary passions that encouraged reflection, the raising of profound political questions in manageable size, and a reverence for the glory of the past.

164. See n. 116, above.

165. See "The Quest for Useful Knowledge in Eighteenth-Century America," Chapter II, above.

166. See "Opponents of Classical Learning in America during the Revolutionary Period," Chapter IV, above; A. Owen Aldridge, "Thomas Paine and the Classics"; H. Young, "Theory of American Education in the Revolutionary Period 1743–1809," pp. 159–171; Edwin A. Miles, "The Young Nation and the Classical World," *Journal of the History of Ideas* 35 (1974), pp. 259–274. See also in this chapter under "Clamor for Educational Reform"; Edgar C. Reinke, "A Classical Debate of the Charleston, South Carolina, Library Society," *Papers of the Bibliographical Society of America* 61 (1967), pp. 83–99; Howard Mumford Jones, *The Theory of American Literature*, rev. ed. (Ithaca, 1965), pp. 26–33.

167. See, e.g., Linda K. Kerber, *Federalists in Dissent: Imagery and Ideology in Jeffersonian America* (Ithaca, 1970), pp. 131, 134.
168. See, e.g., Sydney E. Ahlstrom, *A Religious History of the American People* (New Haven, 1972), pp. 280–294; Wesley M. Gewehr, *The Great Awakening in Virginia, 1740–1796* (Durham, 1930; rpt. 1965); Alan Heimert and Perry Miller, eds., *The Great Awakening: Documents Illustrating the Crisis and the Consequences* (Indianapolis, 1967); Stephen Nissenbaum, ed., *The Great Awakening at Yale College* (Belmont, Calif., 1972), pp. 29–31; Edwin Scott Gaustad, *The Great Awakening in New England* (New York, 1957), pp. 137–139; Sibley's *Harvard Graduates* (see n. 122, above), e.g., vol. X, pp. 55, 59, 90, for classes of 1736–40.
169. See Kerber, *Federalists in Dissent*, pp. 95–134 ("Salvaging the Classical Tradition").
170. John Taylor, *An Inquiry into the Principles and Policy of the Government of the United States*, ed. John F. Nichols (New Haven, 1950); also ed. Loren Baritz (Indianpolis, 1969). See also John Adams's exchange with Taylor in *Works of John Adams* (Boston, 1850–56), vol. VI, pp. 433–521.
171. *Revolution & Romanticism* (see n. 93, above), pp. 151–187.
172. "The American Enlightenment and the Ancient World: A Study in Paradox" (see n. 102, above); cp. Michael Kammen, *People of Paradox* (New York, 1972); Arthur P. Dudden, "Nostalgia and the American," *Journal of the History of Ideas* 22 (1961), pp. 515–530; Curti, *American Paradox*, pp. 8–10. Curti stresses the conflict between traditional verbal knowledge and the need for new techniques in the conquest of nature and participation in public affairs.
173. See *Digest of Conference on "Classical Traditions in Early America*," published July 20, 1971, by Center for Coördination of Ancient and Modern Studies, University of Michigan, Ann Arbor.
174. Cp. Meyer Reinhold and John W. Eadie, "Research on the Classical Influences on Early America," *Class. World* 67 (1973), pp. 1–3.
175. *American Literature* 36 (1964–65), pp. 222–223.
176. Carl Becker once wrote: "Generally speaking, men are influenced by books which clarify their own thought, which express their motives well, or which suggest to them lines which their minds are already predisposed to accept." Cited by Colbourn in "Thomas Jefferson's Use of the Past," p. 59.
177. See, e.g., Richard B. Ballou, "The Grammar Schools in Seventeenth Century Colonial America," appendix D, "Educational Background of the Signers of the Declaration of Independence," pp. 388–396; and the character sketches by William Pierce of the delegates to the Constitutional Convention, in Farrand, *Records of the Federal Convention of 1787*, vol. III, pp. 87–97.
178. Morison, *Intellectual Life*, p. 29.
179. E. Young, "Subjects of Master's Degree in Harvard College from 1655 to 1791."
180. See above in this chapter under "Colleges."
181. *History of the United States of America During the Administration of Thomas Jefferson* (New York, 1930), vol. I, pp. 76–77.
182. "On the Means of Education and the State of Learning in the United States of America," *Blackwood's Magazine* 4 (1819), pp. 547, 549, 552, 639, 649. Cp. James McLachlan, *American Boarding Schools: A Historical Study* (New York, 1970), pp. 30–32, 48.
183. Meriwether, *Our Colonial Curriculum*, pp. 283, 285 ("The Food that Made the Giants").
184. Cited by Gummere in "John Wise: A Colonial Controversialist" (see n. 46, above), p. 269.
185. *Writings of Thomas Jefferson*, Memorial Edition (Washington, D.C., 1905), vol. XVI, pp. 118–119.

186. *Revolution & Romanticism* (see n. 93, above), p. 176.
187. Daniel J. Boorstin, *The Lost World of Thomas Jefferson* (New York, 1948), p. 219.
188. David Ramsay, *The History of the American Revolution* (Philadelphia, 1789), pp. ii, 316. On Ramsay see *Dictionary of American Biography*, vol. XV, pp. 338–339.

Afterword:
An Essay on Classics in America since the Yale Report
by George A. Kennedy

If the classics in America had a Golden and a Silver Age, as Meyer Reinhold suggests, and if a cycle of Ages represents the usual workings of the Fates among human affairs, we might expect an ensuing Age of Bronze, of Heroes, and of Iron before the emergence of the archaic phase of a new classic culture. The conceit can certainly be amplified and may not be entirely without utility in establishing a chronological framework for some future historian of the subject. The Bronze Age would be the time from 1828 to the end of the War between the States, during which the palaces of classical education remained largely intact in American colleges, though repeatedly assaulted by the forces of barbarism. The legendary figures of this period include Edward Everett, Charles Anthon, Cornelius Felton, Charles Woolsey, and a handful of others. There follows an Age of Heroes, the founders and lawgivers of the institutions of our classical establishment such as the American Philological Association (1869), the Archaeological Institute of America (1879), the American School of Classical Studies in Athens (1881), the American Academy in Rome (1894), and the graduate programs both in older colleges, as they gradually emerged into true universities, and in new universities created by private philanthropy: Cornell in 1865, the Johns Hopkins in 1876, the Leland Stanford in 1891, Chicago in 1892. This is the Age of Gilder-

325

sleeve and Goodwin, of Seymour and Hale, of their successors such as Shorey and Smyth. The Iron Age was ushered in by the First World War with its ensuing isolationism and depression, with the destruction of Latin requirements in the 1930s and 1940s and a lost generation of classicists. But new folk migrations were under way, especially from Germany, and after the Second World War colonies began to be sent out to create classical programs in a rapidly increasing number of new colleges and universities, establishing some basis for a new Classical Age—if education does not destroy itself in a new war between Athenians and Spartans.

This would perhaps seem an overly optimistic estimate, were it not for the remarkable power of classical studies to adapt to new circumstances and indeed in the process to provide leadership to other disciplines, seemingly less threatened. In the disputes over what kind of education was appropriate for American youth which raged both within academia and in the popular press in the second quarter of the nineteenth century, who would have guessed that classical studies would prove itself adept at adaptation? Would survive and even flourish a hundred and fifty years later? The adaptability of the classics as a discipline and the inherent appeal of the material it presents is the main thesis which emerges from a look at developments since 1828. In gross figures, more students study Greek and Latin now than did in 1830, and a vastly increased number of Americans have had some contact with classical literature read in translation, have seen works of classical art, and have a familiarity with classical mythology. Although the teaching of the classics consumed much more of the total energy of formal education in the nineteenth century than it does today, by almost universal testimony that teaching was superficial, dull, and frustrating. Some would regard it as still superficial today, but few who have experienced it would call it dull, and its future is probably no more endangered than is that of any other liberal study.

The question of the appropriate form of education for American youth, and particularly of the place of the classics in that education, was raised in the eighteenth century by Benjamin Franklin, Benjamin Rush, and others,[1] and in the early nineteenth century occupied Thomas Jefferson in his plans for the University of Virginia, but it broke out with a special acrimony in the 1820s and 1830s.[2] It had political, social, pedagogical, literary, aesthetic, religious, and moral dimensions, which cannot be explored in depth here, though some of them should be briefly noted. The United States was a new country, with new needs, some observers claimed; it was best to give instruction in the mother tongue, not in the dead languages of the Old World, and to concentrate on vocational training. The country needed merchants, bankers, manufacturers, and engineers, as well as clergymen, lawyers, and doctors. Instruction in the classics theoretically cultivated powers of reading, writing, and thinking useful in a full life, but in practice instruction was extremely superficial and little was done to give practical application to skills so painfully inculcated. The old leaders of the Federalist period had been classically trained and valued the study; the new leaders, of whom Andrew Jackson is the great model,[3] were largely self-made men of the frontier or the new business community. They were largely indifferent to the classics and some regarded such study as a positive wrong: elitist, aristocratic, decadent. Values and taste were changing too: a new generation of evangelical Christians was more intent on saving souls than on reading the Bible in Hebrew and Greek, a cornerstone of the curriculum at the old colleges, and they were appalled at paganism, nudity in art, and the immoral stories of school texts like Ovid. The colossal semi-nude statue of George Washington, based at Edward Everett's suggestion on the Zeus of Phidias and commissioned by Congress from Horatio Greenough between 1833 and 1841, was regarded as a scandal when unveiled in the Capitol. "It is not *our* Washington," exclaimed Leonard Jarvis, chairman of the committee.[4] Although the Greek Revival style in architecture flourished until the Civil War, popular taste increasingly swung away from the classic toward the gothic despite its English connections, while Sir Walter Scott, Wordsworth, and later Dickens became the models in literature.

In 1828 a resolution was introduced into the Connecticut Senate asking Yale, which was a quasi-public corporation, to drop the dead languages and introduce something more up-to-date. Yale's response was a celebrated report, largely authored by President Jeremiah Day and Professor James L. Kingsley, which admitted the need for curricular change, of which recent examples at Yale were cited, but strongly defended classical studies as the best basis of collegiate education:

> The study of the classics is useful, not only as it lays the foundations of a correct taste, and furnishes the student with those elementary ideas which are found in the literature of modern times, and which he nowhere so well acquires as in their original sources;—but also as the study itself forms the most effectual discipline of the mental faculties. This is a topic so often insisted on, that little need be said of it here. It must be obvious to the most cursory observer, that

the classics afford materials to exercise talent of every degree, from the first opening of the youthful intellect to the period of its highest maturity. The range of classical study extends from the elements of language, to the most difficult questions arising from literary research and criticism. Every faculty of the mind is employed; not only the memory, judgment, and reasoning powers, but the taste and fancy are occupied and improved.[5]

Historians of American education often treat the Yale Report as a swan song, already obsolete when it was written,[6] and it is true that it was denounced by many and that there then followed a development of new educational formats, such as the polytechnical and scientific schools, but it was also defended and imitated in new liberal arts colleges such as Western Reserve, Wabash, Illinois, and California.[7] The weakness of its argument lay not so much in theory, but in practice. In most parts of the country secondary education was exceedingly weak and students came to college ill prepared. There they were drilled in Greek and Latin grammar, often by tutors only slightly older than themselves. Little was done to give meaning to what they studied, and had it not been for the extracurricular debating societies and for the traditional senior course in moral philosophy, often given as lectures by the president of a college, their formal education would have been exceedingly empty of content. Edward Everett was criticized by the Harvard Overseers for his lectures on Greek literature, and at Princeton Evert M. Topping was forced off the faculty in 1846 for the crime of trying to interest students in the study of the Greek language by introducing occasional remarks on Greek literature.[8]

Two famous works reflect with some independence of judgment on the American educational scene of the 1830s. One is Alexis de Tocqueville's *Democracy in America*, the result of his travels here in 1831. De Tocqueville devotes a chapter to the question of why the study of Greek and Latin literature is peculiarly useful in democratic societies. He views classical literature as essentially aristocratic and belletristic. Nothing else, he claims, "puts in bolder relief just those qualities democratic writers tend to lack, and therefore no other literature is better to be studied at such times. . . . Greek and Latin should not be taught in all the schools. But it is important that those who are destined by nature or fate to adopt a literary career or to cultivate taste should be able to find schools where the classics are well taught and true scholars formed. A few excellent universities are a better means to this end than a multitude of bad schools in which the classics are an ill-taught extra, standing in the way of sound instruction in necessary studies."[9] Although de Tocqueville had no direct influence on the course of events in American education, his views were to a considerable extent prophetic of efforts during the next century and his argument remains tenable. The authors of the Yale Report had thought the development of an American literature to be taken seriously in Europe required a classical basis.[10] This was most evident in England, where American writers were largely ignored until the twentieth century. Their eventual acceptance owes much to two expatriates: the non-classical Henry James and the strongly classical T. S. Eliot.

Another celebrated document of the period under discussion is Ralph Waldo Emerson's Phi Beta Kappa address at Harvard in 1837, "The American Scholar." In high seriousness Emerson sought to describe a new kind of scholar who could be characteristically American. This scholar should know the world of nature and the history of the past, but he should engage in action and have deep self-trust in his inner life. Emerson is critical of a withdrawal into an isolated study of the classics; critical of a reliance on foreign influence: "We have listened too long to the courtly muses of Europe"; critical of the traditional scholar: "decent, indolent, complaisant."

> Not so, brothers and friends,—please God, ours shall not be so. We will walk on our own feet; we will work with our own hands; we will speak our own minds. Then shall man be no longer a name for pity, for doubt, and for sensual indulgence. The dread of man and the love of man shall be a well of defense and a wreath of love around all. A nation of men will for the first time exist, because each believes himself inspired by the Divine Soul which also inspired all men.[11]

The view of Walt Whitman was somewhat similar:

> Dead poets, philosophs, priests,
> Martyrs, artists, inventors, governments long since,
> Language-shapers on other shores,
> Nations once powerful, now reduced, withdrawn or desolate,
> I dare not proceed till I respectfully credit what you have
>   left wafted hither.
> I have perused it, own it is admirable, (moving awhile among it,)
> Think nothing can ever be greater,
> Nothing can ever deserve more than it deserves,
> Regarding it all intently a long while, then dismissing it,
> I stand in my place with my own day here.[12]

Emerson and his fellow New England writers—Thoreau, Longfellow, Lowell, Melville—found much that was useful in the classics.[13] A few American classicists have played a role in the affairs of the world, as Emerson desired of the scholar: Edward Everett certainly; George Bancroft, Eben Alexander, Edward Capps, Robert Goheen as ministers or ambassadors. One young graduate of Williams College started his career as a Latin teacher in Ohio and became president of the United States. This was James A. Garfield, who taught in 1858 at the Eclectic Institute which later developed into Hiram College. The main importance of Emerson's appeal, in so far as it relates to classical studies, is that effort, already underway in his time, to seek to increase its depth, its understanding, and its relevance.

The early figures in that effort were those ambitious few who graduated from American colleges and as early as 1815 went off to Germany, the only place in the world where advanced studies were available. There they discovered scientific scholarship based on a philosophy of knowledge, exacting methods, and the creative interrelationships of literature, archaeology, history, and philosophy; research libraries, academic freedom, and the company of serious students committed to scholarly pursuits, none of which existed in the United States. Meyer Reinhold has described the experiences of Edward Everett (1794–1865) and his frustrations on return to the United States.[14] Those of George Ticknor (1791–1865) were similar. The times were simply not ripe to introduce German education into a land without good libraries, with no vehicles of scholarly communication, and with no tradition of research. Although Ticknor's main field became Spanish literature, he studied classical philology in Germany and it was in classical studies that Americans had their first experience of the possibilities of advanced humanistic research.

The efforts to improve college instruction in Greek and Latin probably owe as much to some of the stay-at-homes like Cornelius Felton (1807–62) at Harvard and Charles Anthon (1797–1867) at Columbia, both of whom learned German thoroughly, drew on German scholarship, and produced useful editions of school texts.[15] Anthon, though often belittled even in his own time especially by New Englanders, made a major contribution to the teaching of classics in America through a series of school editions of Greek and Latin authors, and his *Classical Dictionary* retained a convenient utility until the publication of the *Oxford Classical Dictionary* in 1949. Major needs, in addition to texts, were lexica and reference grammars. The most significant single advance was probably *Harper's Latin Dictionary* (1879) by Charlton T. Lewis and Charles Short.[16] Efforts to produce grammars began early in the century with Edward Everett's translation of Buttmann's *Greek Grammar*, but really satisfactory results were not achieved until the work of W. W. Goodwin on *Moods and Tenses* (1859) and the Latin grammars of Harkness (1864), Gildersleeve (1867), and Allen and Greenough (1872).

Although Charles Anthon had attempted one serious work of scholarship in his vast edition of Horace of 1830, it was little appreciated at the time and it was not until the formation of graduate schools and the creation of the American Ph.D. that original scholarship could flourish. Plans for advanced studies in America began as early as 1830 when a "Literary Convention" was held at Yale, but the first American-earned Ph.D. was apparently not awarded until 1861. It was in classics, and the Yale recipient was James Morris Whiton, who submitted a thesis on the topic *Ars longa, brevis vita*. Like a number of other early recipients of the doctorate, Whiton did not spend his life in a university; he joined the editorial staff of the *Outlook* and survived until 1920. The first American woman to earn a Ph.D. also studied the classics. She was Helen Magill, a graduate of Swarthmore, where her father was the second president, and recipient of the Ph.D. in Greek from Boston University in 1877 with a dissertation on Greek drama. She then spent three years at Cambridge University, where she earned third-class honors in the classical tripos, directed the Howard Collegiate Institute for Women in Massachusetts, and taught briefly at Evelyn College, which was organized as a woman's counterpart to Princeton. In 1890 she married Andrew Dickson White, former president of Cornell, and accompanied him to Russia and Germany, where he served as ambassador.[17]

Respect for classical studies retained some popular support in the mid-nineteenth century. A curiosity is *A Life of George Washington in Latin Prose*, the fulfillment of a lifetime hope by Francis Glass, a teacher in a log-cabin school in Ohio, who envisioned it as providing a counterpart to Caesar's *Commentaries* with an American theme. It was published by the respected firm of Harper and Brothers in New York in 1835, accompanied by testimonials to its Latinity and utility by Charles Anthon, John Quincy Adams, and others, but seems not to have been much used.[18] More important for the dissemination of the classics was the provision of the Morrell Act of 1869, which first established the system of land grant colleges, calling for instruction not only in agricultural and technical subjects but in classics. The provision was differently interpreted in different states, but it can be said to have laid the basis for the strength of the classics departments in many state universities, especially in the Midwest. In the twentieth century there have been recurring needs to see that federal legislation on education or the recommendations of national commissions include, or at least do not specifically exclude, classical studies.

Although the Renaissance rediscovered Greek, the major influence on renaissance art, literature, and political theory was Roman. A new awareness of the Greeks emerged in Europe in the eighteenth century, but it is to the Romans that the American Founding Fathers owed their greatest debt. Few of them could abide Plato. Interest in the Greeks steadily increased in the nineteenth century, spurred on by the Greek War of Independence and the greater intellectual and spiritual contents of Greek literature.[19] This was most perceived in Germany, but the English romantic poets show a marked inclination to Hellenism, coupled with a rejection of eighteenth-century ideas of the classic. The recognition of the Greek tragedians as among the greatest authors of all time is largely a phenomenon of the nineteenth century. It is tempting to think that popular recognition of the greatness of tragedy had something to do with the moral dilemmas of the nineteenth century—in America with the experience of the Civil War. Henry Adams, who thought that his Harvard education in the 1850s left his mind empty, made an exception of "two or three Greek plays."[20]

Both in Europe and America the new interest in Greek drama led in the 1880s to experiments in producing them on stage in the original language. There was a lively academic interest in the correct pronunciation of Greek about the same time, which may have been a contributing factor. The great American production was that of the *Oedipus Tyrannus* of Sophocles at Harvard in May, 1881. It was apparently the social event of the season; special trains brought the curious from hundreds of miles away and scalpers had no difficulty selling tickets for as much as fifteen dollars. An English translation was furnished each member of the audience, which over several days totalled about six thousand persons, and according to contemporary accounts they sat spellbound at the overwhelming dramatic power of the play and at the end withdrew in a hushed and reverent silence.[21]

Paradoxically, it was at this time of increased interest in Greek literature that the debate over the place of Greek in the curriculum of schools and colleges reached its acrimonious height, climaxed by abolition of Greek requirements at Harvard College in 1886. Harvard was not in fact the first to abolish the requirement of Greek for admission and in the underclass years,[22] but it was the oldest and most famous American college and what Harvard did and does has always had considerable impact on education elsewhere. Most of the traditional colleges, including Yale, followed her lead in the course of the next ten years, though a few, like the University of Vermont, clung to a Greek requirement well into the twentieth century. Secondary school Greek, especially in public schools, was largely a byproduct of college requirements, and it rapidly faded when they were altered.

A fascinating document in the debate over Greek is the 1883 Phi Beta Kappa address of Charles Francis Adams, Jr., "A College Fetich," which focuses on two arguments: the need for studies other than Greek in the society of the nineteenth century and the lack of permanent results to be seen in the hours of study given to the subject by students.[23] Adams claims that his grandfather, John Quincy Adams, was essentially a hypocrite in his many references to reading the classics in the original, and that of all who had studied Greek at Harvard College in his own lifetime, hardly any could read the language. The efforts of a generation of teachers at Harvard and elsewhere to deepen understanding of Greek, to enrich students' lives with the classics, and to produce new and more interesting texts and more useful reference aids are simply ignored. Stranger, perhaps, Adams and his brother Henry both seem totally oblivious to what in historical perspective was the real benefit of their Harvard studies, their ability with words. The writers of the Yale Report, if any were still alive, could have pointed with pride to the Adams brothers as the very kind of product they sought from a classical education—individuals with a discipline of mind to think clearly, write vigorous and succinct prose, and apply these basic skills to public problems, social issues, historical and literary research, or any of the many areas of activity in which their lives fell, but which could not easily be predicted when they were school boys.

Greek was a victim of the sense of progress of the nineteenth century, which demanded not only a place for new subjects in the curriculum but a sharp symbolic break with the past. The requirement went at the same time that the free elective system was being developed at Harvard under the presidency of Charles William Eliot. This opened the possibility of a greater degree of specialization, which was currently being sought in graduate education—thus effectively abandoning the educational ideals of the Renaissance and the Enlightenment—and it implied a greater trust in the maturity of students to judge their own strengths and needs and thus to plan their education. In the humanities this opened the door to a new subjectivity. The basis of a curriculum was to become not what tradition, society, or teachers thought should be taught but what students wanted to learn. It is both the glory and the cross of Greek that it is hard and that the student must, at least in the initial stages, wrestle with memorizing the correct forms and usage of the language and with what Greek writers actually say, rather than trust a direct romantic response, as can be done, at least superficially, with an English poem or a work of art. Until sometime in the nineteenth century what an individual student thought about literature, philosophy, or art was of no interest to his teacher, and was almost certainly wrong. When the essay topic "What I Did on My Summer Vacation" was first assigned by some teacher is not recorded, but that theme was totally foreign to the teaching of composition or anything else until quite modern times. It results partly from the theory of John Dewey that education must be based on experience, but reflects a pessimism on the part of the teacher in interesting the student in serious ideas and a view of literary composition derived from the Romantics. It is no accident that the teaching of rhetorical theory collapsed about the same time that Greek and Latin began to lose their privileged place in education. Rhetoric became elocution and belles lettres, and the results were similar: generations of students with no grasp of the structure of discourse and with few resources for expressing those personal thoughts and impressions which they were encouraged to believe uniquely mattered.

Scientific philology gained ground in the graduate schools, but the popular classicism of the second half of the nineteenth century was a romantic classicism, well seen in two important novels. The earlier (1859) is *The Marble Faun,* by Nathaniel Hawthorne, in which the city of Rome, as Hawthorne had recently reacted to a visit there, is made the setting for the conflict of virtue and vice, innocence and sin, Puritanism and Catholicism. Rome is a symbol of the decadence and decay of history; the civic and moral virtues of the ancient Romans which had impressed the eighteenth century are forgotten. Out of the crumbling ancient past—the catacombs, the Colisseum by moonlight, the Capitol and the Pantheon—one active force which emerges is pagan naturalism, sensuality, and joy in life as experienced by the Faun, but he is doomed to destruction.

The immense popularity of *Ben Hur* by General Lew Wallace (1880) was due, of course, to the role in it of Jesus, but it too is set in a vividly described classical world, and its readers thrilled to accounts of a Roman naval battle and above all to the chariot race in Antioch. Wallace had little formal education and at the time no first-hand knowledge of the locations he describes, but he was well read, had an eye for detail, and engaged in extensive research in historical and geographical sources.[24] (Some of the book was written while he was serving as territorial governor of New Mexico and engaged in pursuit of Billy the Kid.) Rome, as portrayed in the novel, is a great commercial republic like America, recently emerged from civil war. Much of the thought centers around the question of whether the new dispensation brought by God is to be a political one with Christ as a worldly king, as the hero long believes, or a spiritual one, as he eventually realizes. This theme had significance for Americans in the second half of the nineteenth century. The picture of Rome is in many ways one of admiration for its successes, and good Romans are to be found, though the society of the capital and its rhetorical schools are criticized as inculcating arrogance and blamed for the conversion of Messala from Ben Hur's affectionate boyhood friend to his bitterest enemy. There may be a note of criticism here of elitist American education and society, a world in which the Hoosier Wallace never found the acceptance he desired.

Admiration for Roman imperialism was shared by others in the age of American imperialism. Although it rarely appears in literature, it is a strong influence in architecture, blossoming in the beaux arts buildings of the World's Columbian Exposition at Chicago in 1893 and continuing well into the twentieth century in the building of state capitols, court houses and other government buildings, art museums, libraries, and railroad stations. Its greatest achievement was probably Pennsylvania Station in New York by McKim, Mead & White, completed in 1910 on the model of the Baths of Caracalla. The destruction of that great edifice (over many objections) about 1960 resulted from the collapse of the imperial railroad it served, but the particular form which reconstruction took in the present station is equally a rejection of the values of Roman and American imperialism.

The main activity of American classical scholars in the late nineteenth century was in the direction of advanced study, of serious and original research which would provide the humanities with new knowledge as a counterpart to that being gained in the sciences and which could, if well applied, enrich the teaching of Greek and

Latin at all levels. In retrospect, the classicists could be thought to have felt the criticism, equally addressed to rhetoric, that the discipline had a method, but no content, and to have set out to discover and teach content in literature, philosophy, and archaeology, as well as to refine the methods of philology. The nineteenth century wanted facts, and facts were found.

Although teachers at Harvard, Yale, Cornell, Chicago, California, and other colleges and universities played some role in this process, its legendary and seminal leader was the Olympian figure of Basil Lanneau Gildersleeve (1831–1922). A number of publications treat aspects of his career, and there will perhaps eventually be a full-scale biography. Here it seems chiefly important to point out certain movements of which he was a part and certain ideas or values which he held. He was, first, a Southerner, born in Charleston, South Carolina, in the period when Hugh Swinton Legaré and others were seeking to make it an American Athens or Rome.[25] For twenty years Gildersleeve served as a professor at the University of Virginia, and he was a summertime officer in the Confederate Army. He became a spokesman for southern culture, in which he saw a pervasive classicism which was the source of many of its best features and which was both wider and deeper than that of the North.[26] Secondly, he was among those who had the benefits of graduate education in Germany, receiving a Ph.D. from Göttingen in 1853. This was the generation after the pioneers, and he reached his prime in those decades in which American philanthropy was making possible true universities and libraries.As the first professor appointed at the Johns Hopkins University in 1876, the first new American university created on the German model, he was in a unique position to create a school of advanced studies, and he did so, directing the dissertations of many of the teachers and scholars of the next generations. It was in this connection that he founded the *American Journal of Philology* in 1880 as an outlet for the scholarship of Americans, as a vehicle of communication among them, and in its reviews of monographs, texts, and journals as a link with European scholarship. Thirdly, he was at heart a grammarian, but a grammarian with a special interest in syntax, which he regarded as the basis of the study of style and thus of the expression of ideas. All knowledge was for him a unity in which the smallest fact had its place in a connecting network, and he was equally devoted to understanding the woods and the trees. It is perhaps in this that he most surpassed the other American scholars of his time, in this and in his ability to outlive and outwork them. He thought of his discipline as philology, as his German teachers had conceived it, and it extended beyond Greek and Latin to Sanskrit, to the Germanic and Romance languages, and to English, in which he was a master of expression. Even before going to Hopkins he participated with others in the formation of the American Philological Association, which was the first (1869) American learned society with a disciplinary base and which eventually divided and subdivided and regrouped to create other disciplinary organizations such as the Modern Language Association, the American Historical Society, and the Linguistic Society of America.[27] Every American classicist should read Gildersleeve's first presidential address to the APA in 1870, "University Work in America and Classical Philology," in which he outlines the possibilities as he saw them,[28] as well as Paul Shorey's address at the fiftieth anniversary of the Association in which he compares Gildersleeve, "our leader," favorably to representatives of German and British scholarship, who are taken to be Wilamowitz and Jebb.[29]

The place of classical studies in American education in the early twentieth century was superficially secure. The development of graduate departments continued, and American scholarship began to be taken seriously in Europe. New professional associations were formed and new journals published: the *Classical Journal*, sponsored by the Classical Association of the Middle West and South dates from 1905; the *Classical Weekly* (later the *Classical World*) began appearing in 1907 under the auspices of the Classical Association of the Middle States and Maryland. Latin was required for admission to practically every traditional liberal arts college or university and widely required for the bachelor of arts degree, though there was now a Latin-less bachelor of science. Largely because of the college requirements, Latin was strong in secondary schools. In 1900 it was taken by nearly half of all students in high schools and was second only to algebra in school enrollments. But there were signs of trouble and the journals show an uneasiness, even a defensiveness. By 1910 Latin fell to fifth place, after English literature, composition, history, and algebra in that order, though still ahead of any other foreign language, of which the most popular was German.[30] The feeling that education should be more vocational continued to be strong and the demands of new subjects for a place in the curriculum continued. This was especially true in the new social sciences; they claimed not only a scientific method but a practical application in students' understanding of the world in which they lived. Many of the new disciplines made a contribution to classical

research—economics, for example, in the work of Tenney Frank—
but they threatened the teaching of Latin.

Still more threatening was the new philosophy of education, built
on pragmatism and behaviorism. The arch-priest of this movement
was, of course, John Dewey (1859–1952), who taught at the University of Chicago from 1894 to 1904 and later at Teachers College of
Columbia University. Dewey had studied Greek and Latin at the
University of Vermont and his published criticisms of Latin are not
very pointed. What he generally objected to was the method by
which all foreign languages were being taught. Latin was included
in a new, more direct method in the curriculum of his early Laboratory School at the University of Chicago.[31] Dewey did not believe
that the basis of education should be discipline, memory, and structure, and more ominous for the classics he did not believe that its
goal was the handing on of a tradition. Nor did he believe in
"truth," for which he substituted something called "instrumental-
ism," a process of adjustment between an organism and its environment, for example a student and society. Dewey's philosophy,
and the research of the new psychology and sociology, spawned the
Progressive Education Movement, which held serious threats to
both old methods and old contents. Attacks on and defenses of the
claims of Latinists to produce disciplined minds were published,[32]
and in 1916 and 1917 a full-scale battle resulted.

The principals in the battle were two remarkable individuals,
Abraham Flexner and Andrew Fleming West. Flexner (1866–1959)
is best known for his influence on medical education in the United
States, resulting from a report he wrote for the Carnegie Foundation for Advancement of Teaching in 1910, and for his work as the
first director of the Institute for Advanced Study in Princeton
(1930–39), but his career involved the classics in three different
ways. He graduated from Hopkins in 1883 with a major in Greek
under Gildersleeve, taught Greek at Boys High in Louisville, and in
1890 opened a small private preparatory school in which he en-
riched the classical curriculum and prepared his students for college
a year earlier than was traditionally the case, attracting the favorable attention of Charles William Eliot. After his successful work
for the Carnegie Foundation he became an officer of the prestigious
General Education Board, a Rockefeller philanthropy, and it was in
that capacity that he precipitated the crisis over the place of Latin
in the curriculum in 1916 and 1917. His third involvement with the
classics came with his sponsorship of historical studies at the Institute, to be discussed shortly.

Flexner's autobiography, *I Remember*, was published by Simon and Schuster in 1940 and brought up to date at the very end of his life in a second edition. It describes, among much else of interest, the proposal for a Modern School which developed out of a meeting in 1915 among John D. Rockefeller, Charles William Eliot, Flexner, and a few others and which resulted in the sponsorship by the General Education Board of an experimental school which became the Lincoln School at Columbia Teachers College. In the fall of 1916 the General Education Board published a pamphlet entitled *A Modern School* written by Flexner and outlining the goals and methods he recommended. The proposed curriculum omitted both Greek and Latin,

> not, of course, because their literatures are less important than they are reputed to be, but because their present position in the curriculum rests upon tradition and assumption. For most pupils a positive case can be made out for neither. The literary argument fails, because stumbling and blundering through a few patches of Latin classics do not establish a contact with Latin literature. Nor does present-day teaching result in a practical mastery of Latin useful for other purposes. . . . Nor can the study be generally recommended on the ground that a knowledge of Latin is essential in securing a vigorous or graceful use of the mother tongue, for this is again unsubstantiated opinion. . . . Finally, the disciplinary argument fails, because mental discipline is not a real purpose; moreover, it would for many students constitute an argument against rather than for the study of Latin. Instead of getting orderly training by solving difficulties in Latin composition, these pupils guess, fumble, receive surreptitious assistance or accept on faith the injunctions of teacher and grammar. The only discipline that such students get from their classical studies is a discipline in doing things as they should not be done.[33]

This statement, and what follows in the pamphlet, produced a storm of protest. The *New York Times* denounced it in an editorial of January 21, 1917. Gilbert Murray, when introduced to Flexner, asked, "Are you the good Flexner or the bad?"[34] The good Flexner was Abraham's brother Simon, director of the Rockefeller Institute for Medical Research. Despite the opposition and despite the entrance of the United States into the World War in the spring, plans for a Modern School went forward. It was widely believed that the new curriculum was intended as a model for the country and would be imposed by the powerful influence of the General Education Board. Flexner denied this, but sometimes found the opposition trying. It is rumored that he once exclaimed, "I'm not trying to kill Latin; it's already dead. I'm only trying to bury it."

As leader of the opposition emerged the formidible figure of Andrew Fleming West (1853–1943). West too had been a teacher of classics in a private school and he too had attracted the attention of a college president, James McCosh of Princeton. Even though West had no formal graduate study and only an honorary doctorate, McCosh made him Geiger Professor of Latin at the age of thirty. He was never a distinguished scholar, but he had a magisterial presence and a knack of impressing the influential and wealthy. In 1901 he became the first dean of the Princeton Graduate School, which he set out to give the form of an Oxbridge college in a setting apart from the rest of the university. It was opposition to West's plans that led Woodrow Wilson to resign the presidency of Princeton and ultimately to seek the presidency of the United States. Fresh from his victory in the Graduate School, West readily took on the cause of Latin. He was in his way the William Jennings Bryan of the classics, for under his direction the fight took on some of the substance, though not the homey style, of the quarrel between religion and science which eventuated in the "Monkey Trial" between Bryan and Clarence Darrow in 1922.

In June of 1917 West convened at Princeton a Conference on Classical Studies in Liberal Education, opening it with a declaration of a "new seriousness":

> An awakening of what had seemed dormant interest in the value of different studies has happened this year. It is one of many effects of an underlying cause. The entrance of America into the world war with all its excitement, has made us more thoughtful. It has raised the imperative question: Why are we fighting? . . . We need the higher powers of the human soul: not skill and courage alone, but that guiding wisdom which is more than thought and which springs from undying faith in truth and freedom.[35]

The rhetoric is transparent: a universal outcry against the Modern School is assumed; the declaration of war is capitalized on; Latin is identified with country, truth, and discipline. Dewey and his followers rejected the last two, and it was widely known that Dewey had reservations about the war.

West mustered powerful allies to his cause. Other speakers at the Conference included Roscoe Pound, dean of the Harvard Law School, Henry Cabot Lodge, U.S. senator from Massachusetts who later thwarted U.S. entry into the League of Nations, the president of the American Medical Association, and an impressive collection of scientific, academic, and business leaders of a conservative stance, who one and all praised the classics as what America was fighting for. A supporting letter from Nicholas Murray Butler, a spy in the enemy camp at Columbia, was read by Professor F. F. Abbott, best known for his edition of *Selected Letters of Cicero*, still in common use. Later that year the Princeton University Press published a volume entitled *Value of the Classics* which contains the addresses given, statistical information to demonstrate the strength of the classics in American schools, and 222 pages of supporting "statements" from national leaders collected by West and in unanimous support of the classics. All living ex-presidents of the United States contributed letters. The statement of the incumbent president, Woodrow Wilson, is given first place, but unlike the others consists of two quotations from earlier writings. Wilson was no friend to West and he doubtless had pressing things on his mind in the summer of 1917.

To one unaware of the circumstances *Value of the Classics* reads like a spontaneous celebration of classical studies in American life. Flexner is not mentioned in any of the Addresses or Statements, but the statistical analysis at the end attempts to refute his arraignment of the teaching and study in Latin. The new psychology is treated with scorn, but without identifying any of its leaders.[36] After the war the General Education Board was persuaded to redress its earlier unpatriotic actions by funding an extensive study of the status of Latin in the schools, conducted by the American Classical League, which came into being as a result of the crisis. West served on the advisory board for the study and the results were published in 1924, again by the Princeton University Press, under the title *The Classical Investigation*. It is a thoughtful piece of research in reasonable tones with extensive documentation and practical recommendations to the end that students may learn actually to read Latin and not study the subject simply as a discipline of the mind. Latin in the schools did not decline because it had no public defenders; few professions have ever made so mammoth an effort to plead their case and to accompany their defense with reform from within.

The number of Americans who went to high school increased dramatically in the twentieth century; their backgrounds and goals were increasingly diversified, and it became a major challenge for the schools to find teachers who could cope effectively with instructing them in Latin. The Latin requirements were artificially supported by college requirements, and the 1920s saw an increasing attack on these. The symbolic capitulation came at Yale, analogous to the abolition of the Greek requirement at Harvard. Yale had kept Greek for a few years after Harvard let it go, and Harvard kept Latin longer than many other schools. William Howard Taft, a powerful member of the Yale Corporation, declared that Yale would abolish the Latin requirement only over his dead body. He died in 1930 and the requirement died in 1931.[37]

The experience of the 1920s seems to suggest that despite considerable efforts on the part of teachers to improve results and experiment with new methods, Latin could not continue as the foundation of education at the high school and college levels under the conditions of twentieth-century society. It can, of course, be well taught to those attracted to it for a variety of reasons and students can benefit from any well-taught, serious subject. The rejection of the disciplinary theory of education went too far, and the concepts embodied in Flexner's Modern School, admirable in many ways for their concern with the development of students' intellectual, spiritual, and physical potential, have also failed in practice to achieve their objectives as a universal theory of public education. Late twentieth-century high school students graduate knowing little about themselves or any other subject, unaccustomed to memorization or structural patterns, with no experience of any challenging subject, not even mathematics, whose methods Flexner also called into question, sometimes unable to read or write a reasoned paragraph. If an ability to memorize, a sense of structure and of words, and a basis for disciplined study can be laid at all under existing conditions in the American home and society, it probably has to be laid at an even earlier level of education.

The identification of classical and American values expressed at the Princeton Conference of 1917 had some afterlife in the isolationism which followed the war and in the competition for students by the various language groups which followed World War II. The First War almost totally destroyed German as a secondary school subject; it also produced a peculiar attempt at anti-German propaganda in the War Issues course which was intended to teach college students the fallacies of German culture. This was perhaps the first attempt at interdisciplinary cooperation by professors in several fields, and though given only once during the fall of 1918, during which the war ended, it became the ancestor of Western Civilization courses at Columbia and elsewhere. With German gone, and with an emphasis on contemporary life, the rivals of Latin became first French, then Spanish. Many American students clearly preferred "none of the above." Latin could be claimed to have an advantage over the modern languages in terms of its contribution to English, and this was, of course, stressed and has led to effective elementary Latin programs in Philadelphia, Los Angeles, and elsewhere and also to college courses in Greek and Latin roots, etymology, and word power—another example of the classicists' instinct to land on their feet and to try to draw on the richness of their subject for the needs of students.

But the claim had consistently been made that there was a peculiar tie between the ancient world and modern America, and especially between Rome and America, two democratic republics under law, untouched by the dangerous moral decay of the French, the Spanish, and their ilk. In 1914 the Italian historian Guglielmo Ferrero published a curious work in English entitled *Ancient Rome and Modern America* in which he argued that Europeans could not really understand the Romans unless they had experience of New World society and particularly of the place of private philanthropy in it. The classical journals of the 1930s and 1940s again show considerable attention to forming the link between America and Rome, over-arching the history of the intervening centuries, and this found an interesting expression in what was for long the most popular beginning Latin book, *Latin for Americans,* by B. L. Ullman and Norman E. Henry, in which text and pictures sought to establish the identification of the lives of young Americans with their Roman predecessors. Behind this doubtless stood some intent to rebut the charge that the classics were aristocratic and elitist.

The collapse of the Latin requirements was eventually followed in the 1960s by a more general collapse of any foreign language requirements. The impulse this time came not from philosophers of education but from student resistance to studying subjects which were difficult, required memory, and seemed remote from immediate experience. Repeated efforts were made to resist this movement by persons concerned with America's place in the world's economy and politics, or with the survival of ethnic traditions, or with some vestige of discipline in secondary education, or with a decline in College Board verbal scores which continued for seventeen years, or with the security of the profession of language teachers. An unfortunate complicating factor has been the competition among partisans of various languages. In 1978 the author of this essay rashly agreed to chair a Task Force on the Commonly Taught Languages, sponsored by the Modern Language Association with funds from the National Endowment for the Humanities, and advanced what was intended as a rational scheme, but was greeted as a Swiftian "modest proposal." The basic idea was that an awareness of language usage and some basis for its disciplined control, to be effective at all, had to be introduced at a very early stage in education. Because Latin seemed a useful background for the later study of any other language (and the objection was often advanced that students might waste time studying one language when they would ultimately need another) and because it was culturally neutral without specific associations with contemporary ethnic groups, it was proposed that we should work toward national guidelines under which Latin would be taught in elementary schools as an introduction to language arts. Building on the experience in Philadelphia and elsewhere the emphasis would be on etymology, the relationship of Latin to English and other languages, an elementary sense of the structure of all language, and perhaps some attention to America's debt to classical culture. This would then be followed by the teaching of a modern language in junior high school where the emphasis would be conversational as appropriate to the emerging social consciousness of young people in that age group. The specific language to be taught would be chosen locally on the basis of the language which would have most utility in the community. For many Americans that would be Spanish, but for some Italian, Polish, German, Chinese, Japanese, or another language. In areas where a student was unlikely to encounter speakers of any foreign language it might as well be Latin. Then in senior high school we should encourage the offering of courses emphasizing the literature of a foreign language, primarily intended for college-bound students, but open to all. Some German teachers proved sympathetic to the proposal; they had little to lose. The opposition from Spanish and especially French teachers was fantastic. The incoming president of the MLA denounced the proposal as an attempt to undermine the entire appreciation of French culture in the United States and as destructive of any hope an American might have of a good French accent. The proposal died stillborn, but it still seems rational.

The collapse of the Greek requirements coincided with the first development of advanced research in classics in America. The collapse of other language requirements coincided with the development of post-doctoral research. Private philanthropy again led the way. The John Simon Guggenheim Memorial Foundation was established in 1925 "to further the development of scholars and artists by assisting them to engage in research . . . under the freest possible conditions." Many classical scholars have benefited from these awards. Subsequently opportunities for research were supported by other foundations, by the American Council of Learned Societies (formed in 1919), and finally by the federal government through the Fulbright Act (1946) and later legislation and the founding of the National Endowment for the Humanities (1965).

Equally important, and equally characteristic of the mid-twentieth century, was the foundation of independent centers of research. It is here that Abraham Flexner reappears in the history of classical studies in America to make his greatest contribution. In 1930 Felix Bamberger and Mrs. Felix Fuld entrusted him with an initial five million dollars to set up an Institute of Advanced Study. The site eventually chosen was in Princeton, New Jersey, about a quarter of a mile from the Graduate College where Andrew Fleming West was still living. Flexner consulted scholars widely in America and Europe and eventually decided to start with a small group of mathematicians, but he always had in mind to include Greek studies, which he personally loved, and it was he who, about the same time, persuaded John D. Rockefeller, Jr., to finance the American School's excavations of the Athenian agora. With the advice of Charles Rufus Morey of the Princeton University Art Department, Flexner, who served as director of the Institute from 1930 to 1939, moved to add a School of Humanistic Studies, later known as the School of Historical Studies, to the Institute. Greek archaeology and history were the fields chosen, and a close tie was established between the Institute and the excavations in Athens.[38] The first classical scholar appointed at the Institute was the Hopkins epigrapher Benjamin Meritt, and the first great result was the publication under Meritt's supervision of the greatest of Greek historical inscriptions, *The Athenian Tribute Lists,* in four volumes (1939–53). It is at this point that American classical scholarship first clearly equalled that of the Old World. Other centers of research have since been established elsewhere: the Dumbarton Oaks Center for Byzantine Studies, the Center for Hellenic Studies in Washington, and the National Humanities Center in North Carolina are the most important. They are characteristic institutions of the twentieth century which indicate a basic confidence on the part of leaders of American society in the value of humanistic and classical knowledge. That knowledge, of course, needs to be published, and American university presses, another twentieth-century development, have been major vehicles of dissemination. An important challenge of the final decades of the century is how the mounting costs of traditional publication can be managed and how the computer can be effectively applied, both in the process of research and in its dissemination. A pioneer in this effort has been David Packard, a classicist from the family of one of the early developers of the computer, whose Ibycus System has been adopted by a number of classics departments and research institutes.

Have the classics become more remote from the wider intellectual, literary, and artistic life of the nation in the twentieth century? The period from 1890 to 1920 was something of a low point in classical influences on serious American literature, and its great achievements were largely in realistic fiction. William Vaughn Moody (1869–1910) drew on classical themes in poetic dramas, especially *The Firebringer* (1910), but from our perspective today poetry seems moribund until the emergence of new figures about the time of the First World War. Most of the writers in question had a classical education, and the phenomenon could be viewed as a last flowering of the old tradition, but it has now continued for over fifty years and there may be a sense in which the abolition of requirements freed the air to look seriously at the contents and style of classical literature. Between the two wars there appeared a serious use of classical motifs and allusions in American poetry. T. S. Eliot's classical education was acquired in America, and other great examples are Ezra Pound (not just in *Homage to Sextus Propertius*, but in the *Cantos* and other poems), Robert Frost, and Robert Lowell.[39] John G. Neihardt (1881–1973), "the poet laureate of Nebraska," published a cycle of very fine narrative poems dealing with the early exploration of the West and the relations between whites and Indians which are devoid of classical reference, but which nevertheless represent a deliberate attempt to create an American epic on the model of Homer. Both for their classical style and their depth of characterization, they deserve to be better known than they are. In drama, classical influences have made themselves felt in a way not known since the eighteenth century, especially in Eugene O'Neill's *Mourning Becomes Electra* (1931) and Robinson Jeffers's *Medea* (1946). Historical fiction on classical themes resumed its public appeal with John Erskine's *The Private Life of Helen of Troy* (1925), and has continued to flourish in works by Thornton Wilder, Taylor Caldwell, Gore Vidal, and others, while classical themes have been used in novels in contemporary settings such as John Updike's *The Centaur* (1963). The popular scholarship of Edith Hamilton (1867–1963) brought a basic appreciation of Greek mythology and drama to a wide audience.

Mythology has, indeed, proved to be a major strand in twentieth-century classicism. American students of Greek and Latin learned the myths in the eighteenth century, but either as pretty stories to adorn a page or a painting or as moral lessons. The nineteenth century discovered a profounder meaning in mythology as the disciplines of anthropology and psychology emerged, and the twentieth century has taken this understanding into the creative arts. The classicists were not slow in capitalizing on the early possibilities; Anthon's *Classical Dictionary* is already filled with contemporary interpretations of myths, and Sir James Frazier's *The Golden Bough* (1890) was widely read in America, but teachers clung to Bulfinch's *Mythology* for the first half of the twentieth century. In the large courses in classical mythology which constitute an important service function of most classics departments the narrative myths continue to be the chief attraction to students, rather than their structure, their symbolism, or even their utilizations in literature, the arts, and music. In 1983 it is still not clear how useful contemporary sociological and linguistic approaches to mythology and literary criticism will be to the understanding of the classics. Some classicists are well aware of such schools as structuralism, deconstructionism, and semiotics, but many are repelled by what seems to them an obfuscation by theory of the clarity and directness of classical texts in which their appeal has traditionally been found. American classical scholarship has traditionally been closer to British than to German and closer to German than to French, but with the decline of Britain this allegiance may be reversed and the French, who are major figures in the new schools, may yet come to have an important impact on American scholarship. It was after all in France that Millman Parry did his pioneering work on oral epic which has lead to one of the great critical advances of the twentieth century in the understanding of Homer.

The second half of the twentieth century has also been characterized by a more profound understanding of ancient character and society on a historical basis. E. R. Dodds's *The Greeks and the Irrational* (1951) did much for this effort and can be included as almost American in that it was originally delivered as one of the series of Sather Lectures at Berkeley. We have found in the Greeks not just the *stille Grosse* and *edele Dunkelheit* of Winckelmann, but human beings with passions and conflicts, nobility anddarker sides. This awareness has helped make it possible for classical studies to venture out into still other fields of research and teaching involving sociology and psychology. New ground was broken by Sarah B.

Pomeroy in *Goddesses, Whores, Wives, and Slaves: Women in Classical Antiquity* (1975) and by Frank M. Snowden in *Blacks in Antiquity: Ethiopians in the Greco-Roman Experience* (1970). Another feature of ancient life which has been allowed to come to the surface is homosexuality. Since it is such a prominent part of Greek and Latin epigram, lyric, and satire, and to be found as well in epic and philosophy, a case could be made that reading the classics has been through centuries of suppression one of the few vehicles by which a young man, in particular, could discover that his sexual preference was not some unique sin in himself, but a feeling shared with others, including some of the greatest figures of all time. Texts for school use were of course often bowdlerized, but at least in the case of Plato and Catullus the passion could be found by the curious. An interesting American instance of this is James Turney Allen's *First Year of Greek*, originally published in the otherwise very macho year of 1917. The reading selections are largely based on Plato's *Lysis* and involve love between males, which the student is encouraged to translate "friendship." Since then the sexual revolution has made possible a franker acknowledgment of an important ingredient of Greek life, and a greater understanding of human life. In particular, Petronius, one of the greatest masters of Latin style, has assumed his rightful place in the curriculum, and a meeting of the Petronian Society is a regular feature of the annual assembly of the American Philological Association.

Finally, a very important influence on American understanding of the classics throughout two-thirds of the twentieth century has been the arrival here of scholars and teachers seeking freedom of thought and escape from persecution in Europe, especially Russia, Germany, and Austria. The great names are those of Michael Rostovzeff (1870–1952) and Werner Jaeger (1888–1961), but there have been many others with European training who have diversified and deepened American scholarship.[40] There has also been an exodus from Britain as opportunities there decreased following the Second World War.

All these observations, selective and even personal as they must be, are intended as suggestions for some future historian of classical studies who will round out the work of Meyer Reinhold on the earlier period. A few words about Meyer himself deserve to be said, for he has been a part of the history of classics in America as well as its historian. He first acquired his knowledge of the classics in the distinctively American setting of the public schools and the City University of New York in the 1920s. He pursued graduate studies at

Columbia University in the early 1930s, where he was profoundly influenced by Professors Charles Knapp and William Westermann and by his fellow students and friends M. I. Finley and Naphtali Lewis. He spent the years 1933–35 in Rome as Fellow of the American Academy. Since then he has taught thousands of students classical languages and literatures, ancient history, and the classical heritage of America—at Brooklyn College, Southern Illinois University, and the University of Missouri at Columbia, where he became a campus legend, and presently as Visiting University Professor at Boston University. He has made distinguished contributions to scholarship for fifty years, especially in his fine book on Marcus Agrippa, and to the availability of classical sources to English-speaking scholars and teachers, especially in the two-volume work *Roman Civilization*, which he edited with Naphtali Lewis. He has published works which find important uses in the teaching of mythology and drama, two areas of the classics which are noted above as highly characteristic of our century, and he has been the model, guide, and friend of generations of students and colleagues. Taken as a whole, his work demonstrates that variety, vitality, and richness of the classical tradition which has made it possible for the classics to surmount all artificial supports, to find constantly new interests, and to contribute to American life in ways undreamed of earlier.

Notes

1. See "Opponents of Classical Learning in America during the Revolutionary Period," Chapter IV, above.
2. See "The Silver Age of Classical Studies in America, 1790–1830," Chapter VI, above.
3. For an amusing account of Jackson's visit to Harvard in 1833 and the Latin, real or imagined, it provoked, see Josiah Quincy, Jr., "President Jackson Gives 'Em a Little Latin," in *The Harvard Book: Selections from Three Centuries*, ed. William Bentinck-Smith (Cambridge, Mass., 1953), pp. 276–280.
4. Harold E. Dickson, *Arts of the Young Republic* (Chapel Hill, N.C., 1968), pp. 82–84; pl. 194.
5. Richard Hofstadter and Wilson Smith, eds., *American Higher Education: A Documentary History* (Chicago, 1961), vol. I, p. 289.
6. Frederick Rudolph, *Curriculum: A History of the American Undergraduate Course of Study since 1636* (San Francisco, 1977), pp. 66–75.
7. Rudolph, *Curriculum*, p. 73; James Insley Osborne and Theodore Gregory Gronert, *Wabash College: The First Hundred Years, 1832–1932* (Crawfordsville, Ind., 1932), pp. 41–44.
8. Rudolph, *Curriculum*, pp. 89–90.
9. Alexis de Tocqueville, *Democracy in America*, trans. George Lawrence, ed. J. P. Mayer and Max Lerner (New York, 1966), p. 445.
10. Hofstadter and Smith, *American Higher Education*, vol. I, pp. 288–290.

11. Ralph Waldo Emerson, "The American Scholar," in *An American Primer*, ed. Daniel J. Boorstin (Chicago, 1966), p. 318.
12. "Starting from Paumanok, 5," in Walt Whitman, *Complete Poetry and Selected Prose and Letters* (London, 1938), p. 16.
13. E.g., Edmund G. Berry, *Emerson's Plutarch* (Cambridge, Mass., 1961); Ethel Seybold, *Thoreau: The Quest and the Classics* (New Haven, 1951).
14. See "A 'New Morning': Edward Everett's Contributions to Classical Learning," Chapter VII, above.
15. Stephen Newmyer, "Charles Anthon: Knickerbocker Scholar," and David Wiesen, "Cornelius Felton and the Flowering of Classics in New England," *Classical Outlook* 59 (1981–82), pp. 41–44; 44–48.
16. Francis J. Syphen, Jr., "A History of Harper's Latin Dictionary," *Harvard Library Bulletin* 20 (1972), pp. 349–366.
17. Edward T. James, ed., *Notable American Women* (Cambridge, Mass., 1971), vol. III, pp. 588–589.
18. Reissued, with an introduction by John Francis Latimer, in company with *A Grammatical and Historical Supplement* and *A Composite Translation of A Life of George Washington in Latin Prose*, ed. John Francis Latimer (Washington, D.C., 1976).
19. See "Philhellenism in America in the Early National Period," Chapter VIII, above.
20. *The Education of Henry Adams,* ed. Ernest Samuels (Boston, 1973), p. 60.
21. Brief account in R. C. Jebb, *Sophocles: I. The Oedipus Tyrannus,* 2nd ed. (Cambridge, 1887), pp. xlviii–xlix, based on Henry Norman, *An Account of the Harvard Greek Play* (Boston, 1882). See Doris E. Pluggé, *History of Greek Play Production in American Colleges and Universities from 1881 to 1936* (New York, 1938); James E. Ford, "The Rebirth of Greek Tragedy and the Decline of the Humanities," *Georgia Review* 34 (1980), pp. 545–555.
22. Some land grant colleges initially required Greek, then gave it up, e.g., Kansas State in 1872; Indiana University had dropped Greek in 1873. Strictly speaking, Harvard did not abolish the Greek requirement, but allowed substitution of advanced mathematics and physics. See Rudolph, *Curriculum,* pp. 180–183.
23. Charles Francis Adams, *Three Phi Beta Kappa Addresses* (Boston, 1907), pp. 3–48. In the third of the addresses, "Some Modern Tendencies" (1906), Adams said, "I would prescribe one of the classic tongues, Greek or Latin, as a compulsory study to the day of graduation" (p. 133). This was understandably taken as a recantation of the thesis of "A College Fetich," but Adams denies this (Preface, p. v.). Adams claims that as an undergraduate he had "a fancy for Greek," but "those were the days of Professors Felton and Sophocles, and the methods of instruction in Greek at Harvard were simply beneath contempt" (*Charles Francis Adams, 1835–1915: An Autobiography* [Boston, 1916], p. 26).
24. Irving McKee, *"Ben Hur" Wallace: The Life of General Lew Wallace* (Berkeley, 1947), passim.
25. Richard Lounsbury, *"Ludibria Rerum Mortalium*: Charleston Intellectuals and Their Classics," in *Intellectual Life in Ante-Bellum Charleston,* ed. Michael O'Brien (Charleston, in press). The role of the classics in the slavery dispute was considerable; see David S. Wiesen, "The Contribution of Antiquity to American Racial Thought," *Classical Traditions in Early America,* ed. John W. Eadie (Ann Arbor, 1976), pp. 191–212.
26. Best seen in *The Creed of the Old South* (Baltimore, 1915), which is a reprint of two articles which originally appeared in the *Atlantic Monthly* of January, 1892, and September, 1897. See George Kennedy, "A Southerner in the Peloponnesian War," in *The Classical Tradition in the South,* Special Issue of *Southern Humanities Review* (1977), pp. 21–25.

27. See Lucius Rogers Shero, *The American Philological Association: An Historical Sketch* (Lancaster, Pennsylvania, 1964).
28. Originally published in the *Princeton Review* (May, 1879); reprinted in Basil Lanneau Gildersleeve, *Essays and Studies, Educational and Literary* (Baltimore, 1890), pp. 87–123.
29. Paul Shorey, "Fifty Years of Classical Studies in America," *Transactions and Proceedings of the American Philological Association* 50 (1919), pp. 32–61.
30. See the statistical table in *Value of the Classics*, ed. Andrew F. West (Princeton, 1917), p. 359, derived from the Report of the United States Commissioner of Education for 1916, vol. II, p. 489.
31. Nancy A. Mavrogenes, "The Teaching of Greek and Latin according to Francis Parker and John Dewey," *Classical Outlook* 60 (1982), pp. 3–6.
32. The sociologist A. G. Keller judiciously weighed the claims and concluded that Latin was worth the cost ("The Case of Latin," *Yale Review* 6 [1916–17], pp. 135–149).
33. Abraham Flexner, *A Modern College and A Modern School* (Garden City, N.Y., 1923), pp. 123–124.
34. Abraham Flexner, *An Autobiography* (New York, 1960), p. 159.
35. West, *Value of the Classics*, p. 3.
36. See esp. West, *Value of the Classics*, p. 23.
37. Rudolph, *Curriculum*, p. 214.
38. See "The School of Historical Studies," a mimeographed brochure issued by the Institute for Advanced Study in 1980, pp. 6–7. Flexner's own account of the development of the school mentions E. A. Lowe (actually the third appointed) and Hetty Goldman (actually the fifth) as though they preceded Meritt (Flexner, *Autobiography*, p. 254).
39. On Frost, see Helen Bacon, " 'In- and Outdoor Schooling': Robert Frost and the Classics," in *Robert Frost: Lectures on the Centennial of His Birth* (Washington, D.C., 1975), pp. 3–25; "For Girls: From 'Birches' to 'Wild Grapes,' " *Yale Review* (Autumn, 1977), pp. 13–29; "Dialogue of Poets: *Mens Animi* and the Renewal of Words," *Massachusetts Review* 19 (1978), pp. 319–334; "The Contemporary Reader and Robert Frost: The Heavenly Guest of 'One More Brevity' and *Aeneid* 8," *St. Johns Review* (Summer, 1981), pp. 3–10. On Lowell, see Meyer Reinhold, "Robert Lowell's Uses of Classical Myths," *Helios* 7 (1980), pp. 1–18; Stephen Newmyer, "Robert Lowell and the Weeping Philosopher," *Classical and Modern Literature* 1 (1981), pp. 121–131.
40. See William M. Calder III, "Die Geschichte der klassischen Philologie in den Vereinigten Staaten," *Jahrbuch für Amerikastudien* 11 (1966), pp. 232–236.

Selected Bibliography

The Classics in American Culture

Bailyn, Bernard. *The Ideological Origins of the American Revolution*. Cambridge, Mass., 1967.

Bridenbaugh, Charles, and Bridenbaugh, Jessica. *Rebels and Gentlemen: Philadelphia in the Age of Franklin*. New York, 1942.

Calder, William M. III. "Die Geschichte der klassischen Philologie in den Vereinigten Staaten." *Jahrbuch für Amerikastudien* 11 (1966), pp. 213–217.

Clough, Wilson O., ed. *Intellectual Origins of American National Thought: Pages from the Books Our Founding Fathers Read*. 2nd ed. New York, 1961.

Commager, Henry Steele. "Leadership in Eighteenth-Century America and Today." *Daedalus* 90 (1961), pp. 650–673.

———. "The American Enlightenment and the Ancient World: A Study in Paradox." *Proc. Mass. Hist. Soc.* 83 (1971), pp. 3–15.

Curti, Merle. "The Transmission of Ancient Classics." In *The Growth of American Thought*. 3rd ed. New York, 1960.

Eadie, John W., ed. *Classical Traditions in Early America*. Ann Arbor, 1976.

Else, Gerald F. "The Classics in the New World." *News Letter, American Council of Learned Societies* 16, no. 5 (1965), pp. 1–6.

Gummere, Richard M. "A Scottish Classicist in America." *Publ. Colon. Soc. Mass.*, vol. 35 (1947), *Transactions*, 1942–46, pp. 146–161.

———. *The American Colonial Mind and the Classical Tradition: Essays in Comparative Culture*. Cambridge, Mass., 1963.

———. "The Classics in a Brave New World." *Harvard Studies in Classical Philology* 62 (1957), pp. 119–139.

———. "The Heritage of the Classics in Colonial North America." *Proc. Amer. Philos. Soc.* 99 (1955), pp. 68–78.

———. *Seven Wise Men of Colonial America*. Cambridge, Mass., 1967.

Jones, Howard Mumford. "The Appeal of Antiquity." In *Revolution & Romanticism*. Cambridge, Mass., 1974.

Kennedy, George A. "Towards a Methodology for Study of Classics in America." In *The Usefulness of Classical Learning in the Eighteenth Century*, edited by Susan Ford Wiltshire. University Park, Pa., 1977.

Kerber, Linda K. "Salvaging the Classical Tradition." In *The Federalists in Dissent: Imagery and Ideology in Jeffersonian America*. Ithaca, N.Y., 1970.

Miles, Edwin A. "The Young American Nation and the Classical World." *Journal of the History of Ideas* 35 (1974), pp. 259–274.

Miller, Samuel. *A Brief Retrospect of the Eighteenth Century*. 2 vols. New York, 1803.

Morison, Samuel E. *The Intellectual Life of Colonial New England*. New York, 1956.

Reinhold, Meyer. *The Classick Pages: Classical Reading of Eighteenth-Century Americans*. University Park, Pa., 1975.

Sandys, John E. *A History of Classical Scholarship.* Vol. III, pp. 450–470. Cambridge, 1908. Reprint 1967.

Stoughton, Herbert P. "The Study of the Classics in the United States in the 17th, 18th, 19th, and 20th Centuries." *Humanitas* [Coimbra, Portugal] 2 (1948–49), pp. 345–350.

Urzidil, Johannes. *Amerika und die Antike.* Zurich, 1964.

Wheeler, James T. "Reading Interests of the Professional Classes in Colonial Maryland, 1700–1776." *Maryland Historical Magazine* 36 (1941), pp. 184–201, 281–306.

Wright, Louis B. *The Culture of the American Colonies, 1607–1763.* New York, 1957.

———. "The Purposeful Reading of Our Colonial Ancestors." *ELH: Journal of English Literary History* 4 (1937), pp. 85–111.

Wright, Thomas G. *Literary Culture in Early New England, 1620–1730.* New Haven, 1920.

The Cult of Antiquity in Early America

Benario, Herbert W. "Gordon's Tacitus." *Classical Journal* 72 (1976–77), pp. 107–114.

Cohn-Haft, Louis. "The Founding Fathers and Antiquity: A Selective Passion." *Smith College Studies in History* 66 (1980), pp. 137–153.

Else, Gerald F. "The Classical Humanities in the Making of America." *Journal of the California Classical Association, Northern Section* (1977–78), pp. 5–15.

Ingalls, Beatrice K. "George Sandys' Translation of Ovid's Metamorphoses." Ph.D. dissertation, Radcliffe, 1949.

Kaiser, Leo M. "On the Latin Attainments of Colonel Landon Carter of Sabine Hall." *Va. Mag. Hist. & Biog.* 85 (1977), pp. 51–54.

Luce, John T. "The Idea of an American National Character: The Influence of Greece and Rome." *Journal of the California Classical Association, Northern Section* (1977–78), pp. 3–45.

MacKendrick, Paul. "This Rich Source of Delight: The Classics and the Founding Fathers." *Classical Journal* 72 (1976–77), pp. 97–106.

Marson, Philip. *Breeder of Democracy.* Cambridge, Mass., 1970. Pp. 3–188 on Boston Latin School.

Mcdonald, Forrest. "A Founding Father's Library." *Literature of Liberty* 1 (1978), pp. 4–15.

Mullett, Charles F. "Ancient Historians and 'Enlightened' Reviewers." *Review of Politics* 21 (1959), pp. 550–565.

Noyes, Richard. "A Note on a Founding Father's Library: The Books of Benjamin Giles." *Historical New Hampshire* 34 (1979), pp. 244–252.

Rexine, John E. "The Boston Latin School Curriculum in the 17th and 18th Centuries." *Classical Journal* 72 (1976–77), pp. 261–266.

Rudolph, Frederick. *Curriculum: A History of the American Undergraduate Course of Study since 1636.* San Francisco, 1977. Pp. 29–36, 56 on the curriculum at Harvard and Yale.

Wright, Louis B. "Richard Lee II, A Belated Elizabethan in Virginia." *Huntington Library Quarterly* 2 (1938), pp. 1–35.

Winans, Robert B. *A Descriptive Checklist of Book Catalogues Separately Printed in America 1693–1800.* Worcester, 1981. See Winans's index under "Classics," "Greek Books," "Latin Books," "School Books."

The Quest for Useful Knowledge

Oleson, Alexandra, and Brown, Sanborn C., eds. *The Pursuit of Knowledge in the Early American Republic: American Scientific and Learned Societies from Colonial Times to the Civil War.* Baltimore, 1976.

The Classics and Early American Political Thought

Ames, R. A., and Montgomery, H. C. "The Influence of Rome on the American Constitution." *Classical Journal* 30 (1934–35), pp. 19–27.

Bailyn, Bernard, ed. "A Dialogue between an American and a European Englishman, by Thomas Hutchinson" [1768]. *Perspectives in American History* 9 (1975), pp. 343–410.

Bradford, M. E. "A 'Better Guide than Reason': The Politics of John Dickinson." *Modern Age* 2 (1977), pp. 39–49.

———. "A Teaching for Republicans: Roman History and the Nation's First Identity." *Intercollegiate Review* 11 (1976), pp. 67–81.

Chinard, Gilbert. "Polybius and the American Constitution." *Journal of the History of Ideas* 1 (1940), pp. 38–58.

Corwin, Edward S. *The "Higher Law" Background of American Constitutional Law.* Ithaca, 1955.

Gribbin, William. "Rollin's Histories and American Republicanism." *Wm. & Mary Quart.*, 3rd ser., 29 (1972), pp. 611–622.

Gummere, Richard M. "The Classical Ancestry of the United States Constitution." *American Quarterly* 14 (1961), pp. 3–18.

Guttridge, G. H. *English Whiggism and the American Revolution.* University of California Publications in History, vol. XVIII. Berkeley, 1928.

Howe, Daniel Walker. *The Political Culture of the American Whigs.* Chicago, 1979.

Hunt, Edmund B. "The Rebels and the Ancients: The Use of Ancient Classics in American Polemical Literature, 1763–1776." Ph.D. dissertation, Ohio State, 1974.

Johnson, James William. *The Formation of English Neo-Classical Thought.* Princeton, 1967.

Kennedy, George. "Classical Influence on the Federalist." In *Classical Traditions in Early America*, edited by John W. Eadie. Ann Arbor, 1976.

LeBoutillier, C. G. *American Democracy and Natural Law.* New York, 1950.

Mullett, Charles F. "Classical Influences on the American Revolution." *Classical Journal* 35 (1939–40), pp. 92–104.

Murphy, John P. "Rome at the Constitutional Convention." *Classical Outlook* 51 (1974), pp. 112–114.

Peardon, Thomas Preston. *The Transition in English Historical Writing, 1760–1830.* Studies in History, Economics, and Public Law, Columbia University, no. 390. New York, 1966.

Rexine, John E. "Classical Political Theory and the U.S. Constitution." *Greek Orthodox Theological Review* 21 (1976), pp. 321–340.

Wood, Gordon S. *The Creation of the American Republic 1776–1787.* Chapel Hill, 1969.

The Classics and the Quest for Virtue

Agresto, John T. "Liberty, Virtue and Republicanism, 1776–1787." *Review of Politics* 39 (1977), pp. 473–504.

Billian, George A. *Elbridge Gerry: Founding Father and Republican Statesman.* New York, 1976.

Goodman, Paul. "Elbridge Gerry: The Founding Father, and the Republic of Virtue." *Reviews in American History* 5 (1977), pp. 496–502.

Jones, Howard Mumford. *O Strange New World: American Culture: The Formative Years.* New York, 1964. Pp. 227–272, "Roman Virtue."

Classical Studies in America 1790–1830

Agard, Walter R. "Classics on the Midwest Frontier." *Classical Journal* 51 (1955), pp. 103–110.

Baker, Paul R. *The Fortunate Pilgrims: Americans in Italy 1800–1860.* Cambridge, Mass., 1964.

Cremin, Lawrence A. *American Education. The National Experience, 1783–1876.* New York, 1979.

Crowley, John E. "Classical and Other Traditions for the Understanding of Change in Post-Revolutionary America: The Idea of Decline." In *Classical Traditions in Early America,* edited by John W. Eadie. Ann Arbor, 1976.

Diehl, Carl. *Americans and German Scholarship, 1770–1870.* New Haven, 1978.

Isbell, Egbert R. "The Catholepistemiad, or University, of Michigania." In *University of Michigan Historical Essays,* edited by A. E. R. Boak. Ann Arbor, 1937.

Latimer, John F. "American Classical Scholarship and Caleb Alexander." *Trans. Amer. Philolog. Assn.* 80 (1949), pp. 403–422.

Miles, Edwin A. "The Whig Party and the Menace of Caesar." *Tennessee Historical Quarterly* 27 (1968), pp. 361–379.

———. "The Young American Nation and the Classical World." *Journal of the History of Ideas* 35 (1974), pp. 259–274.

Rudolph, Frederick. *Curriculum: A History of the American Undergraduate Course of Study Since 1636.* San Francisco, 1977.

Sypher, Francis J., Jr. "A History of Harper's Latin Dictionary." *Harvard Library Bulletin* 20 (1972), pp. 347–366.

Turk, Milton H. "Without Classical Studies." *Journal of Higher Education* 4 (1933), pp. 339–346.

American Education and the Classics

Axtell, James. *The School Upon a Hill: Education and Society in Colonial New England.* New Haven, 1974.

Bailyn, Bernard. *Education in the Formation of American Society.* Chapel Hill, 1960.

Ballou, Richard B. "The Grammar Schools in 17th Century Colonial America." Ph.D. dissertation, Harvard, 1940.

Clarke, John. *Letters to a Student in the University at Cambridge, Massachusetts.* Boston, 1795.

Cleary, Marie. "Thomas Bulfinch, *The Age of Fable,* and the Continuity of the Classics in American Education." Ph.D. dissertation, University of Massachusetts, Amherst, 1982.

Cohen, Sheldon D. *A History of Colonial Education, 1607–1776.* New York, 1974.

Cremin, Lawrence A. *American Education: The Colonial Experience, 1607–1783.* New York, 1970.

Fink, Jerome S. "The Purpose of the American Colonial Colleges." Ph.D. dissertation, Stanford, 1958.

Gummere, Richard M. "Some Classical Sidelights on Colonial Education." *Classical Journal* 35 (1959–60), pp. 223–232.

Hansen, Allen O. *Liberalism and American Education in the Eighteenth Century.* New York, 1936. Reprint 1965.

Herbst, Jurgen. "The American Revolution and the American University." *Perspectives in American History* 10 (1976), pp. 279–354.

Hofstadter, Richard, and Smith, Wilson, eds. *American Higher Education: A Documentary History.* 2 vols. Chicago, 1961.

Holmes, Pauline. *A Tercentenary History of the Boston Latin School 1635–1935.* Cambridge, Mass., 1935.

Jenks, Henry F. *Catalogue of the Boston Latin School.* Boston, 1886.

Knight, Edgar W. *A Documentary History of Education in the South Before 1860.* 5 vols. Chapel Hill, 1949–53.

May, Henry F. *The Enlightenment in America.* New York, 1976.

Marson, Philip. *Breeder of Democracy*. Cambridge, Mass., 1970. Pp. 3–188 on Boston Latin School.

McLachlan, James. "The *Choice of Hercules:* American Student Societies in the Early 19th Century." In *The University in Society,* edited by Lawrence Stone, vol. II, pp. 449–494. Princeton, 1974.

———. "Classical Names, American Identities: Some Notes on College Students and the Classical Tradition in the 1770s." In *Classical Traditions in Early America,* edited by John W. Eadie. Ann Arbor, 1976.

Meriwether, Colyer. *Our Colonial Curriculum, 1607–1776.* Washington, D.C., 1907.

Middlekauff, Robert. *Ancients and Axioms: Secondary Education in Eighteenth-Century New England.* New Haven, 1963.

———. "A Persistent Tradition: The Classical Curriculum in Eighteenth-Century New England." *Wm. & Mary Quart.,* 3rd ser., 18 (1961), pp. 54–67.

Morford, Mark. "Early American School Editions of Ovid." *Classical Journal* 78 (1982–83), pp. 150–158.

Morison, Samuel Eliot. *Harvard College in the Seventeenth Century.* 2 vols. Cambridge, Mass., 1936.

Murdock, Kenneth B. "The Teaching of Latin and Greek at the Boston Latin School in 1712." *Publ. Colon. Soc. Mass.,* vol. XXVII (1931), *Transactions,* 1927–30, pp. 21–29.

Pomfret, John E. "Student Interests at Brown University 1789–1790." *New Engl. Quart.* 5 (1932), pp. 135–147.

Rudolph, Frederick. *Curriculum: A History of the American Undergraduate Course of Study Since 1636.* San Francisco, 1977.

———, ed. *Essays in Education in the Early Republic.* Cambridge, Mass., 1965.

Shipton, Clifford K. "Secondary Education in the Puritan Colonies." *New Engl. Quart.* 7 (1934), pp. 646–661.

Smith, William. *A General Idea of the College of Mirania.* New York, 1753.

Smith, Wilson, ed. *Theories of Education in Early America, 1635–1819.* Indianapolis, 1973.

Straub, Jean S. "Teaching in the Friends' Latin School of Philadelphia in the Eighteenth Century." *Pa. Mag. Hist. & Biog.* 91 (1967), pp. 434–456.

Vine, Phyllis. "The Social Function of Eighteenth Century Higher Education." *History of Education Quarterly* 16 (1976), pp. 409–424.

Vassar, Rena L. "Elementary and Latin Grammar School Education in the American Colonies 1607–1700." Ph.D. dissertation, University of California, Berkeley, 1958.

Wolf, Edwin L. "The Classical Languages in Colonial Philadelphia." In *Classical Traditions in Early America,* edited by John W. Eadie. Ann Arbor, 1976.

Yost, Mary A. "Classical Studies in American Colonial Schools 1635–1776." *Classical Outlook* 54 (1976), pp. 40–43.

Young, Homer A. "Theory of American Education during the Revolutionary Period, 1743–1809." Ph.D. dissertation, University of Texas, 1949.

Books and Libraries

Bridenbaugh, Carl. "The Press and the Book in Eighteenth Century Philadelphia." *Pa. Mag. Hist. & Biog.* 65 (1941), pp. 1–30.

———, and Bridenbaugh, Jessica. *Rebels and Gentlemen: Philadelphia in the Age of Franklin.* New York, 1942. Chap. III, "Books and Libraries."

Bruce, Philip A. *Institutional History of Virginia in the Seventeenth Century.* 2 vols. New York, 1910.

Davis, Richard Beale. *Intellectual Life in Jefferson's Virginia, 1790–1830.* Chapel Hill, 1964.

Dexter, Franklin B. "Early Private Libraries in New England." *Proc. Amer. Antiq. Soc.,* n.s., 18 (1907), pp. 135–137.

Dix, William S. "The Princeton University Library in the Eighteenth Century." *Princeton University Library Chronicle* 40 (1978), pp. 1–102.

Edmunds, Albert J. "The First Books Imported by America's First Great Library: 1732." *Pa. Mag. Hist. & Biog.* 30 (1906), pp. 300–308.

Edgar, Walter B. "Some Popular Books in Colonial South Carolina." *South Carolina Historical Magazine* 72 (1971), pp. 174–178.

Ford, Worthington C. *The Boston Book Market 1679–1700.* Boston, 1917.

Jennings, John M. *The Library of the College of William and Mary in Virginia 1693–1793.* Charlottesville, 1968.

Keys, Thomas E. "Popular Authors in the Colonial Library." *Wilson Library Bulletin* 14 (1940), pp. 726–727.

Korty, Margaret B. *Benjamin Franklin and Eighteenth-Century Libraries. Trans. Amer. Philos. Soc.,* n.s., vol. LV, pt. 9. Philadelphia, 1965.

Kraus, Joe W. "Book Collections of Five Colonial College Libraries." Ph.D. dissertation, University of Illinois, 1960.

Lamberton, E. V. "Colonial Libraries of Pennsylvania." *Pa. Mag. Hist. & Biog.* 42 (1918), pp. 193–234.

McCorison, Marcus A., ed. *The 1764 Catalogue of the Redwood Library of Newport, Rhode Island.* New Haven, 1965.

Norton, Arthur O. "Harvard Text-Books and Reference Books of the Seventeenth-Century." *Publ. Colon. Soc. Mass.,* vol. XXVII (1934), *Transactions,* 1930–33, pp. 361–438.

Potter, Alfred C. "The Harvard College Library, 1723–1735." *Publ. Colon. Soc. Mass.,* vol. XXV (1925), *Transactions,* 1922–24, pp. 1–13.

Shores, Louis. *Origins of the American College Library, 1638–1800.* Nashville, 1934.

Weeks, Stephen B. *Libraries and Literature in North Carolina in the Eighteenth Century.* Washington, D.C., 1895.

Smart, George K. "Private Libraries in Colonial Virginia." *American Literature* 10 (1938–39), pp. 24–52.

Wheeler, Joseph T. "Books Owned by Marylanders, 1700–1776." *Maryland History Magazine* 35 (1940), pp. 337–353.

――――. "Reading Interests of Maryland Planters and Merchants, 1700–1776." *Maryland History Magazine* 37 (1942), pp. 26–41.

――――. "Reading Interests of the Professional Classes in Colonial Maryland, 1700–1776." *Maryland History Magazine* 36 (1941), pp. 184–201, 281–306.

Wright, Louis B. *The First Gentlemen of Virginia: Intellectual Qualities of the Early Colonial Ruling Class.* San Marino, 1940.

――――. "The 'Gentlemen's Library' in Early Virginia: The Literary Interests of the First Carters." *Huntington Library Quarterly* 1 (1937), pp. 3–61.

Wolf, Edwin, 2nd. "The Library of Ralph Assheton: The Book Background of a Colonial Philadelphia Lawyer." *Papers of the Bibliographical Society of America* 58 (1964), pp. 345–379.

The Classics in the Southern States

Benario, Herbert W. "The Classics in Southern Higher Education." In *The Classical Tradition in the South,* Special Issue of *Southern Humanities Review* (1977), pp. 15–20.

Berrigan, Joseph R. "The Impact of the Classics upon the South." *Classical Journal* 64 (1964), pp. 18–20.

Bradford, M. E. "That Other Republic: *Romanitas* in Southern Literature." In *The Classical Tradition in the South,* Special Issue of *Southern Humanities Review* (1977), pp. 4–13.

Bruce, Dickson D., Jr. "The Conservative Use of History in Early National Virginia." *Southern Studies* 19 (1980), pp. 128–146.

Coon, Charles L. *North Carolina Schools and Academies 1790–1840: A Documentary History.* Raleigh, 1915.

Davis, Richard Beale. *Intellectual Life in the Colonial South 1585–1763.* 3 vols. Knoxville, 1978.

———. *A Colonial Southern Bookshelf: Reading in the Eighteenth Century.* Athens, Ga., 1979.

Gamle, Robert. "The White Column Tradition: Classical Architecture and the Southern Mystique." In *The Classical Tradition in the South,* Special Issue of *Southern Humanities Review* (1977), pp. 41–59.

Hiden, Martha W. "Education and the Classics in the Life of Colonial Virginia." *Va. Mag. Hist. & Biog.* 49 (1941), pp. 20–38.

———. "Latin in Colonial Virginia." *Classical Weekly* 22 (1927–28), pp. 41–45.

Johnson, George H. "A Book for General Lee." *Virginia Cavalcade* (Autumn, 1980), pp. 88–95.

Miles, Edwin A. "The Old South and the Classical World." *North Carolina Historical Review* 48 (1971), pp. 258–275.

Steiner, Barnard C. "Early Classical Scholars in Maryland." *Classical Weekly* 14 (1922), pp. 185–190.

Thiveat, John H. "James Priestley: Classical Scholar of the Old South." *Tennessee Historical Quarterly* 39 (1980), pp. 421–439.

Umbreit, Allen G. "Education in the Southern Colonies." Ph.D. dissertation, State University of Iowa, 1932.

Wiltshire, Susan Ford. "Jefferson, Calhoun, and the Slavery Debate: The Classics and the Two Minds of the South." In *The Classical Tradition in the South,* Special Issue of *Southern Humanities Review* (1977), pp. 33–40.

The Slavery Debate

Wiesen, David S. "The Contribution of Antiquity in American Social Thought." In *The Classical Traditions in Early America,* edited by John W. Eadie. Ann Arbor, 1976.

———. "Herodotus and the Modern Debate over Race and Slavery." *The Ancient World* 3, no. 1 (1980), pp. 3–16.

Wiltshire, Susan Ford. "Jefferson, Calhoun, and the Slavery Debate: The Classics and the Two Minds of the South." In *The Classical Tradition in the South,* Special Issue of *Southern Humanities Review* (1977), pp. 33–40.

Prominent Americans and the Classics

John Adams

Adams Family Correspondence. Edited by L. H. Butterfield. 4 vols. Cambridge, Mass., 1963–73.

Adams Family Papers. Massachusetts Historical Society, Boston. Microfilm reels 187, 188, 193: literary commonplace book, catalogue of his library in 1790, literary notes and drafts, from 1756 to 1816.

The Adams-Jefferson Letters. Edited by Lester J. Cappon. 2 vols. Chapel Hill, 1959.

Catalogue of the John Adams Library in the Public Library of the City of Boston. Boston, 1907.

Diary and Autobiography of John Adams. Edited by L. H. Butterfield. 4 vols. Cambridge, Mass., 1962.

Gummere, Richard M. "The Classical Politics of John Adams." *Boston Public Library Quarterly* 9, no. 4 (1957), pp. 167–182.

———. "John Adams, Togatus." *Philological Quarterly* 13 (1934), pp. 203–210.

Haraszati, Zoltán. *John Adams and the Prophets of Progress.* Cambridge, Mass., 1952.
Robathan, Dorothy M. "John Adams and the Classics." *New Engl. Quart.* 19 (1946), pp. 91–98.
Schutz, John A., and Adair, Douglass, eds. *The Spur of Fame: Dialogues of John Adams and Benjamin Rush, 1805–1813.* San Marino, 1966.
Shaw, Peter. *The Character of John Adams.* Chapel Hill, 1976.
[Wiltshire], Susan Ford. "Thomas Jefferson and John Adams on the Classics." *Arion* 6 (Spring, 1967), pp. 116–132.
The Works of John Adams. 10 vols. Boston, 1850–1856.

John Quincy Adams

Adams Family Papers. Massachusetts Historical Society, Boston. Microfilm reels 4, 7–10, 13, 199, 217–220, 222, 223, 225, 237–239: his notebooks, commonplace books, copybooks, translations, verse compositions, diary of readings in classical authors, from 1789–1841.
Diary of John Quincy Adams. Edited by David Grayson et al. Cambridge, Mass., 1981–.

Hugh Henry Brackenridge

Kaiser, Leo M. "An Aspect of Hugh Henry Brackenridge's Classicism." *Early American Literature* 15 (1980–81), pp. 260–270.

Ralph Waldo Emerson

Berry, Edmund G. *Emerson's Plutarch.* Cambridge, Mass., 1961.
———. "Plutarque dans l'Amérique du XIXe Siècle." In *Actes du VIIIe Congrès, Association Guillaume Budé, 1968.* Paris, 1969.

Benjamin Franklin

Best, John A. *Benjamin Franklin on Education.* Teachers College, Columbia University Classics in Education, no. 14. New York, 1962.
Gray, Austin K. *Benjamin Franklin's Library.* New York, 1937.
Gummere, Richard M. "Socrates at the Printing Press: Benjamin Franklin and the Classics." *Classical Weekly* 26 (1932), pp. 57–59.
Keiter, M. Roberta W. "Benjamin Franklin as an Educator." Ph.D. dissertation, Maryland, 1957.
Papers of Benjamin Franklin. Edited by Leonard W. Labaree. New Haven, 1959–.
Woody, Thomas. *Educational Views of Benjamin Franklin.* New York, 1931.

Philip Freneau

Brown, Ruth W. "Classical Echoes in the Poetry of Philip Freneau." *Classical Journal* 45 (1949), pp. 29–34.

Alexander Hamilton

Adair, Douglass. "A Note on Certain of Hamilton's Pseudonyms." *Wm. & Mary Quart.*, 3rd ser., 12 (1955), pp. 282–297.
Papers of Alexander Hamilton. Edited by Harold C. Syrett. New York, 1961–.
Stourzh, Gerald. *Alexander Hamilton and the Idea of Popular Government.* Stanford, 1970.
Works of Alexander Hamilton. Edited by Henry Cabot Lodge. 12 vols. New York, 1904.

Nathaniel Hawthorne

Hutchinson, Earl R., Sr. "Antiquity and Mythology in *The Scarlet Letter:* The Primary Sources." *Arizona Quarterly* 36 (1980), pp. 197–210.
_____. "Antiquity in *The Scarlet Letter:* The Primary Sources." *University of Hartford Studies in Literature* 13 (1981), pp. 99–110.

Thomas Jefferson

Adair, Douglass. "Intellectual Origins of Jeffersonian Democracy: Republicanism, the Class Struggle, and the Virtuous Farmer." Ph.D. dissertation, Yale, 1943.
Berman, Eleanor D. "Jefferson as Litterateur and Critic." In *Thomas Jefferson Among the Arts*. New York, 1947.
Boorstin, Daniel J. *The Lost World of Thomas Jefferson*. New York, 1948.
Cappon, Lester J., ed. *The Adams-Jefferson Letters*. 2 vols. Chapel Hill, 1959.
Chinard, Gilbert, ed. *The Literary Bible of Thomas Jefferson: His Commonplace Book of Philosophers and Poets*. Baltimore, 1928.
_____. "Thomas Jefferson as a Classical Scholar." *Johns Hopkins Alumni Magazine* 18 (1929–30), pp. 291–303.
Colbourn, H. Trevor. "Thomas Jefferson's Use of the Past." *Wm. & Mary Quart.*, 3rd ser., 15 (1958), pp. 56–70.
Cunliffe, Marcus. "Thomas Jefferson and the Dangers of the Past." *Wilson Quarterly* 6, no. 1 (1982), pp. 96–107. Also in *Forms and Functions of History in American Literature: Essays in Honor of Ursula Brumm*, edited by Winifred Fluck et al. Berlin, 1980.
Dickson, Harold E. "Th. J. Art Collector." In *Jefferson and the Arts: An Extended View*, edited by William H. Adams. Washington, D.C., 1976.
Guiness, Desmond, and Sadler, Julius T., Jr. *Mr. Jefferson, Architect*. New York, 1973.
Honeywell, Roy J. *The Educational Work of Thomas Jefferson*. Harvard Studies in Education, no. 16. Cambridge, Mass., 1931.
Kimball, Fiske. *Thomas Jefferson, Architect*. Boston, 1916.
Kimball, Marie. *Jefferson: The Road to Glory 1743-1776*. New York, 1943. Pp. 83–116 on Jefferson's reading.
Lee, Gordon C., ed. *Crusade Against Ignorance: Thomas Jefferson on Education*. Teachers College, Columbia University Classics on Education, no. 16. New York, 1961.
Lehmann, Karl. *Thomas Jefferson, American Humanist*. New York, 1947.
Nichols, Frederic D. "Jefferson: The Making of an Architect." In *Jefferson and the Arts: An Extended View*, edited by William H. Adams. Washington, D.C., 1976.
Papers of Thomas Jefferson. Edited by Julian P. Boyd. Princeton, 1950–.
Sowerby, E. Millicent, ed. *Catalogue of the Library of Thomas Jefferson*. 5 vols. Washington, D.C., 1952–59.
Wilson, Douglas L. "The American *agricola*: Jefferson's Agrarianism and the Classical Tradition." *South Atlantic Quarterly* 80 (1981), pp. 339–354.
[Wiltshire], Susan Ford. "Thomas Jefferson and John Adams on the Classics." *Arion* 6 (Spring, 1967), pp. 116–132.
Wolff, Philippe. "Le Voyage de Thomas Jefferson en Provence-Langedoc en 1787." *Annales Historiques de la Révolution Française* 48 (1976), pp. 608–611.
Wright, Louis B. "Thomas Jefferson and the Classics." *Proc. Amer. Philos. Soc.* 87 (1943–44), pp. 223–233.
The Writings of Thomas Jefferson. Memorial Edition. 20 vols. Washington, D.C., 1905.

James Logan

Tolles, Frederick B. "Quaker Humanist: James Logan as a Classical Scholar." *Pa. Mag. Hist. & Biog.* 79 (1955), pp. 415–438.
Wolf, Edwin, 2nd. *The Library of James Logan.* Philadelphia, 1975.
————. "The Romance of James Logan's Books." *Wm. & Mary Quart.*, 3rd ser., 13 (1956), pp. 342–353.

Cotton Mather

Gustaaf van Cromphout. "Cotton Mather as Plutarchan Biographer." *American Literature* 46 (1974–75), pp. 465–481.
————. "*Manductio ad Ministerium:* Cotton Mather as Neoclassicist." *American Literature* 52 (1981), pp. 361–379.
Kaiser, Leo M. "On the Latin Verse Passages in Cotton Mather's Magnalia." *Early American Literature* 10 (1975–76), pp. 301–306.
Mather, Cotton. *Magnalia Christi Americana.* 2 vols. Hartford, 1820 [1st American edition from London edition of 1702].
————. *Magnalia Christi Americana Books I and II.* Edited by Kenneth B. Murdock. Cambridge, Mass., 1980.

Herman Melville

Sweeney, Gerard M. *Melville's Use of Classical Mythology.* Highlands, N.J., 1975.

Thomas Paine

Aldridge, A. Owen. "Thomas Paine and the Classics." *Eighteenth Century Studies* 1 (1968), pp. 370–380.
Gummere, Richard M. "Thomas Paine: Was He Really Anti-classical?" In *Seven Wise Men of Colonial America.* Cambridge, Mass., 1967.

Benjamin Rush

The Autobiography of Benjamin Rush. Edited by George W. Corner. Princeton, 1948.
Bonar, James. "Benjamin Rush and the Theory and Practice of Republican Education in Pennsylvania." Ph.D. dissertation, Johns Hopkins, 1965.
D'Elia, Donald J. *Benjamin Rush: Philosopher of the American Revolution. Trans. Amer. Philos. Soc.,* vol. LXIV, pt. 5. Philadelphia, 1974.
Good, Harry S. *Benjamin Rush and His Services to American Education.* Berne, Ind., 1918.
Goodman, Nathan S. *Benjamin Rush: Physician and Citizen, 1746–1813.* Philadelphia, 1934.
Hawke, David F. *Benjamin Rush, Revolutionary Gadfly.* Indianapolis, 1971.
Letters of Benjamin Rush. Edited by L. H. Butterfield. 2 vols. Philadelphia, 1951.
Schutz, John A., and Adair, Douglass, eds. *The Spur of Fame: Dialogues of John Adams and Benjamin Rush, 1805–1813.* San Marino, 1966.

Charles Thomson

Hendricks, J. Edwin. *Charles Thomson and the Making of a New Nation, 1729–1824.* Rutherford, N.J., 1979.
White, Cyril M. "Charles Thomson: The Irish-Born Secretary of the Continental Congress." *Studies* [Ireland] 68 (1979), pp. 33–45.

Henry Thoreau

Kaiser, Leo M. "Thoreau's Translation of *The Seven Against Thebes.*" *Emerson Society Quarterly* 17 (1959), pp. 2–28.
Seybold, Ethel. *Thoreau: The Quest and the Classics.* New Haven, 1951.
Van Anglen, Kevin P. "The Sources of Thoreau's Greek Translations." *Studies in the American Renaissance* (Boston, 1980), p. 291–299.

James Wilson

The Works of James Wilson. Edited by Robert G. McCloskey. 2 vols. Cambridge, Mass., 1967.

Ancient History

Burns, Edward M. "The Philosophy of History of the Founding Fathers." *The Historian* 16 (1954), pp. 142–161.
Callcott, George H. *History in the United States 1800–1860.* Baltimore, 1970.
Colbourn, H. Trevor. *The Lamp of Experience: Whig History and the Intellectual Origins of the American Revolution.* Chapel Hill, 1965.
Jameson, J. Franklin. *The History of Historical Writing in America.* Boston, 1891.
Ward, Addison. "The Tory View of Roman History." *Studies in English Literature 1500–1900* 4 (1964), pp. 425–443.
Wiesen, David S. "Ancient History in Early American Education." In *The Usefulness of Classical Learning in the Eighteenth Century,* edited by Susan Ford Wiltshire. University Park, Pa., 1976.

Rhetoric, Oratory, Law

Botein, Stephen. "Cicero as Role Model for Early American Lawyers: A Case Study in Classical 'Influence.'" *Classical Journal* 73 (1978), pp. 313–231.
Ferguson, Robert A. "The Legal Mind in Early American Literature." Ph.D. dissertation, Harvard, 1974.
Hoffman, Richard J. "Classics in the Courts of the United States, 1790–1800." *American Journal of Legal History* 22 (1978), pp. 55–84.
Stein, Peter. "The Attraction of the Civil Law in Post-Revolutionary America." *Virginia Law Review* 52 (1966), pp. 403–434.

Classics and Education of Women

"Female Education." *Harvard Lyceum* 1 (1810–11), pp. 320–326.
Kerber, Linda K. *Women in the Republic: Intellect and Ideology in Revolutionary America.* Chapel Hill, 1980.

American Indians and the Classics

Lafitau, Father Joseph François. *The Customs of the American Indians Compared with the Customs of Primitive Times* [1724]. Edited and translated by William N. Fenton and Elizabeth L. Moon. Toronto, 1974.

Classical Art, Symbols, Iconography, Music

Anderson, William B. "The 'Temple of Minerva' and Francis Hopkinson: A Reappraisal of America's First Poet-Composer." *Proc. Amer. Philos. Soc.* 120 (1976), pp. 166–177. On a grand opera performed in Philadelphia, March, 1781.
Ceracchi, Giuseppe. *A Description of the Monument Consecrated to Liberty.* Philadelphia, 1795. Proposal for a marble monument 100 ft. high with many classical symbols and figures.

Craven, Wayne. "The Grand Manner in Early Nineteenth-Century American Painting: Borrowings from Antiquity, the Renaissance, and the Baroque." *American Art Journal* 11, no. 2 (1979), pp. 5–43.

———. "Horatio Greenough's Statue of Washington and Phidias's Olympian Zeus." *Art Quarterly* 26 (1963), pp. 429–440.

Crawford, John Stephen. "The Classical Orator in Nineteenth Century American Sculpture." *American Art Journal* 62 (1974), pp. 56–72.

———. "The Classical Tradition in American Sculpture: Structure and Surface." *American Art Journal* 11, no. 3 (1979), pp. 38–52.

Flexner, James Thomas. "Benjamin West's American Neo-Classicism." *New York Historical Society Quarterly* 36 (1952), pp. 5–41.

Pierson, William H., Jr. *American Buildings and Their Architects.* Garden City, 1970.

Sawitzky, William. "The American Work of Benjamin West." *Pa. Mag. Hist. & Biog.* 62 (1938), pp. 433–462.

Schleiner, Winfried. "The Infant Hercules: Franklin's Design for a Medal Commemorating American Liberty." *Eighteenth Century Studies* 10 (1976–77), pp. 236–244.

Snyder, Martin D. "The Icon of Antiquity." In *The Usefulness of Classical Learning in the Eighteenth Century*, edited by Susan Ford Wiltshire. University Park, Pa., 1976.

Tolnick, J. "Public Patronage." In *The Classical Spirit in American Portraiture.* Providence, 1976.

Neo-Latin

Glass, Francis. *A Life of George Washington in Latin Prose.* Edited by J. N. Reynolds. New York, 1835. Edited by John F. Latimer (with Introduction). Washington, D.C., 1976.

Kaiser, Leo M. "A President Accepts." *Classical Outlook* 52 (1974), pp. 40–41.

———. "An Unpublished 17th Century American Latin Poem." *Seventeenth-Century News* 23 (1965), pp. 163–164.

———. "Apta et Concinna Oratio: The 1703 Commencement Address of John Leverett." *Manuscripta* 19 (1975), pp. 159–170.

———. "A Census of American Latin Verse, 1625–1825." *Proc. Amer. Antiq. Soc.* 91 (1981), pp. 197–299.

———. "Contributions to a Census of American Latin Prose, 1634–1800." *Humanistica Lovaniensia* 31 (1982), pp. 164–189.

———. "The First American Translations from Seneca's Tragedies." *Classical Bulletin* 59 (1983), pp. 6–8.

———. "The First American Translation of the *Odes* and *Epodes* of Horace." *Classical Journal* 60 (1965), pp. 220–230.

———. "The Inaugural Address of Edward Wigglesworth as First Hollis Professor of Divinity." *Harvard Library Bulletin* 27 (1979), pp. 319–329.

———. "John Beveridge, Latin Poet of Two Worlds." *Classical Journal* 58 (1963), pp. 251–256.

———. "Latin Epitaphs for a *Corpus Inscriptionum Graecarum Latinarumque Americae*." *Classical Journal* 51 (1955–56), pp. 69–81, 141–144, 294–301, 342–344.

———. "Leverett on Holyoke, *Ornamentum, Emolumentum*." *Harvard Library Bulletin* 28 (1980), pp. 182–184.

———. "The Question of Lamb." *Harvard Library Bulletin* 28 (1980), pp. 16–18. Latin oration by student J. Lamb.

———. "Seventeenth Century American Latin Prose: John Leverett's Welcome to Governor Sir Edmund Andros." *Manuscripta* 18 (1974), pp. 30–37.

_____. "Thirteen Early American Latin Elegies: A Critical Edition." *Humanistica Lovaniensia* 23 (1974), pp. 346–381.

_____. "'We Are All Filled with the Greatest Hope': An Installation Speech of Gov. Joseph Dudley." *Harvard Library Bulletin* 27 (1979), pp. 443–444.

Kittredge, G. L., and Samuel E. Morison. "Urian Oakes' Salutatory Oration: Commencement of 1677." *Publ. Colon. Soc. Mass.* 31 (1935), pp. 405–436.

Lance, William. *Georgii Washingtonis Vita.* Charleston, 1836.

Oliver, Revilo P. "A Voice in the Wilderness." In *Classical, Medieval and Renaissance Studies in Honor of Berthold Louis Ullman,* edited by Charles Henderson, Jr. Rome, 1960. On Francis Glass.

Rand, Edward K. "John Wilson's Latin Verses on John Harvard." *Harvard Graduate Magazine* 42 (1933), pp. 41–46.

Research on the Classical Tradition in America

Atwater, Elizabeth A. "A History of Classical Scholarship in America." Ph.D. dissertation, Pittsburgh, 1938. Largely biographical and bibliographical collection.

Reinhold, Meyer, and Eadie, John W. "Research on the Classical Influences on Early America." *Classical World* 67 (1973), pp. 1–3.

Index

Meyer Reinhold, professor emeritus of classical studies and Byler Distinguished Professor at the University of Missouri, is currently Visiting University Professor of Classical Studies at Boston University. Among his many publications are *Classics, Greek and Roman* (1946); *Roman Civilization* (1951–55); *Classical Drama* (1959); *Past and Present: The Continuity of Classical Myths* (1972); *The Classick Pages: Classical Reading of Eighteenth-Century Americans* (1975); *Diaspora: The Jews among the Greeks and Romans* (1983).

The manuscript was edited for publication by Carol Altman Bromberg. The book was designed by Don Ross. The typeface for the text and for the display is Autologic's APS-5 Times Roman. The book is printed on 55 lb. Glatfelter text paper and is bound in Holliston Mills' Roxite Linen cloth over binder's boards.

Manufactured in the United States of America.